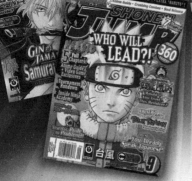
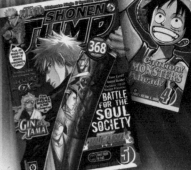

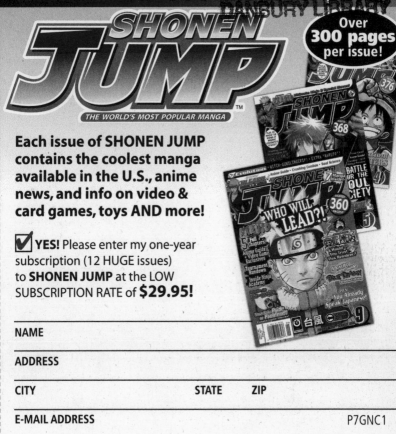

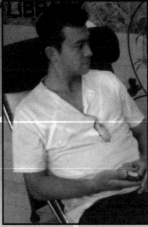

Thanks to everyone's support I finally reached the 30-volume milestone I've been striving for. This would not have been possible without you, so once again, thank you. I promise to keep working hard!!

– Takeshi Konomi, 2005

About Takeshi Konomi

Takeshi Konomi exploded onto the manga scene with the incredible **THE PRINCE OF TENNIS**. His refined art style and sleek character designs proved popular with **Weekly Shonen Jump** readers, and **THE PRINCE OF TENNIS** became the number one sports manga in Japan almost overnight. Its cast of fascinating male tennis players attracted legions of female readers even though it was originally intended to be a boys' comic. The manga continues to be a success in Japan and has inspired a hit anime series, as well as several video games and mountains of merchandise.

THE PRINCE OF TENNIS
VOL. 30
The SHONEN JUMP Manga Edition

STORY AND ART BY
TAKESHI KONOMI

Translation/Joe Yamazaki
Touch-up Art & Lettering/Vanessa Satone
Design/Sam Elzway
Editor/Leyla Aker

Editor in Chief, Books/Alvin Lu
Editor in Chief, Magazines/Marc Weidenbaum
VP, Publishing Licensing/Rika Inouye
VP, Sales & Product Marketing/Gonzalo Ferreyra
VP, Creative/Linda Espinosa
Publisher/Hyoe Narita

Printed in the U.S.A.

Published by VIZ Media, LLC
P.O. Box 77010
San Francisco, CA 94107

SHONEN JUMP Manga Edition
10 9 8 7 6 5 4 3 2 1
First printing, March 2009

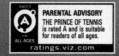

PARENTAL ADVISORY
THE PRINCE OF TENNIS
is rated A and is suitable
for readers of all ages.
ratings.viz.com

THE WORLD'S
MOST POPULAR MANGA

www.viz.com

www.shonenjump.com

THE PRINCE OF TENNIS

VOL. 30

The Boys from Okinawa

Story & Art by

Takeshi Konomi

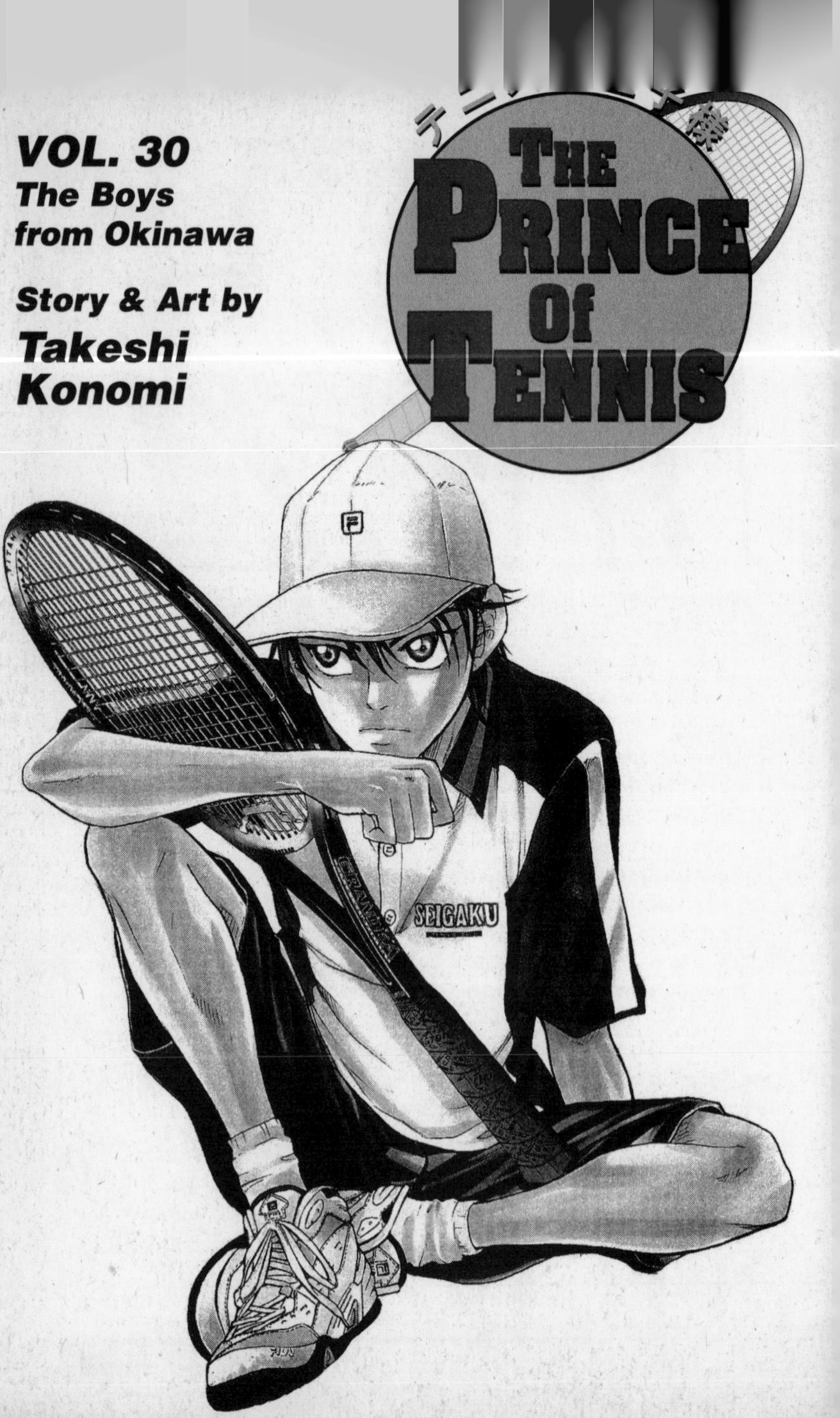
SEIGAKU

ENNIS CLUB

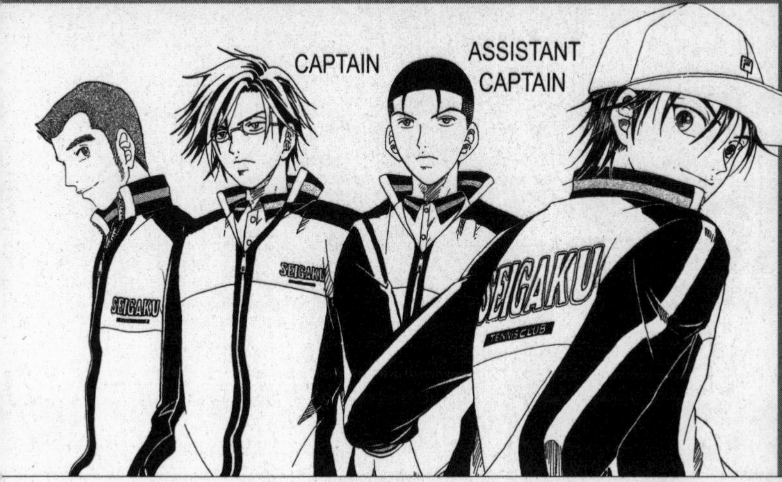
CAPTAIN
ASSISTANT CAPTAIN

• TAKASHI KAWAMURA • KUNIMITSU TEZUKA • SHUICHIRO OISHI • RYOMA ECHIZEN •

STORY & CHARACTERS

Seishun Academy student Ryoma Echizen is a tennis prodigy, with wins in four consecutive U.S. Junior Tennis Tournaments under his belt. He became a starter as a 7th grader and led his team to the District Preliminaries! Despite a few mishaps, Seishun won the District Prelims and the City Tournament, and earned a ticket to the Kanto Tournament. The team came away victorious from its first-round matches, but captain Kunimitsu injured his shoulder and went to Kyushu for treatment. Despite losing Kunimitsu and assistant captain Shuichiro to injury, Seishun pulled together as a team, winning the Kanto Tournament and earning a slot at the Nationals!

With Kunimitsu recovered and back on the team, Seishun enters the Nationals with their strongest lineup to face Okinawa's Higa Junior High! Ryoma, playing in No. 3 Singles against the giant Kei Tanishi, struggles against Kei's immensely powerful Big Bang serve in a 1–1 tie game...

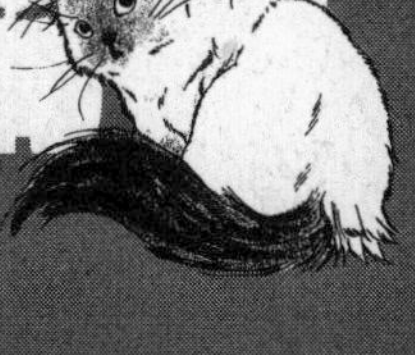

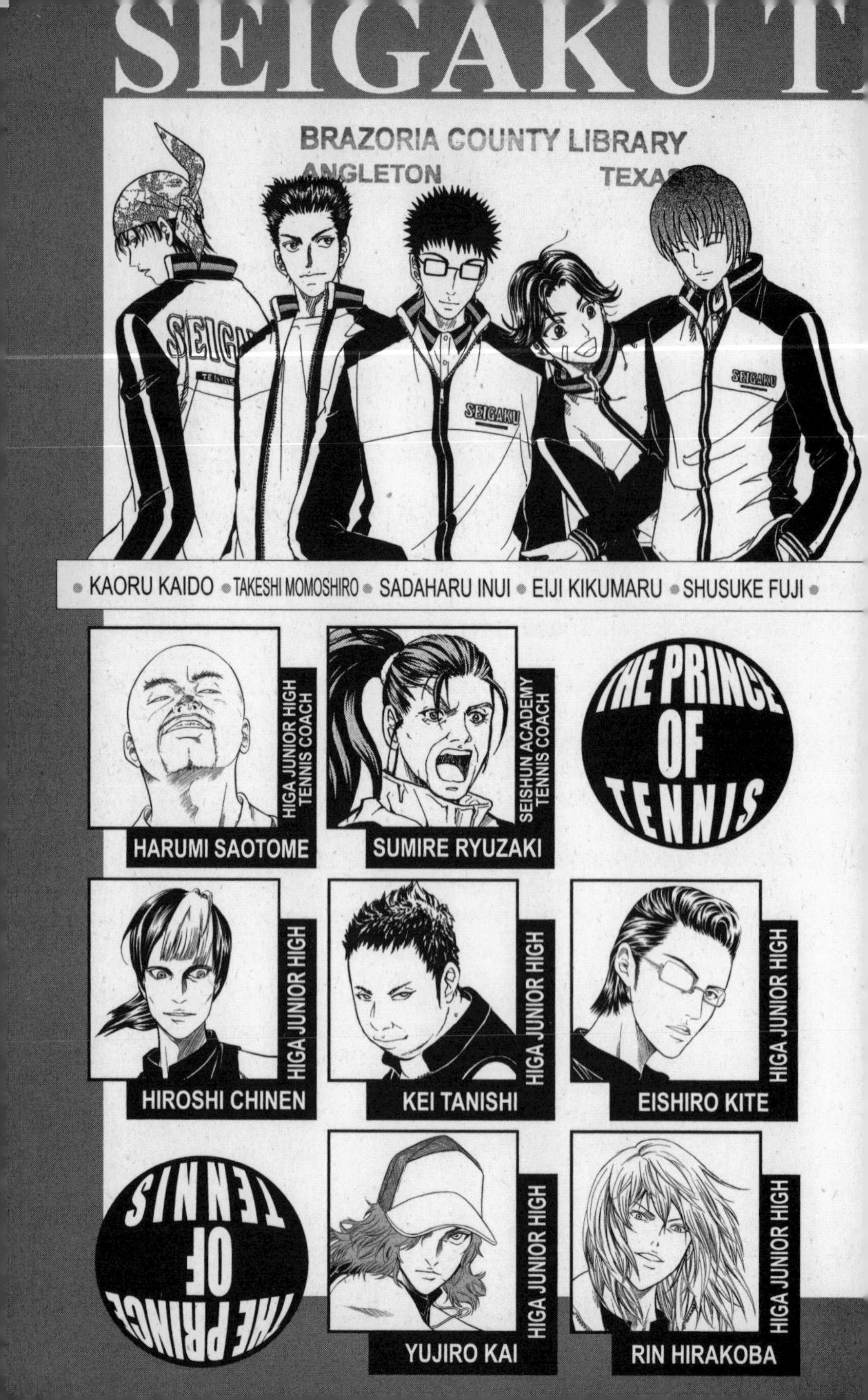
SEIGAKU T
KAORU KAIDO • TAKESHI MOMOSHIRO • SADAHARU INUI • EIJI KIKUMARU • SHUSUKE FUJI
THE PRINCE OF TENNIS
SEISHUN ACADEMY TENNIS COACH
SUMIRE RYUZAKI
HIGA JUNIOR HIGH TENNIS COACH
HARUMI SAOTOME
HIGA JUNIOR HIGH
EISHIRO KITE
HIGA JUNIOR HIGH
KEI TANISHI
HIGA JUNIOR HIGH
HIROSHI CHINEN
HIGA JUNIOR HIGH
RIN HIRAKOBA
HIGA JUNIOR HIGH
YUJIRO KAI
THE PRINCE OF TENNIS

CONTENTS Vol. 30
The Boys from Okinawa

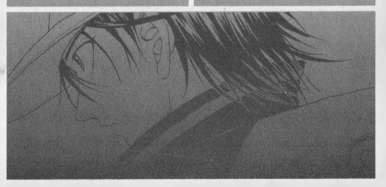

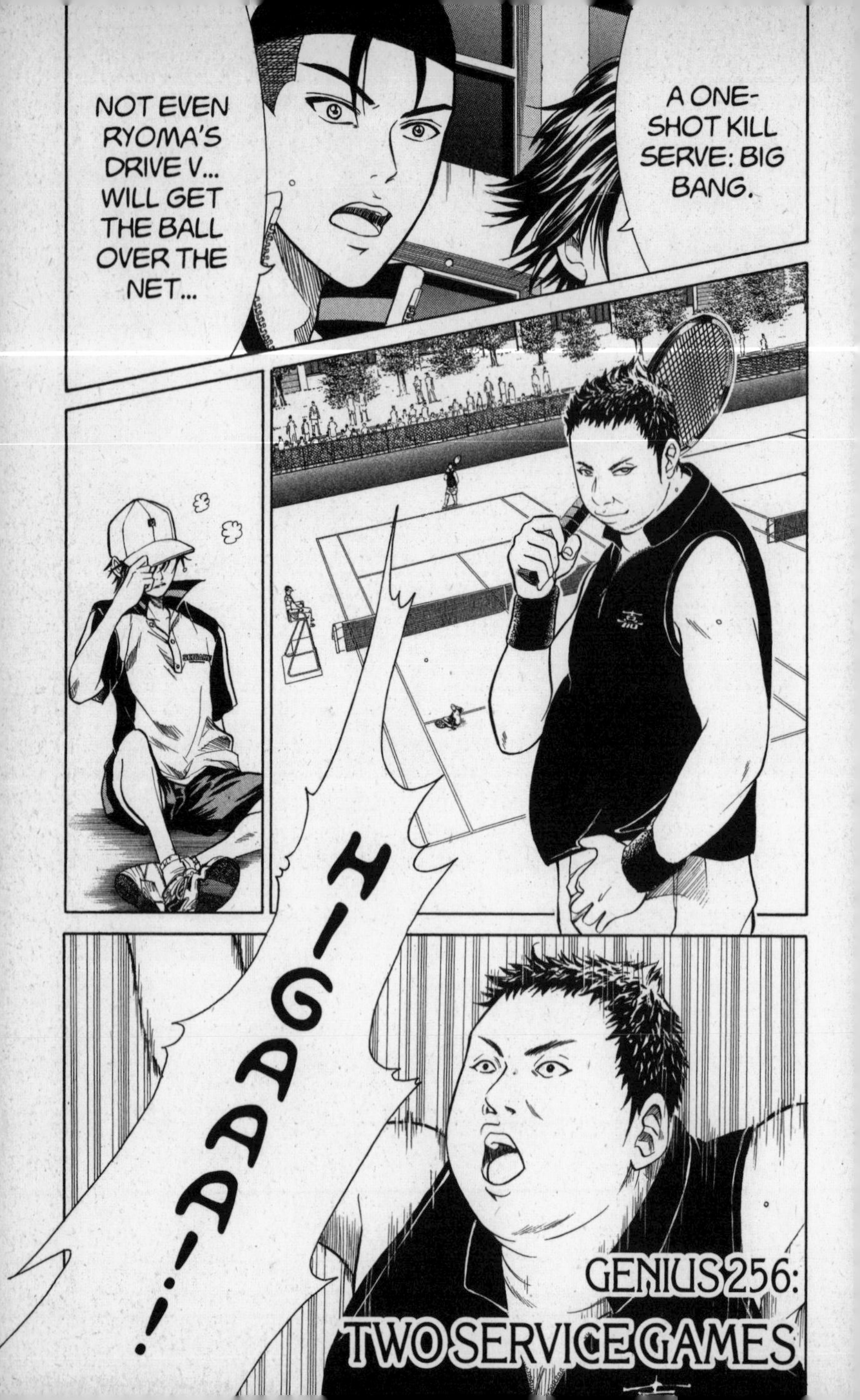
A ONE-SHOT KILL SERVE: BIG BANG.
NOT EVEN RYOMA'S DRIVE V... WILL GET THE BALL OVER THE NET...
HIGAAAA!!!
GENIUS 256:
TWO SERVICE GAMES

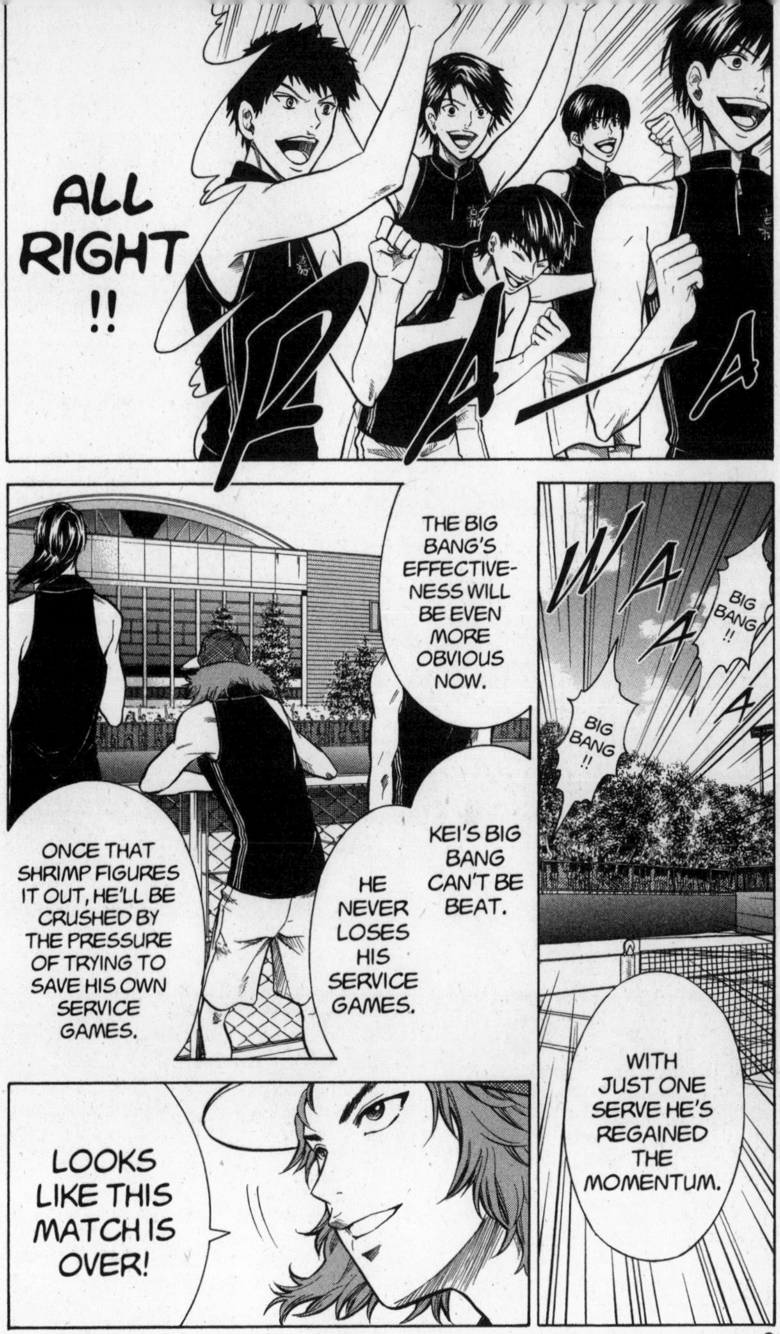
ALL RIGHT !!
WAAA
BIG BANG !!
BIG BANG !!
WITH JUST ONE SERVE HE'S REGAINED THE MOMENTUM.
THE BIG BANG'S EFFECTIVENESS WILL BE EVEN MORE OBVIOUS NOW.
KEI'S BIG BANG CAN'T BE BEAT.
HE NEVER LOSES HIS SERVICE GAMES.
ONCE THAT SHRIMP FIGURES IT OUT, HE'LL BE CRUSHED BY THE PRESSURE OF TRYING TO SAVE HIS OWN SERVICE GAMES.
LOOKS LIKE THIS MATCH IS OVER!

READ THIS WAY

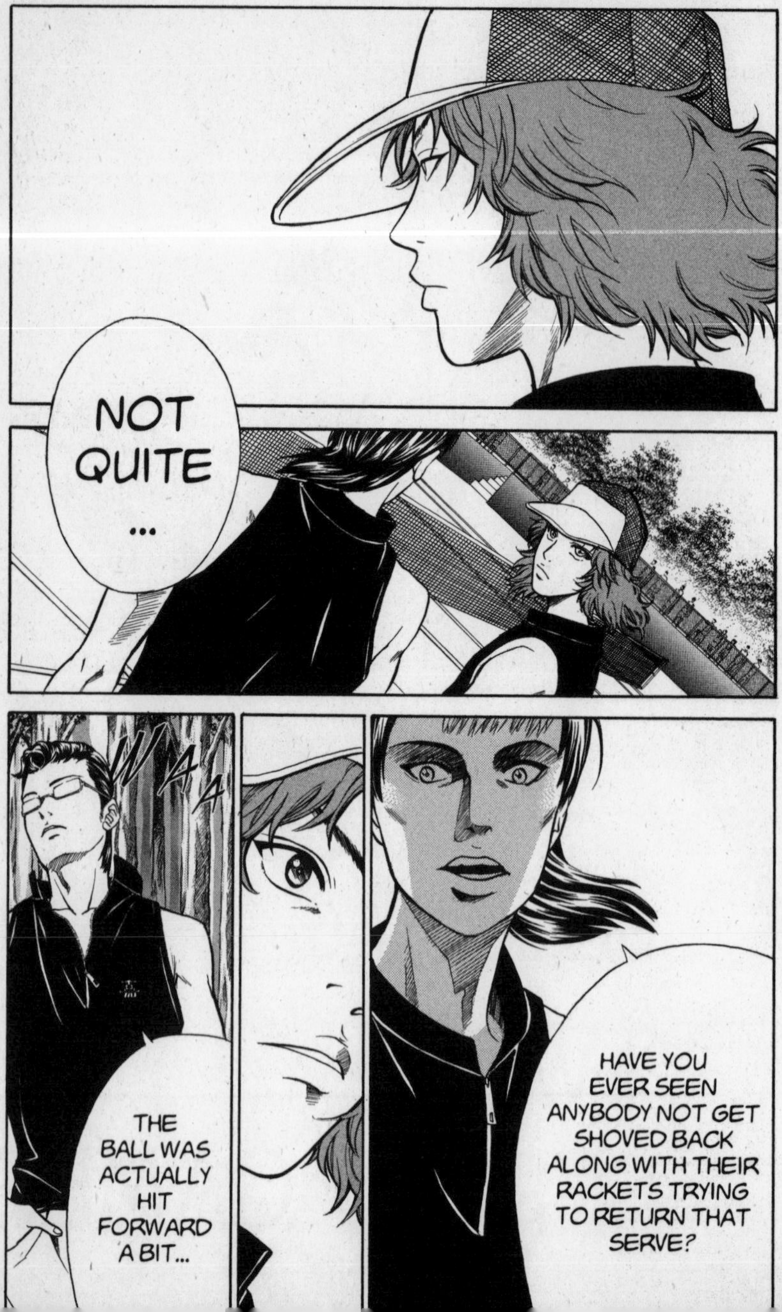
NOT QUITE ...
HAVE YOU EVER SEEN ANYBODY NOT GET SHOVED BACK ALONG WITH THEIR RACKETS TRYING TO RETURN THAT SERVE?
WAA
THE BALL WAS ACTUALLY HIT FORWARD A BIT...

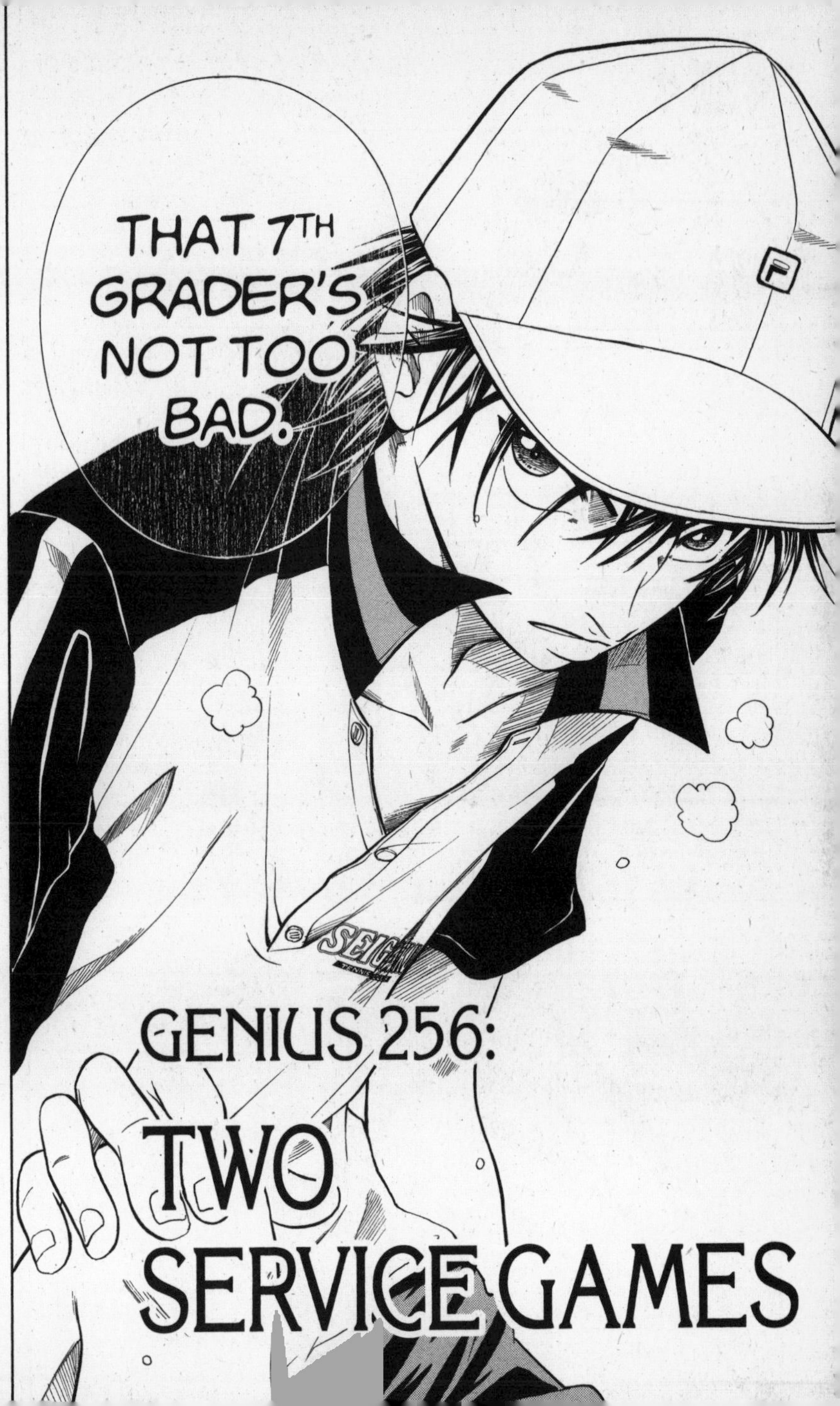
THAT 7TH GRADER'S NOT TOO BAD.
GENIUS 256:
TWO SERVICE GAMES

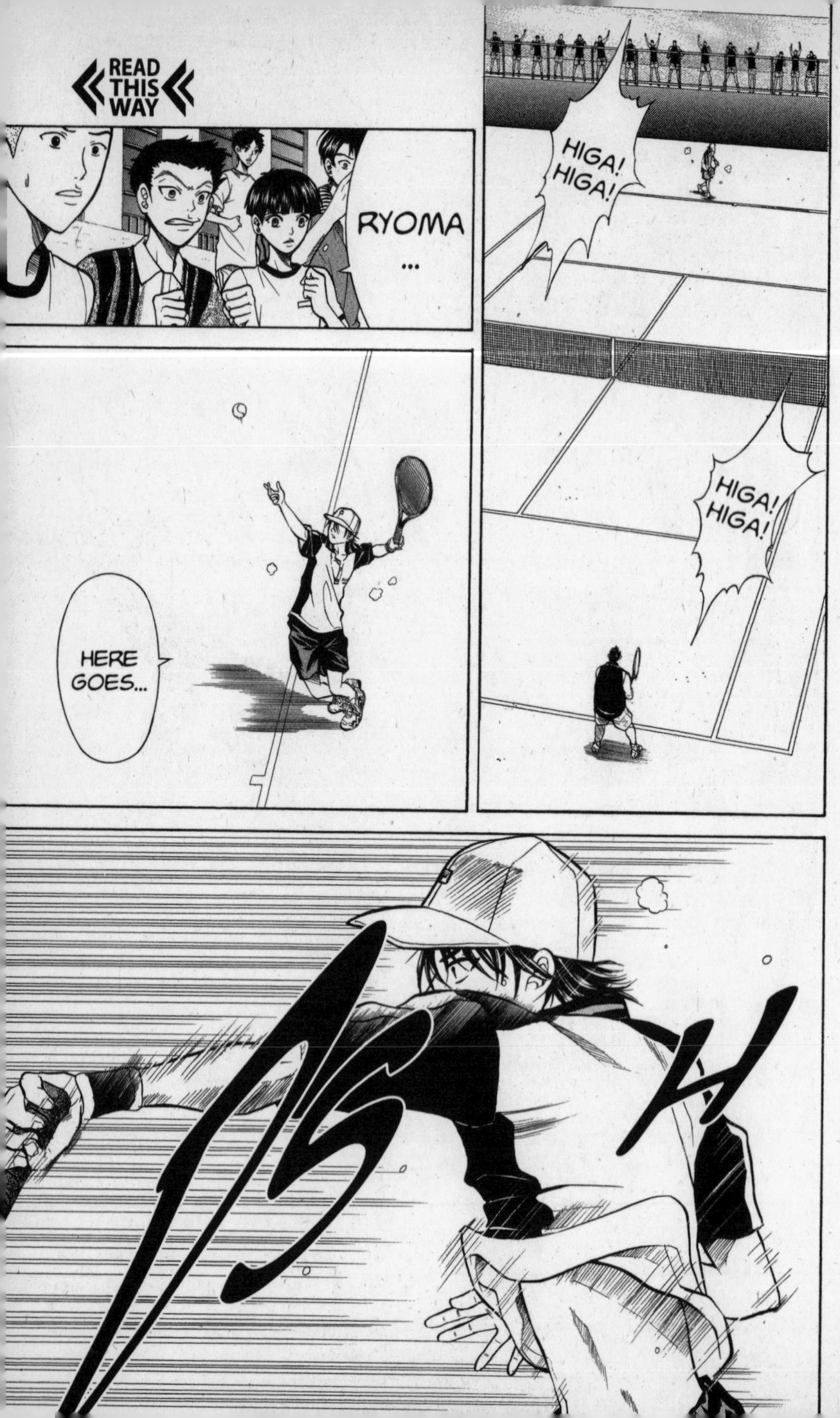
READ THIS WAY
HIGA! HIGA!
HIGA! HIGA!
RYOMA ...
HERE GOES...

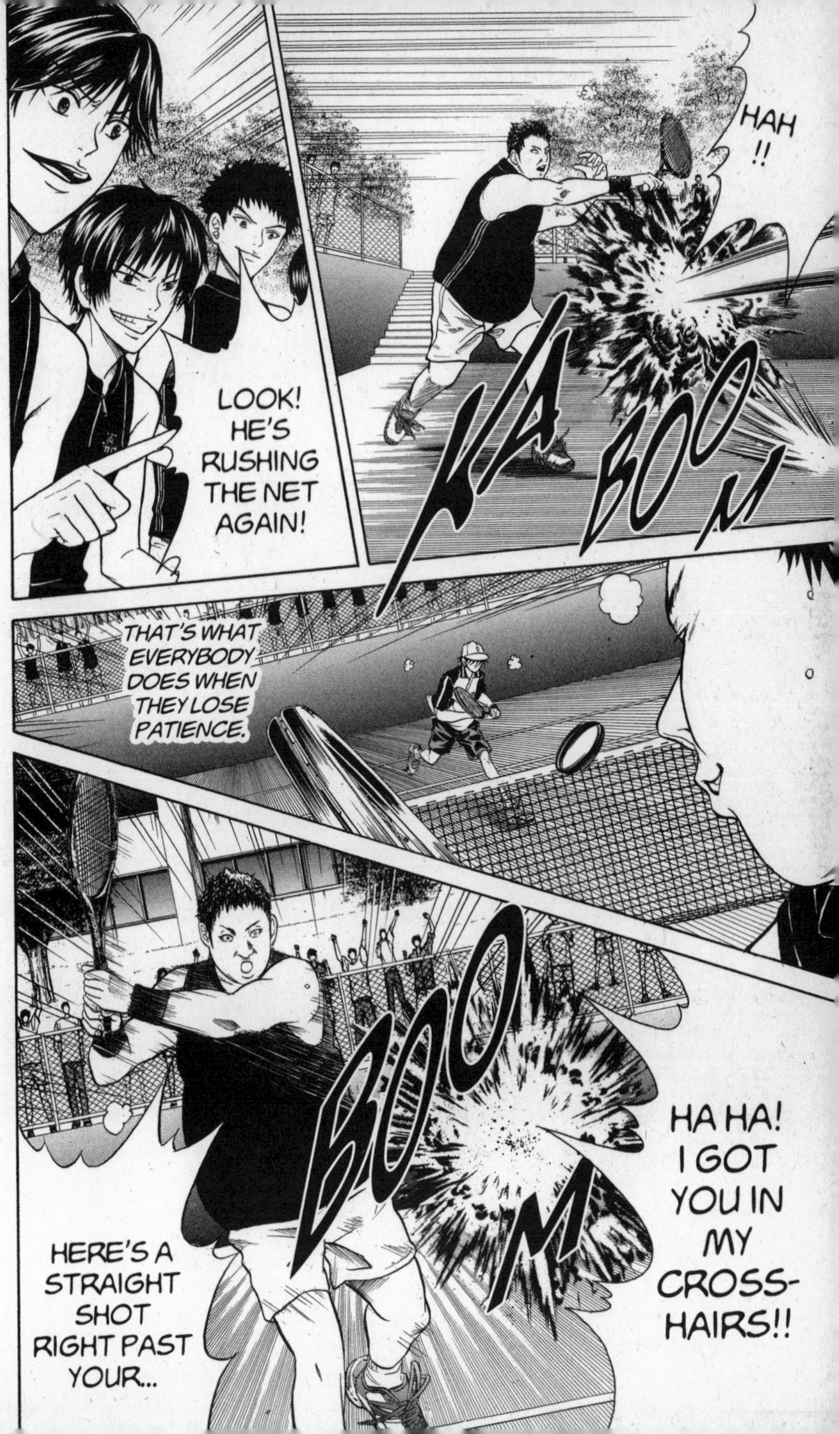
HAH!!
KA BOOM
LOOK! HE'S RUSHING THE NET AGAIN!
THAT'S WHAT EVERYBODY DOES WHEN THEY LOSE PATIENCE.
HA HA! I GOT YOU IN MY CROSS-HAIRS!!
HERE'S A STRAIGHT SHOT RIGHT PAST YOUR...
BOOM

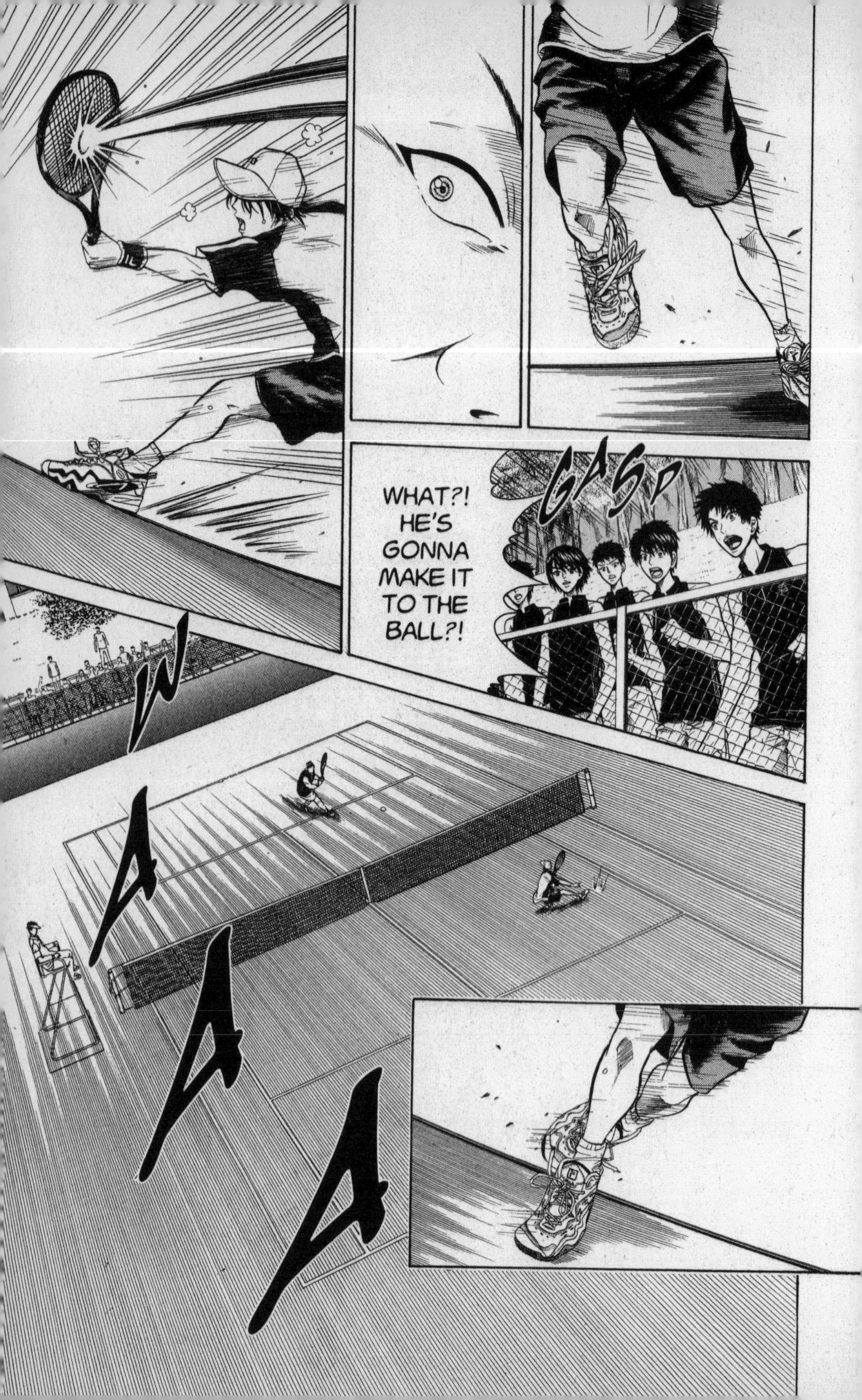
GASP
WHAT?! HE'S GONNA MAKE IT TO THE BALL?!

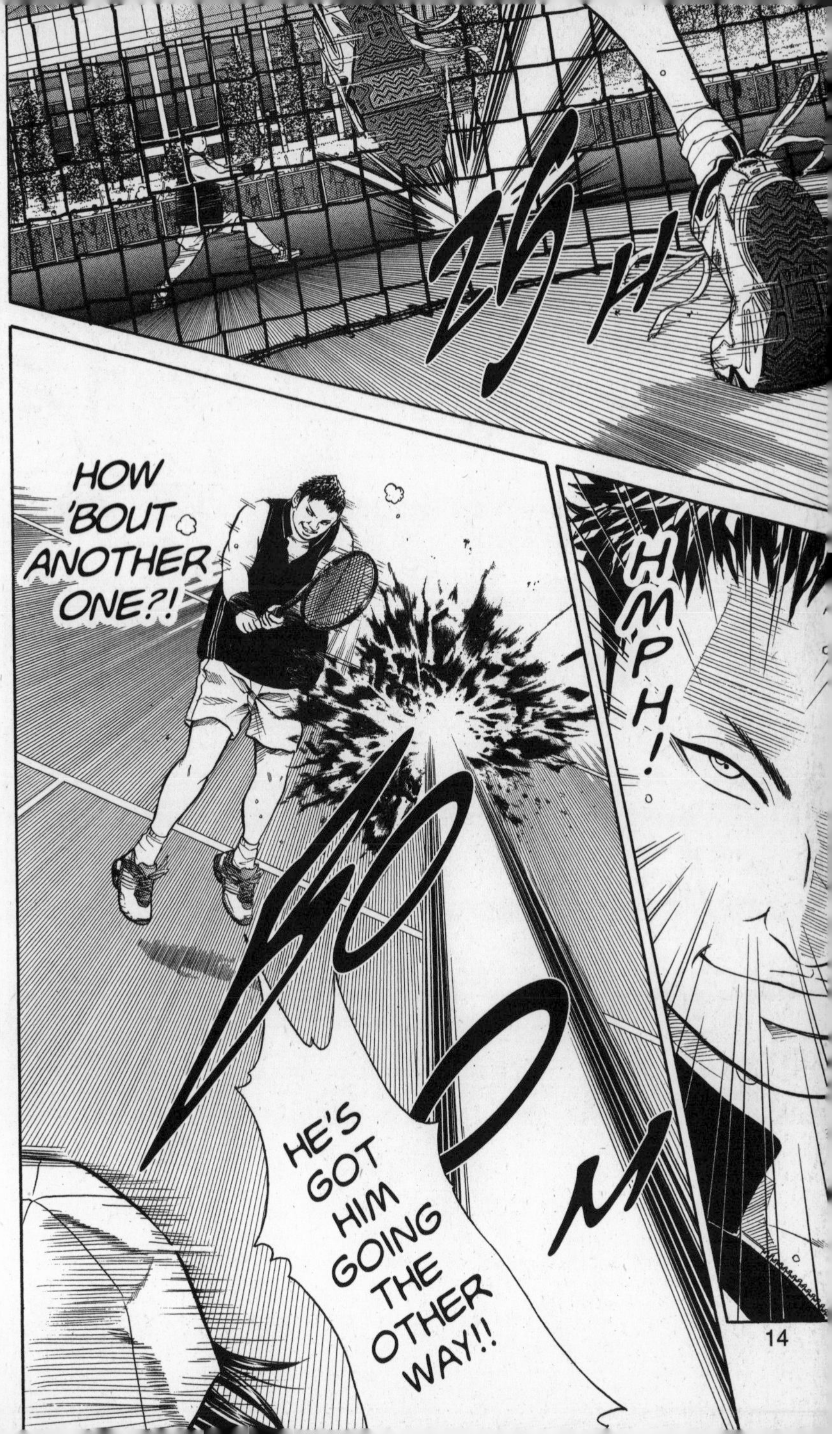
ZSSH
HMMPH!
HOW 'BOUT ANOTHER ONE?!
HE'S GOT HIM GOING THE OTHER WAY!!

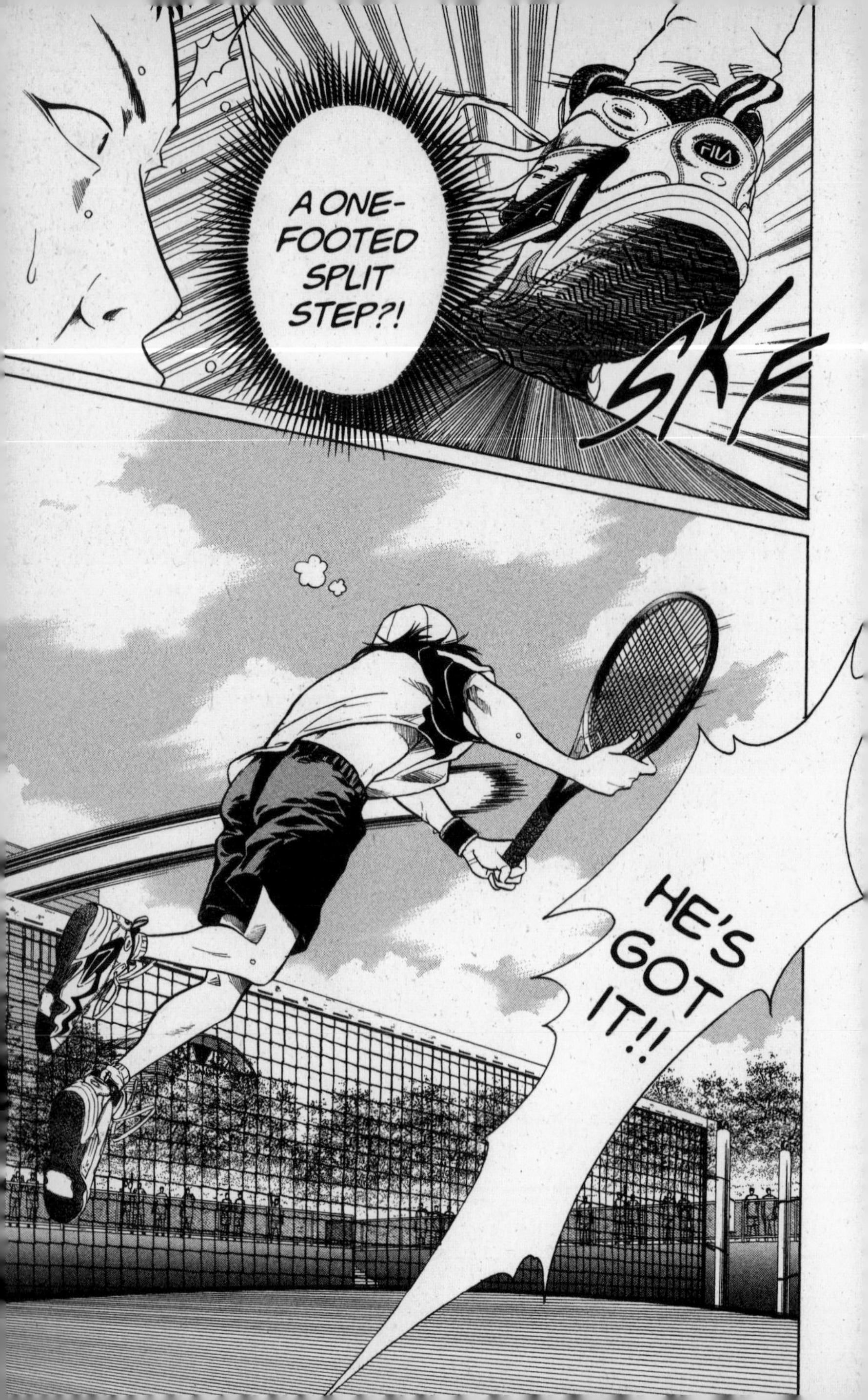
A ONE-FOOTED SPLIT STEP?!
SKF
HE'S GOT IT!!

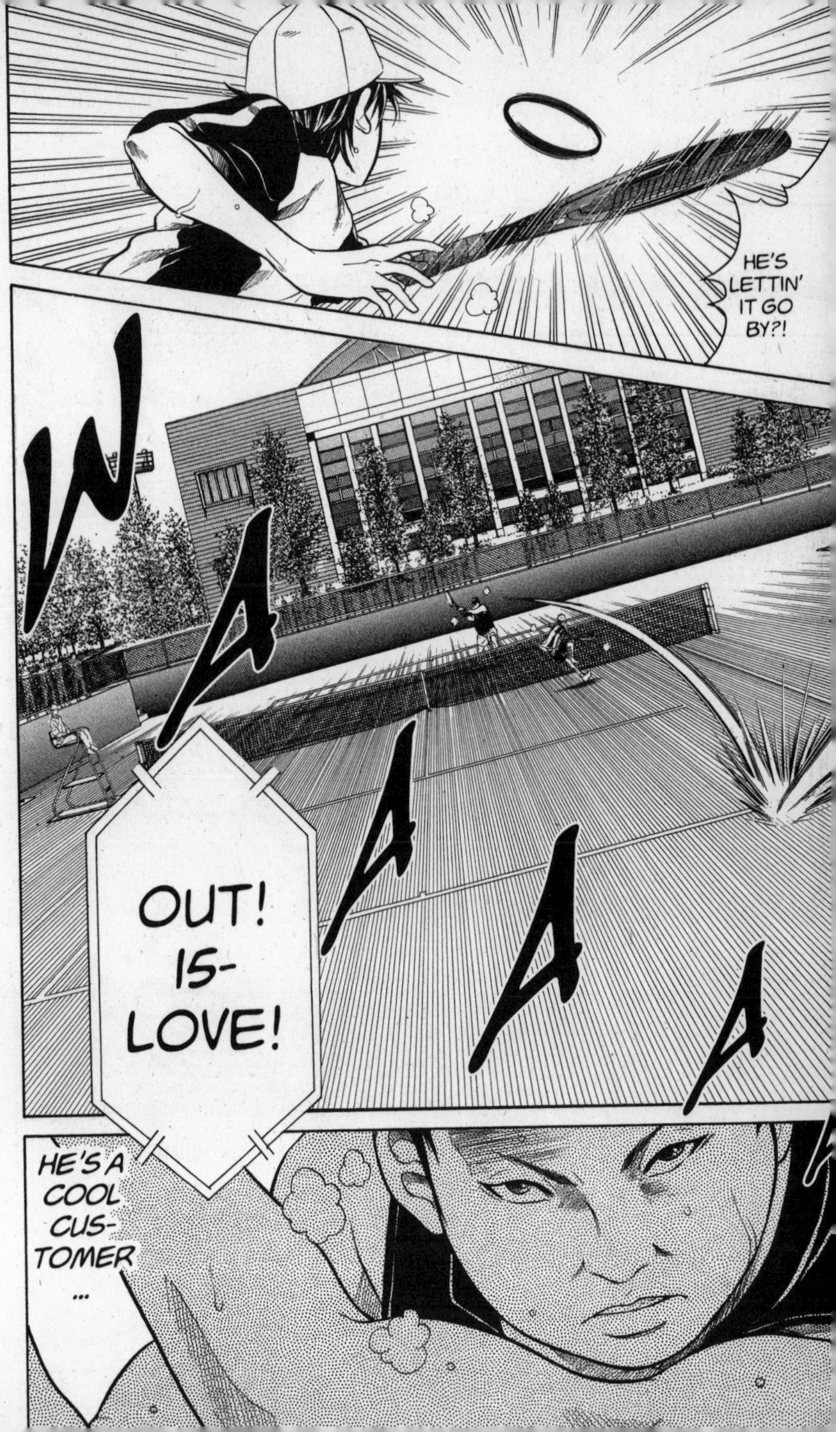
HE'S LETTIN' IT GO BY?!
WAAAAAA
OUT! 15-LOVE!
HE'S A COOL CUS-TOMER ...

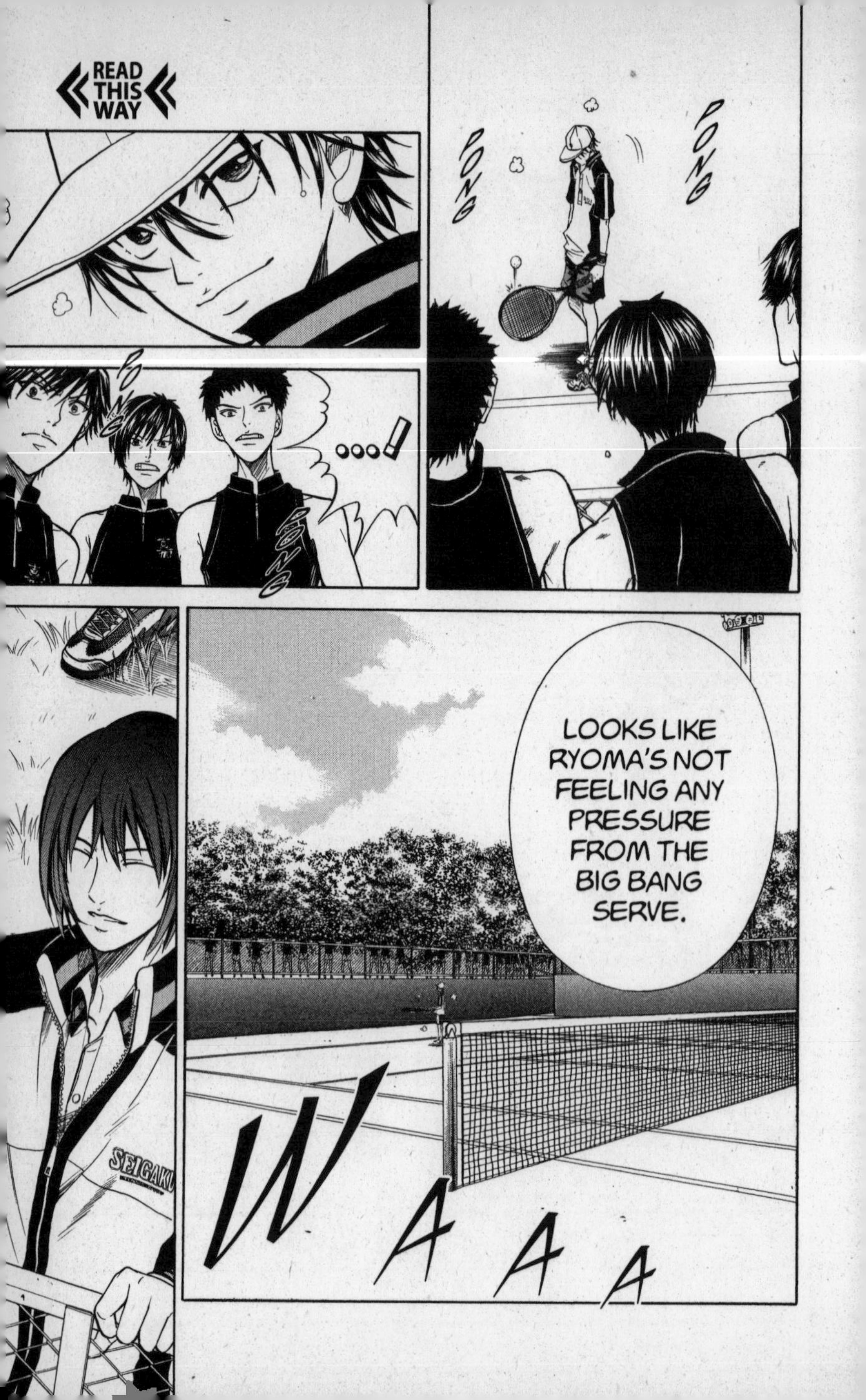
READ THIS WAY
PONG
PONG
...!
PONG
PONG
LOOKS LIKE RYOMA'S NOT FEELING ANY PRESSURE FROM THE BIG BANG SERVE.
WAAAA
SEIGAKU

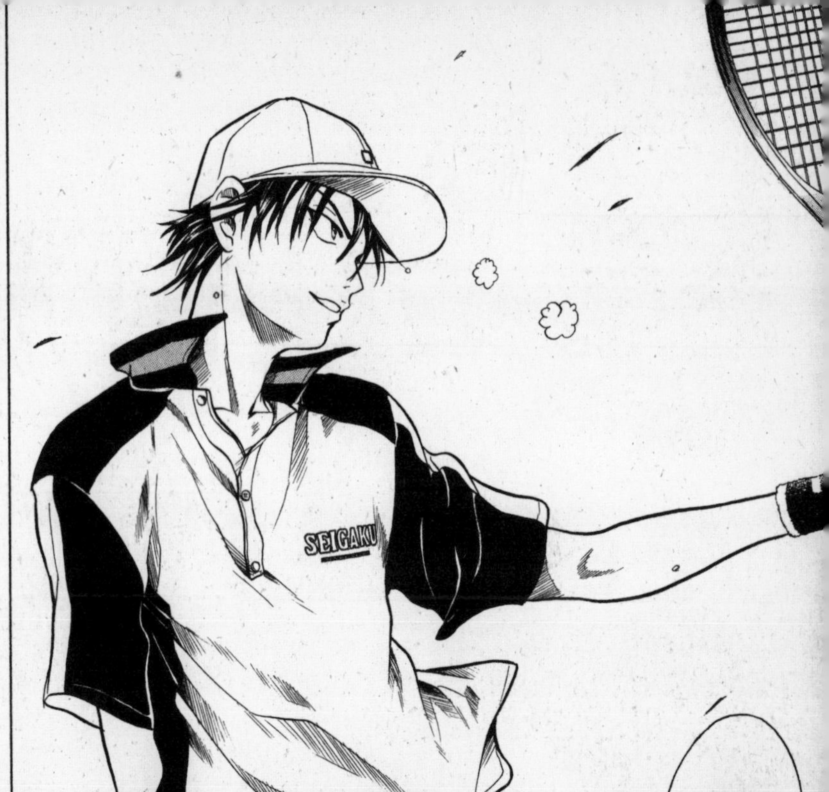
HEY ...
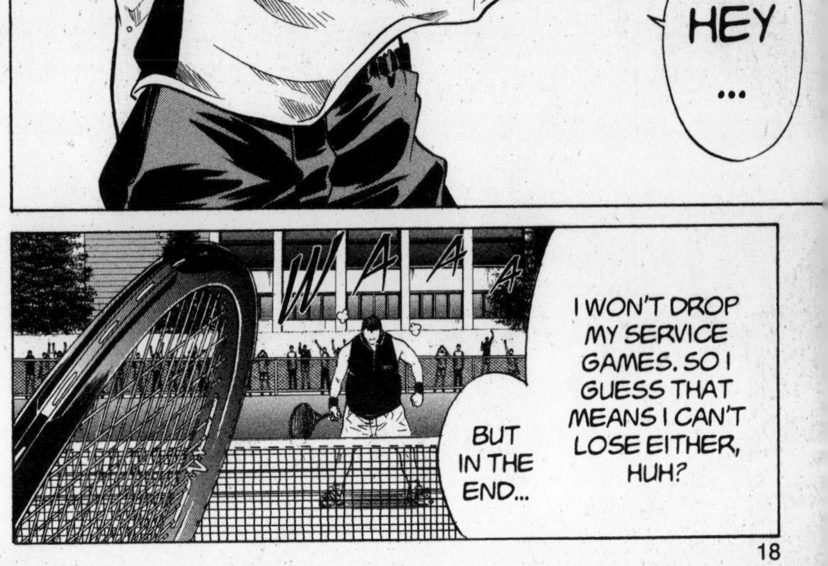
WAAA
I WON'T DROP MY SERVICE GAMES. SO I GUESS THAT MEANS I CAN'T LOSE EITHER, HUH?
BUT IN THE END...

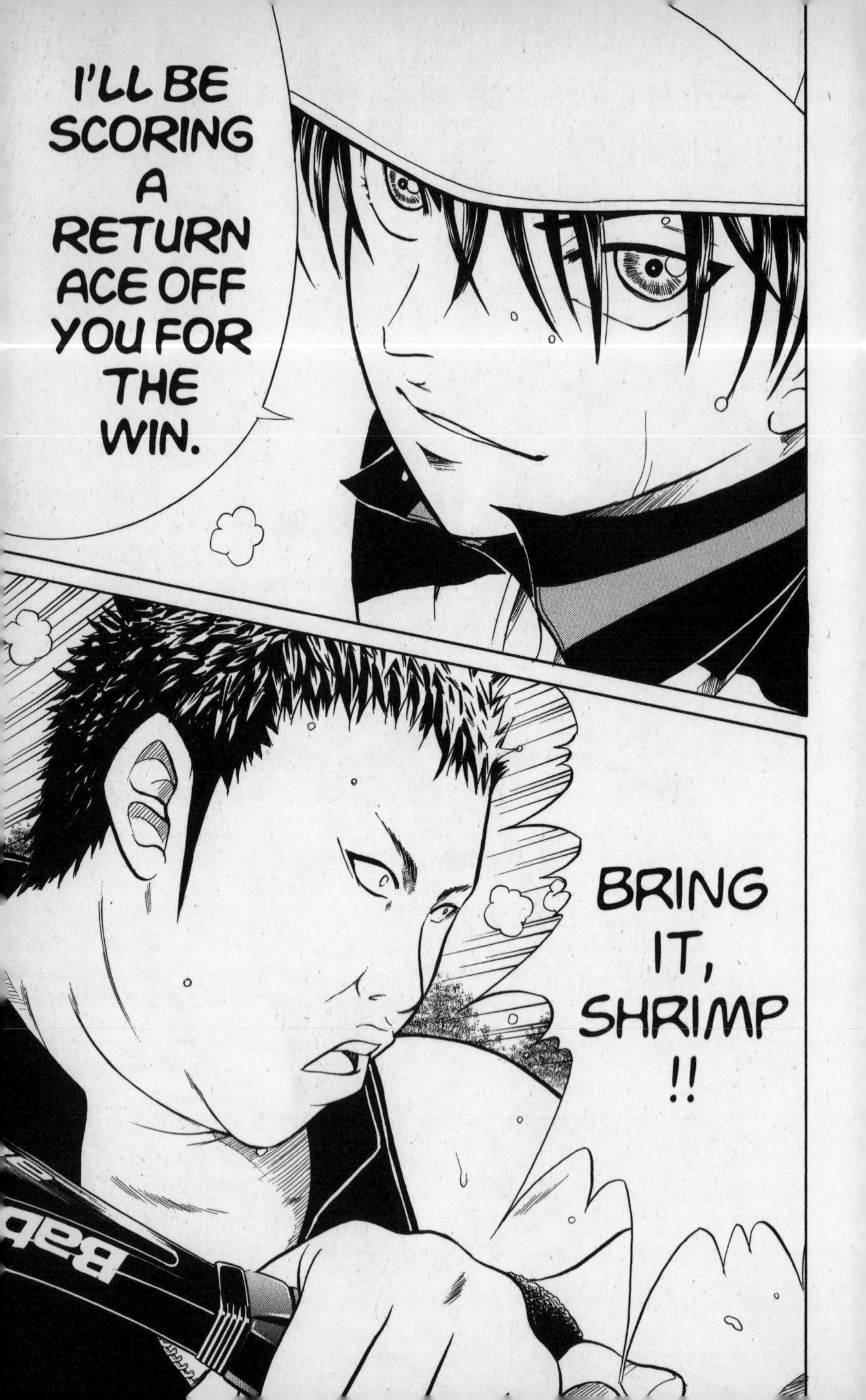
I'LL BE SCORING A RETURN ACE OFF YOU FOR THE WIN.
BRING IT, SHRIMP!!

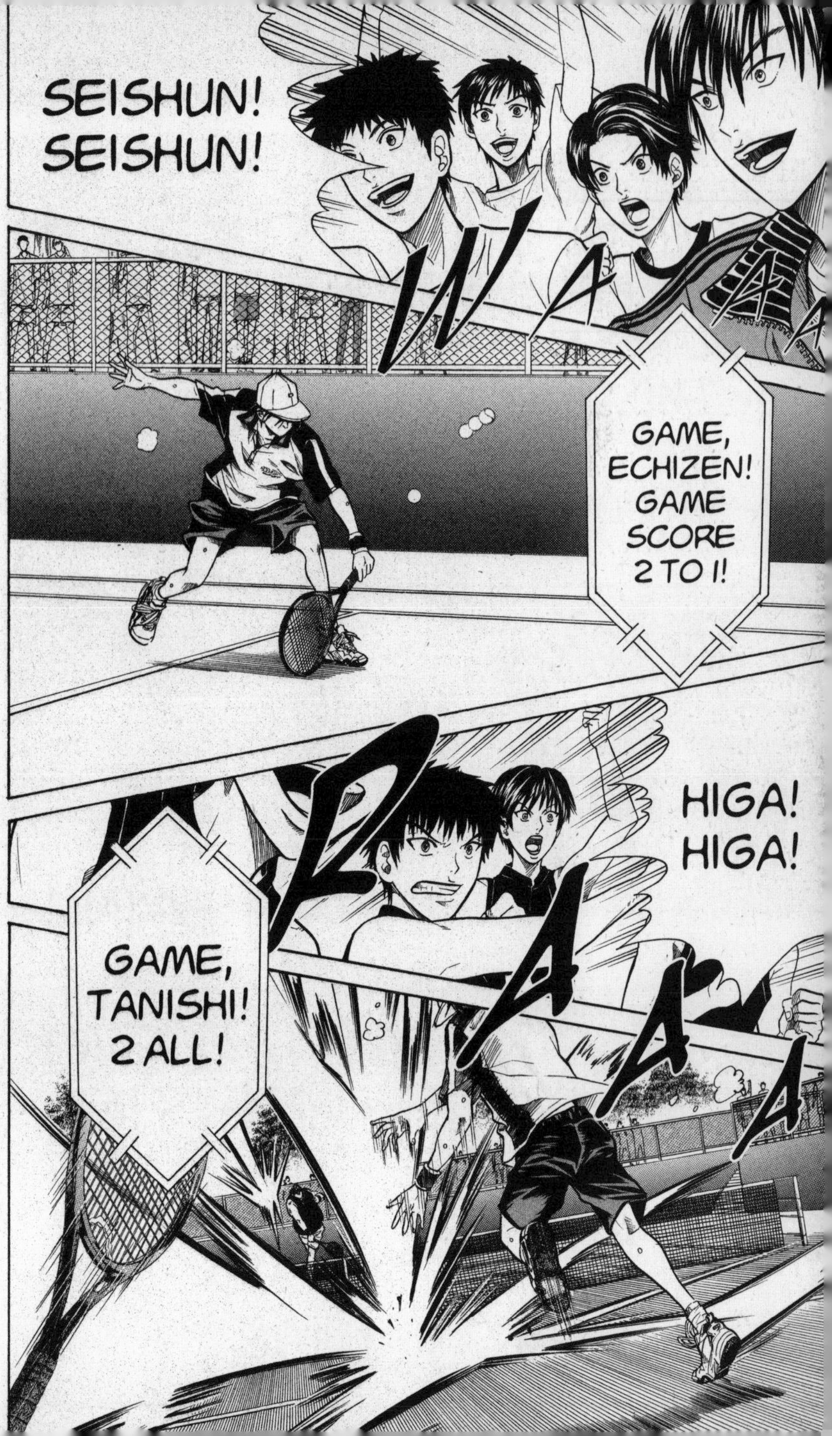
SEISHUN! SEISHUN!
GAME, ECHIZEN! GAME SCORE 2 TO 1!
HIGA! HIGA!
GAME, TANISHI! 2 ALL!

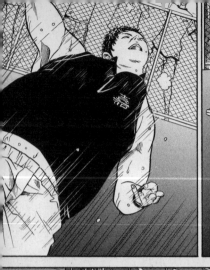
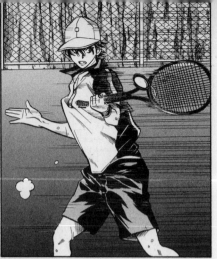

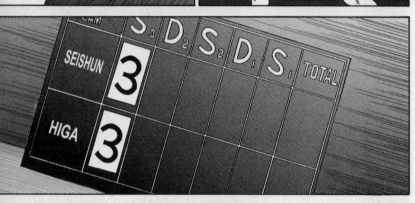

TEAM	S₃	D₂	S₂	D₁	S₁	TOTAL
SEISHUN	3					
HIGA	3					

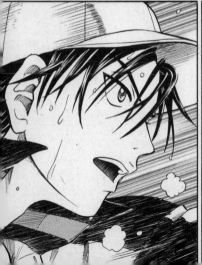
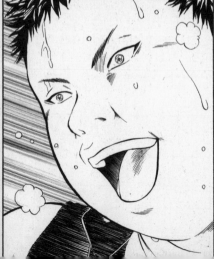

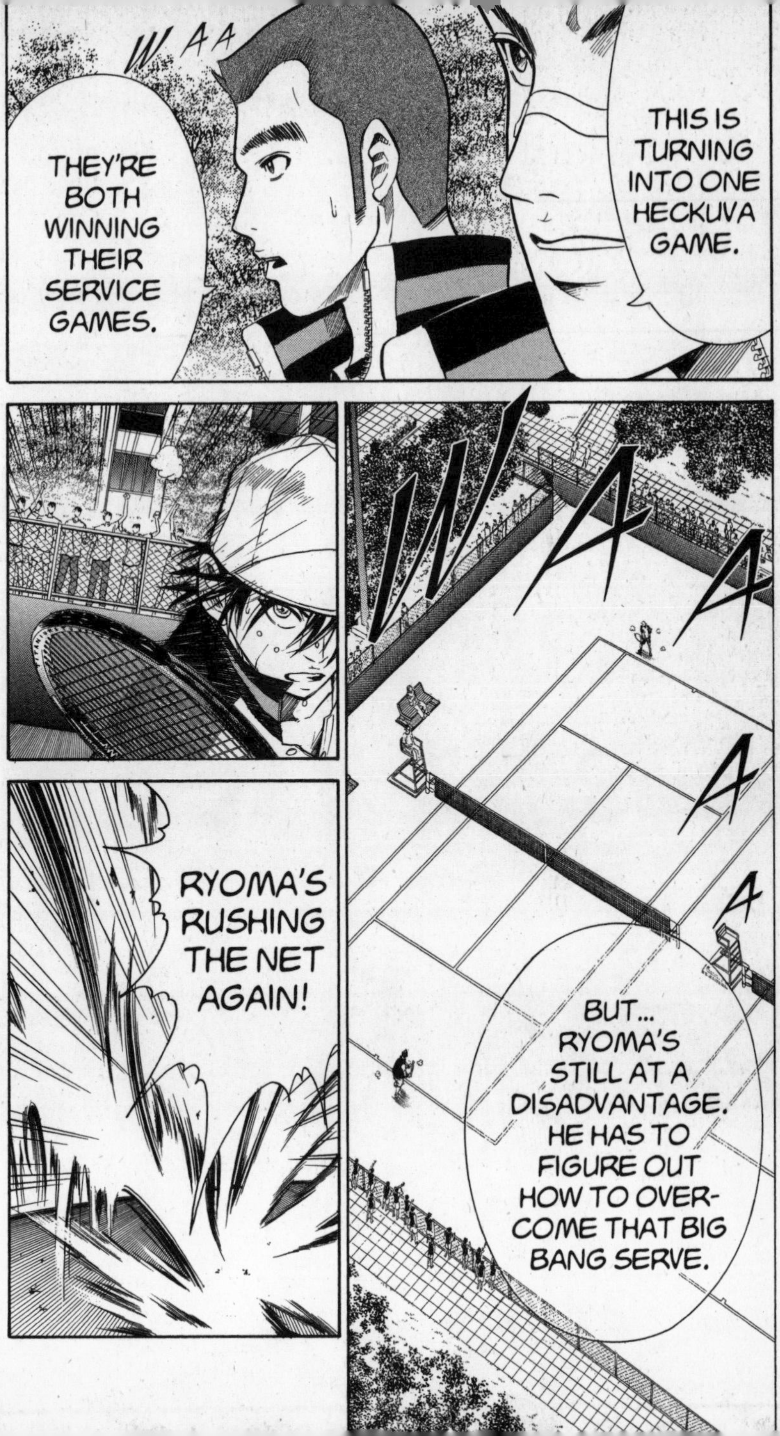
WAA
THIS IS TURNING INTO ONE HECKUVA GAME.
THEY'RE BOTH WINNING THEIR SERVICE GAMES.
WAAAA
BUT... RYOMA'S STILL AT A DISADVANTAGE. HE HAS TO FIGURE OUT HOW TO OVER-COME THAT BIG BANG SERVE.
RYOMA'S RUSHING THE NET AGAIN!

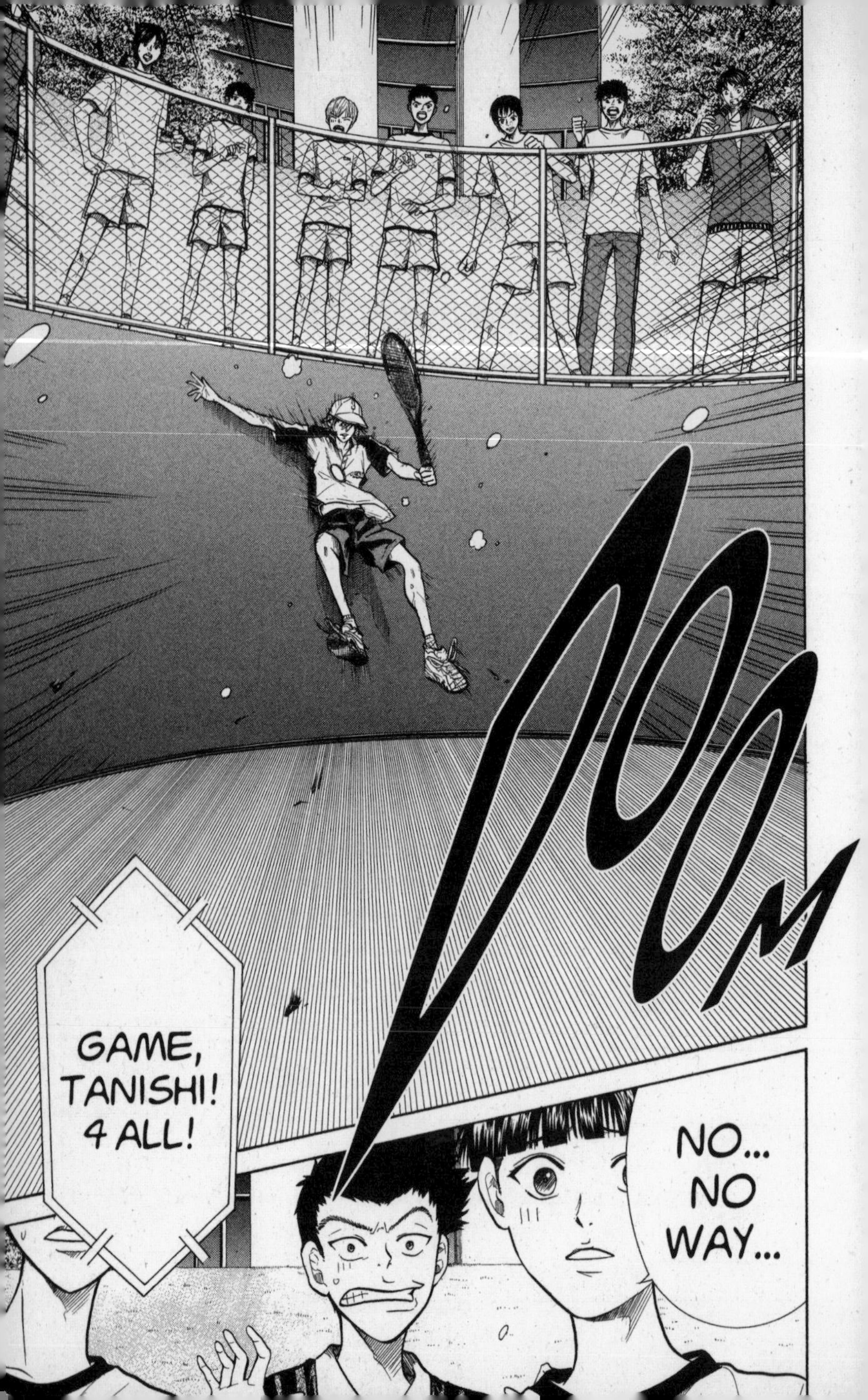
GAME, TANISHI! 4 ALL!
NO... NO WAY...

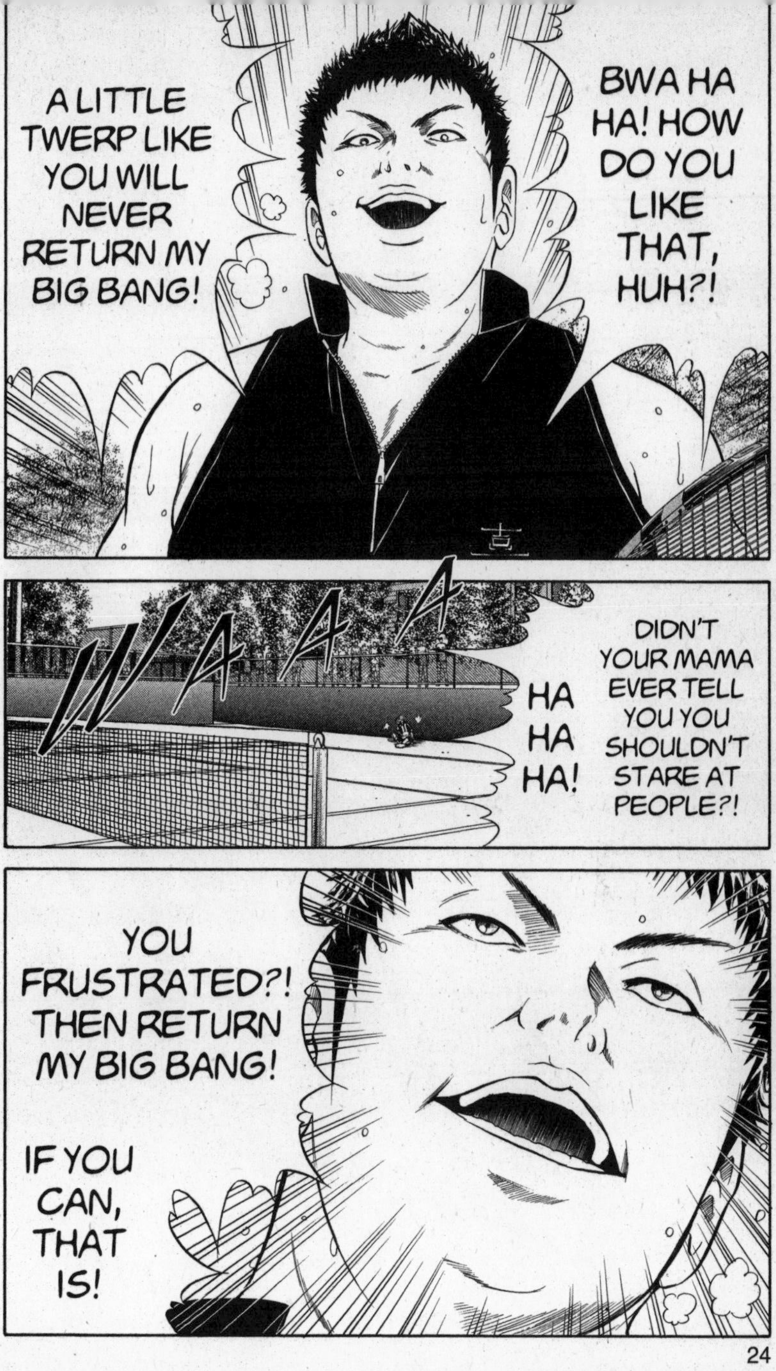
BWA HA HA! HOW DO YOU LIKE THAT, HUH?!
A LITTLE TWERP LIKE YOU WILL NEVER RETURN MY BIG BANG!
DIDN'T YOUR MAMA EVER TELL YOU YOU SHOULDN'T STARE AT PEOPLE?!
HA HA HA!
WAAAA
YOU FRUSTRATED?! THEN RETURN MY BIG BANG!
IF YOU CAN, THAT IS!

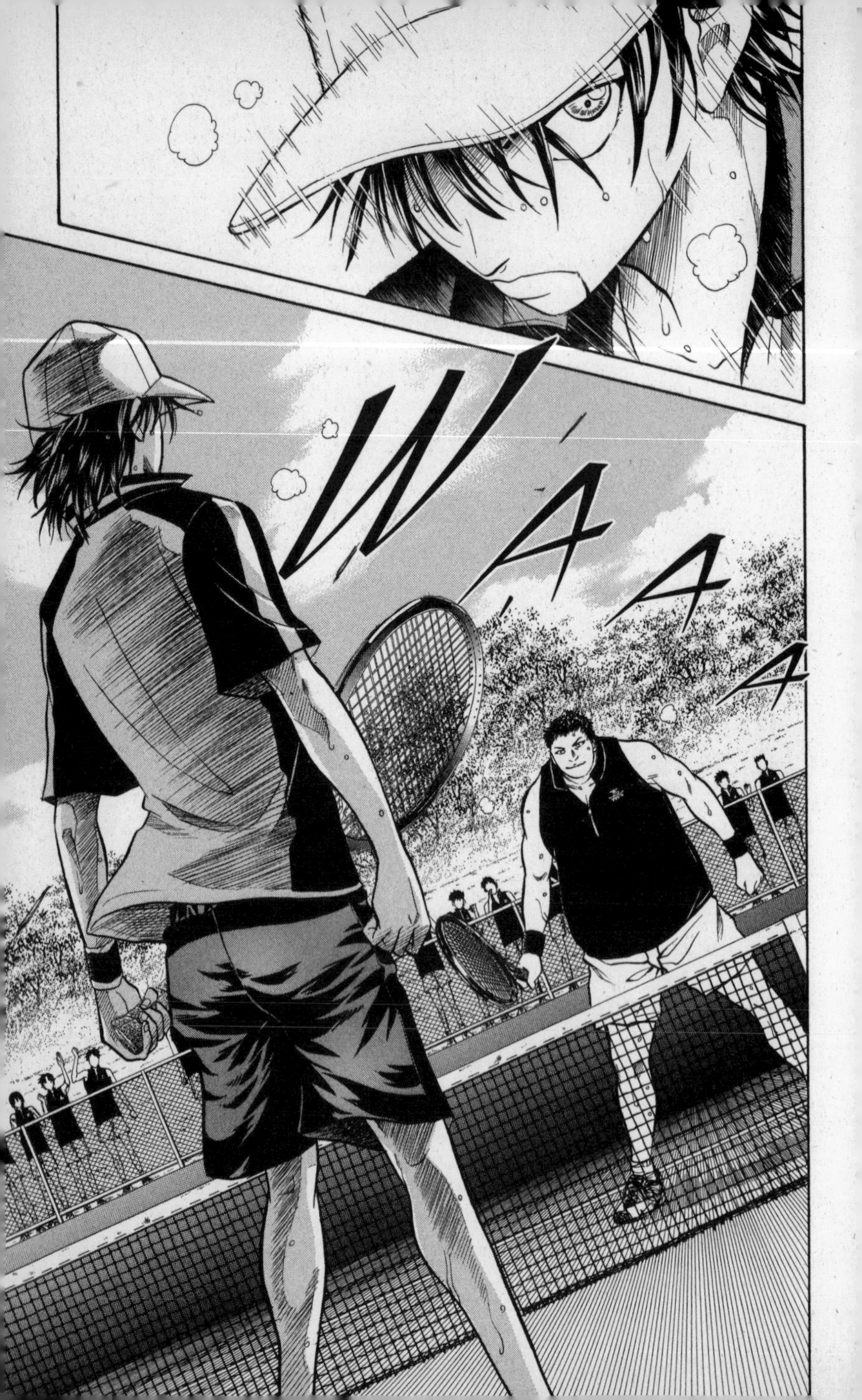
WAAAA

テニスの王子様

THE PRINCE OF TENNIS

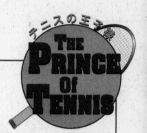

Thank you for reading *The Prince of Tennis*, volume 30.

As I mentioned in the previous volume, the anime's scheduled to be back in March 2006!! BOOM BOOM BOOM

It'll return with the Nationals story arc, so both the manga fans and anime fans should enjoy it. You'll be seeing the games against Okinawa's Higa! But this time it'll be an OVA* instead of a television broadcast. We tried as hard as we could to get it broadcast so it could be seen by as many people as possible, but it just couldn't be helped. Anyway, because it'll be an OVA, the quality will be good. Keep an eye out for it! There'll be some updates in *Weekly Shonen Jump* magazine, so check it out!! And in the winter, a *Prince of Tennis* romance adventure game will be released from Konami. It's completely geared toward women, so all you guys out there, don't buy it! [*laughs*]

Oh, I'd also like to take this opportunity to make a correction and an apology. There was an error in the results of the 2005 Valentine's Day Chocolate Ranking announced in volume 29. The total for Yushi Oshitari, who finished 3rd, was not 241 but rather 214. So he actually did not place 2nd. I apologize for the error. The correction will be made in the reprint.

*An OVA is an "Original Video Animation" movie.—Ed.

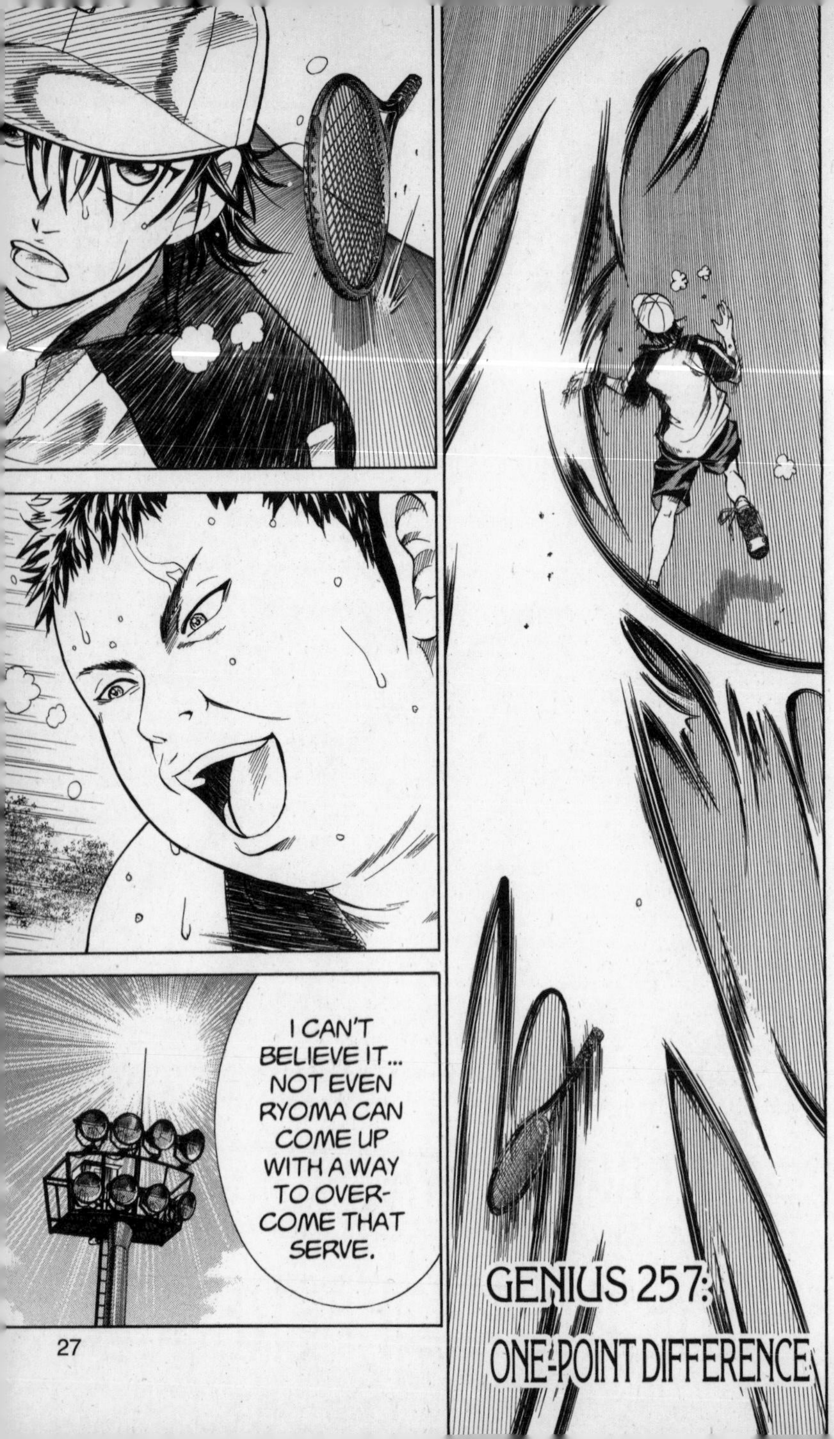
GENIUS 257:
ONE-POINT DIFFERENCE
I CAN'T BELIEVE IT... NOT EVEN RYOMA CAN COME UP WITH A WAY TO OVER-COME THAT SERVE.

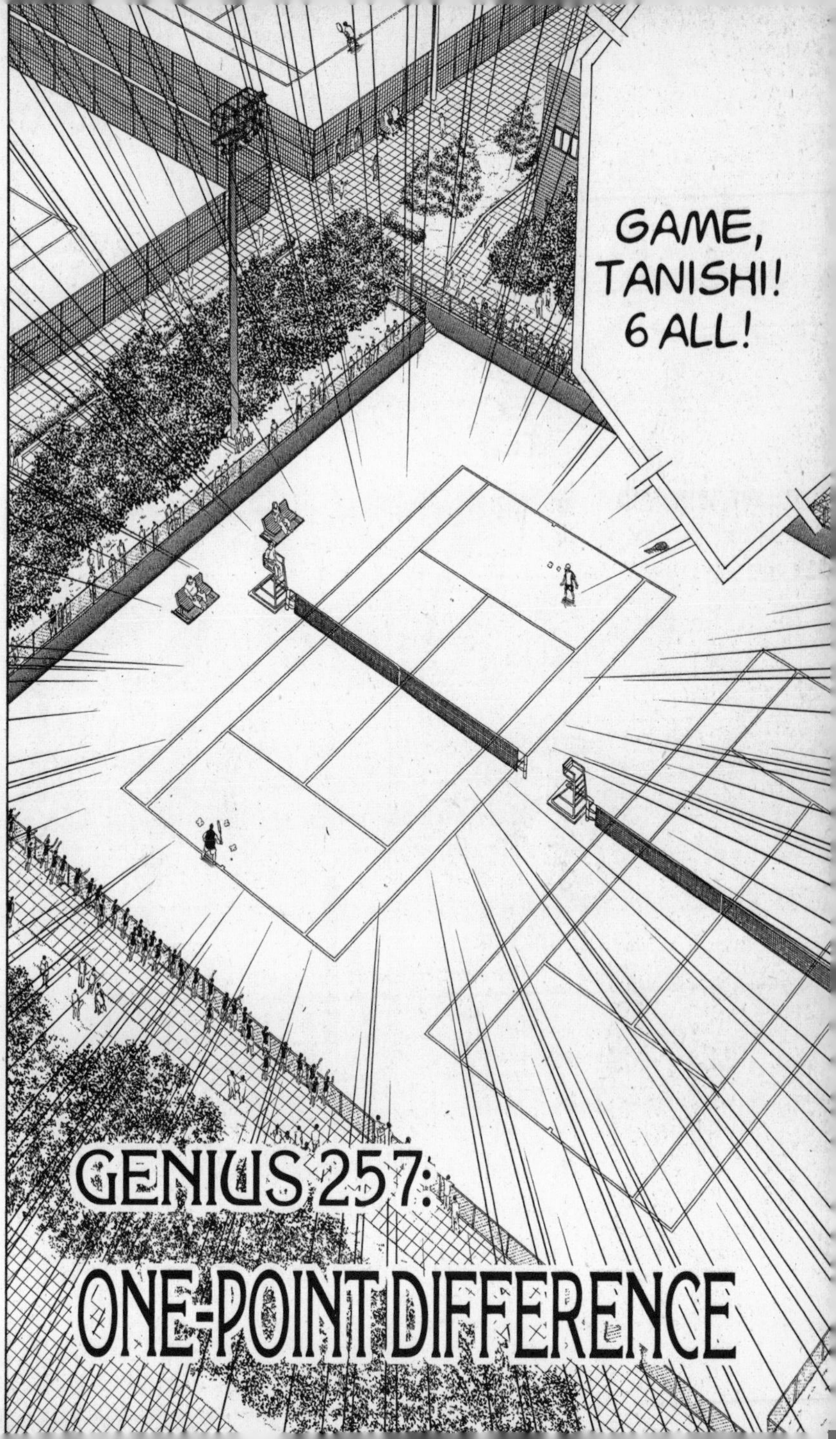
GAME, TANISHI! 6 ALL!
GENIUS 257:
ONE-POINT DIFFERENCE

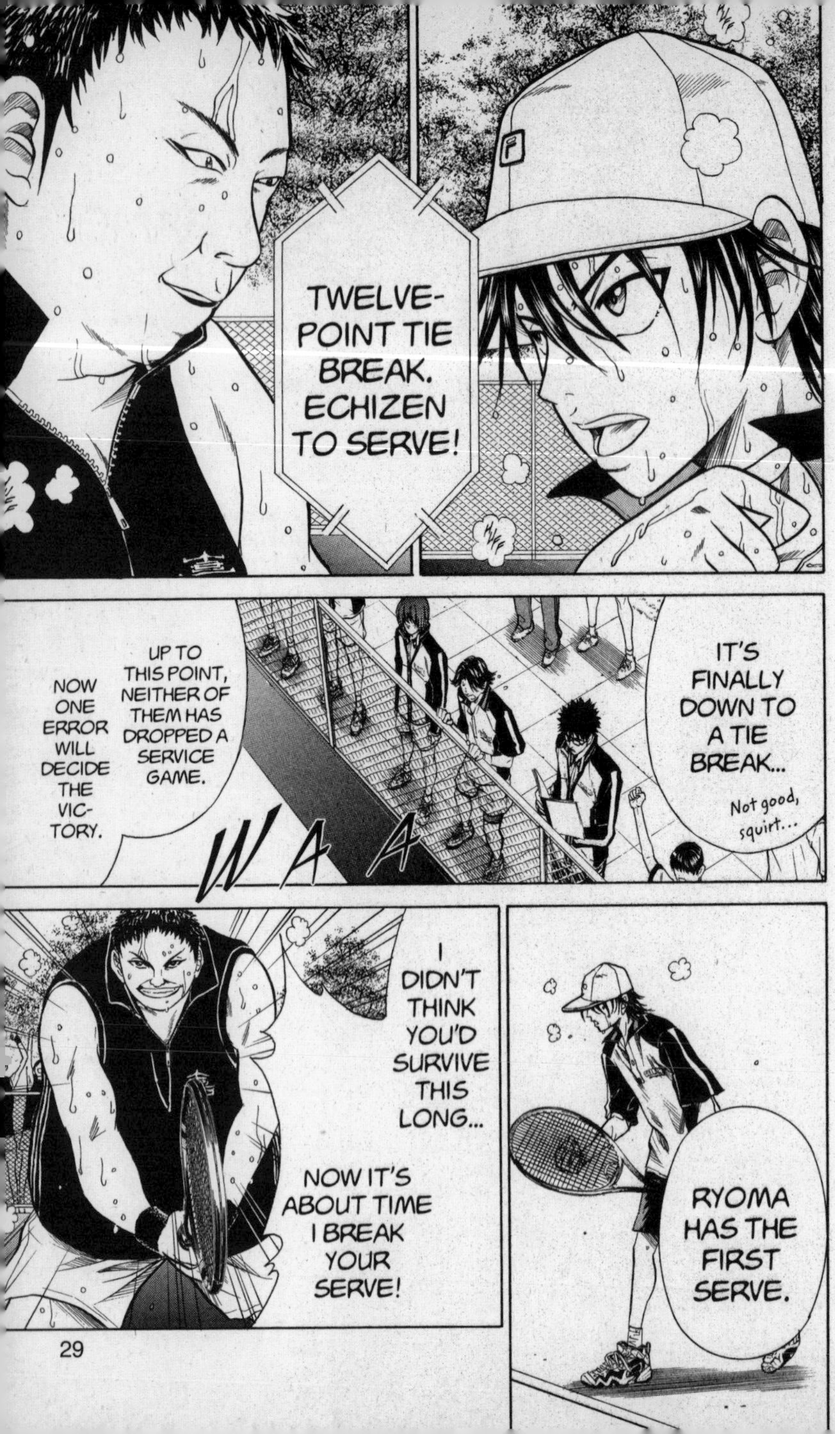
HUFF
TWELVE-POINT TIE BREAK. ECHIZEN TO SERVE!
HUFF
IT'S FINALLY DOWN TO A TIE BREAK...
Not good, squirt...
UP TO THIS POINT, NEITHER OF THEM HAS DROPPED A SERVICE GAME.
NOW ONE ERROR WILL DECIDE THE VIC-TORY.
WAA
RYOMA HAS THE FIRST SERVE.
I DIDN'T THINK YOU'D SURVIVE THIS LONG...
NOW IT'S ABOUT TIME I BREAK YOUR SERVE!

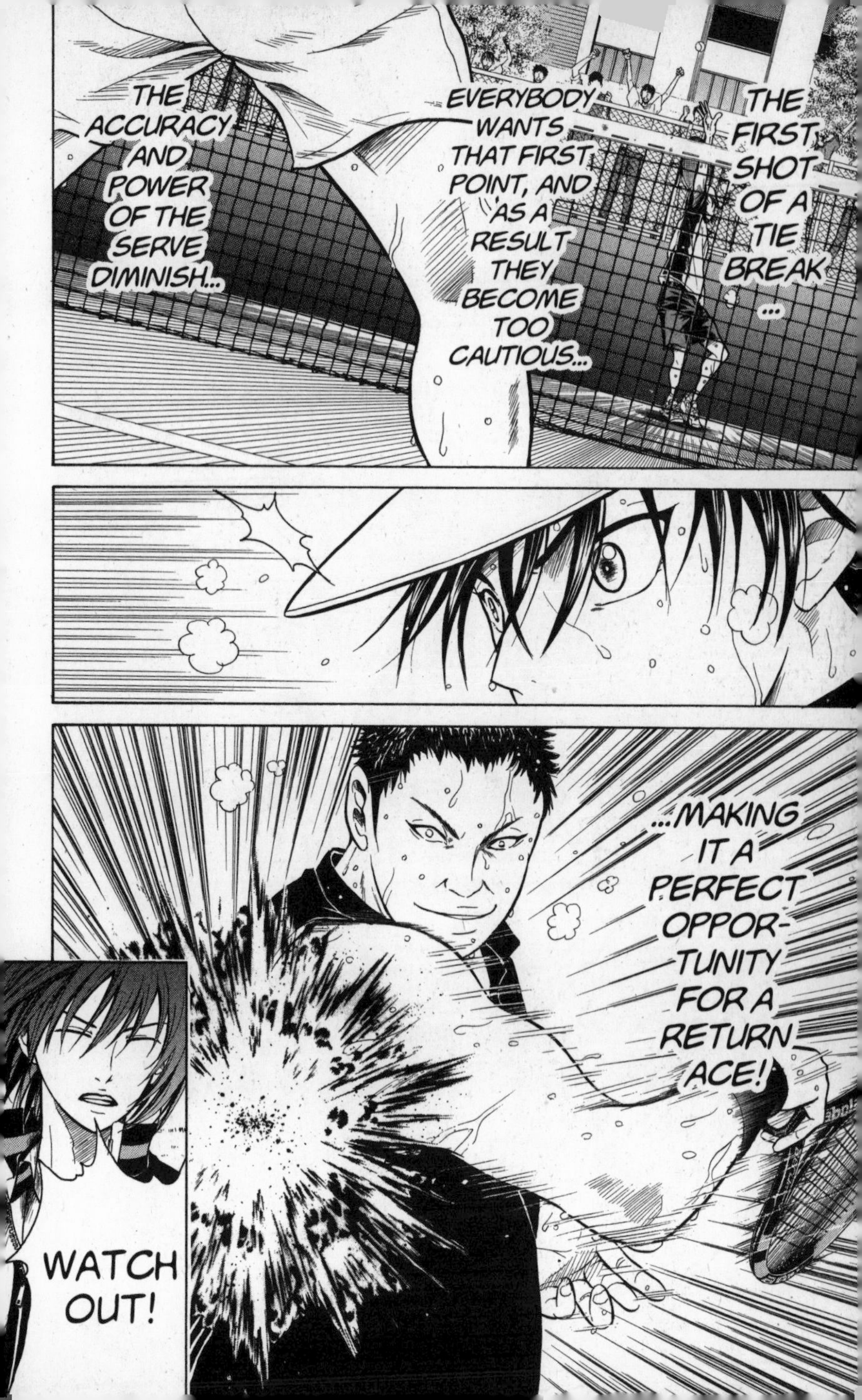
THE FIRST SHOT OF A TIE BREAK...
EVERYBODY WANTS THAT FIRST POINT, AND AS A RESULT THEY BECOME TOO CAUTIOUS...
THE ACCURACY AND POWER OF THE SERVE DIMINISH...
...MAKING IT A PERFECT OPPOR-TUNITY FOR A RETURN ACE!
WATCH OUT!

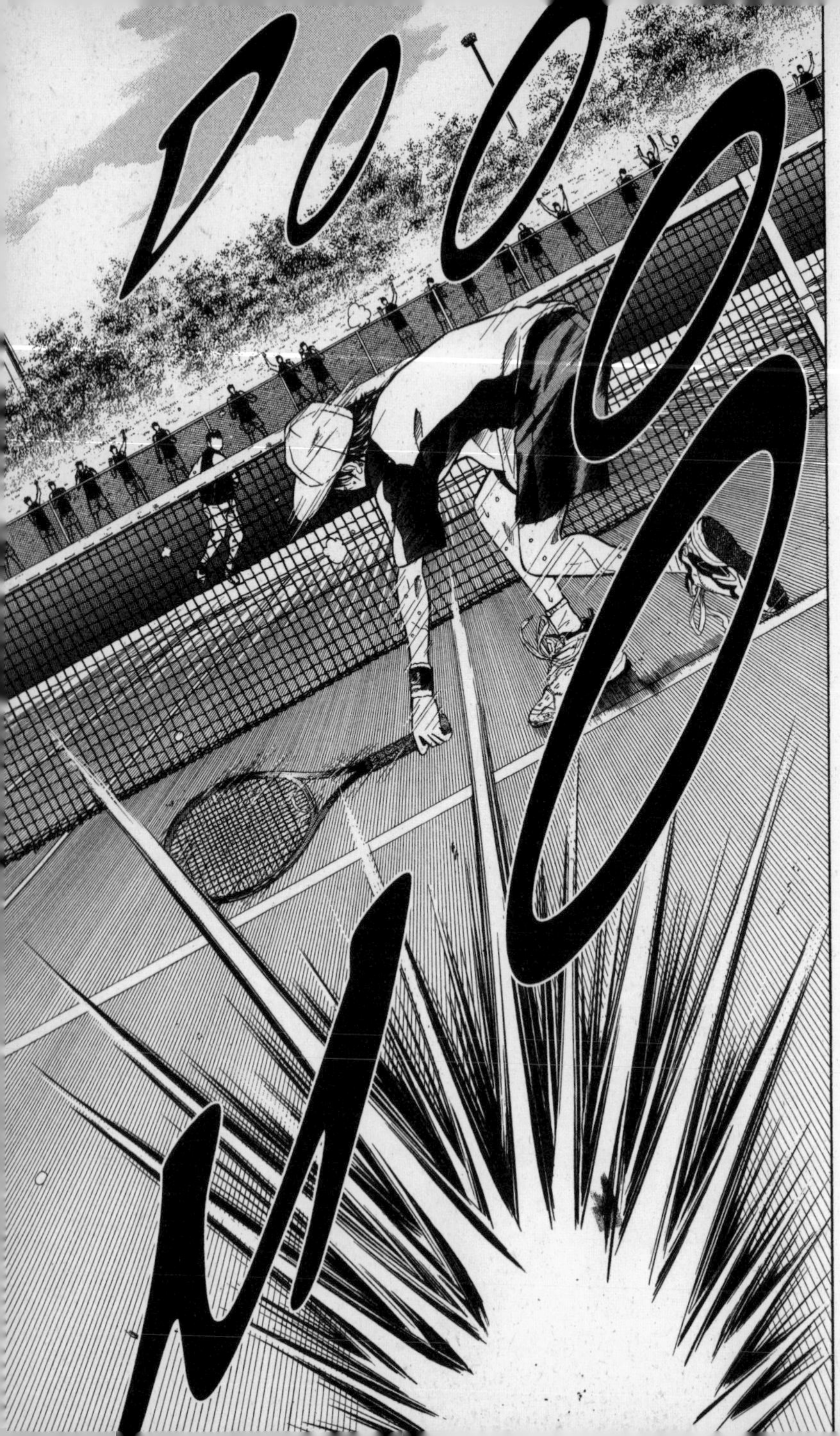

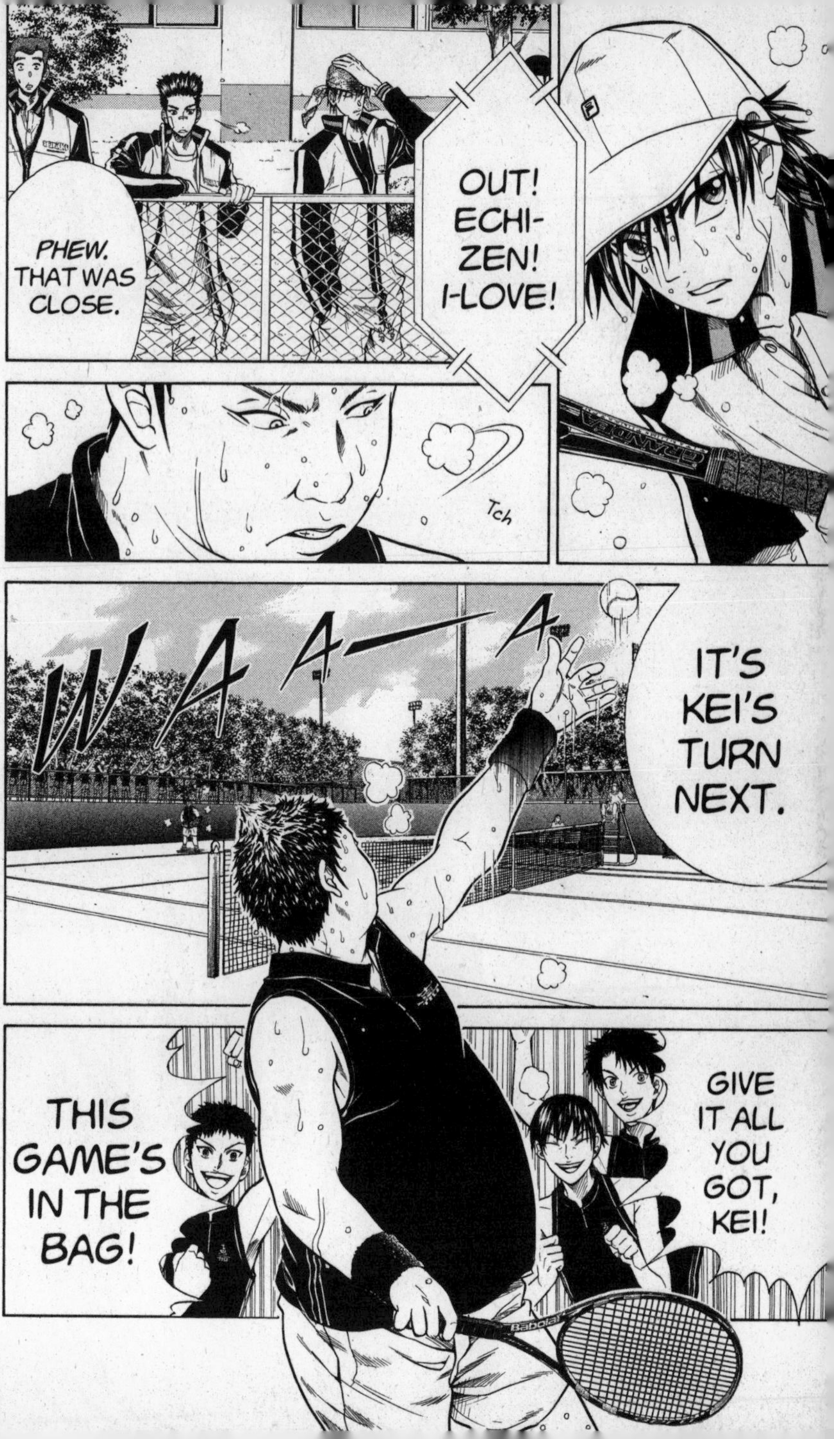
OUT! ECHIZEN! I-LOVE!
PHEW. THAT WAS CLOSE.
Tch
WAA—A
IT'S KEI'S TURN NEXT.
GIVE IT ALL YOU GOT, KEI!
THIS GAME'S IN THE BAG!

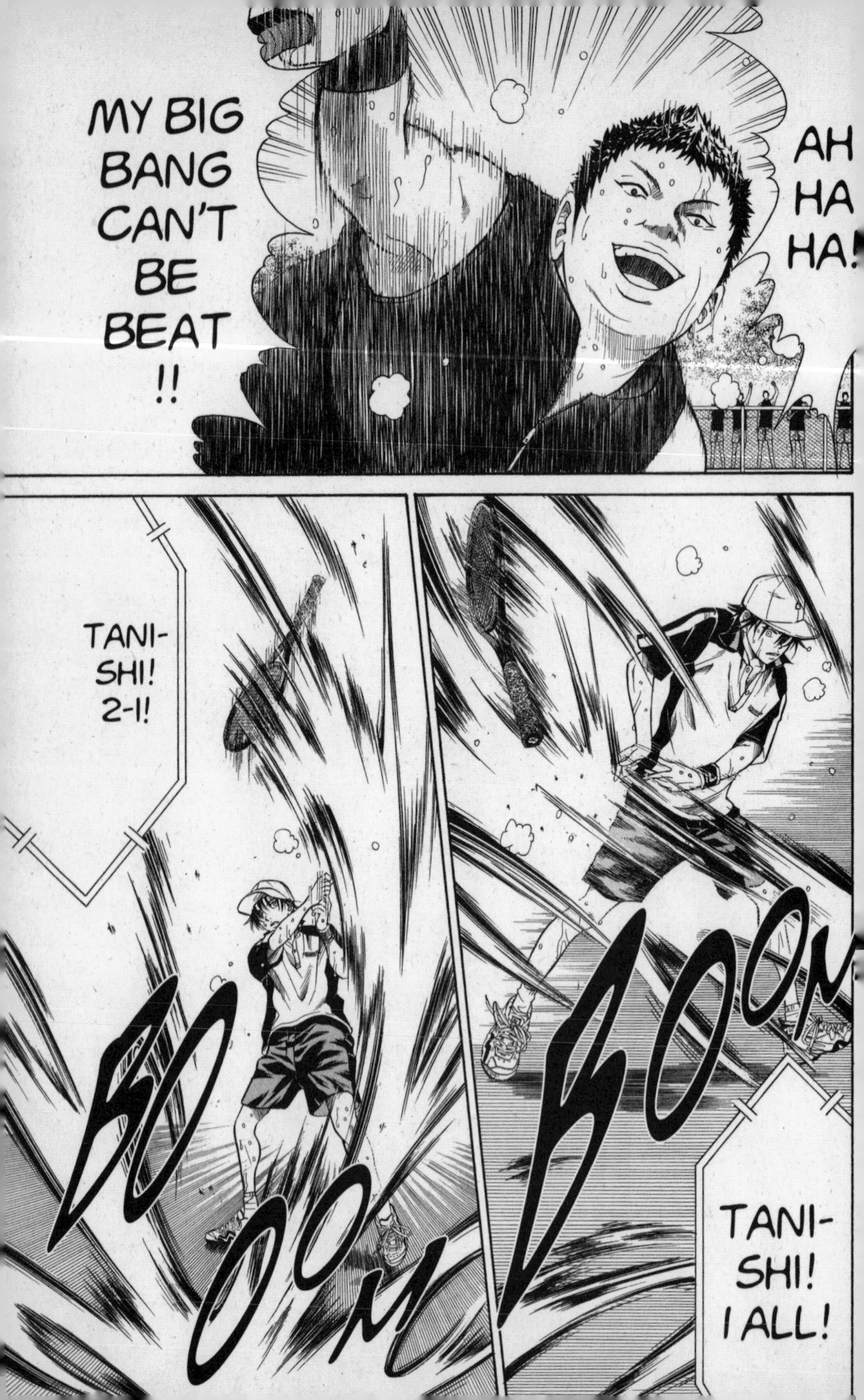
AH HA HA!
MY BIG BANG CAN'T BE BEAT!!
BOOM
TANI-SHI! 1 ALL!
TANI-SHI! 2-1!
BOOM

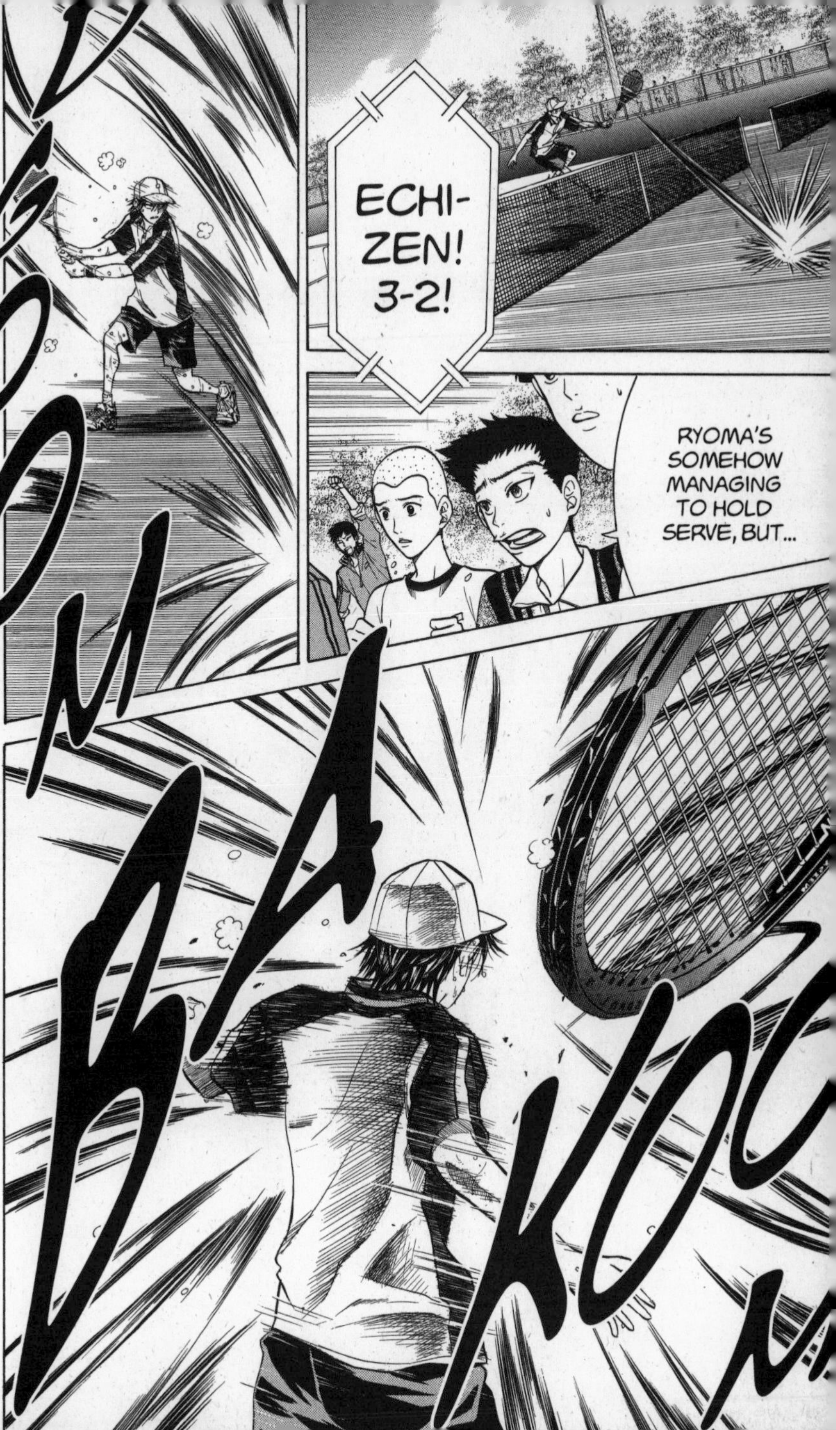
ECHI-ZEN! 3-2!
RYOMA'S SOMEHOW MANAGING TO HOLD SERVE, BUT...

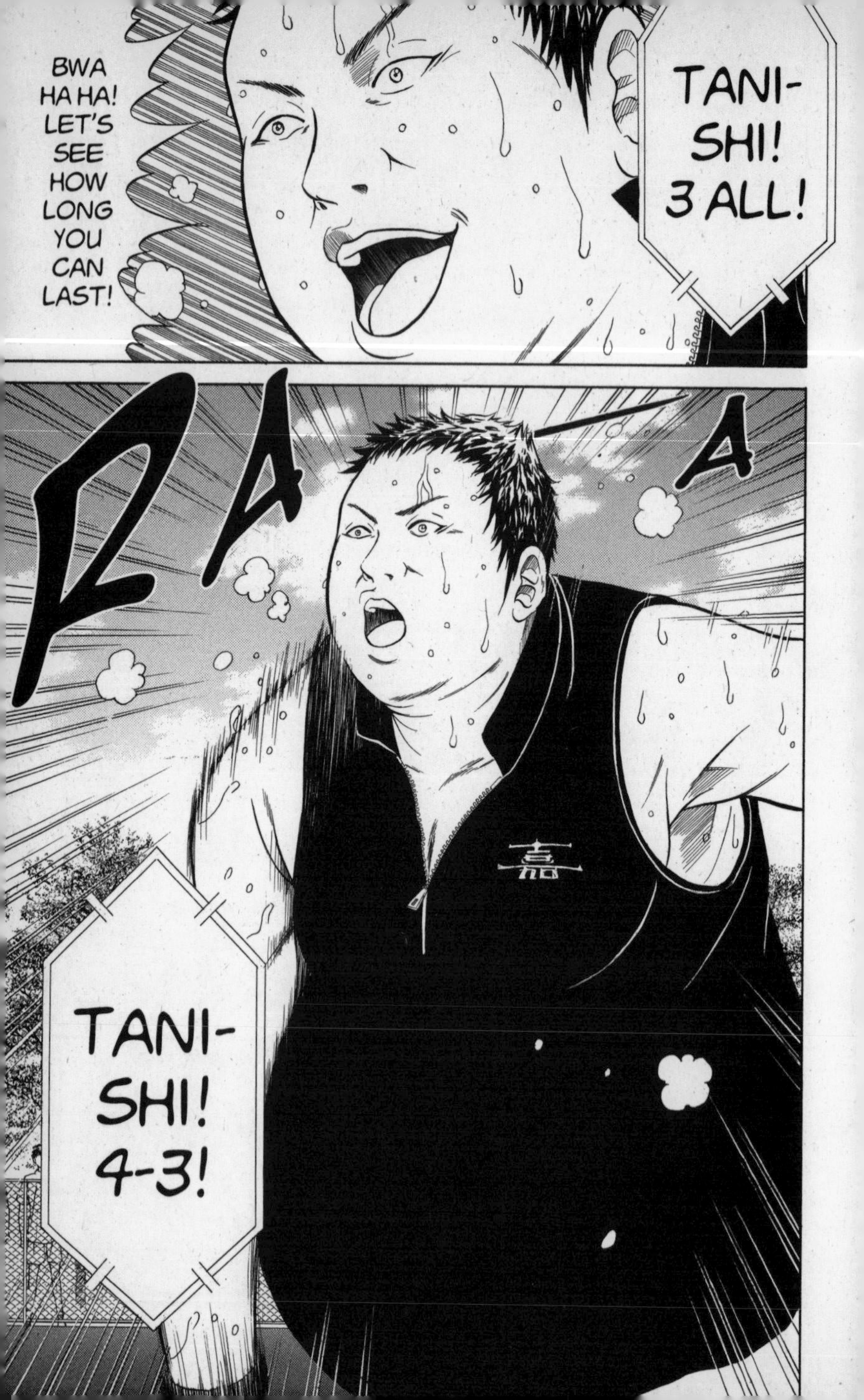
TANI-SHI! 3 ALL!
BWA HA HA! LET'S SEE HOW LONG YOU CAN LAST!
RAA
TANI-SHI! 4-3!

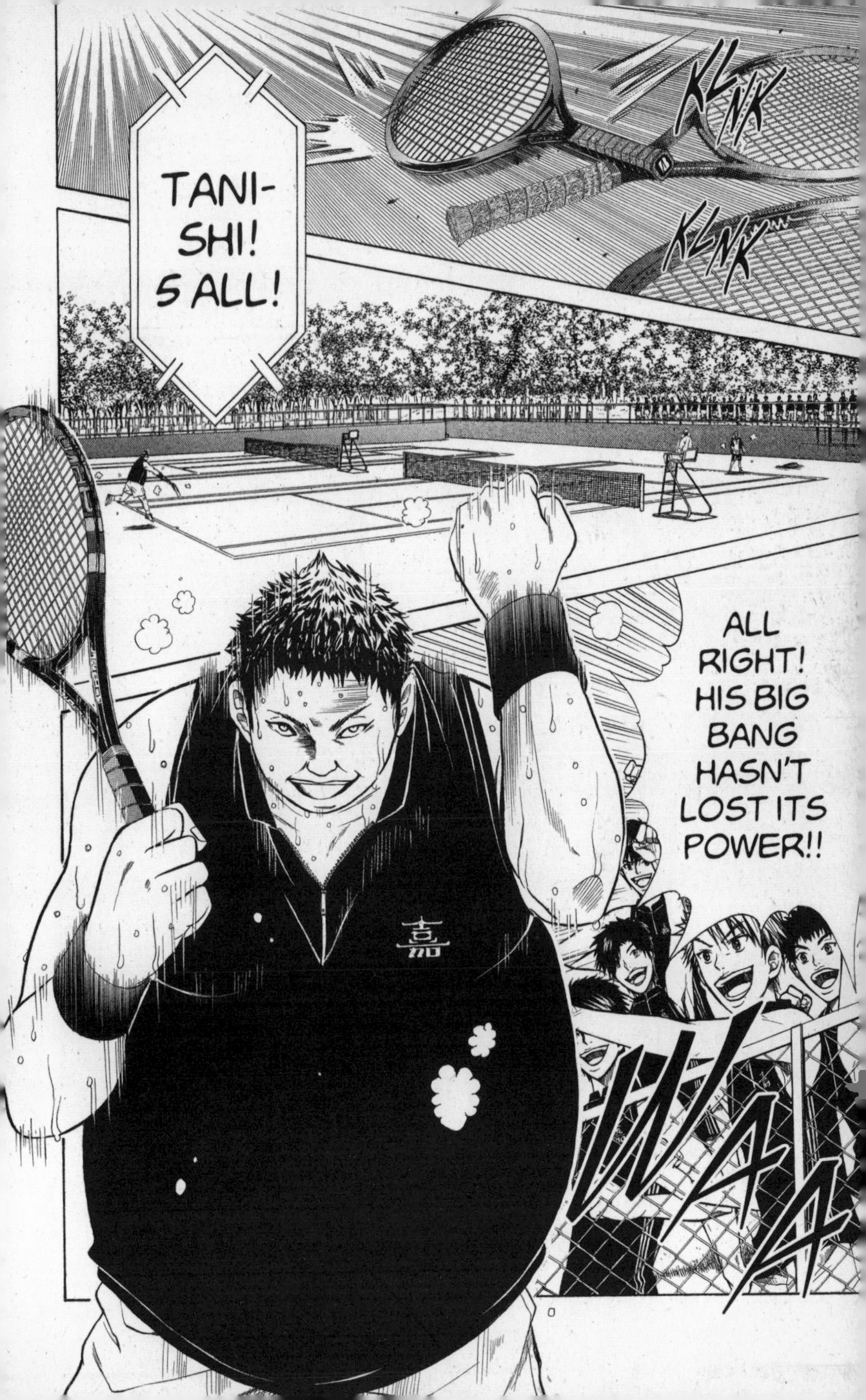
KLNK
KLNK
TANI-SHI! 5 ALL!
ALL RIGHT! HIS BIG BANG HASN'T LOST ITS POWER!!
嘉
WAAA

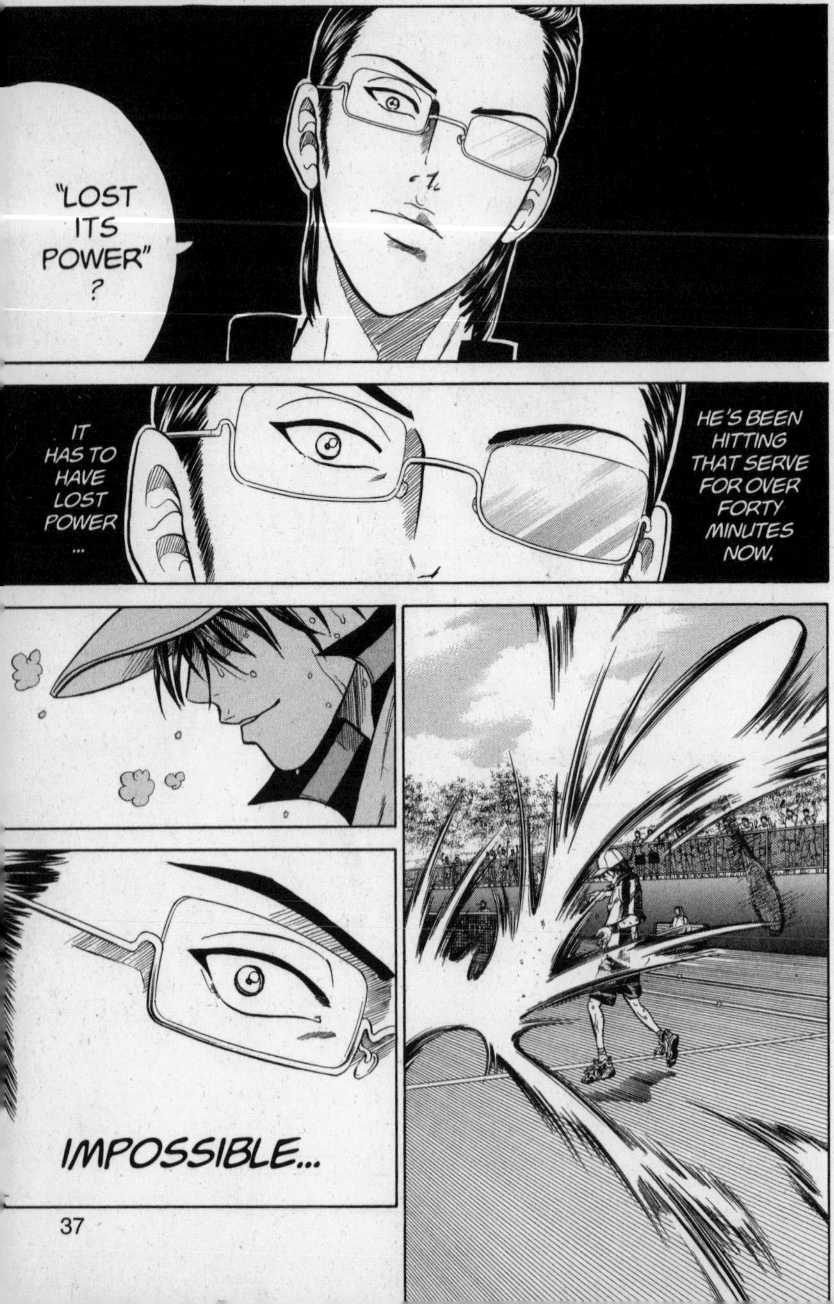
READ THIS WAY
"LOST ITS POWER" ?
HE'S BEEN HITTING THAT SERVE FOR OVER FORTY MINUTES NOW.
IT HAS TO HAVE LOST POWER ...
IMPOSSIBLE...

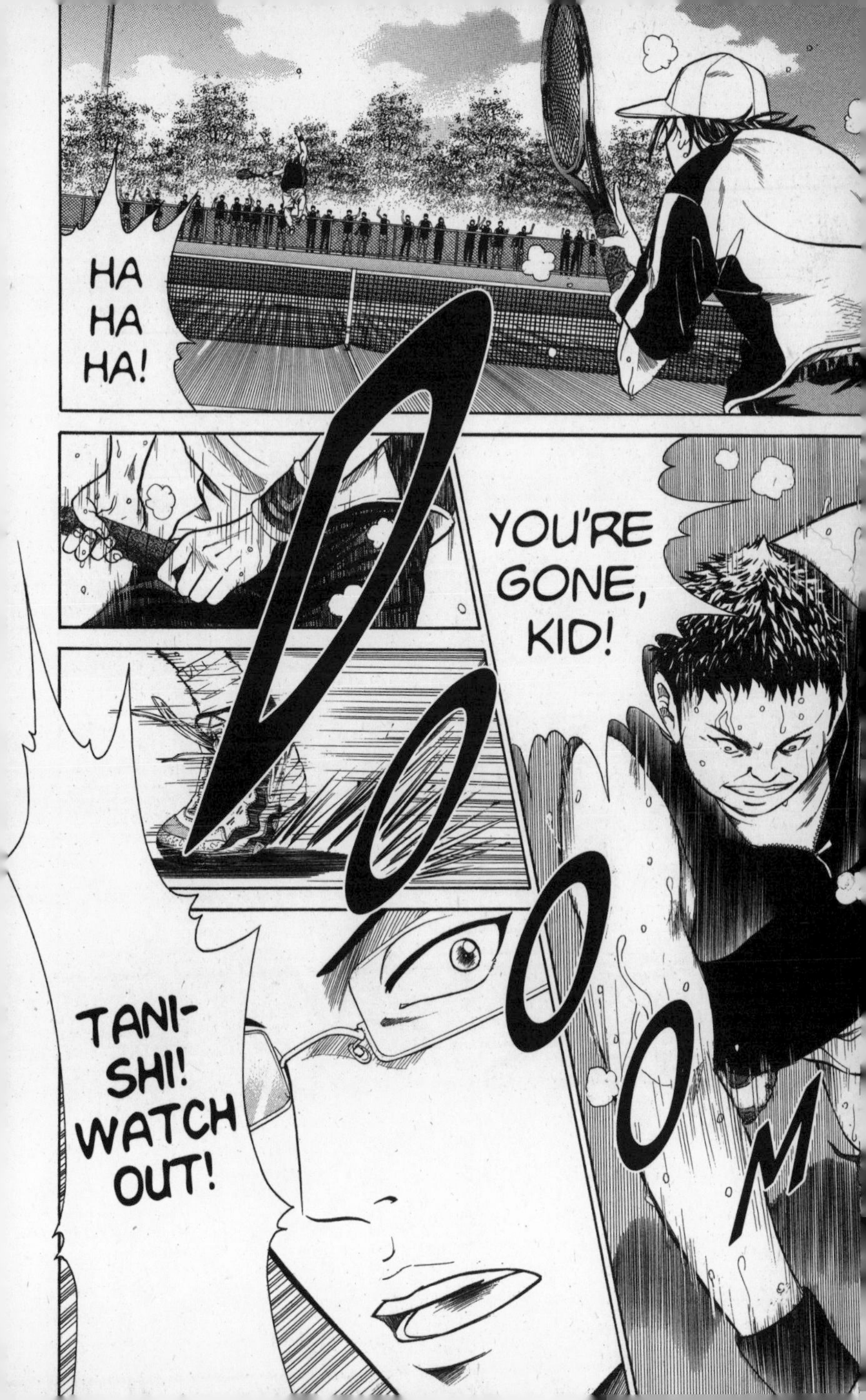
HA HA HA!
YOU'RE GONE, KID!
DOOOOOM
TANI-SHI! WATCH OUT!

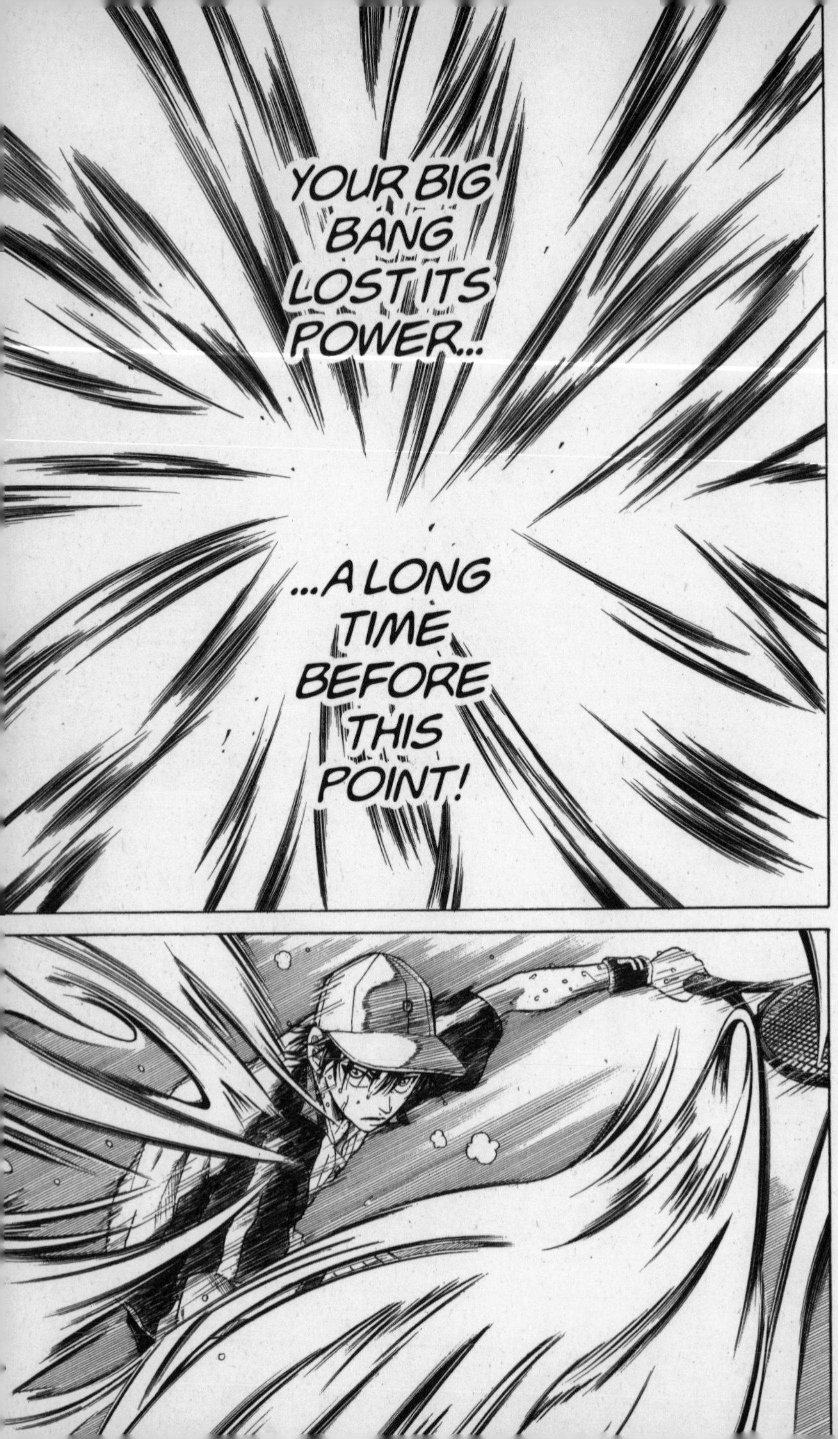
YOUR BIG BANG LOST ITS POWER...
...A LONG TIME BEFORE THIS POINT!

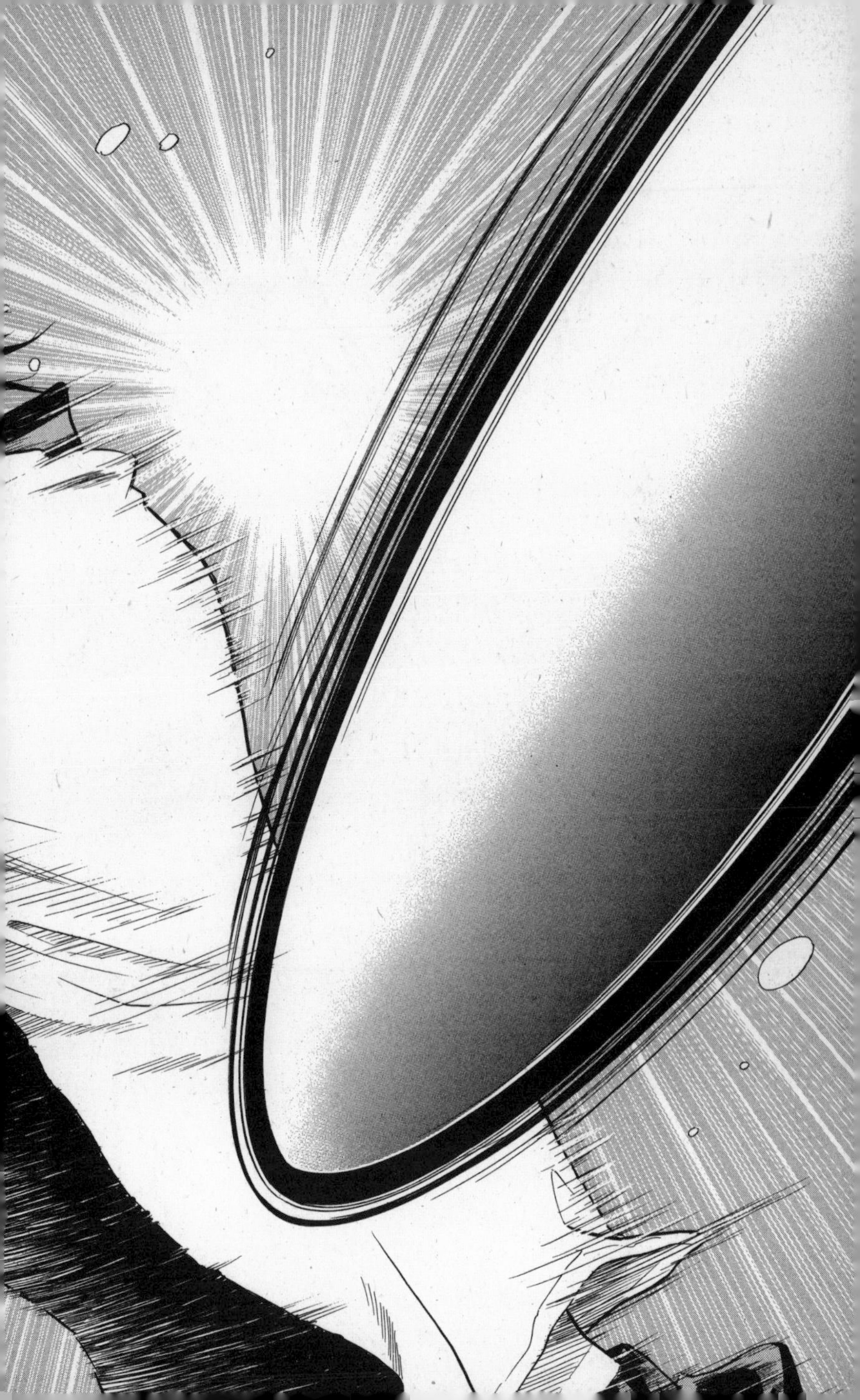

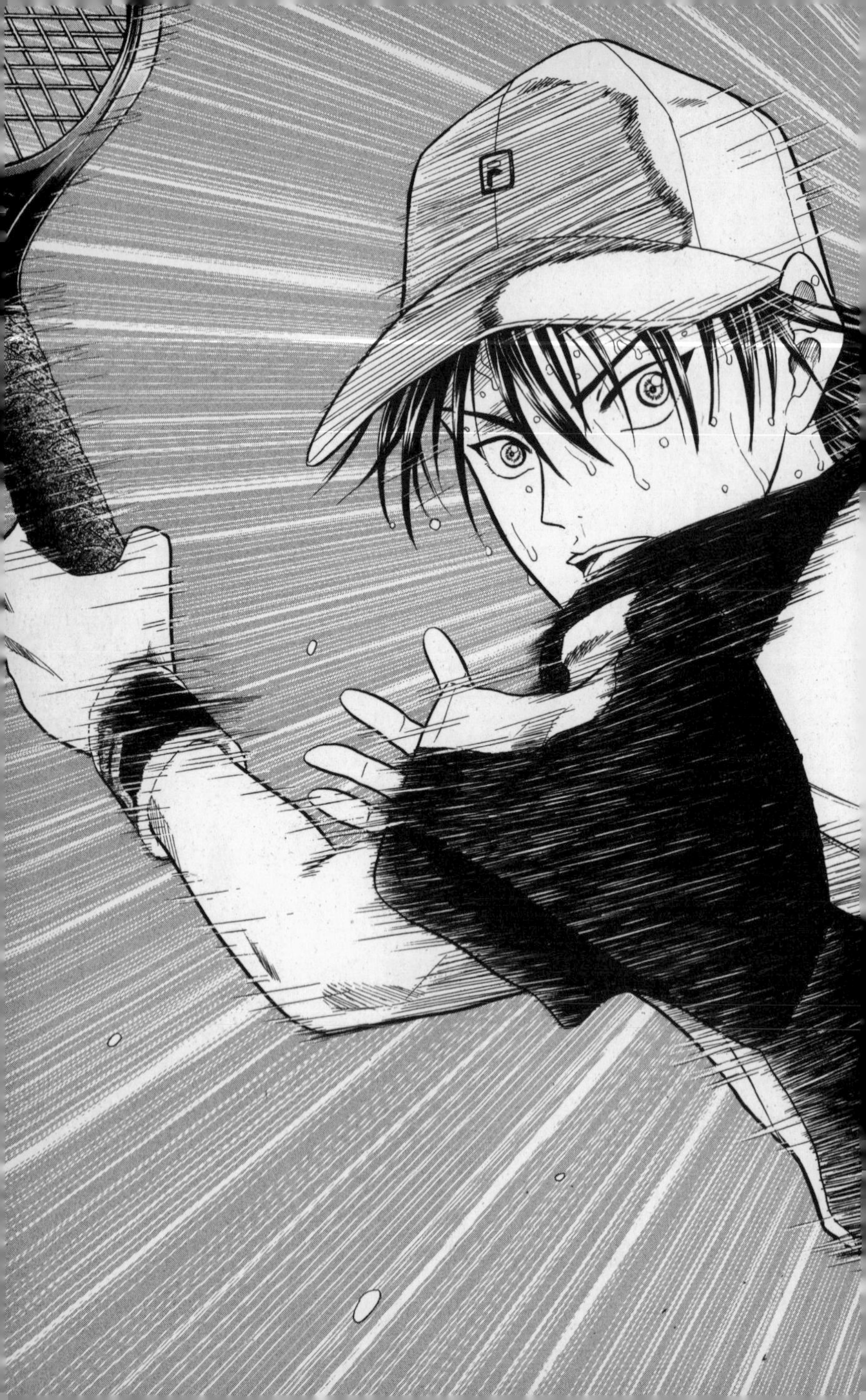

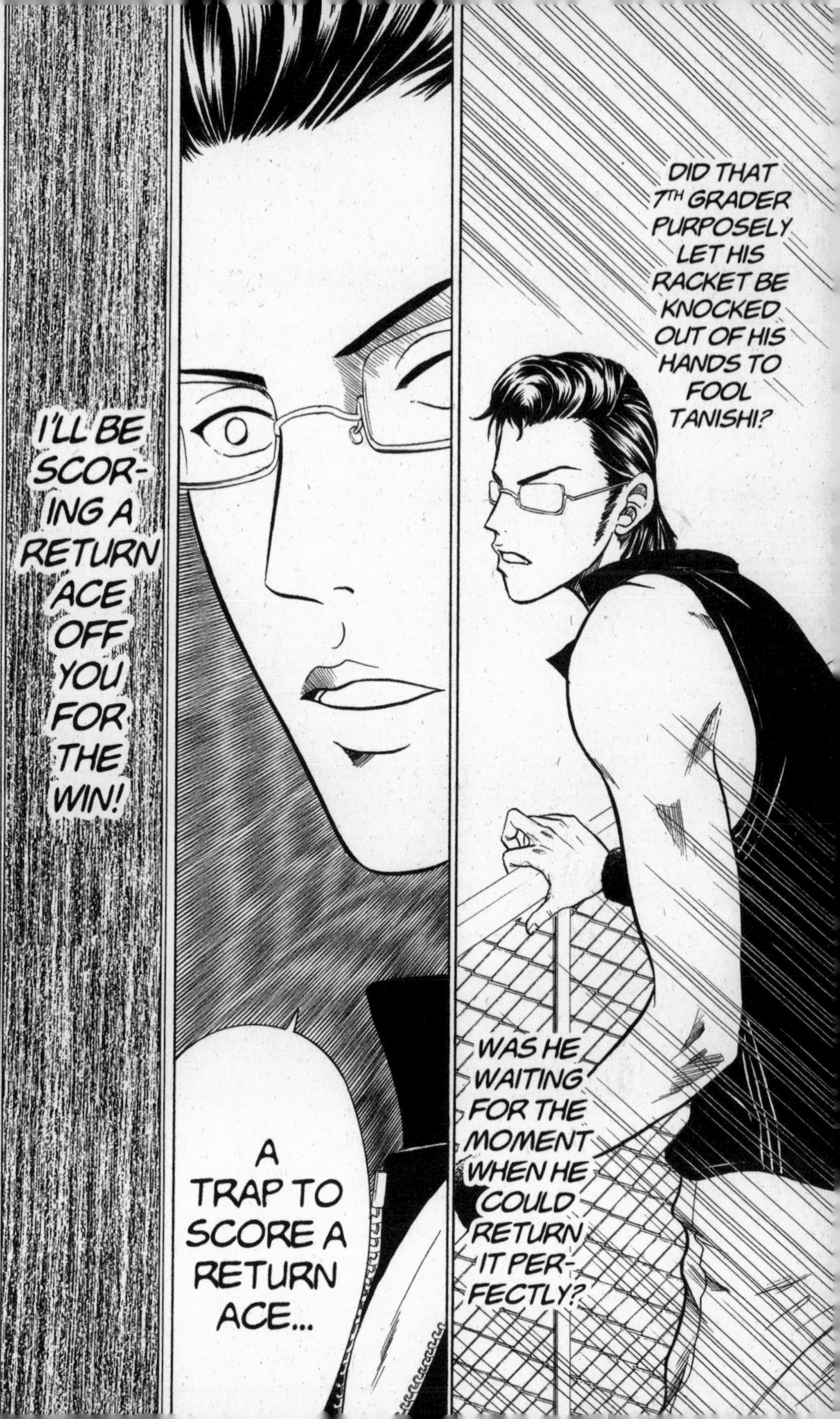
DID THAT 7TH GRADER PURPOSELY LET HIS RACKET BE KNOCKED OUT OF HIS HANDS TO FOOL TANISHI?
WAS HE WAITING FOR THE MOMENT WHEN HE COULD RETURN IT PER-FECTLY?
A TRAP TO SCORE A RETURN ACE...
I'LL BE SCOR-ING A RETURN ACE OFF YOU FOR THE WIN!

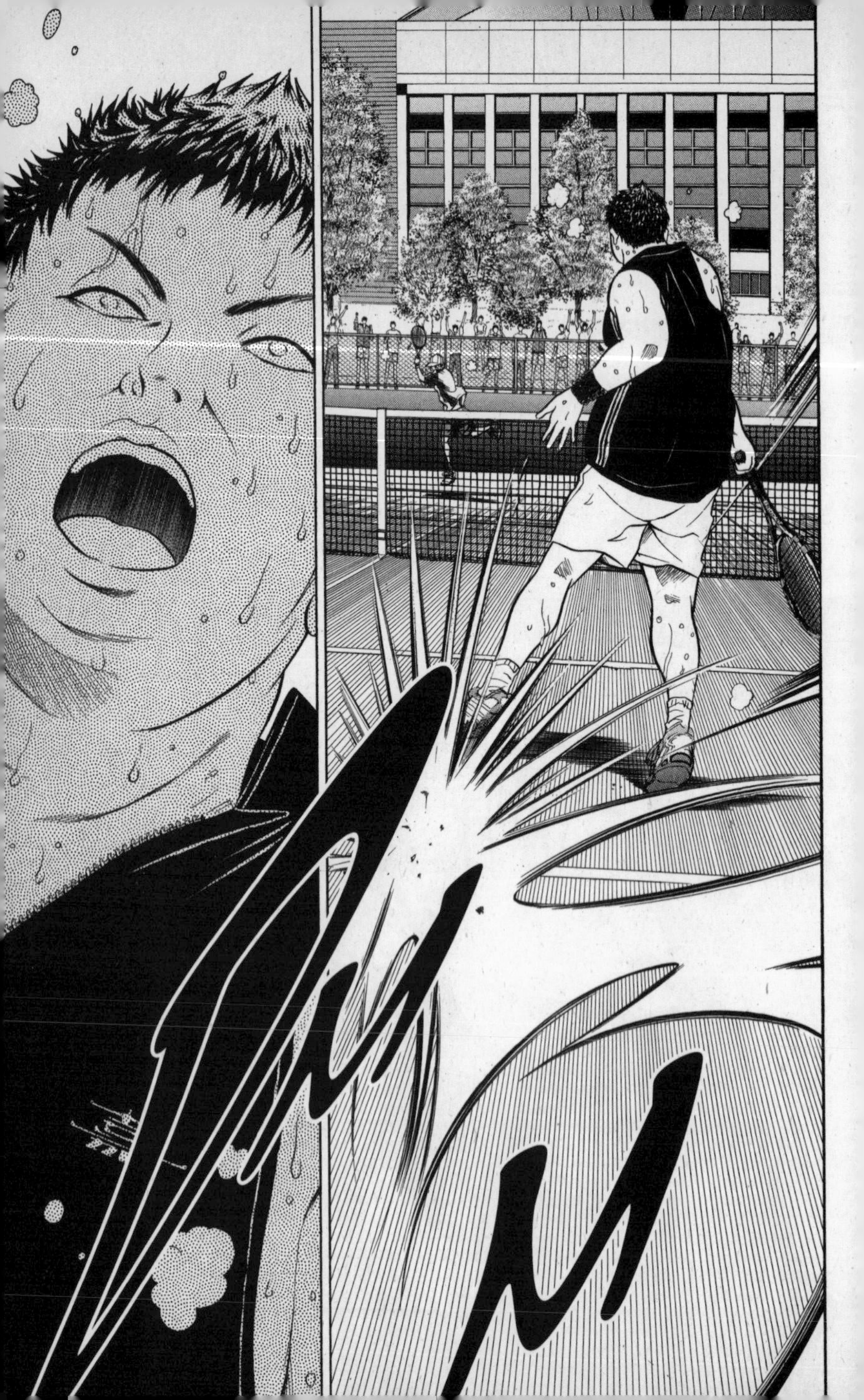

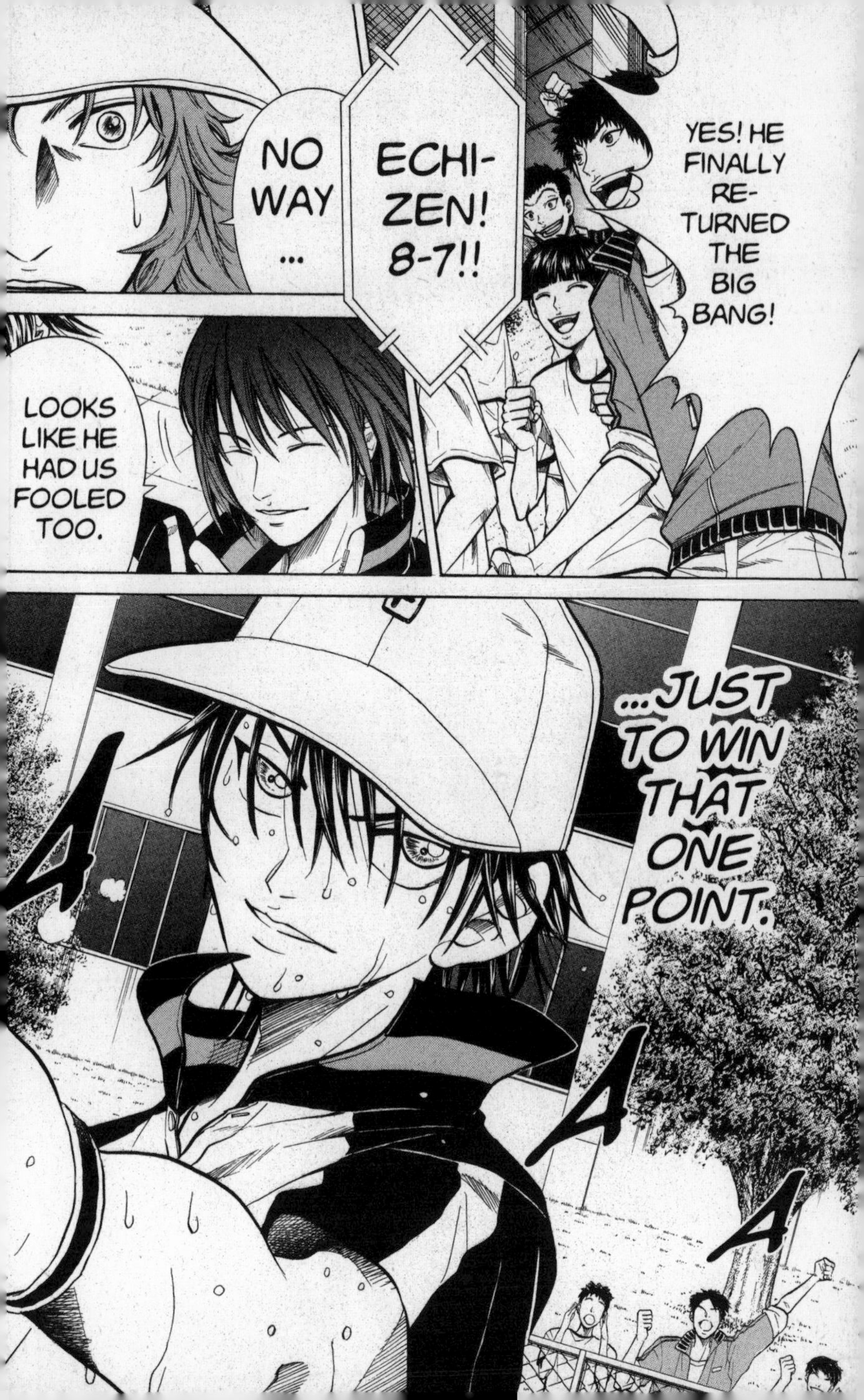
YES! HE FINALLY RE-TURNED THE BIG BANG!
ECHI-ZEN! 8-7!!
NO WAY ...
LOOKS LIKE HE HAD US FOOLED TOO.
...JUST TO WIN THAT ONE POINT.

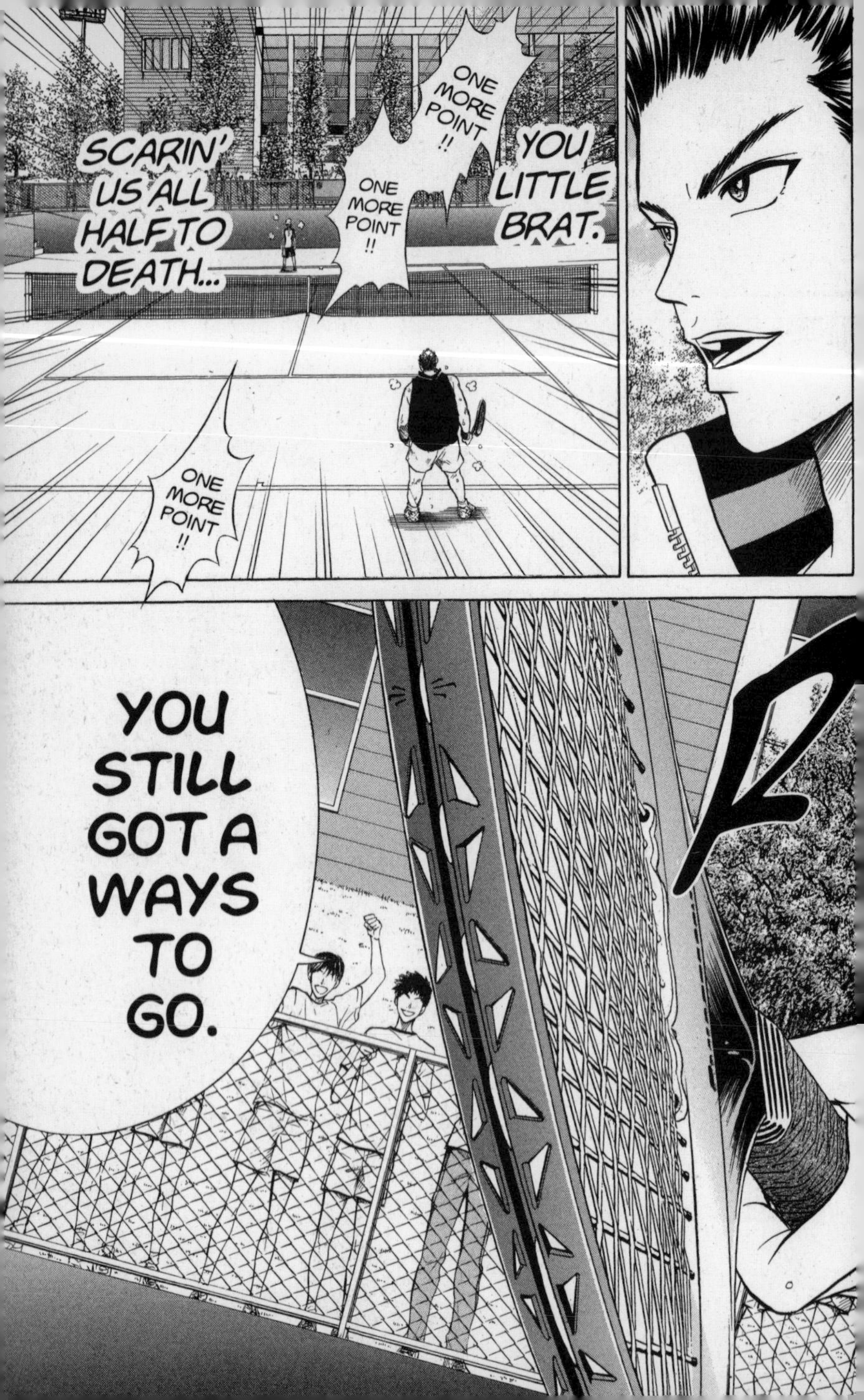
ONE MORE POINT!!
YOU LITTLE BRAT.
ONE MORE POINT!!
SCARIN' US ALL HALF TO DEATH...
ONE MORE POINT!!
YOU STILL GOT A WAYS TO GO.

テニスの王子様

THE PRINCE OF TENNIS

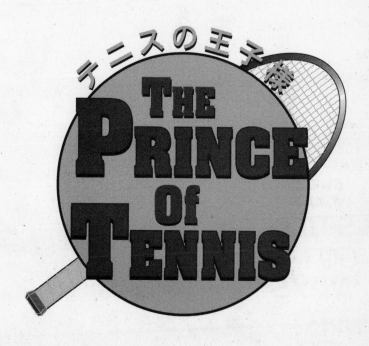

GENIUS 258: LAST RESORT

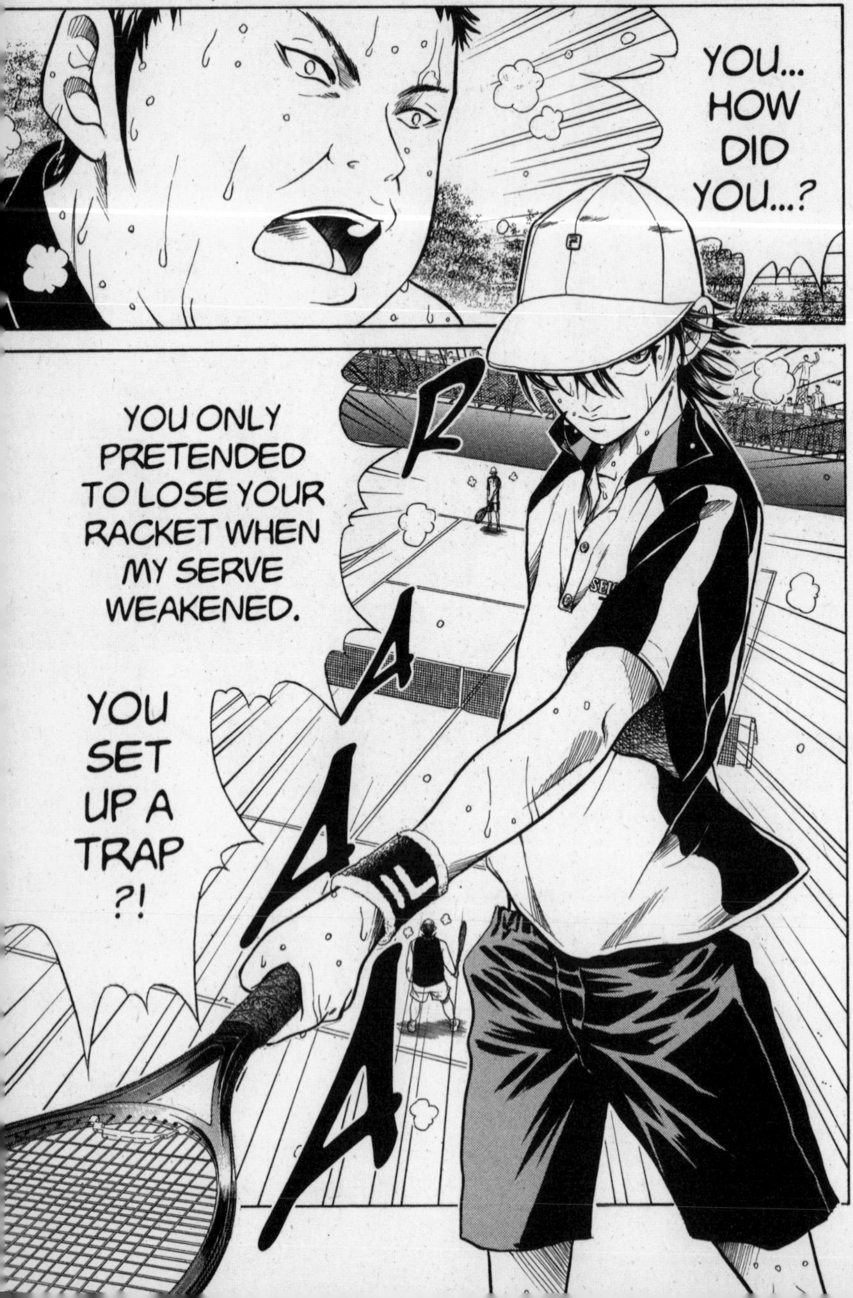
YOU... HOW DID YOU...?
YOU ONLY PRETENDED TO LOSE YOUR RACKET WHEN MY SERVE WEAKENED.
YOU SET UP A TRAP ?!

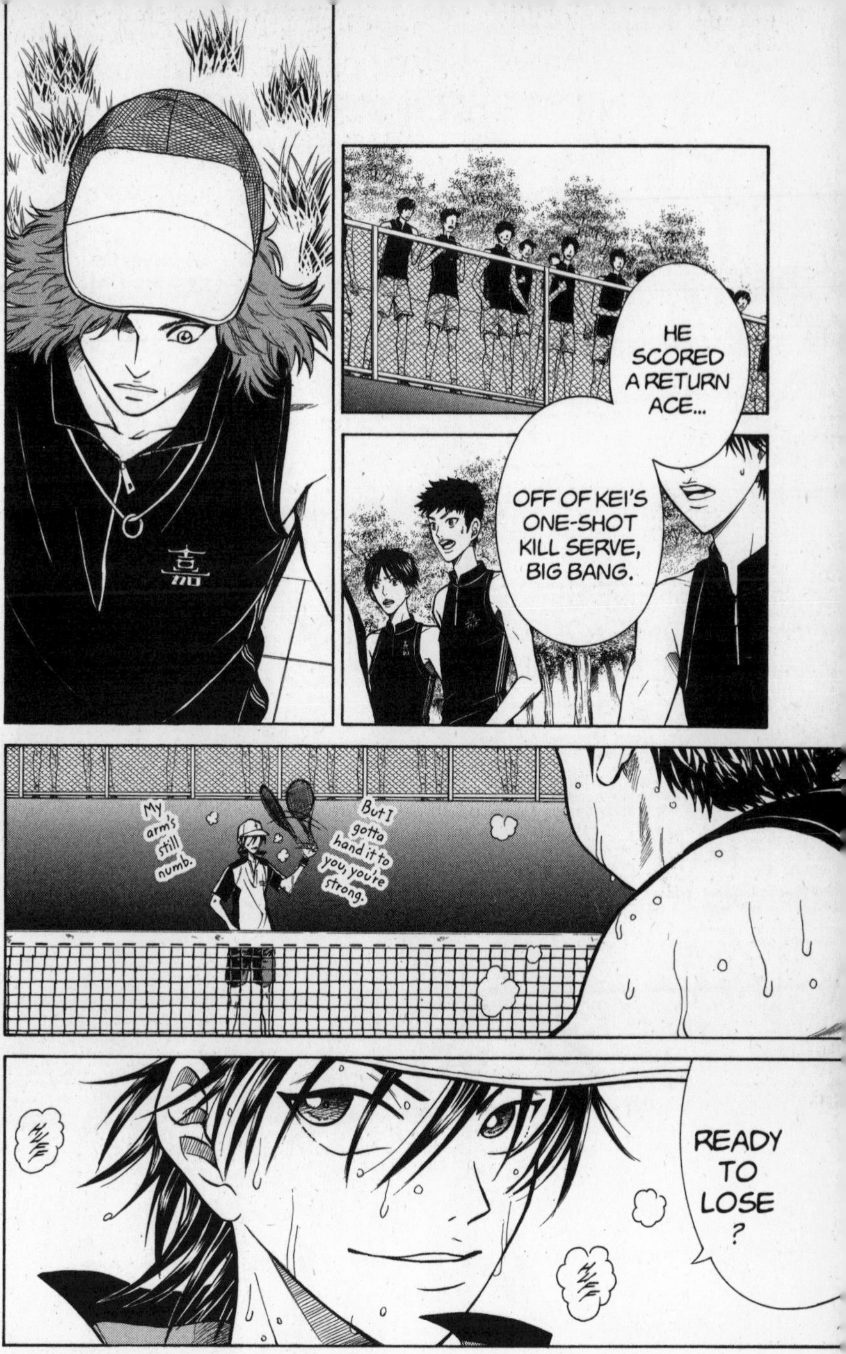
HE SCORED A RETURN ACE...
OFF OF KEI'S ONE-SHOT KILL SERVE, BIG BANG.
But I gotta hand it to you, you're strong.
My arm's still numb.
READY TO LOSE?

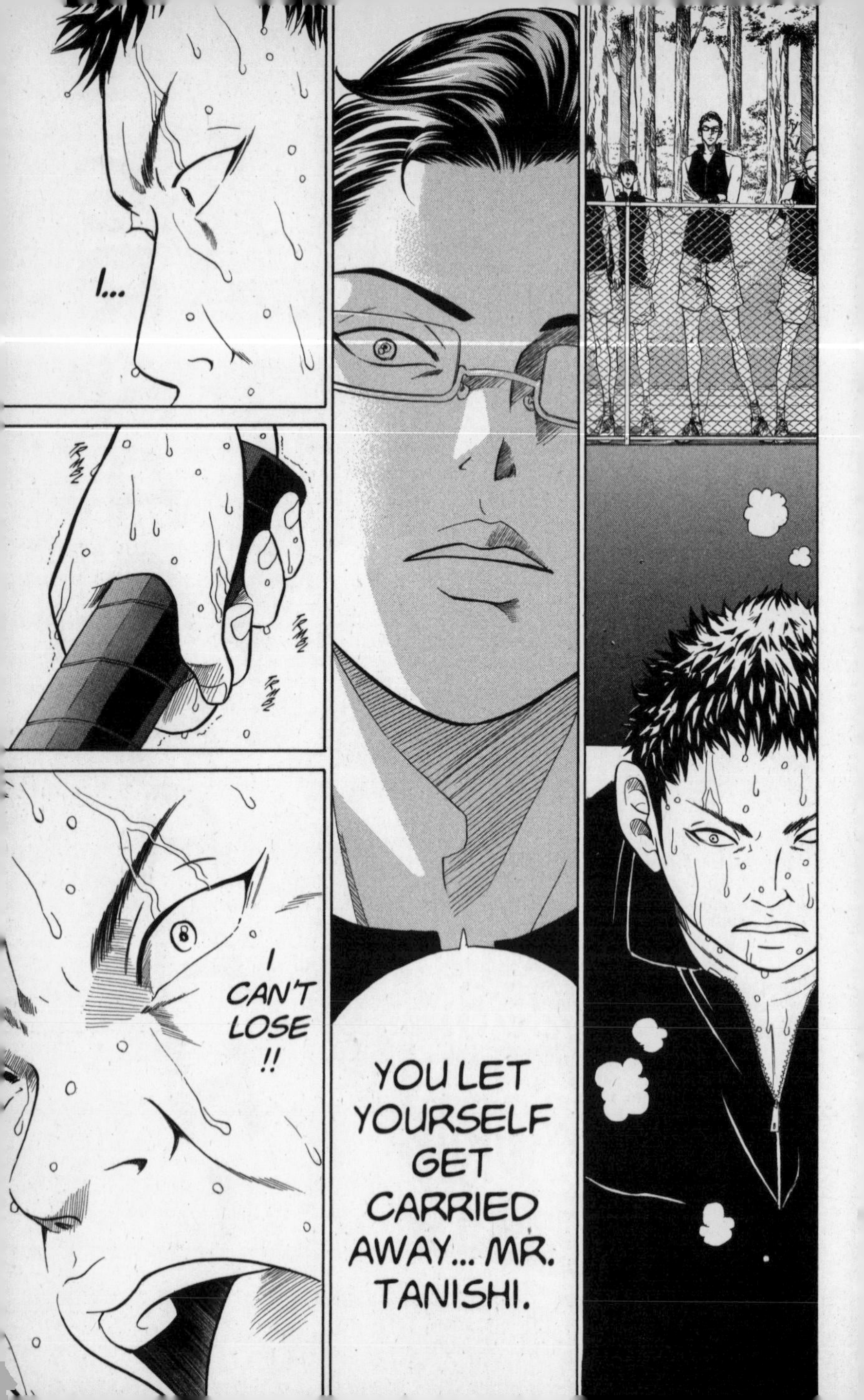
YOU LET YOURSELF GET CARRIED AWAY... MR. TANISHI.
I...
I CAN'T LOSE!!

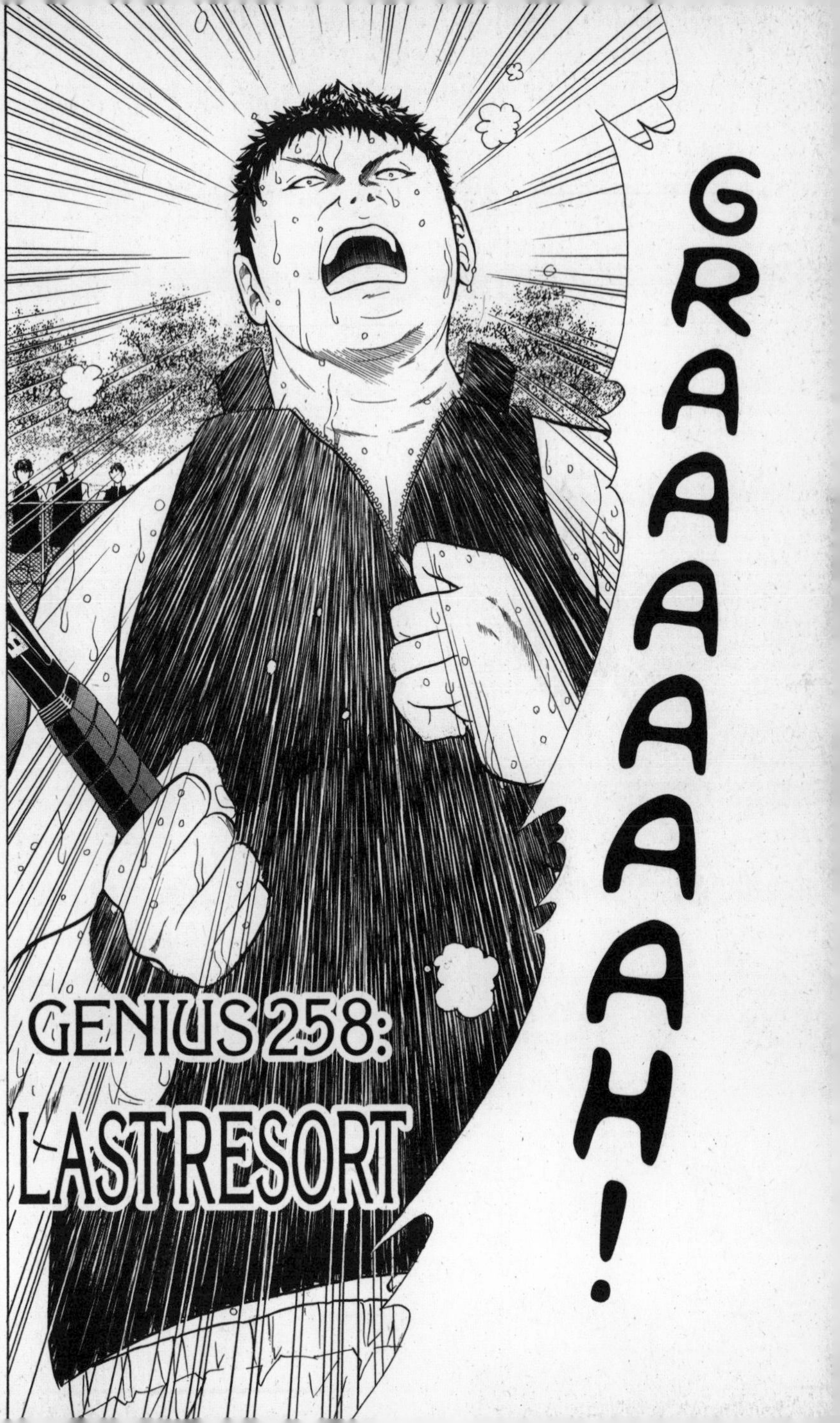
GRAAAAAAAH!
GENIUS 258:
LAST RESORT

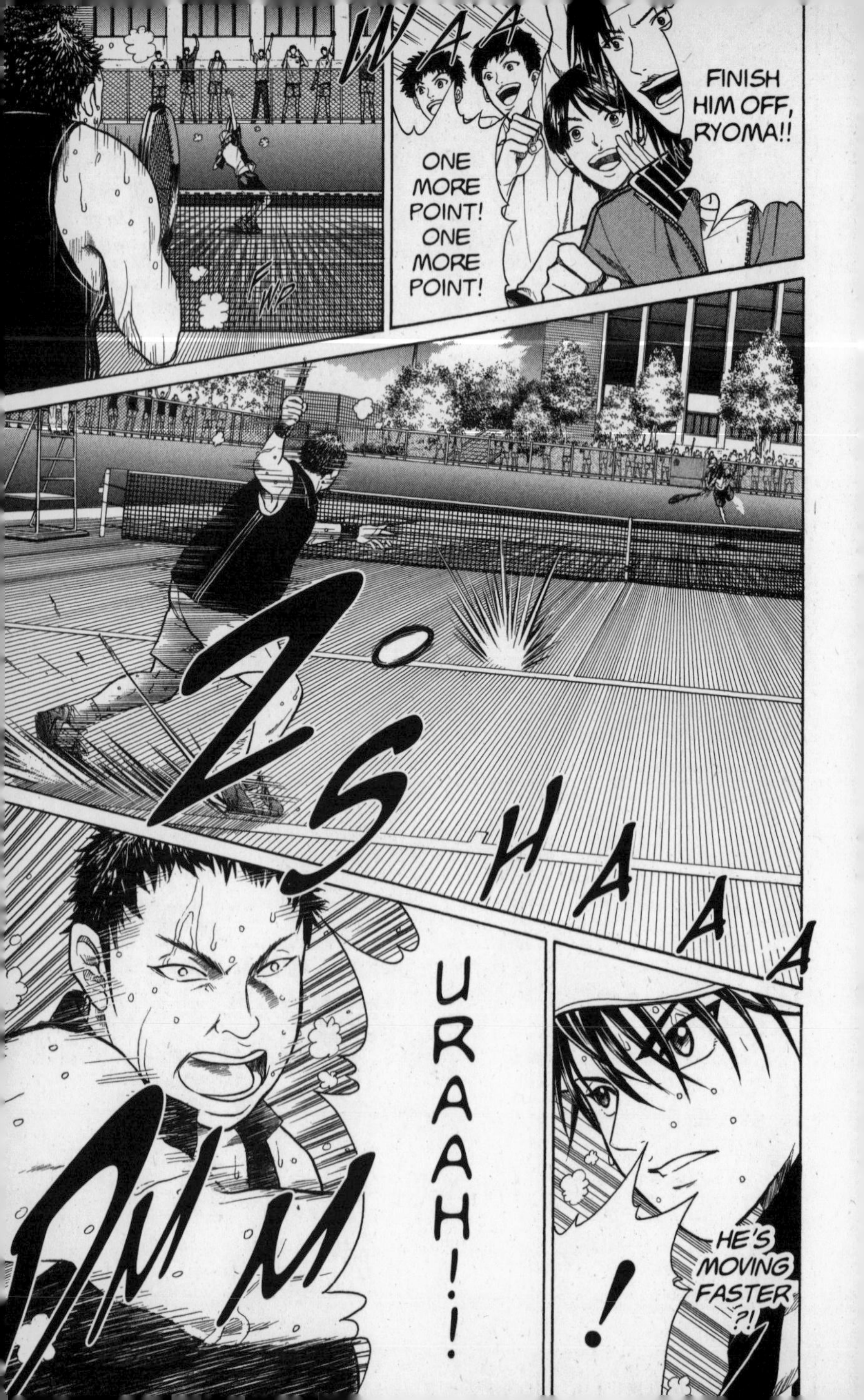
FINISH HIM OFF, RYOMA!!
ONE MORE POINT! ONE MORE POINT!
WAA
FWP
ZSHAAA
HE'S MOVING FASTER ?!
!
URAAH!!

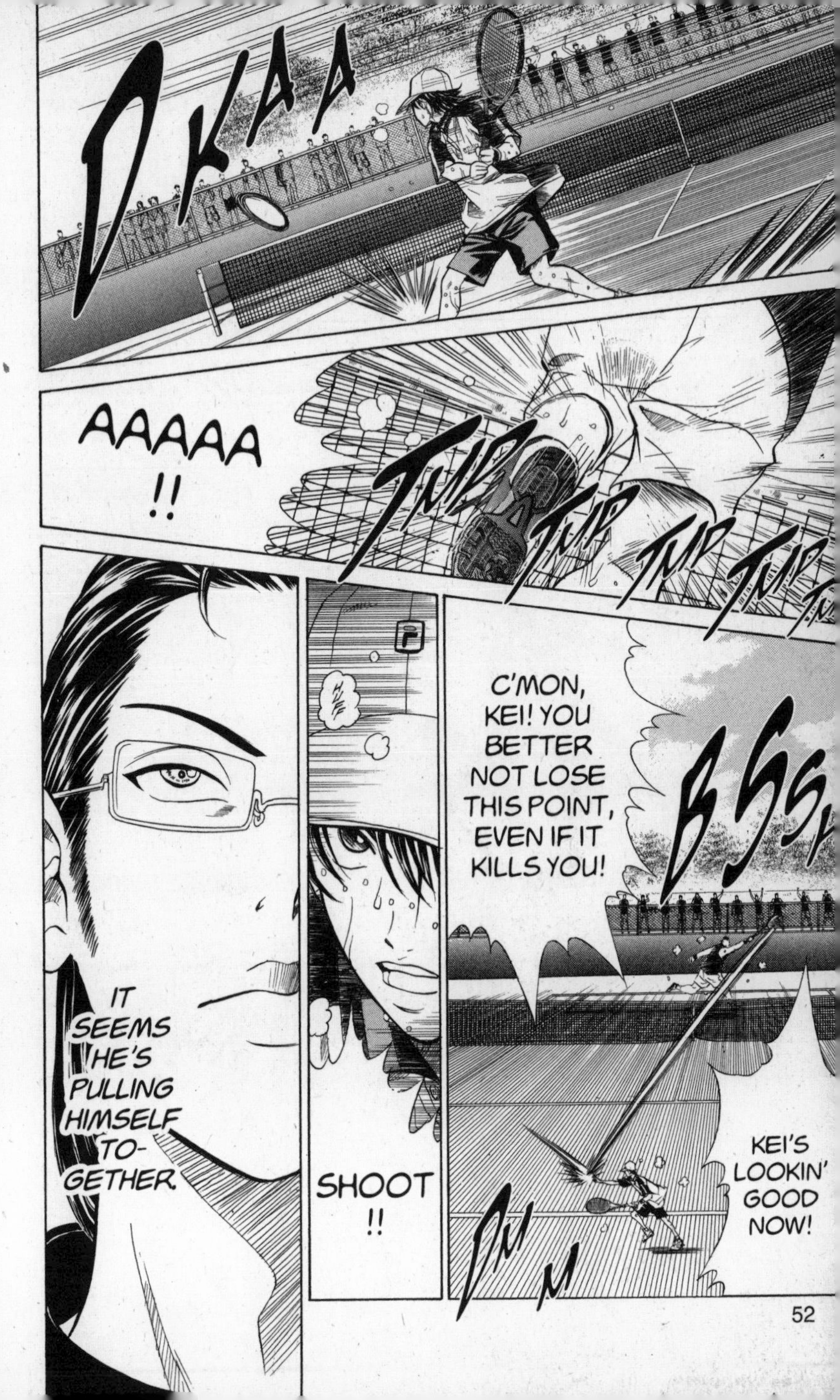
DKAA
AAAAA!!
TMP TMP TMP TMP
C'MON, KEI! YOU BETTER NOT LOSE THIS POINT, EVEN IF IT KILLS YOU!
KEI'S LOOKIN' GOOD NOW!
SHOOT!!
IT SEEMS HE'S PULLING HIMSELF TO-GETHER.

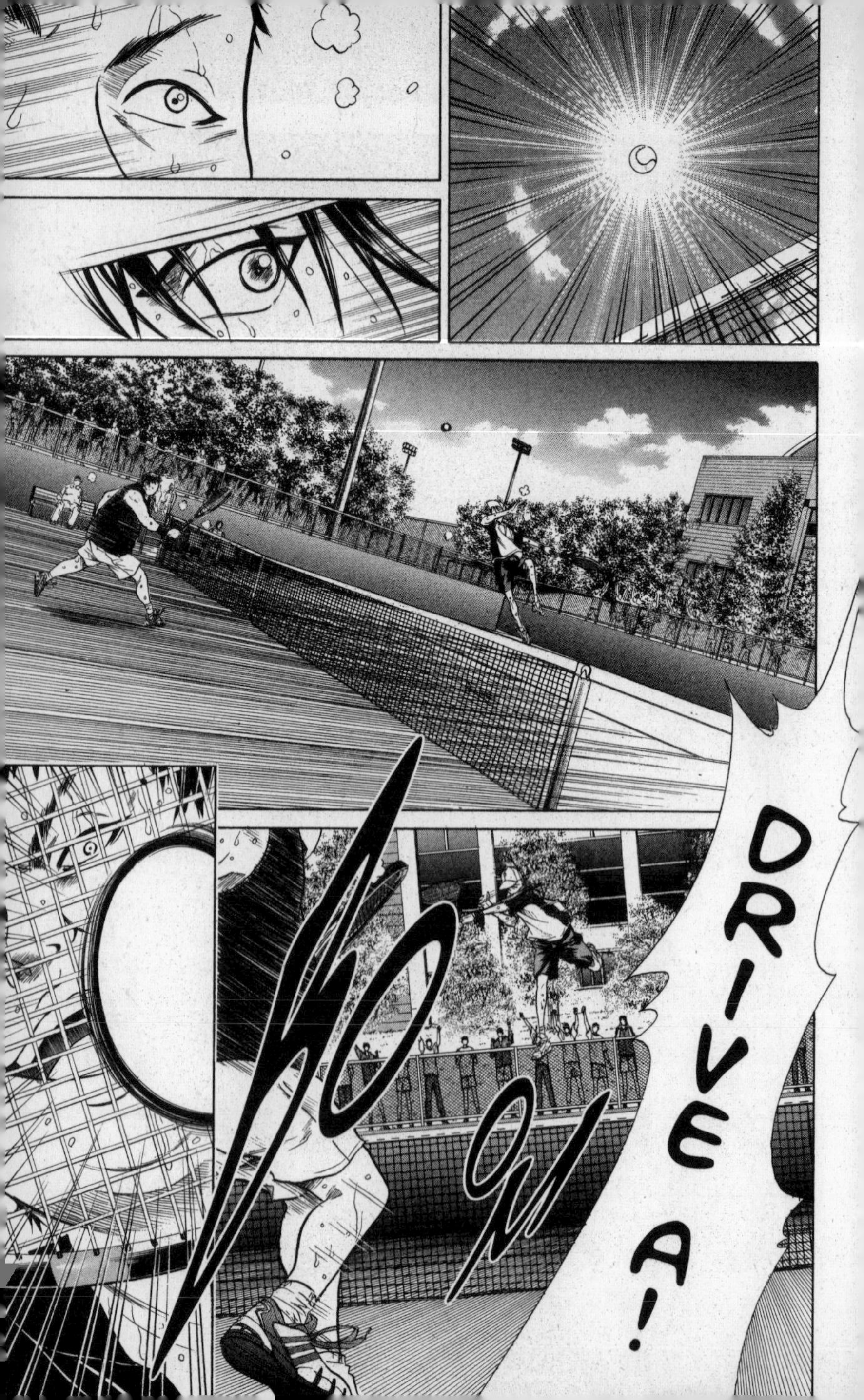
DRIVE A!

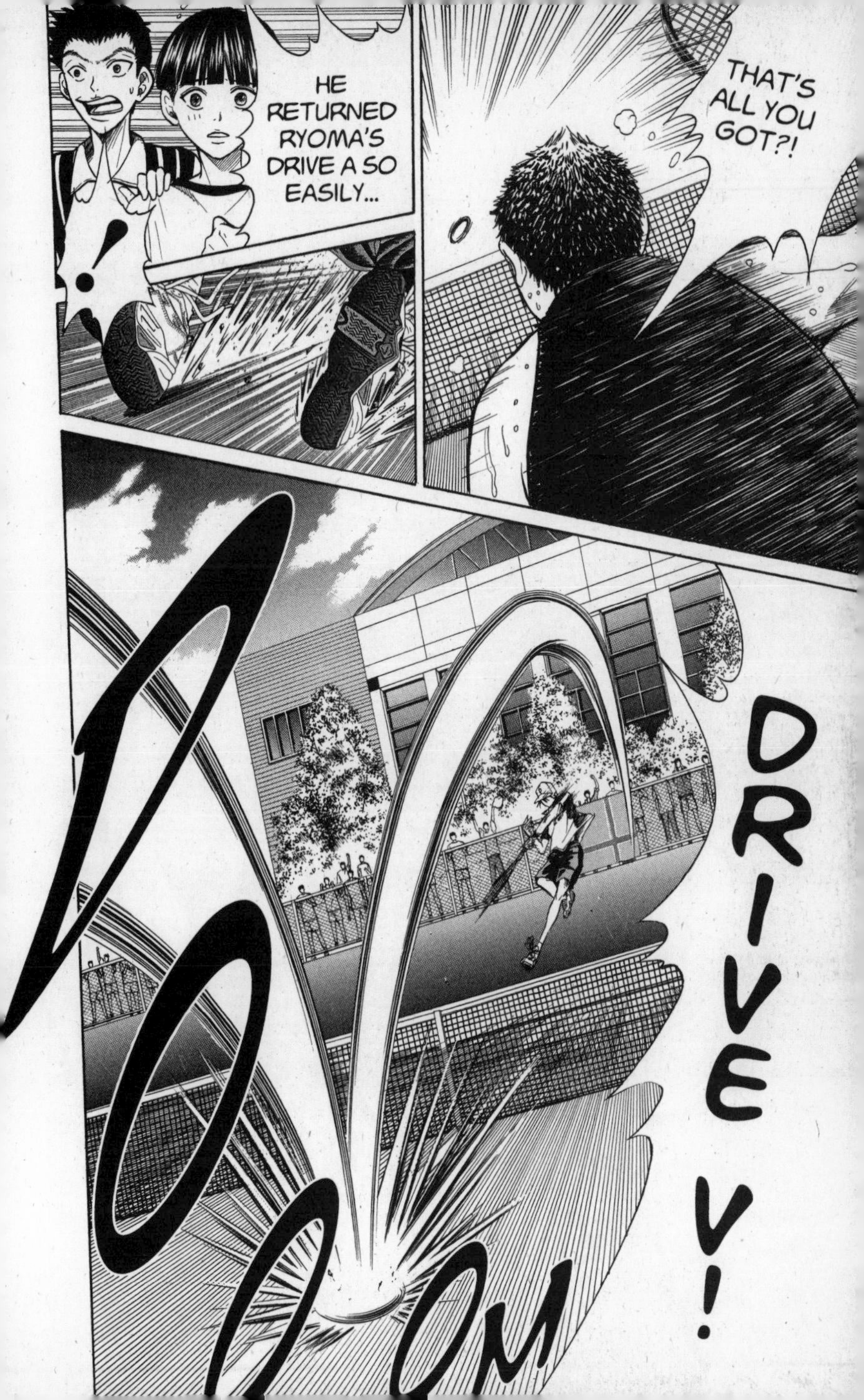
THAT'S ALL YOU GOT?!
HE RETURNED RYOMA'S DRIVE A SO EASILY...
DRIVE V!

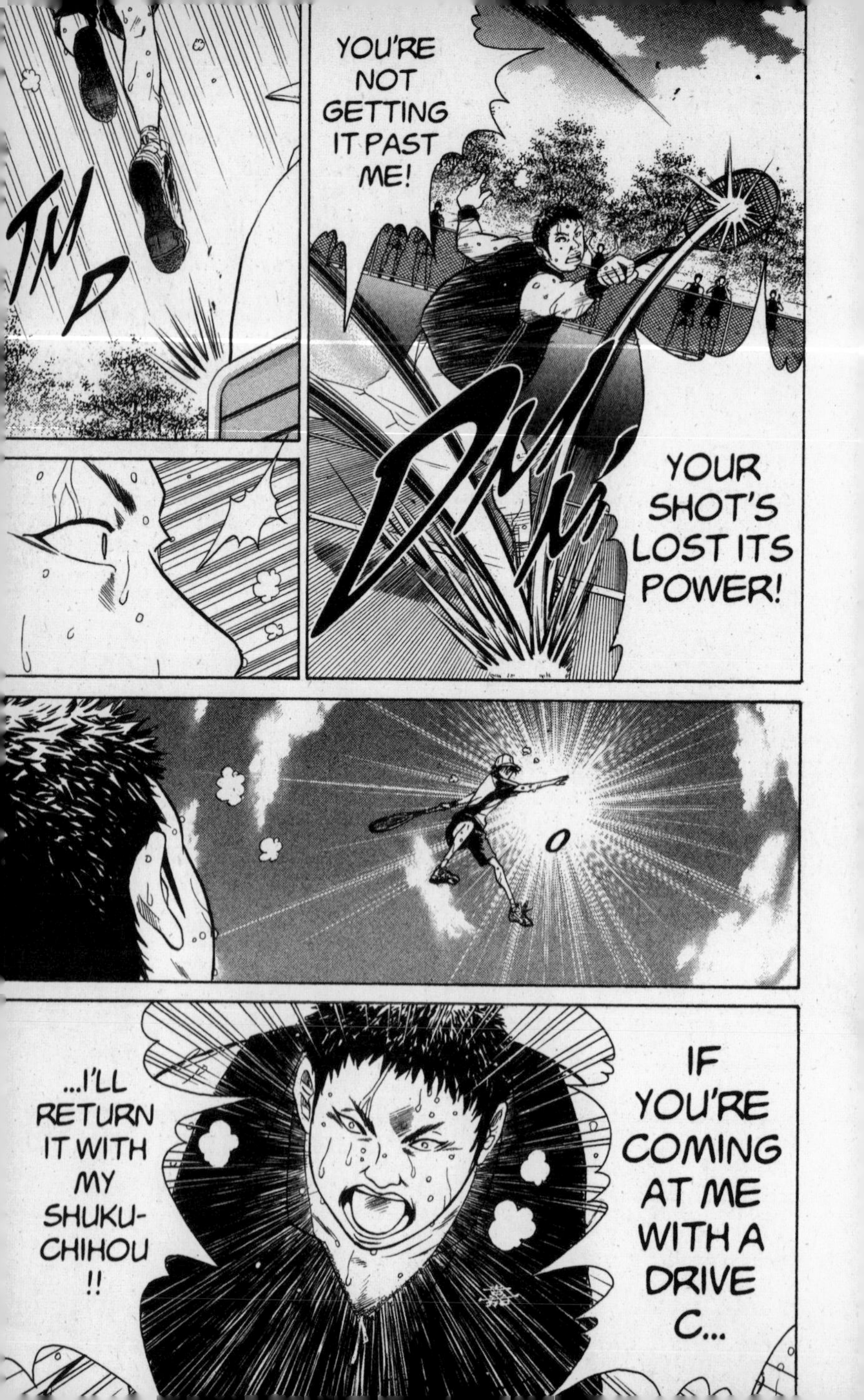
YOU'RE NOT GETTING IT PAST ME!
YOUR SHOT'S LOST ITS POWER!
IF YOU'RE COMING AT ME WITH A DRIVE C...
...I'LL RETURN IT WITH MY SHUKU-CHIHOU!!

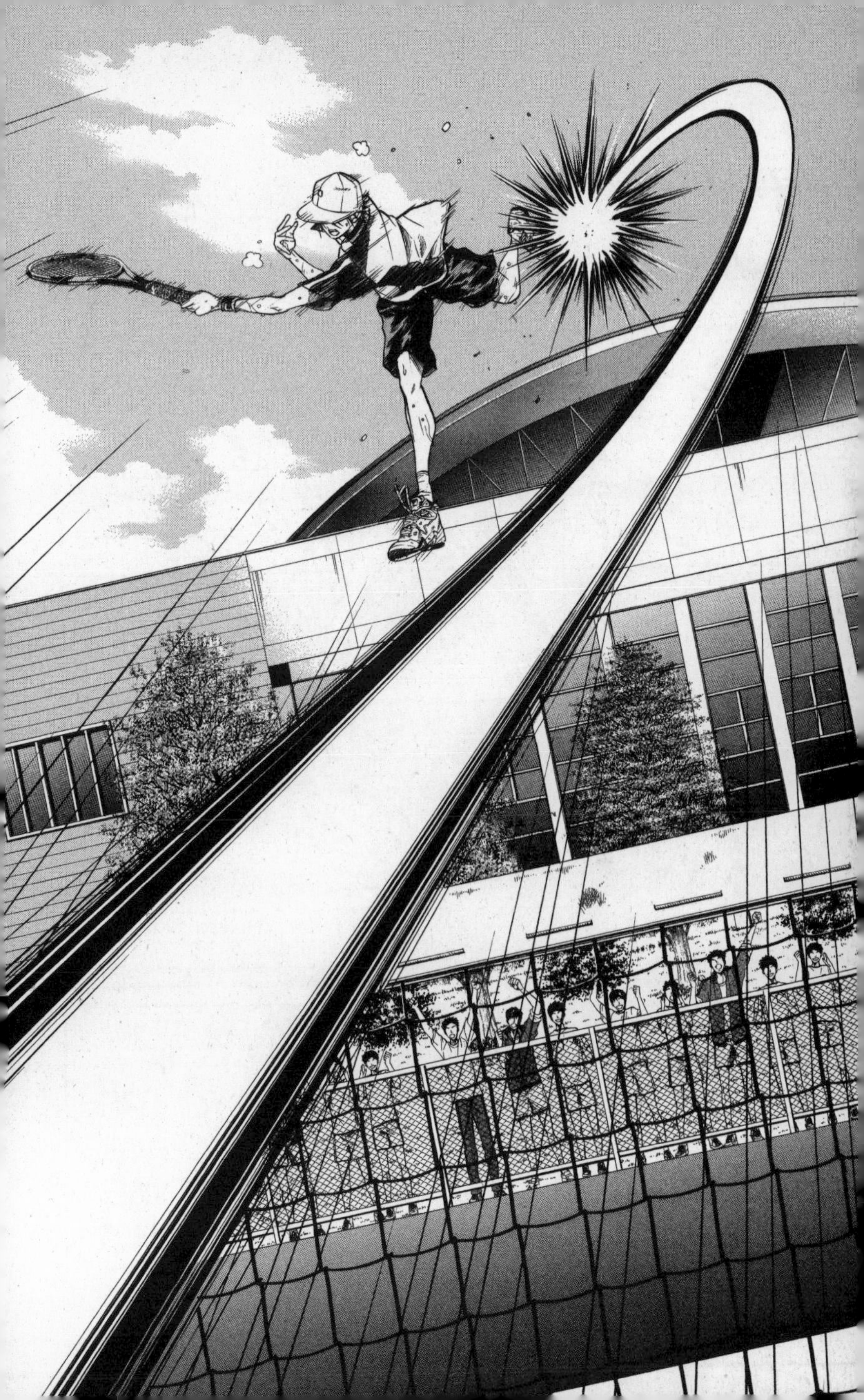

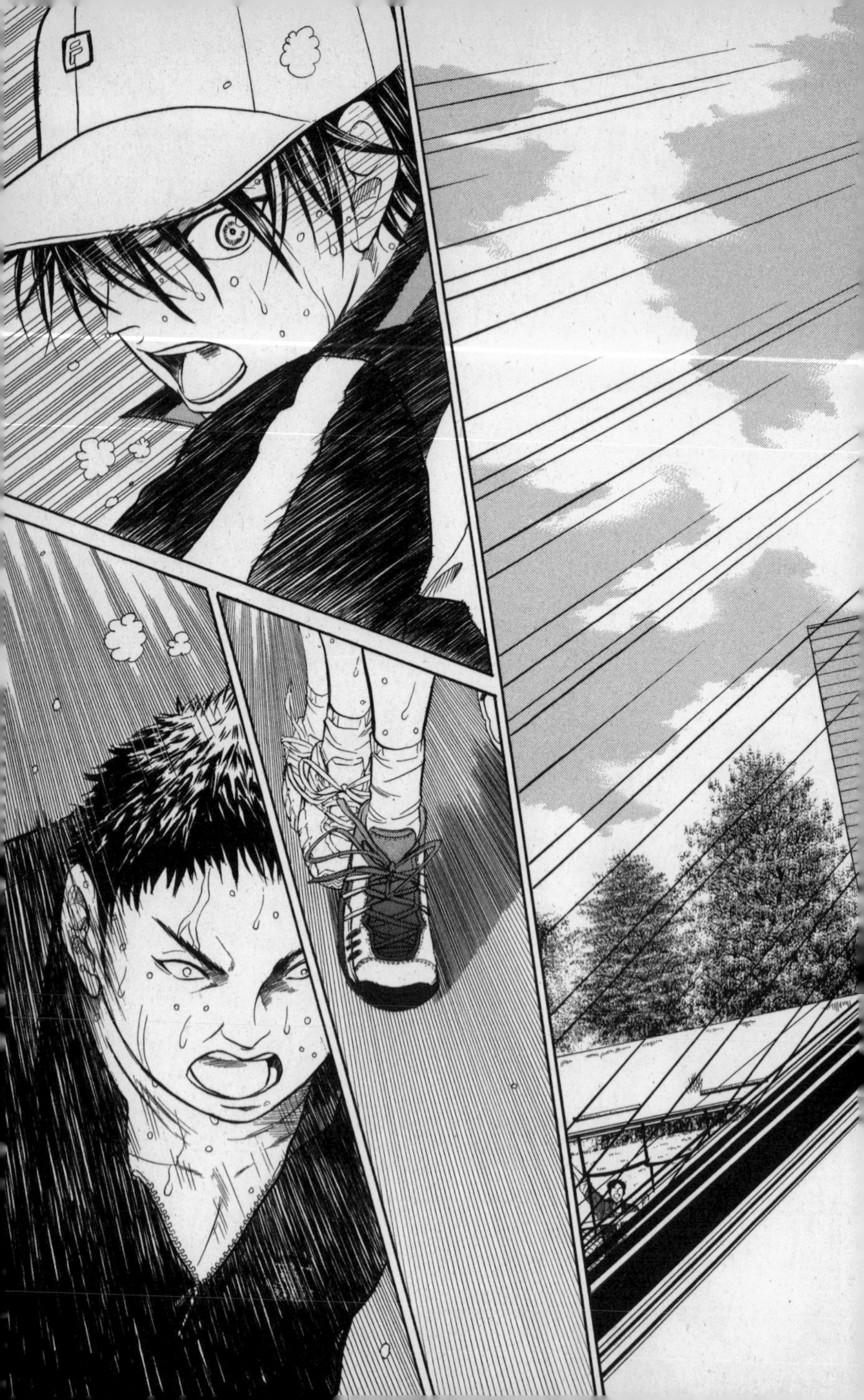

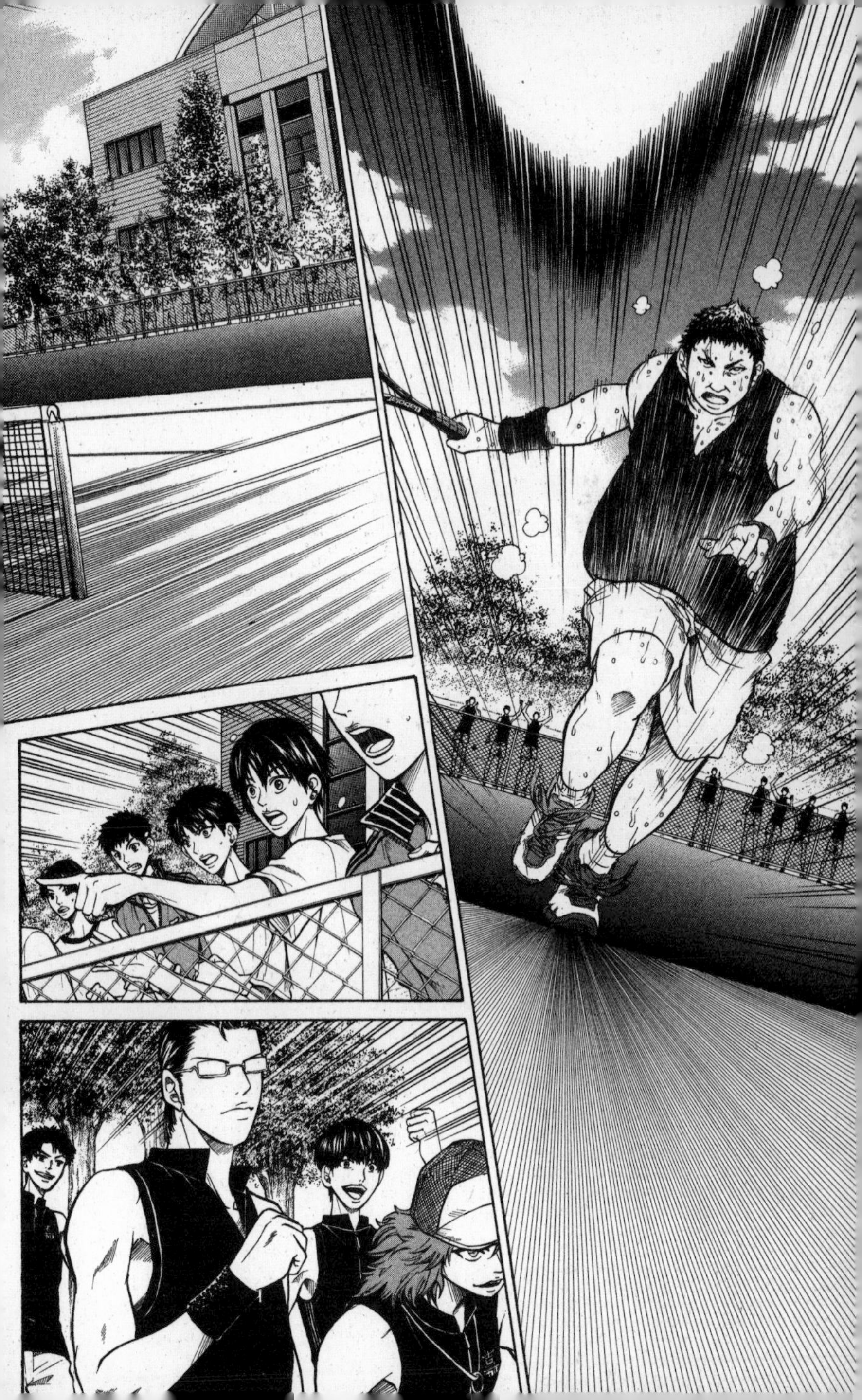

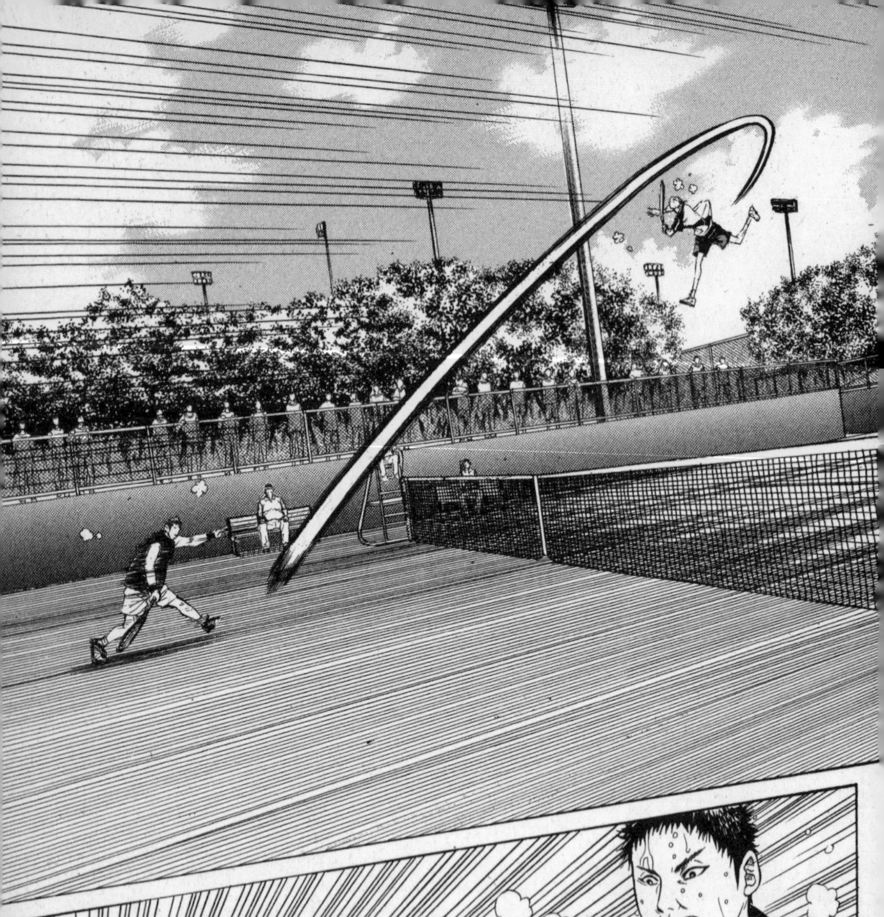
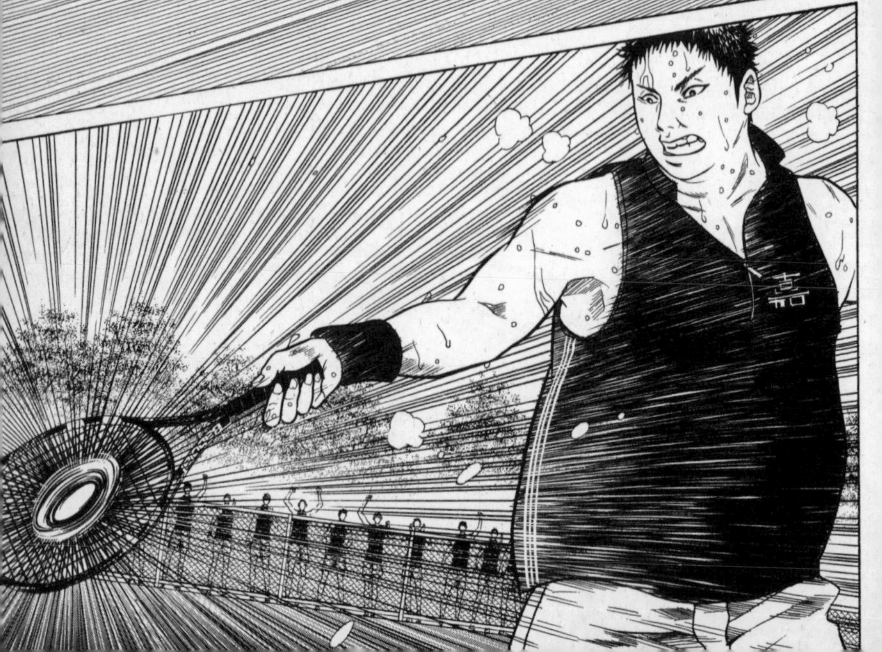

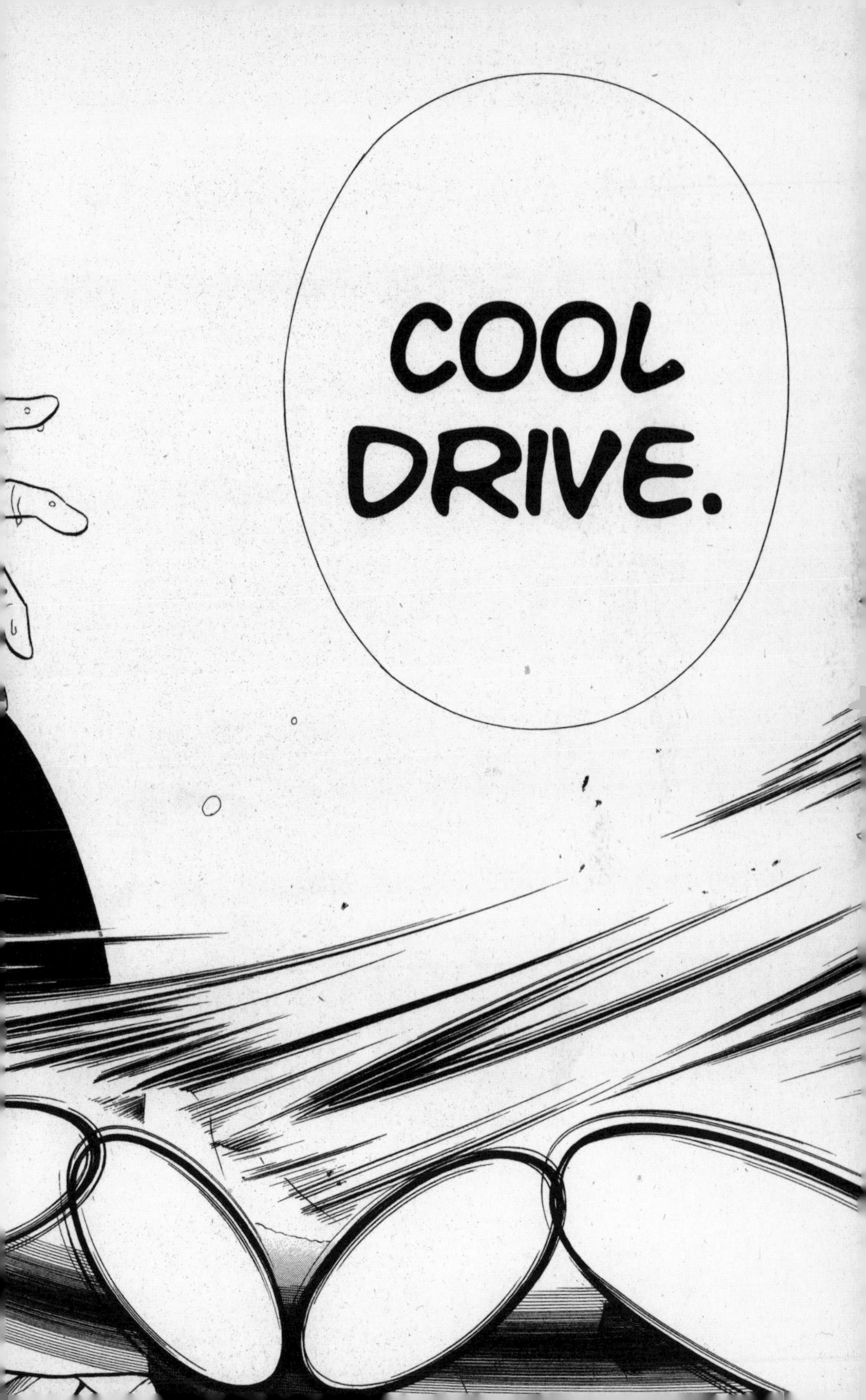
COOL DRIVE.

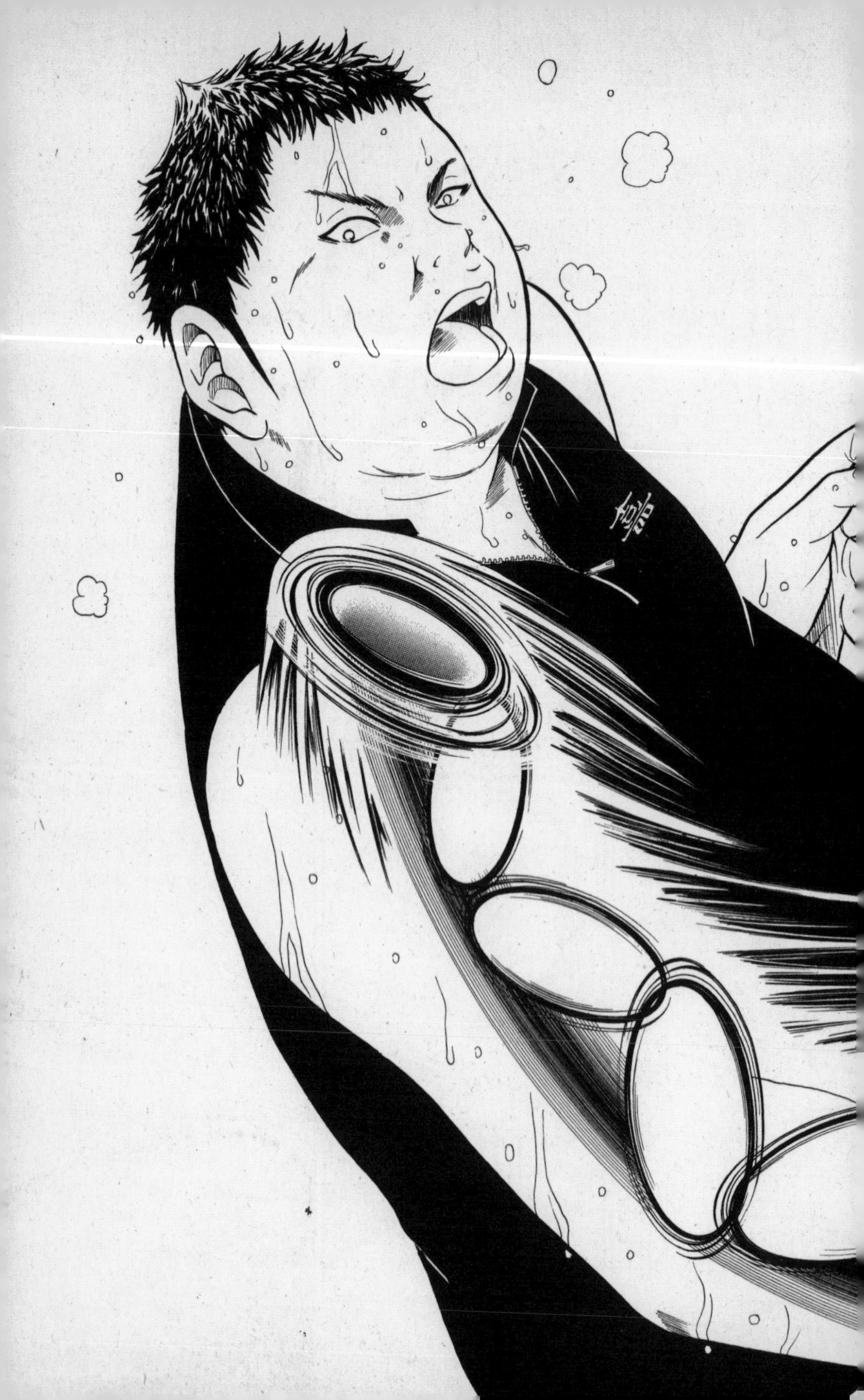

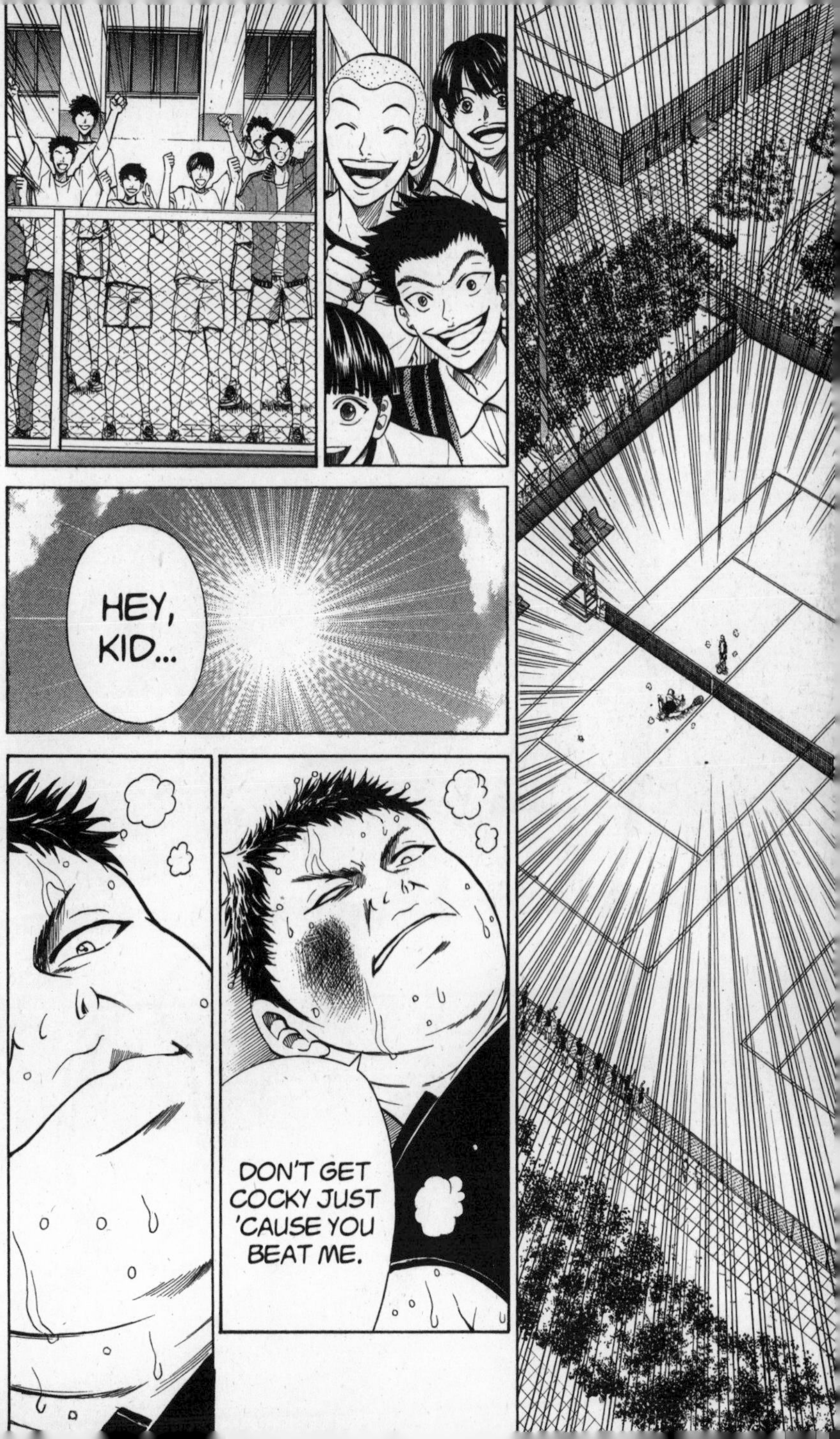
HEY, KID...
DON'T GET COCKY JUST 'CAUSE YOU BEAT ME.

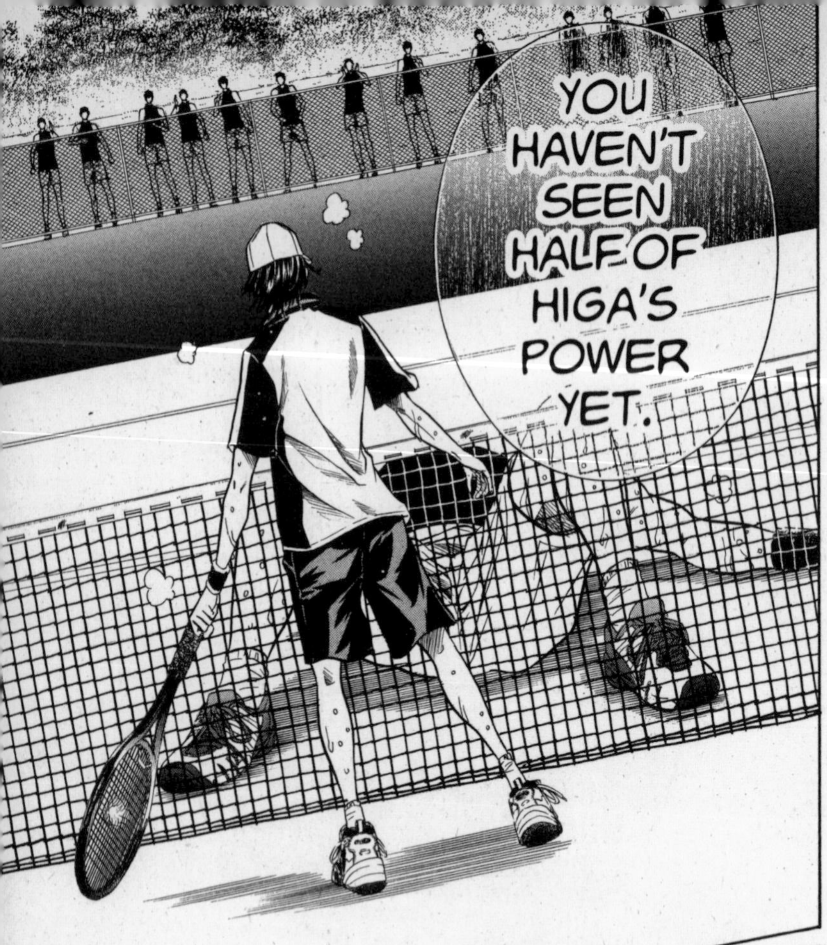
YOU HAVEN'T SEEN HALF OF HIGA'S POWER YET.

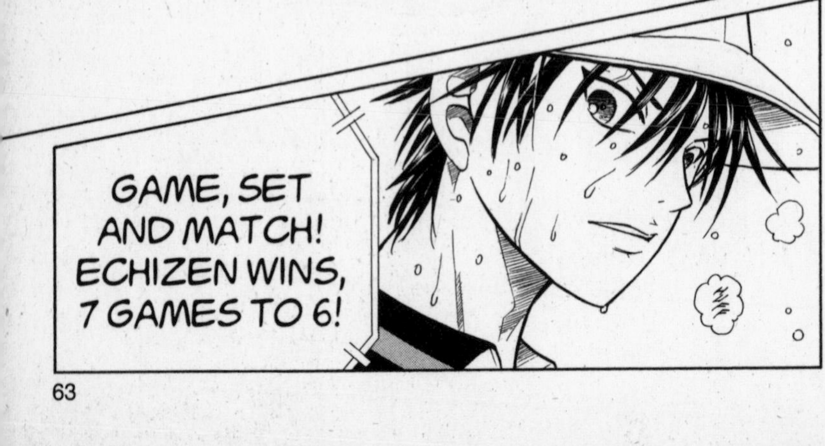
GAME, SET AND MATCH! ECHIZEN WINS, 7 GAMES TO 6!

テニスの王子様

THE PRINCE OF TENNIS

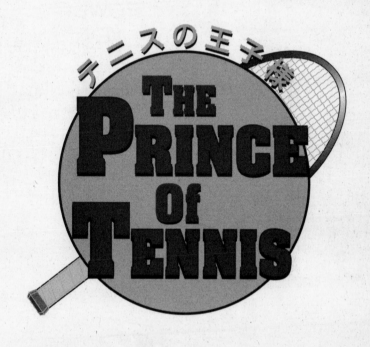

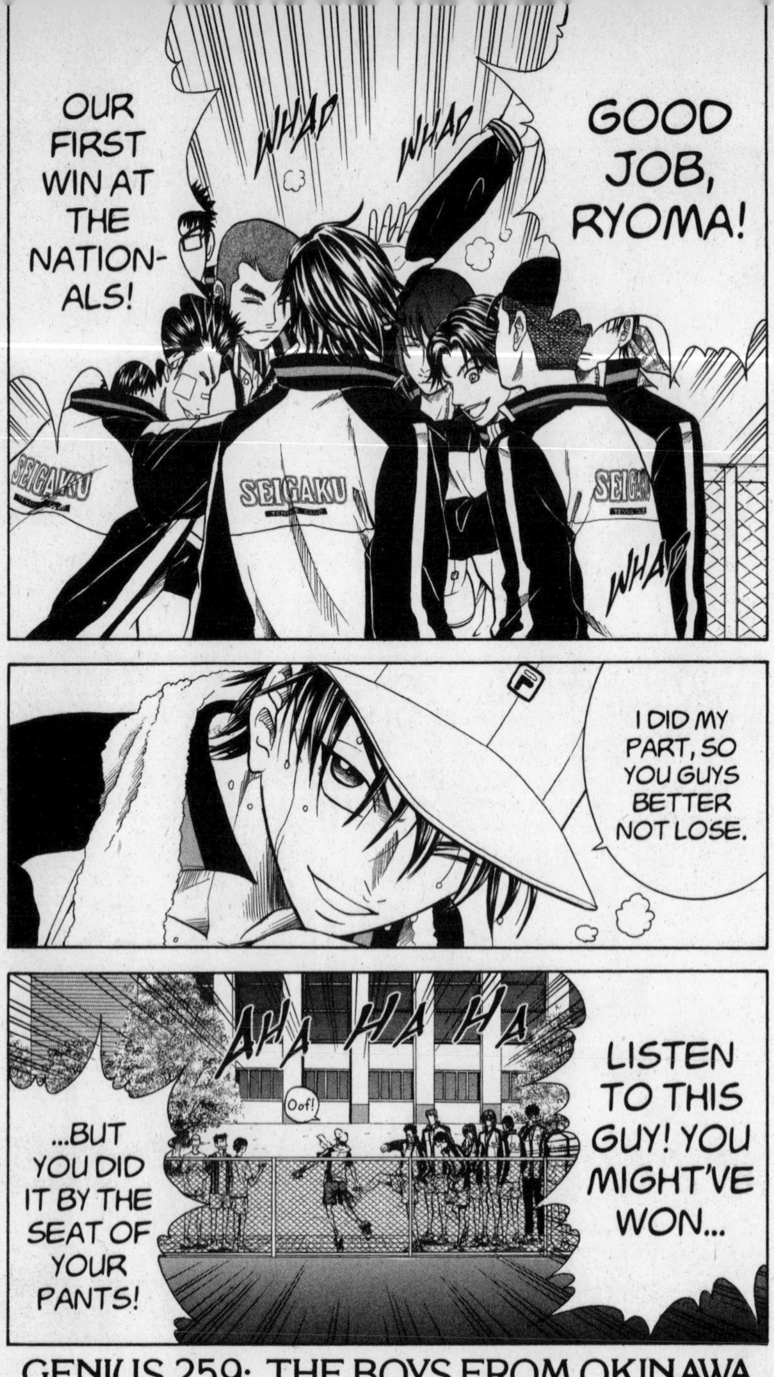
GOOD JOB, RYOMA!
WHAP
WHAP
OUR FIRST WIN AT THE NATIONALS!
WHAP
I DID MY PART, SO YOU GUYS BETTER NOT LOSE.
AHA HA HA HA
LISTEN TO THIS GUY! YOU MIGHT'VE WON...
Oof!
...BUT YOU DID IT BY THE SEAT OF YOUR PANTS!

GENIUS 259: THE BOYS FROM OKINAWA

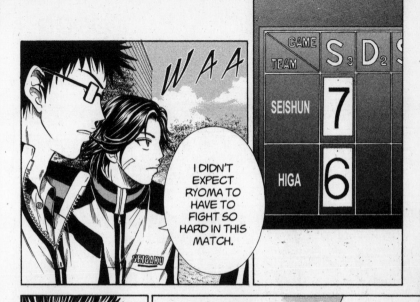

WAA

	GAME	S₃	D₂	
SEISHUN		7		
HIGA		6		

I DIDN'T EXPECT RYOMA TO HAVE TO FIGHT SO HARD IN THIS MATCH.

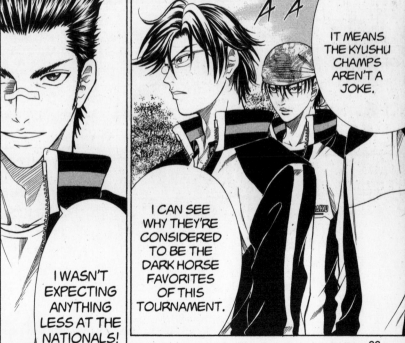

AA

IT MEANS THE KYUSHU CHAMPS AREN'T A JOKE.

I CAN SEE WHY THEY'RE CONSIDERED TO BE THE DARK HORSE FAVORITES OF THIS TOURNAMENT.

I WASN'T EXPECTING ANYTHING LESS AT THE NATIONALS!

66

READ THIS WAY

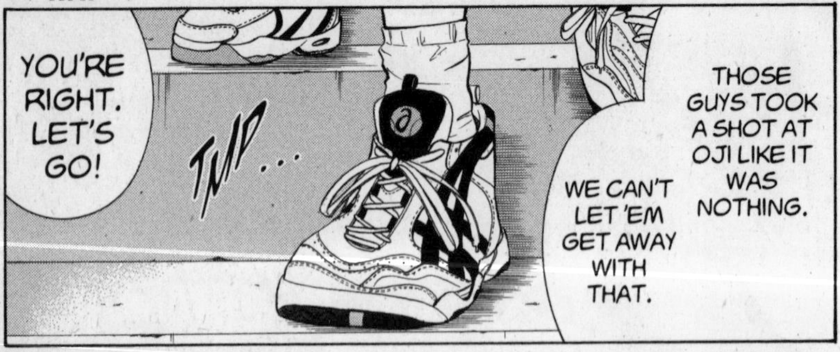
THOSE GUYS TOOK A SHOT AT OJI LIKE IT WAS NOTHING.
WE CAN'T LET 'EM GET AWAY WITH THAT.
TMP...
YOU'RE RIGHT. LET'S GO!

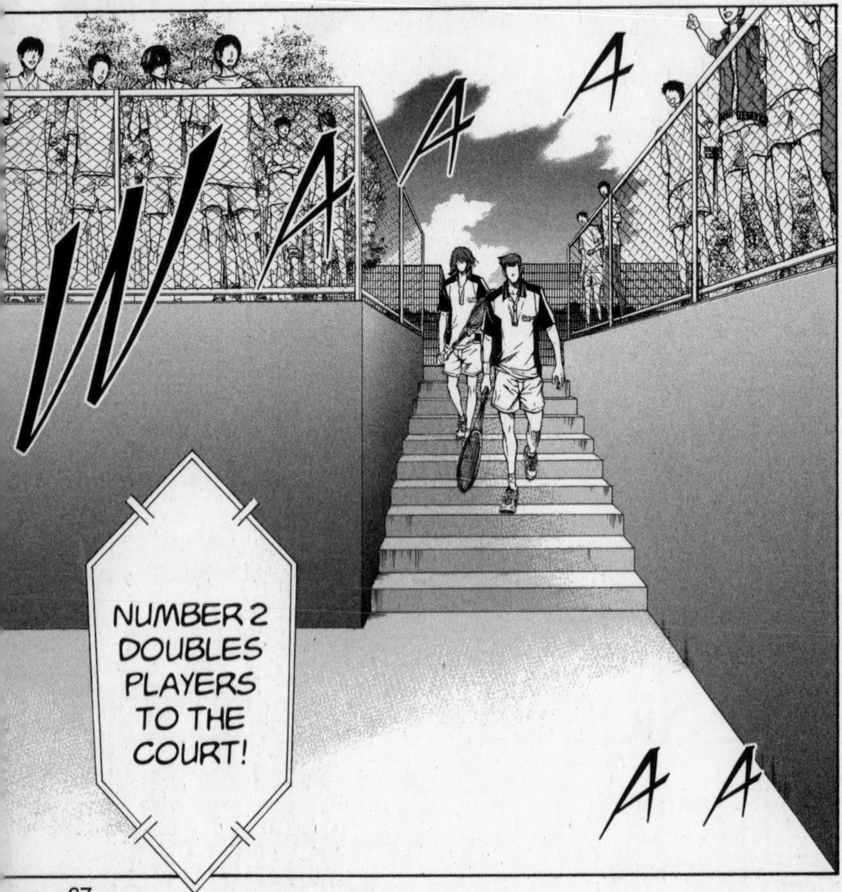
WAAA
NUMBER 2 DOUBLES PLAYERS TO THE COURT!
AA

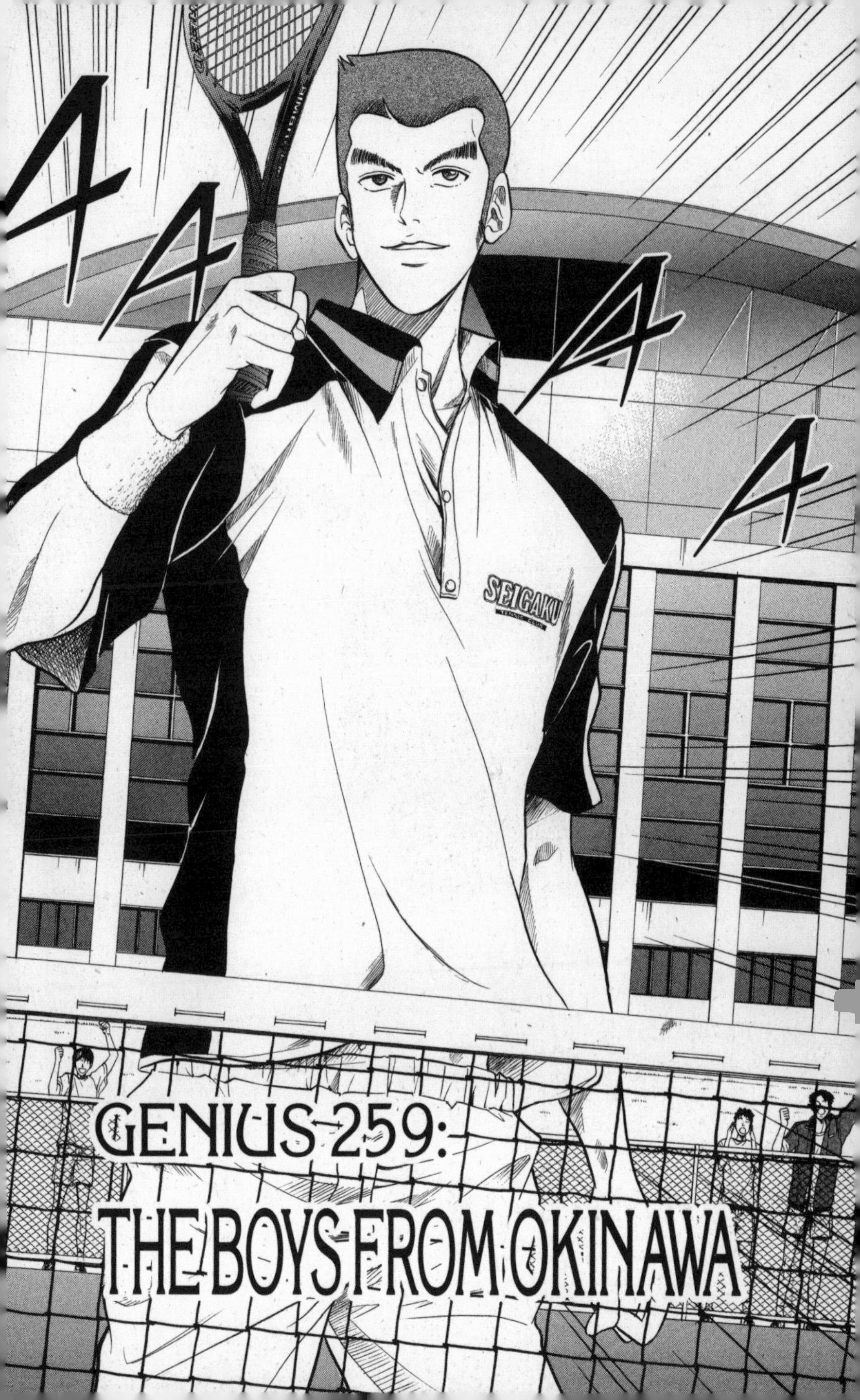
AAAAA
SEIGAKU
TENNIS CLUB
GENIUS 259:
THE BOYS FROM OKINAWA

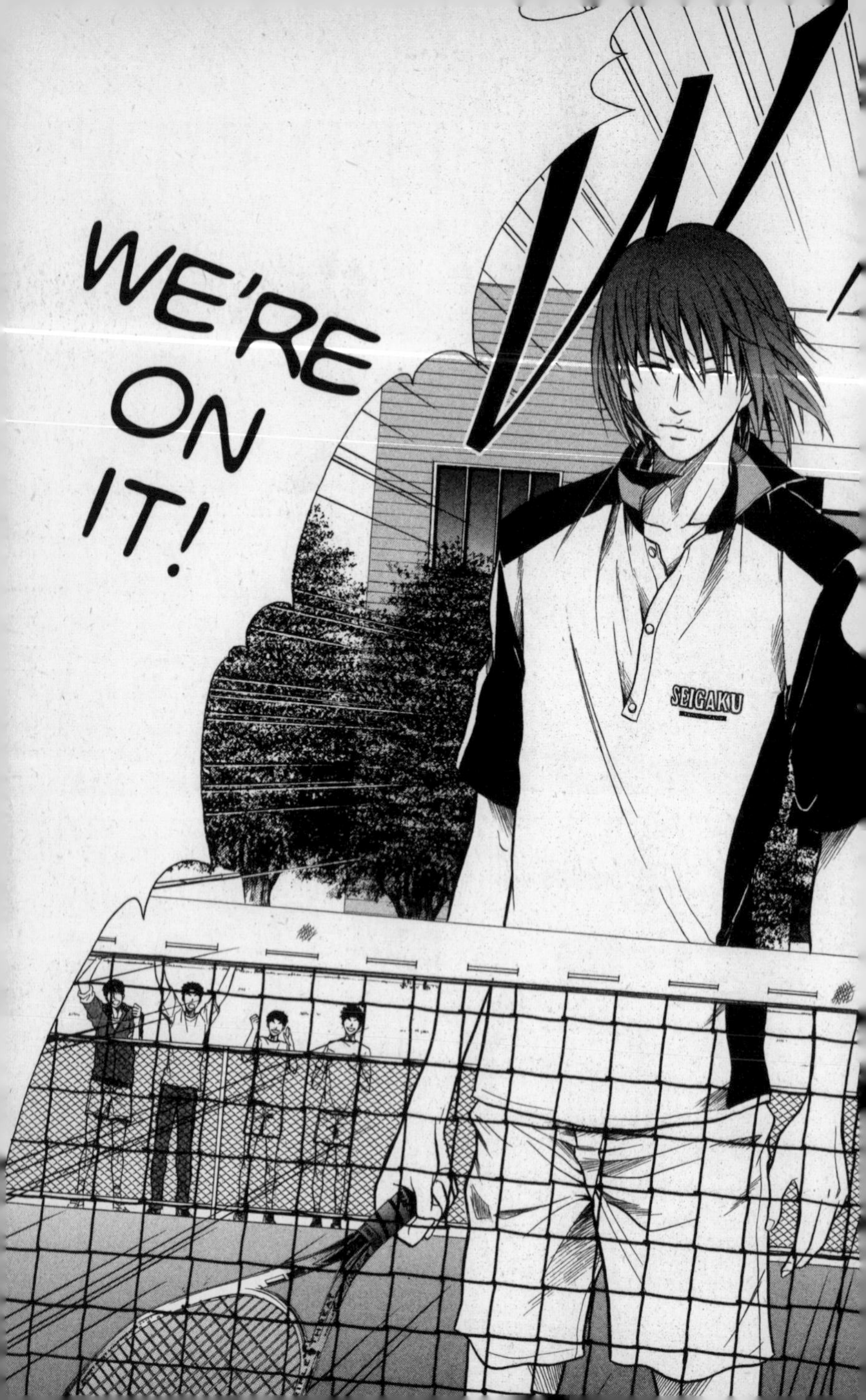
WE'RE ON IT!
SEIGAKU

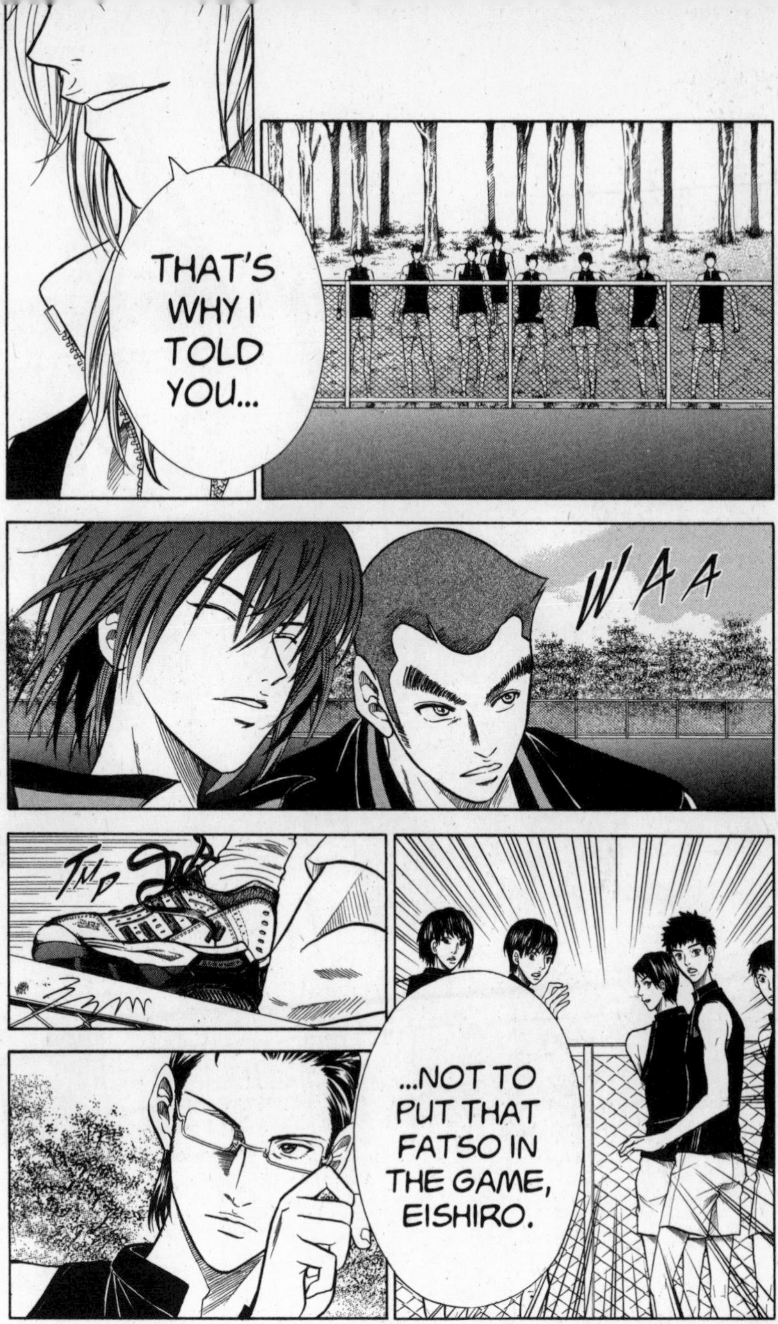
THAT'S WHY I TOLD YOU...
WAA
TMP
...NOT TO PUT THAT FATSO IN THE GAME, EISHIRO.

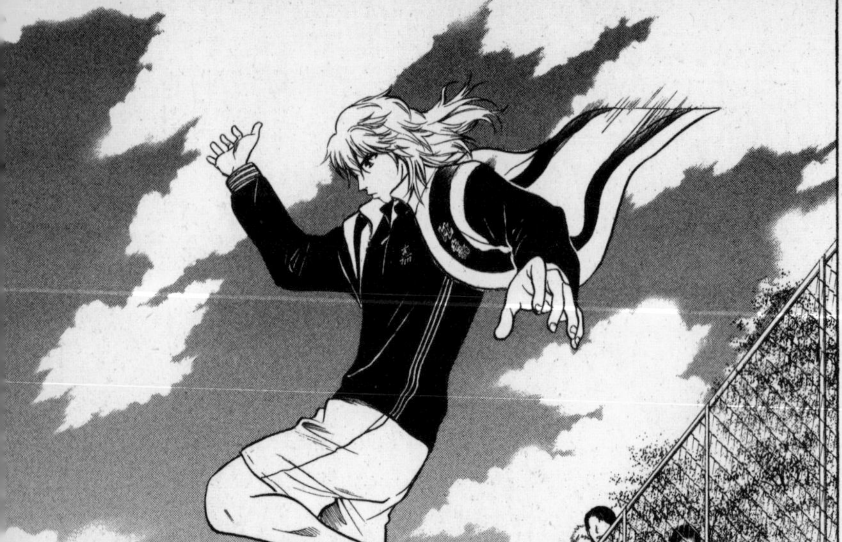
HUP.

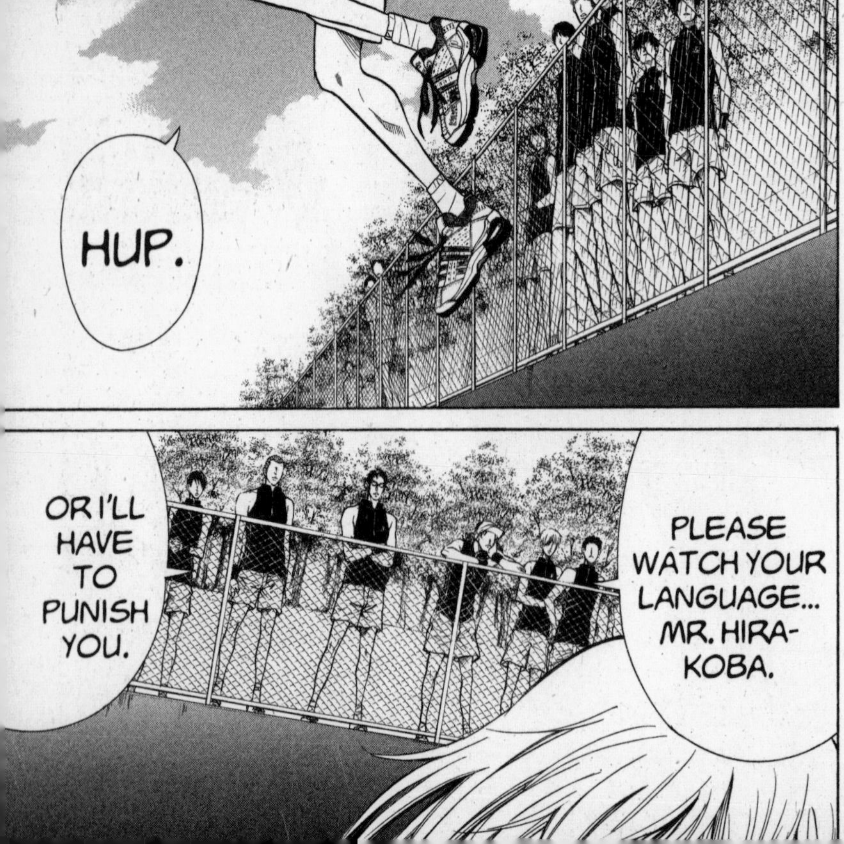
PLEASE WATCH YOUR LANGUAGE... MR. HIRA-KOBA.
OR I'LL HAVE TO PUNISH YOU.

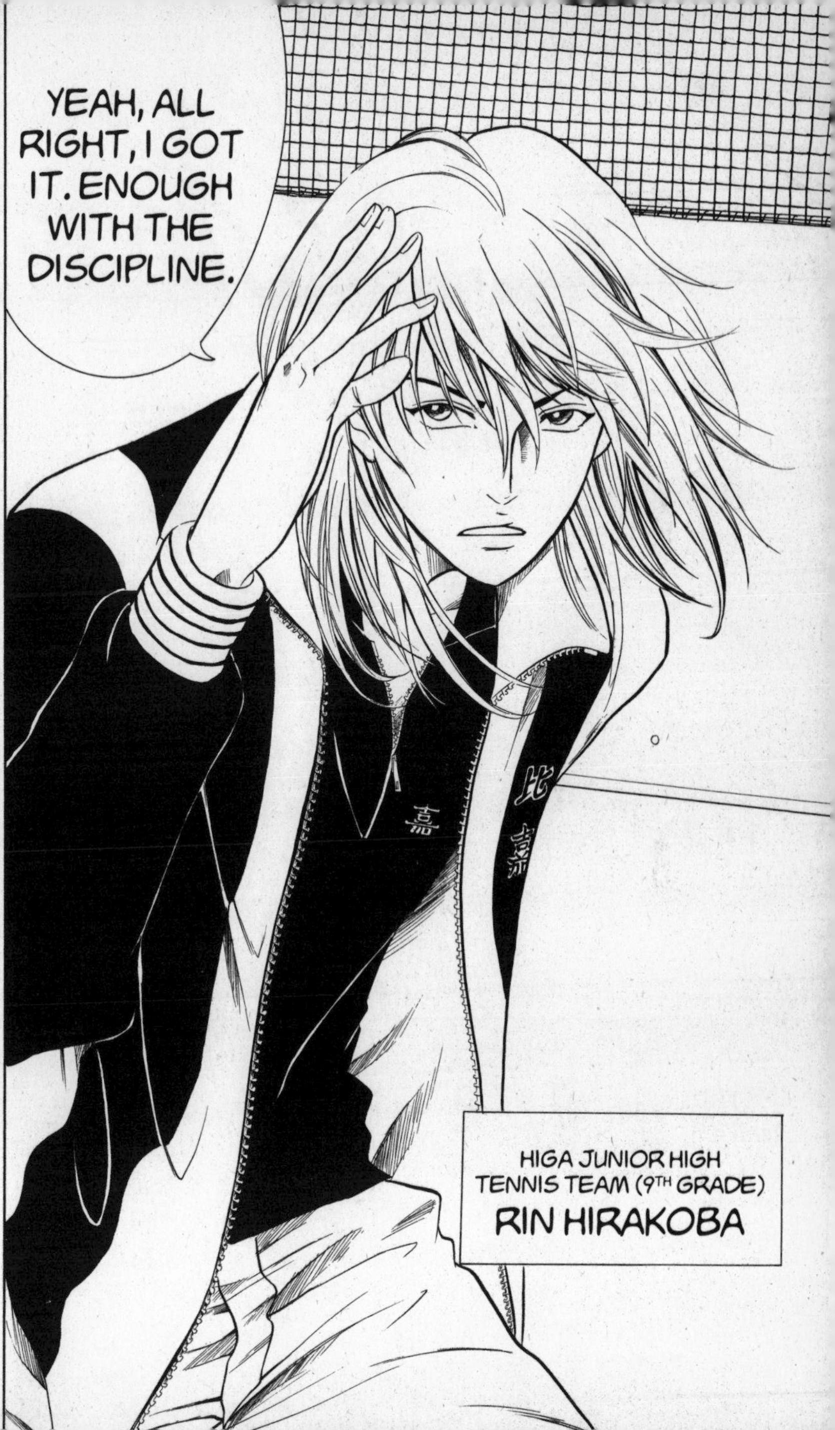
YEAH, ALL RIGHT, I GOT IT. ENOUGH WITH THE DISCIPLINE.
HIGA JUNIOR HIGH TENNIS TEAM (9TH GRADE) RIN HIRAKOBA

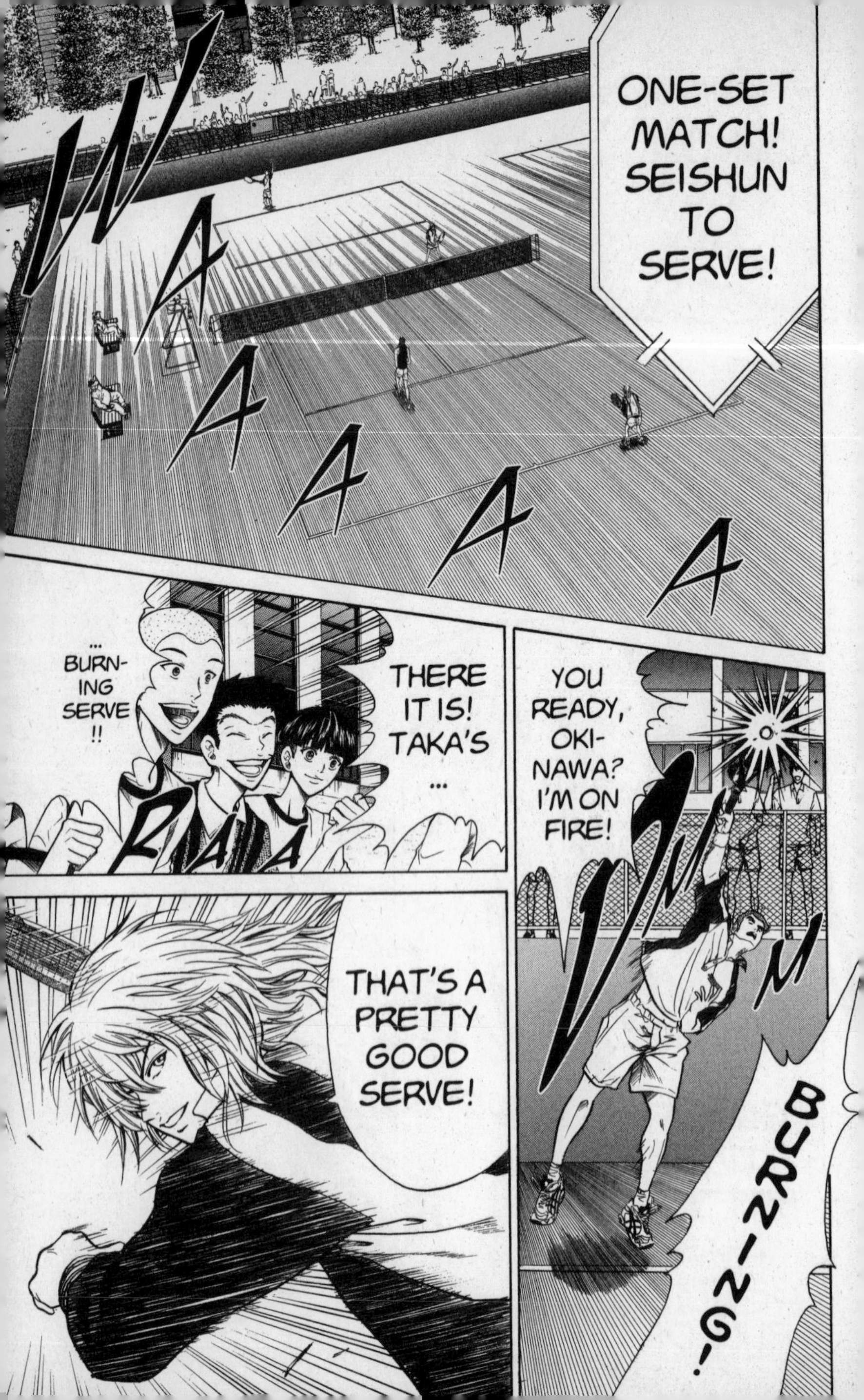
WAAAAAA
ONE-SET MATCH! SEISHUN TO SERVE!
YOU READY, OKINAWA? I'M ON FIRE!
BURNING!
THERE IT IS! TAKA'S ...
... BURNING SERVE!!
THAT'S A PRETTY GOOD SERVE!

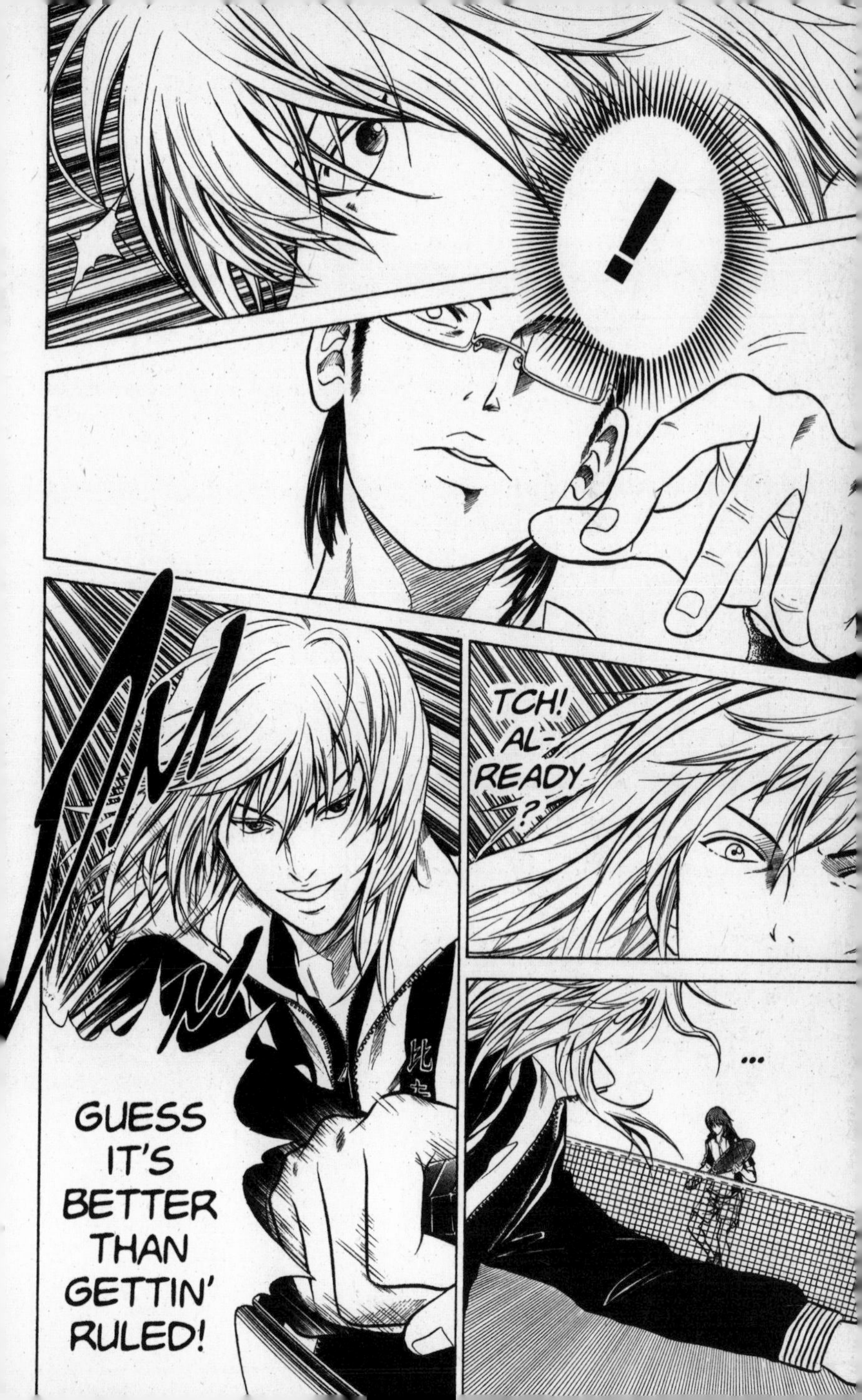
!
TCH! AL-READY?
...
GUESS IT'S BETTER THAN GETTIN' RULED!

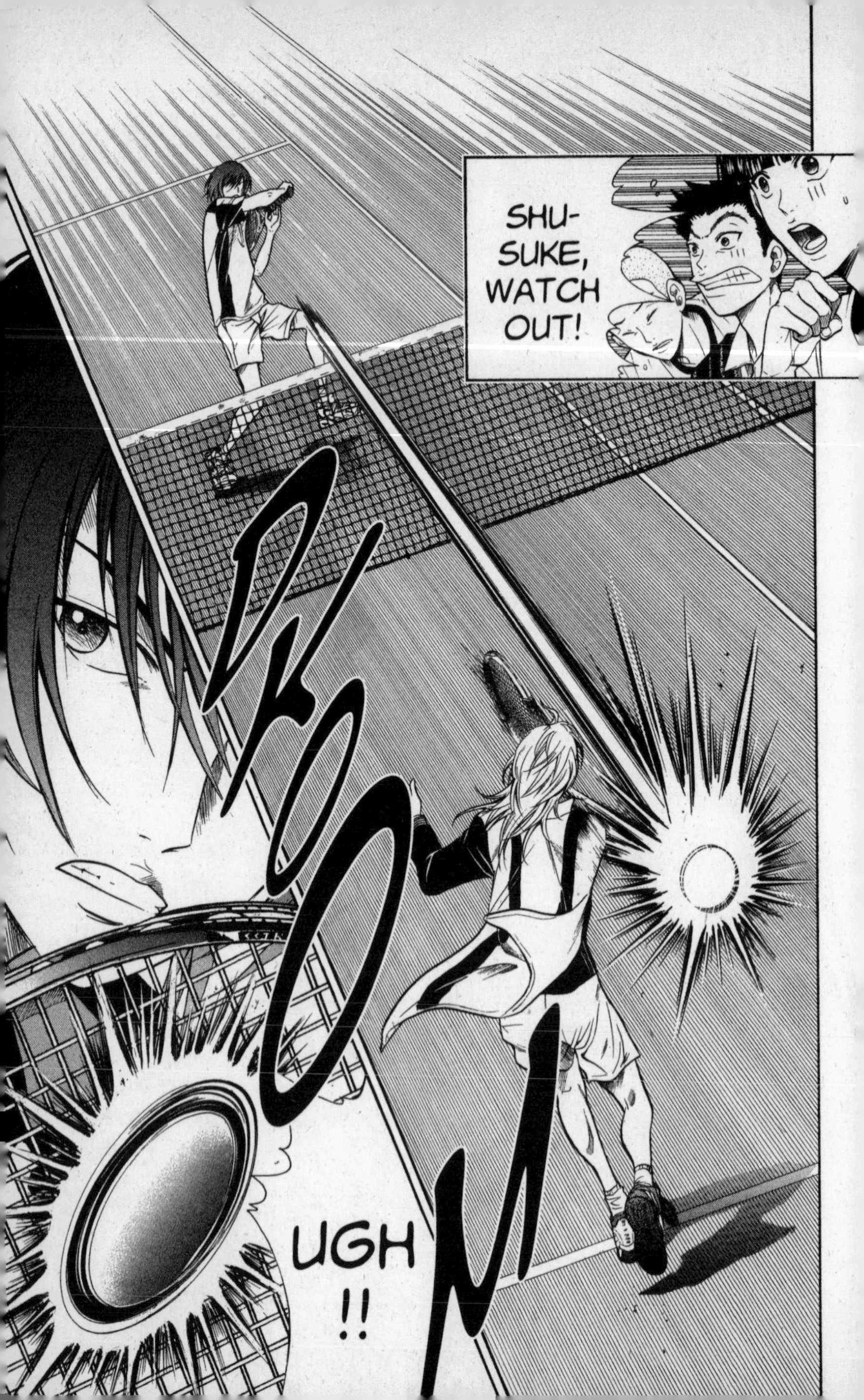
SHU-SUKE, WATCH OUT!
UGH !!

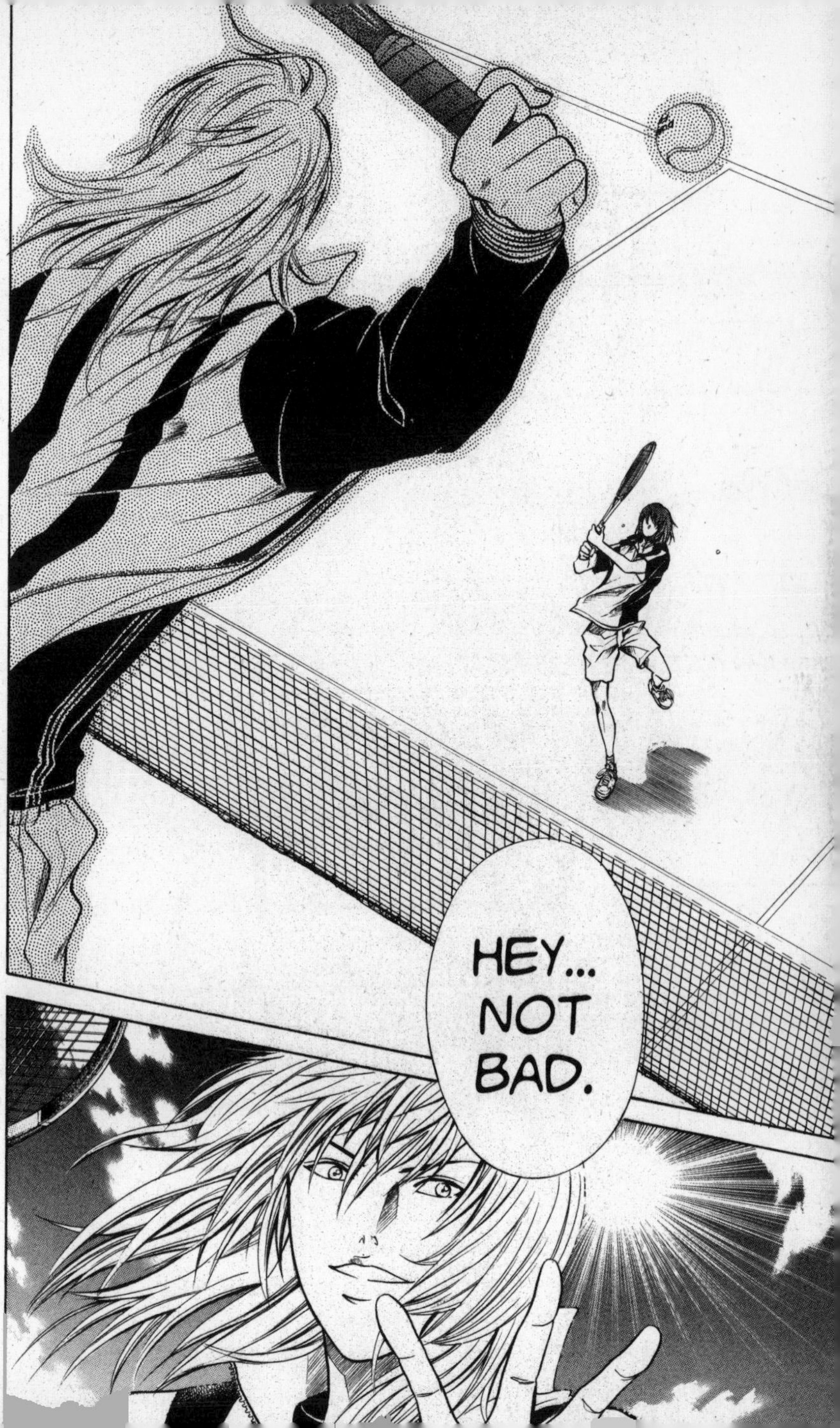
HEY... NOT BAD.

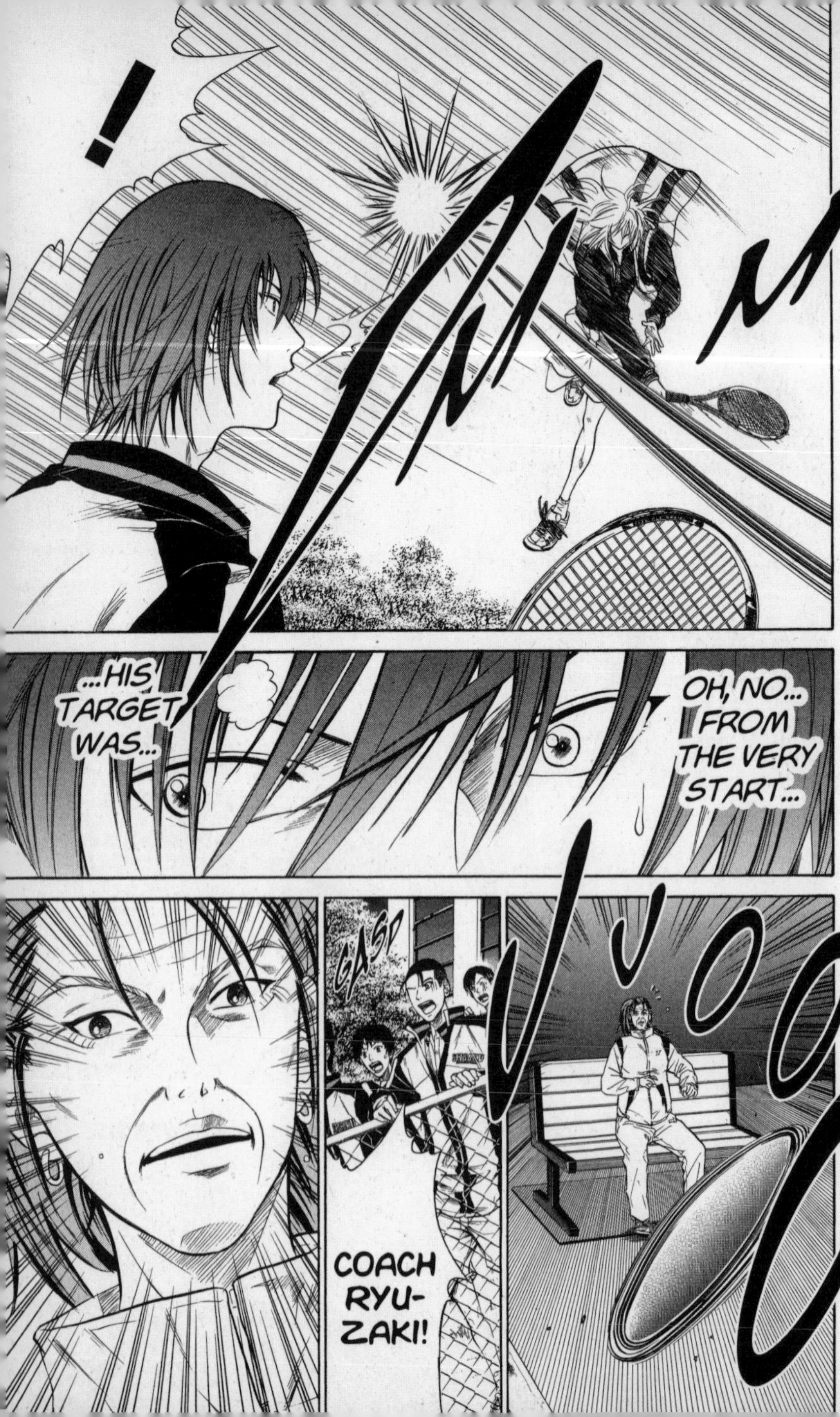
!
OH, NO... FROM THE VERY START...
...HIS TARGET WAS...
GASP
COACH RYU-ZAKI!

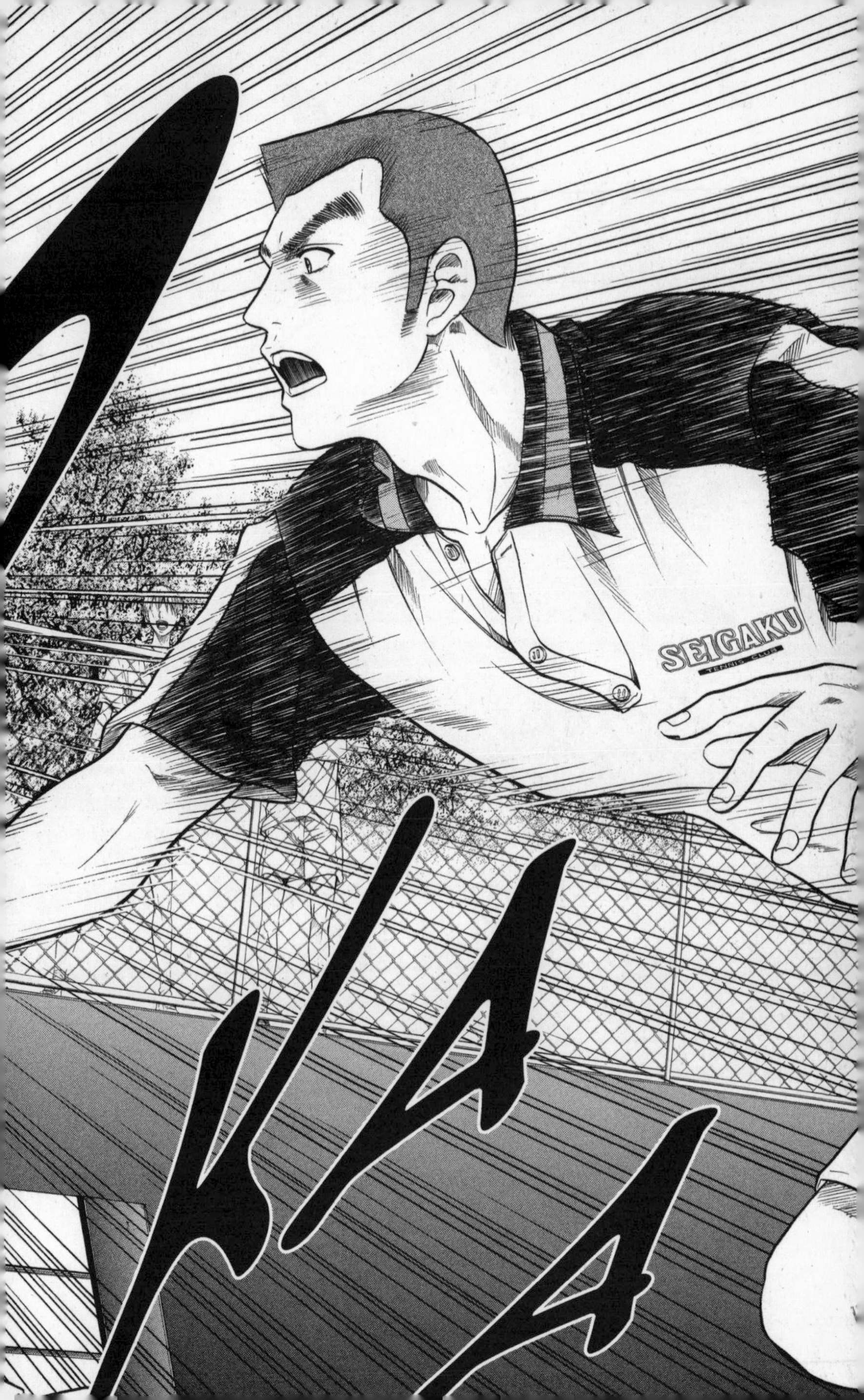
SEIGAKU
TENNIS CLUB

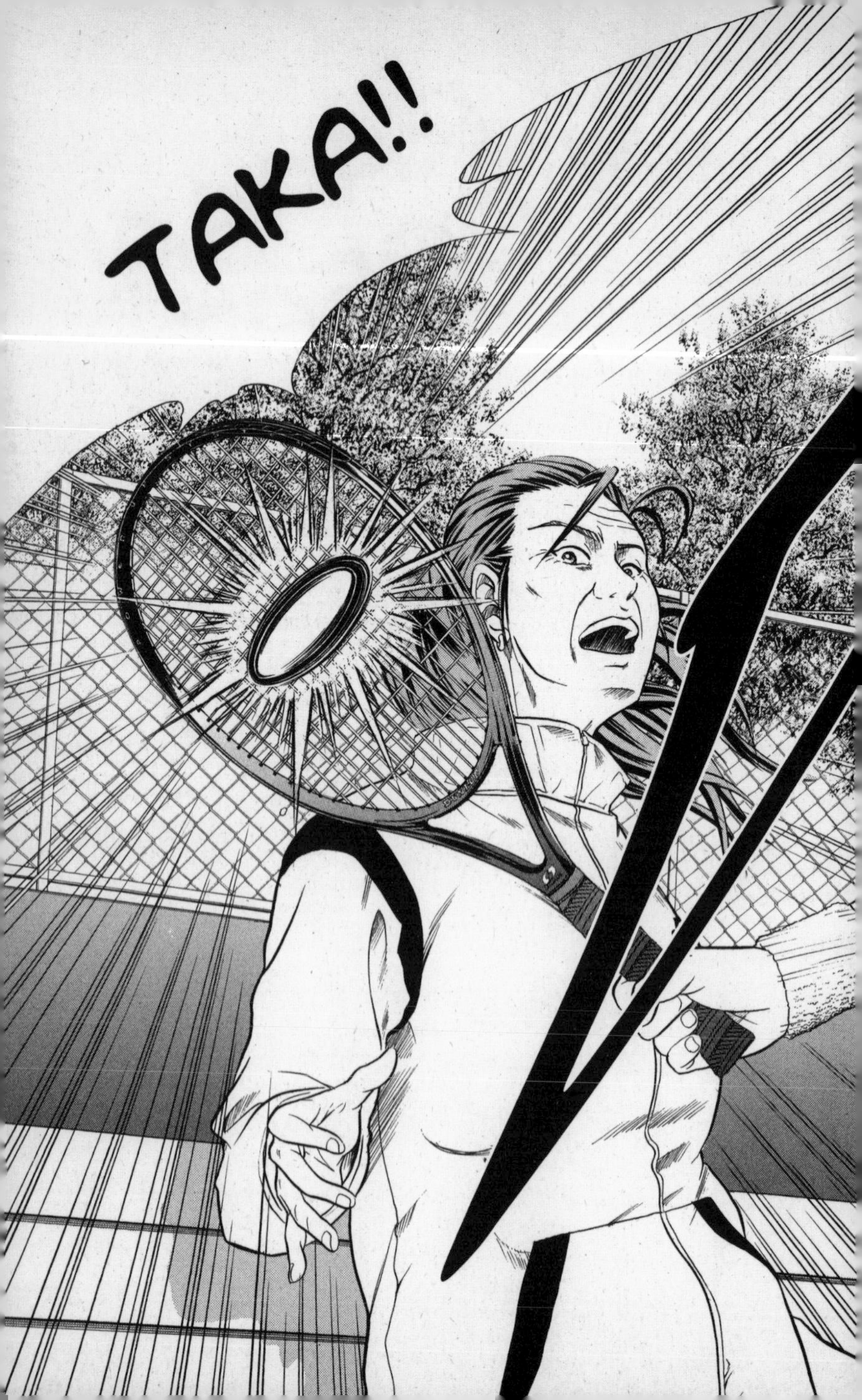
TAKA!!

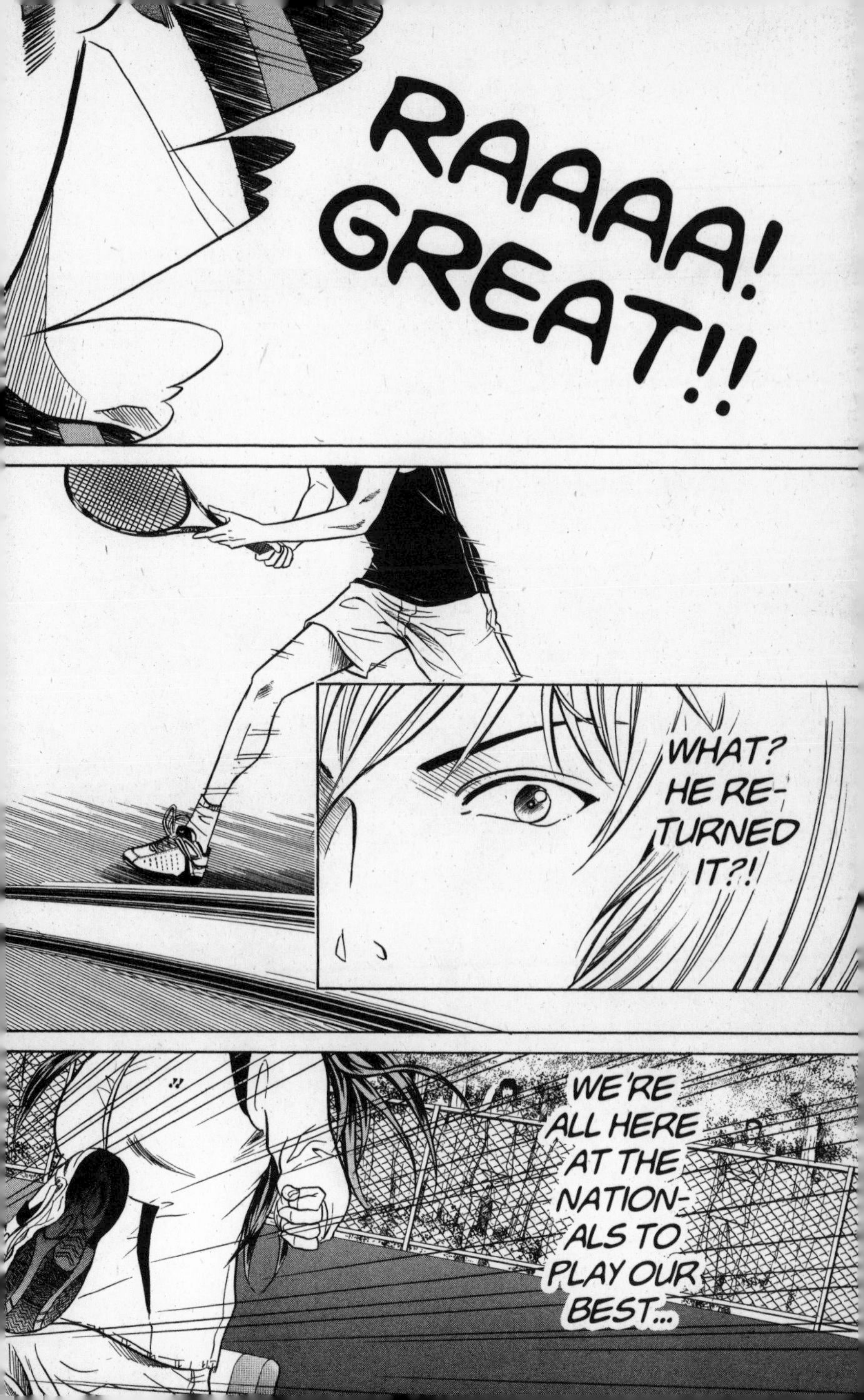
RAAAAA! GREAT!!
WHAT? HE RE-TURNED IT?!
WE'RE ALL HERE AT THE NATION-ALS TO PLAY OUR BEST...

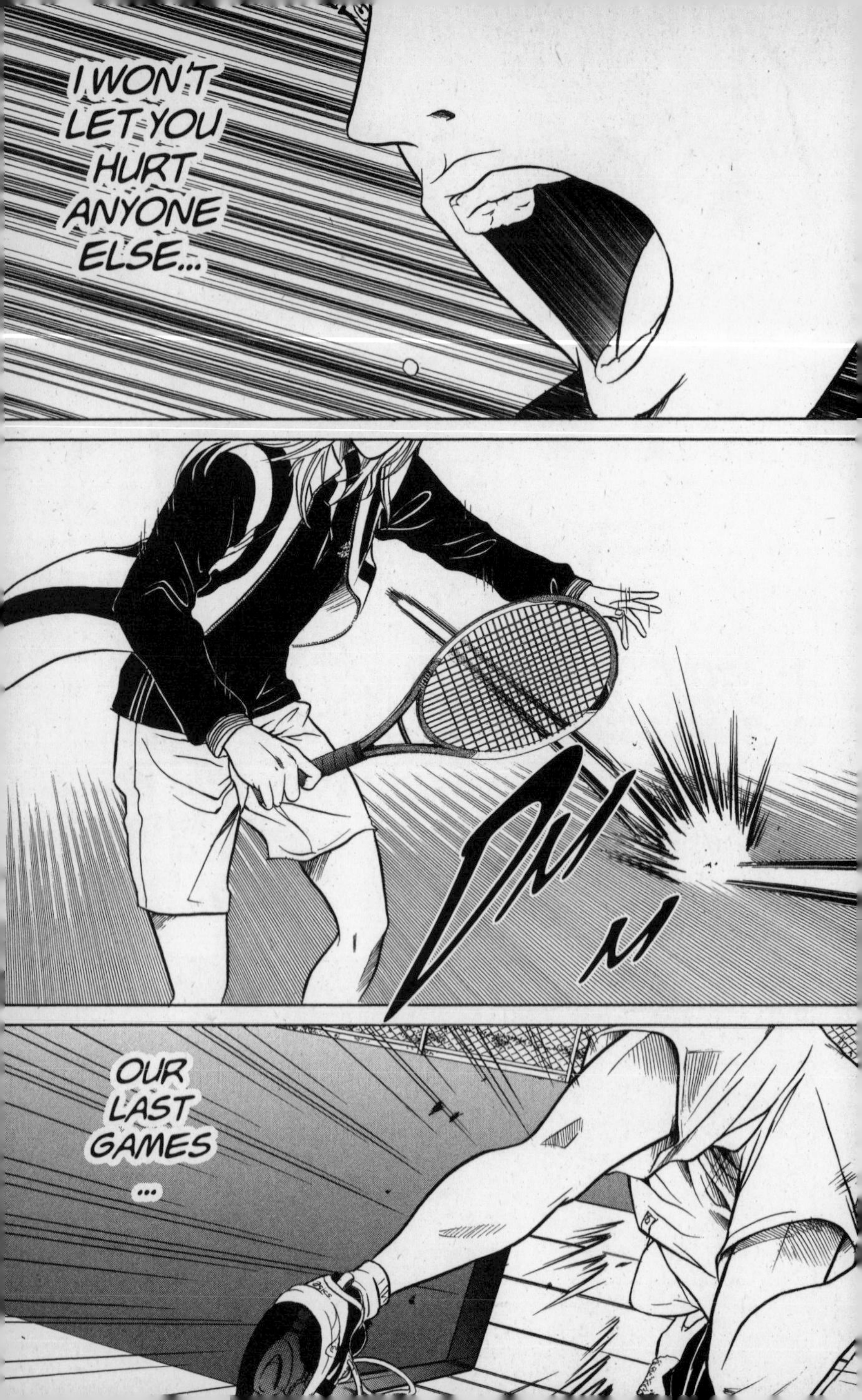
I WON'T LET YOU HURT ANYONE ELSE...
OUR LAST GAMES ...

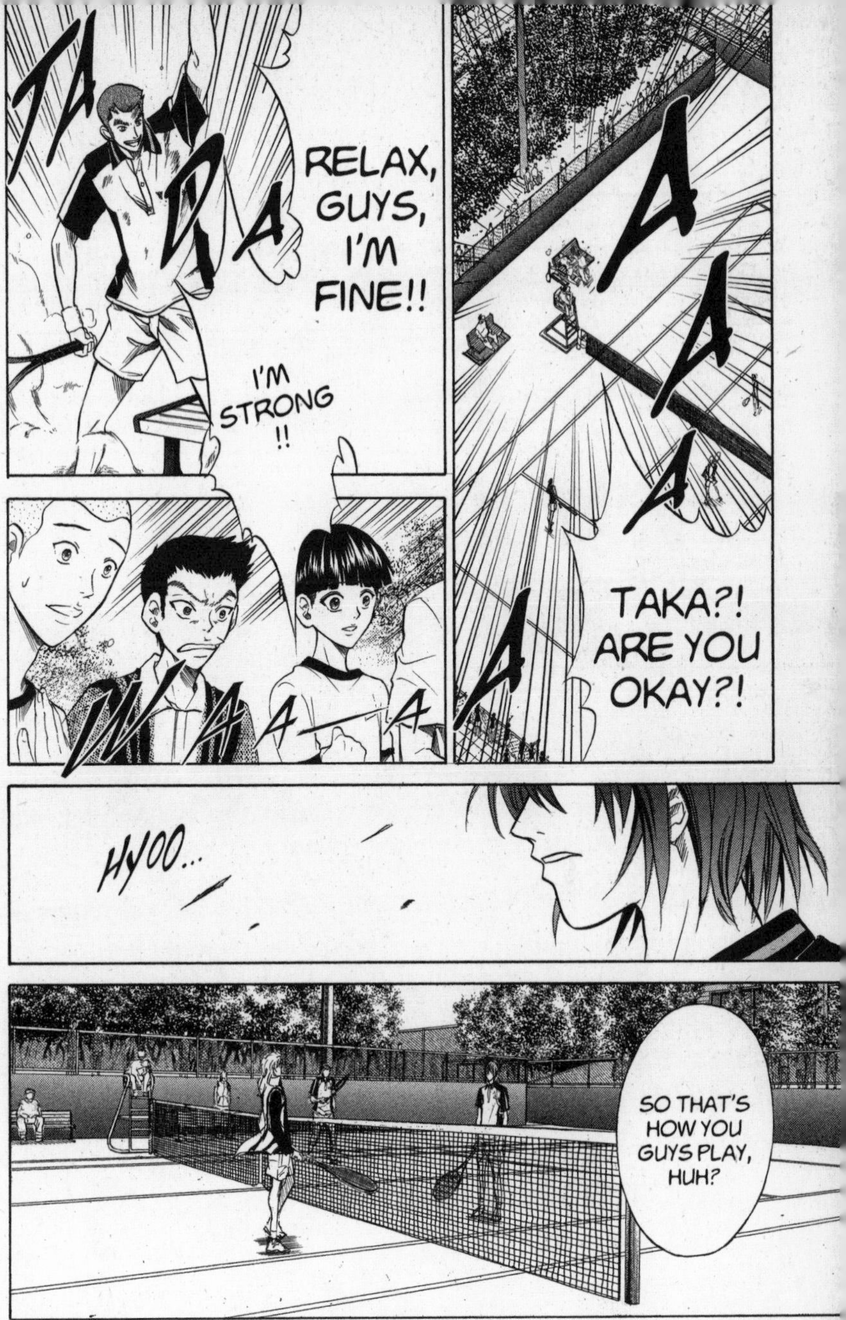
AAAAA
TAKA?! ARE YOU OKAY?!
TADAA
RELAX, GUYS, I'M FINE!!
I'M STRONG !!
WAA—A
HYOO...
SO THAT'S HOW YOU GUYS PLAY, HUH?

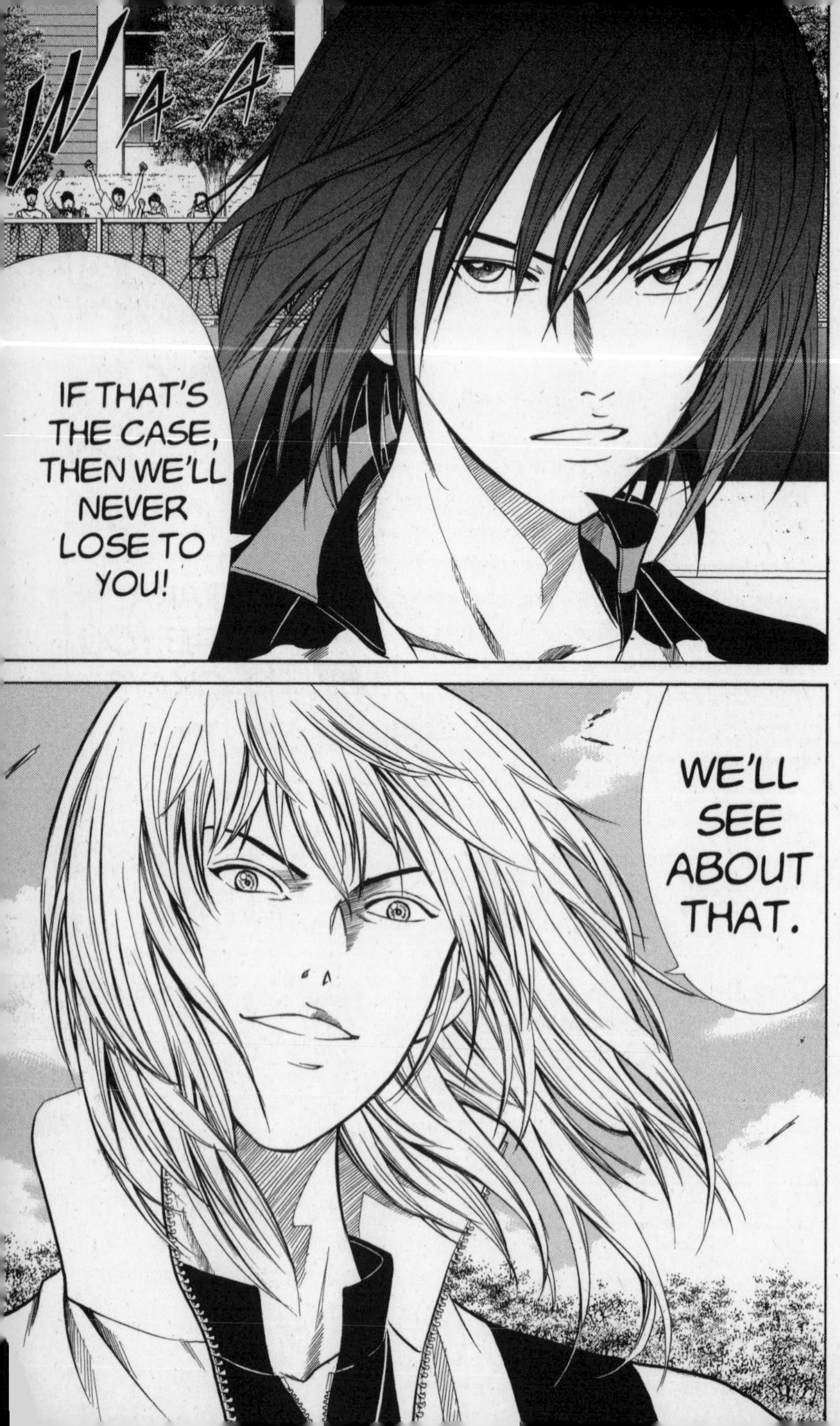
WAA
IF THAT'S THE CASE, THEN WE'LL NEVER LOSE TO YOU!
WE'LL SEE ABOUT THAT.

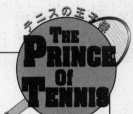

テニスの王子様
THE PRINCE OF TENNIS

The Prince of Tennis Illustration Collection 30.5!!

It's coming out! This time it's a collection of illustrations!! I believe it hits the stands some time in early December* along with volume 31. I've accumulated lots and lots of art and now it's finally going to be released. I put a lot of hard work into it; without a doubt it's one of my best books ever. There'll be more details about it in *Weekly Shonen Jump* magazine, so make sure to check it out. And of course I'm planning on drawing as many new illustrations All the main characters as I can. The book will include every color illustration and cut, and also some never-before-seen *Jump* covers of Ryoga Echizen. It'll be full of goodies, so please check it out!

I'll be busier than ever in the fall, so I got some time off this summer. I went to the beach, went fishing, went to some hot springs, and now I'm fully recharged! ✧ The National Tournament is just getting started, so I've got a lot of hard work ahead of me!

Okay, then! Here's the usual: keep supporting *The Prince of Tennis* and Ryoma!

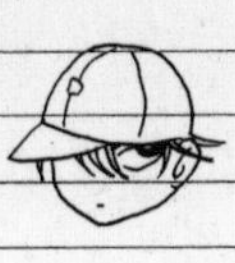

テニスの王子様
T. KONOMI

*This book was released in Japan in 2005.—Ed.

Send fan letters to: Takeshi Konomi, *The Prince of Tennis*, c/o VIZ Media LLC, P.O. Box 77010, San Francisco, CA 94107

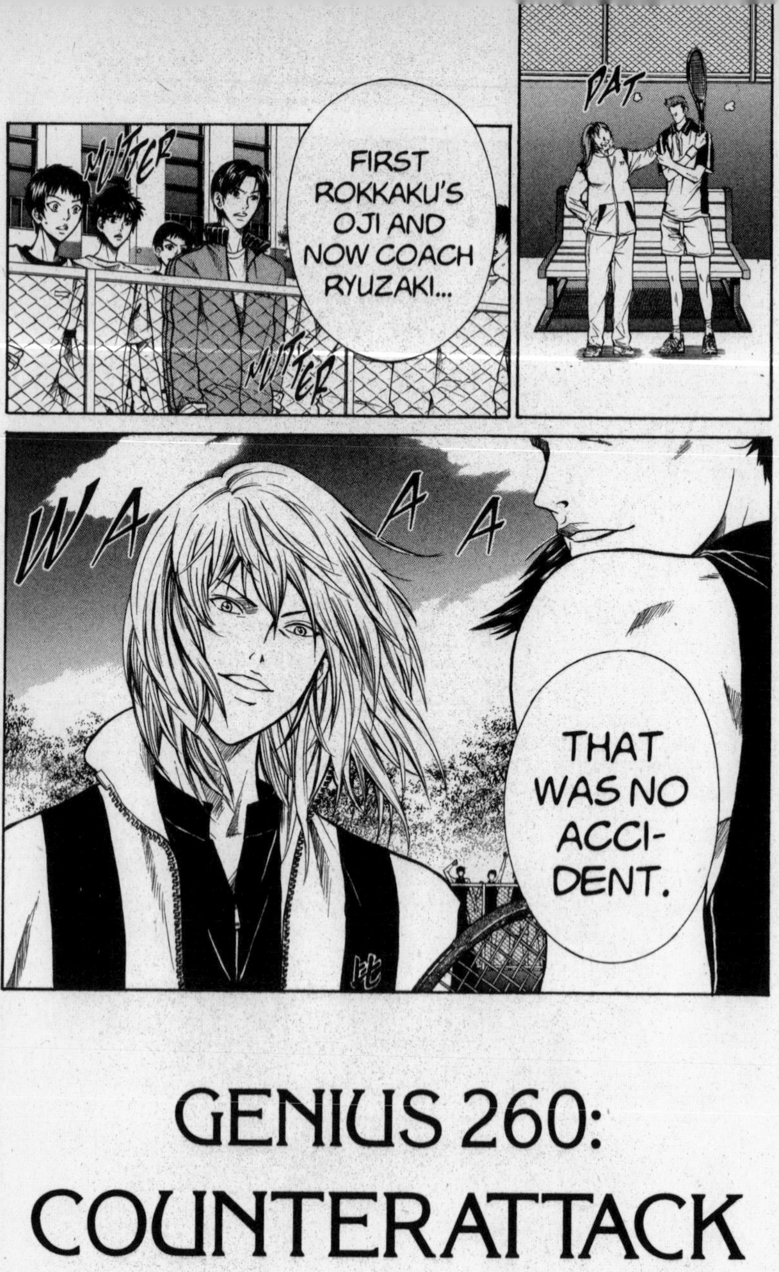
PAT
MUTTER
FIRST ROKKAKU'S OJI AND NOW COACH RYUZAKI...
MUTTER
WA A A
THAT WAS NO ACCI-DENT.

GENIUS 260: COUNTERATTACK

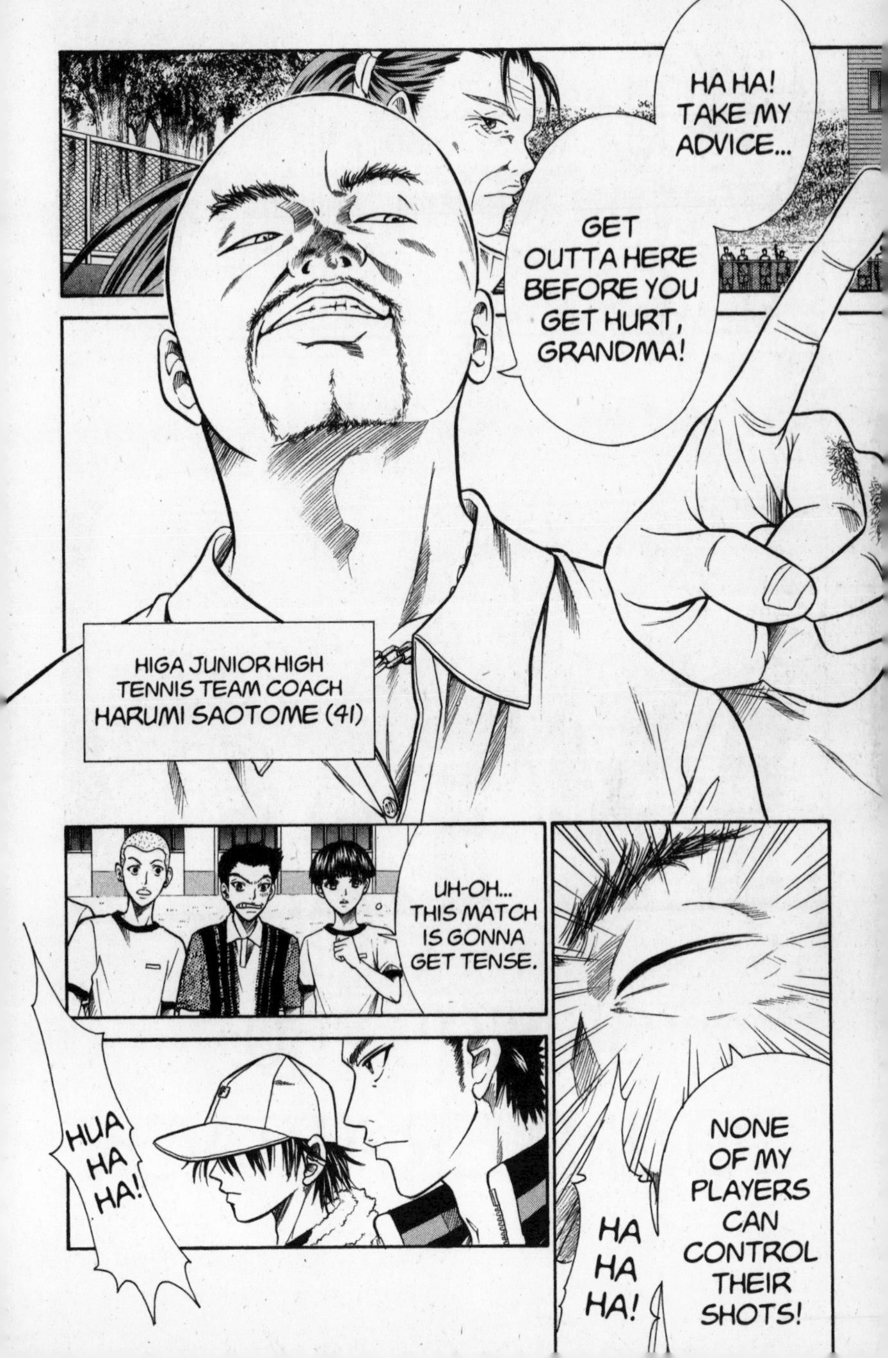
HA HA! TAKE MY ADVICE...
GET OUTTA HERE BEFORE YOU GET HURT, GRANDMA!
HIGA JUNIOR HIGH TENNIS TEAM COACH HARUMI SAOTOME (41)
NONE OF MY PLAYERS CAN CONTROL THEIR SHOTS!
HA HA HA!
UH-OH... THIS MATCH IS GONNA GET TENSE.
HUA HA HA!

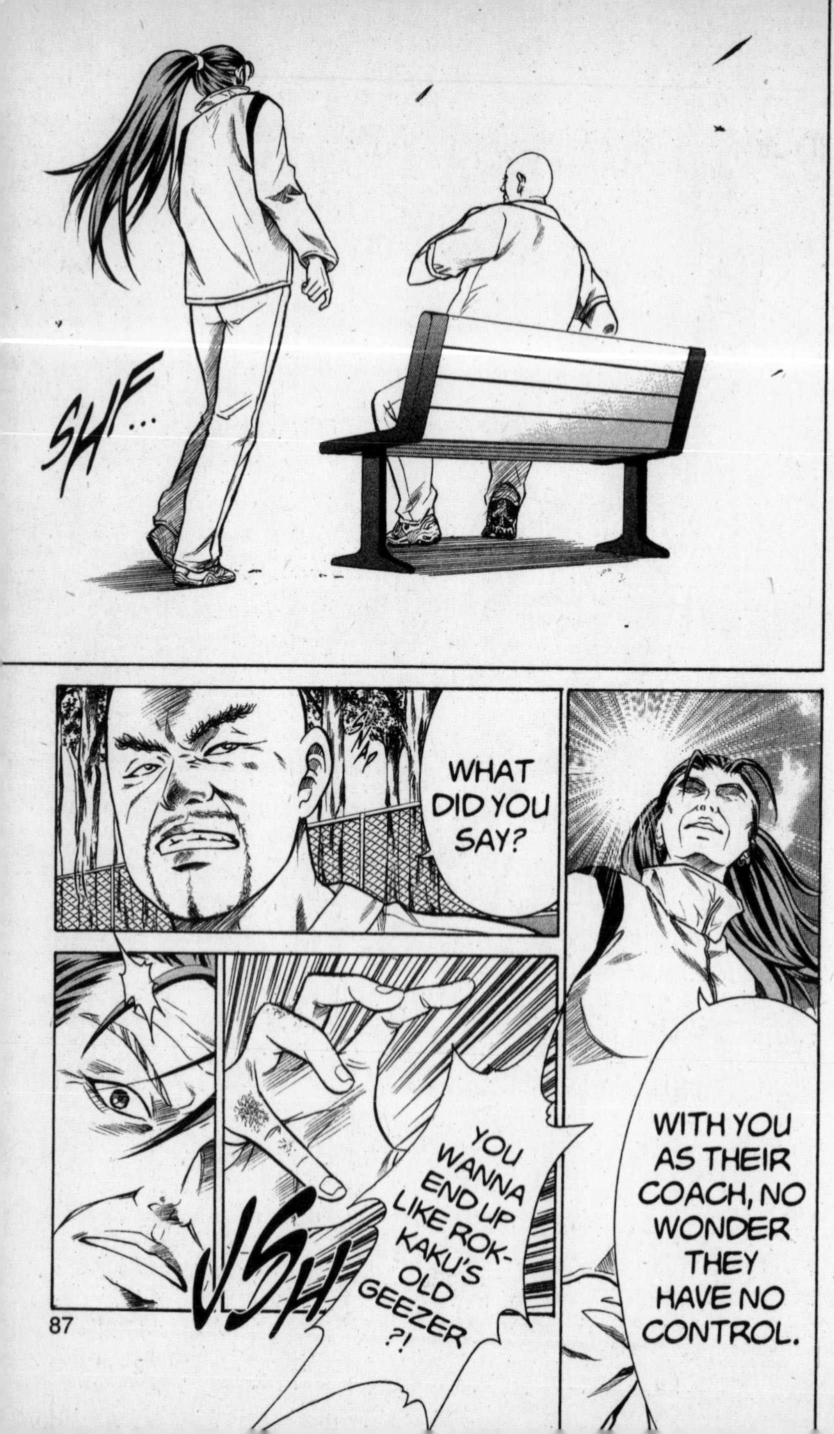
SHF...
WITH YOU AS THEIR COACH, NO WONDER THEY HAVE NO CONTROL.
SNAP
WHAT DID YOU SAY?
YOU WANNA END UP LIKE ROK-KAKU'S OLD GEEZER?!
VSH

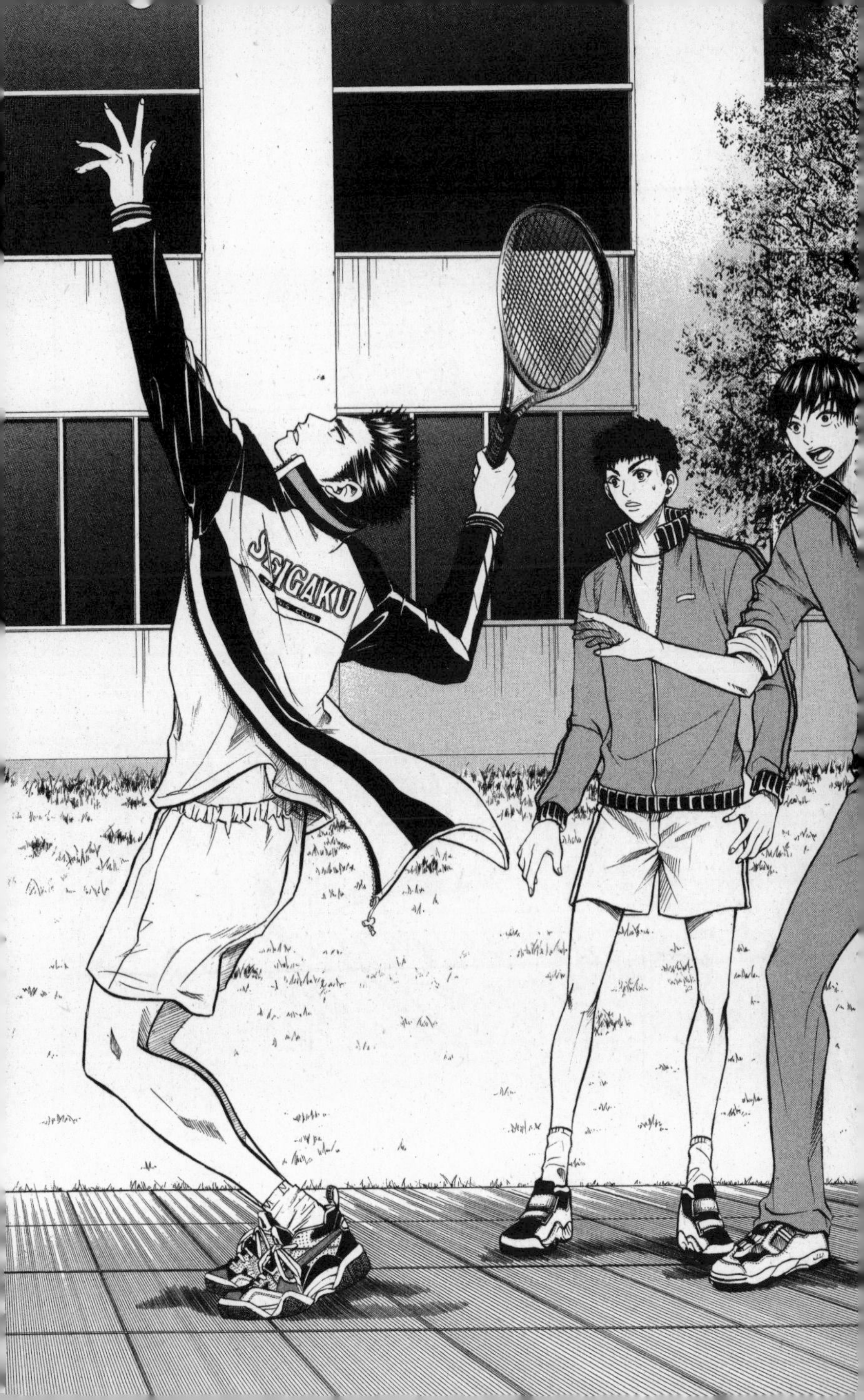
SEIGAKU

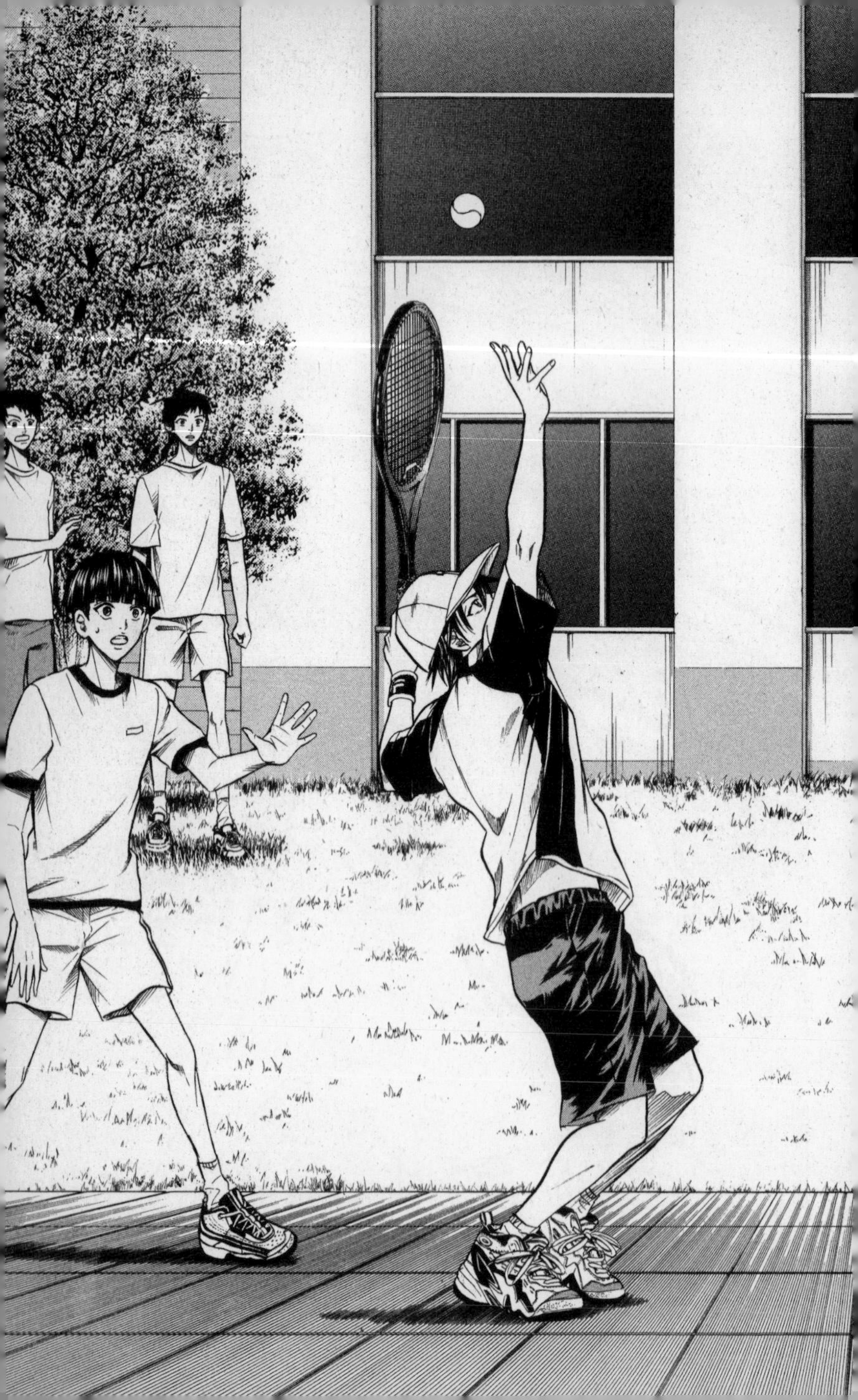

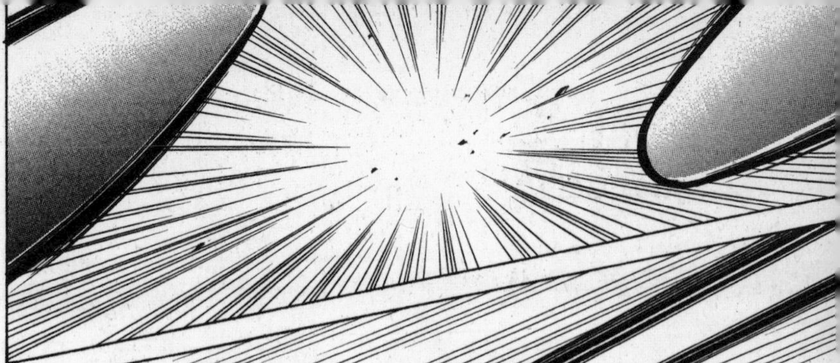

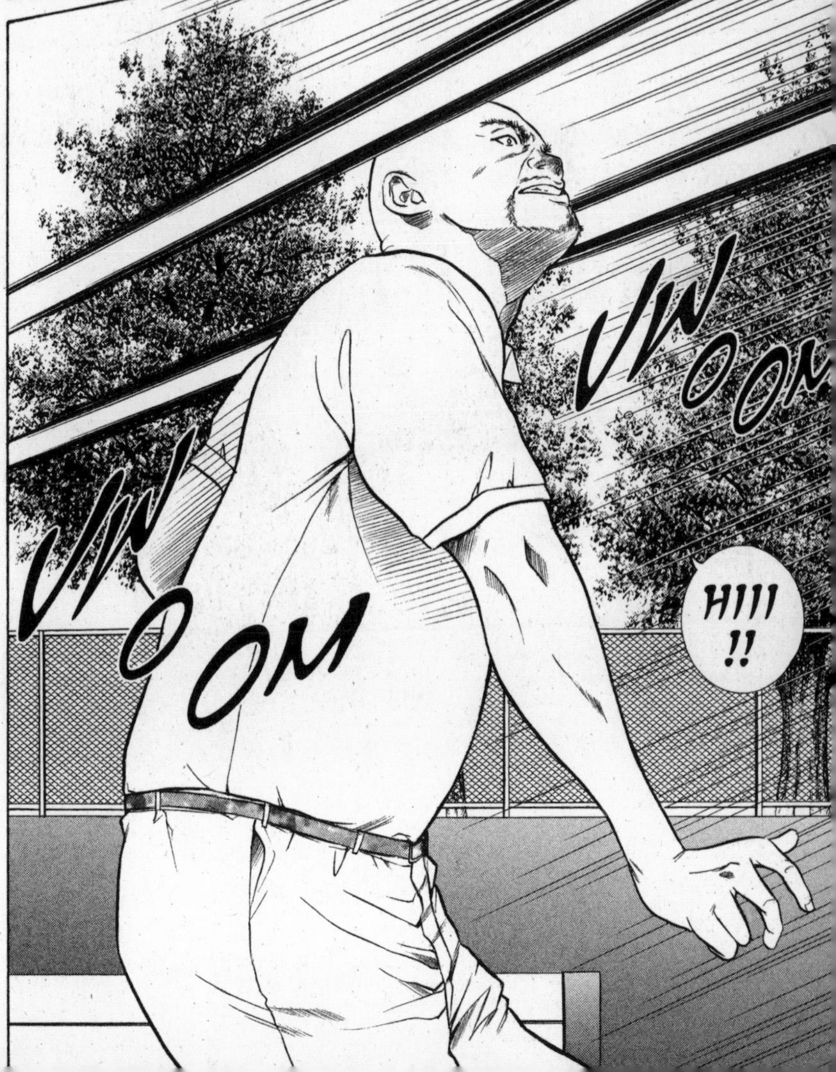
VWOOM
VWOOM
HIII !!

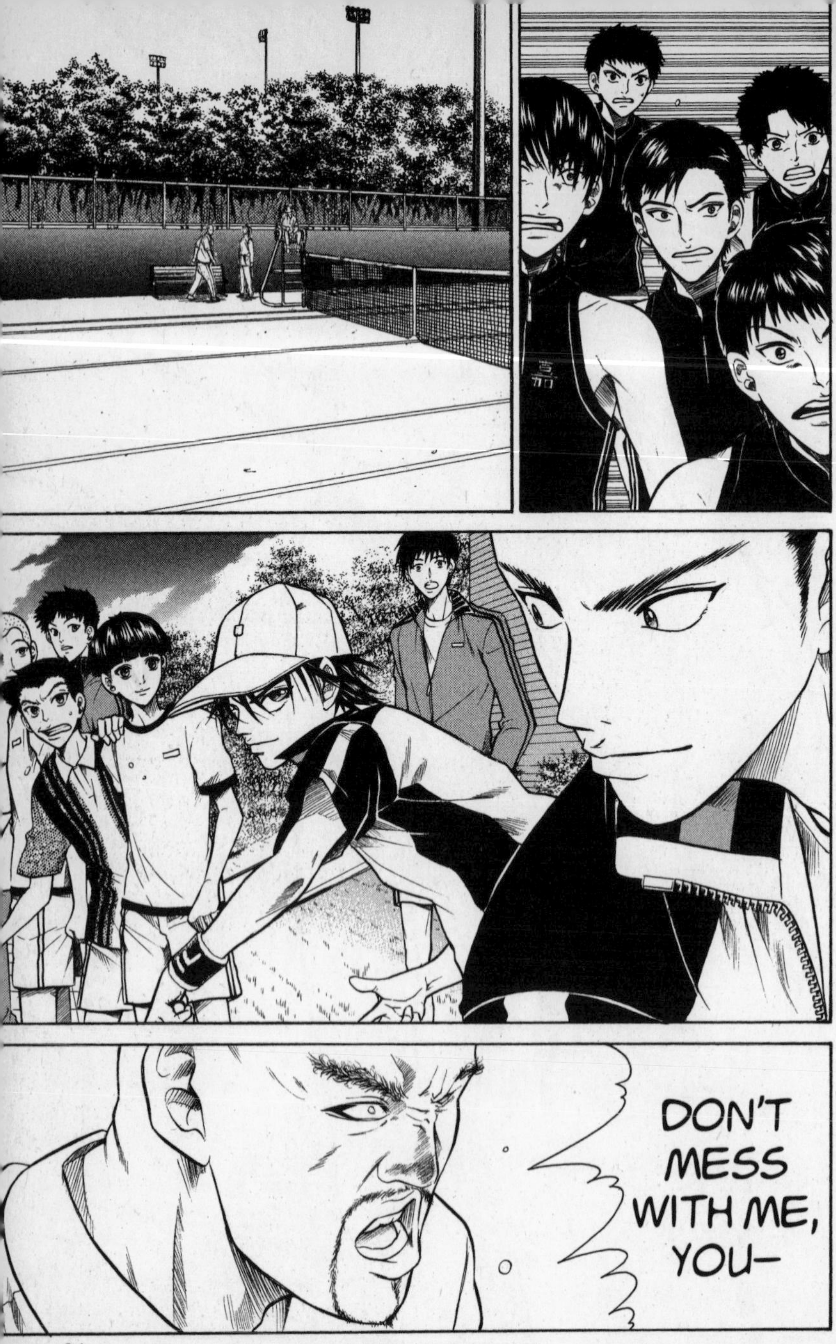
DON'T MESS WITH ME, YOU–

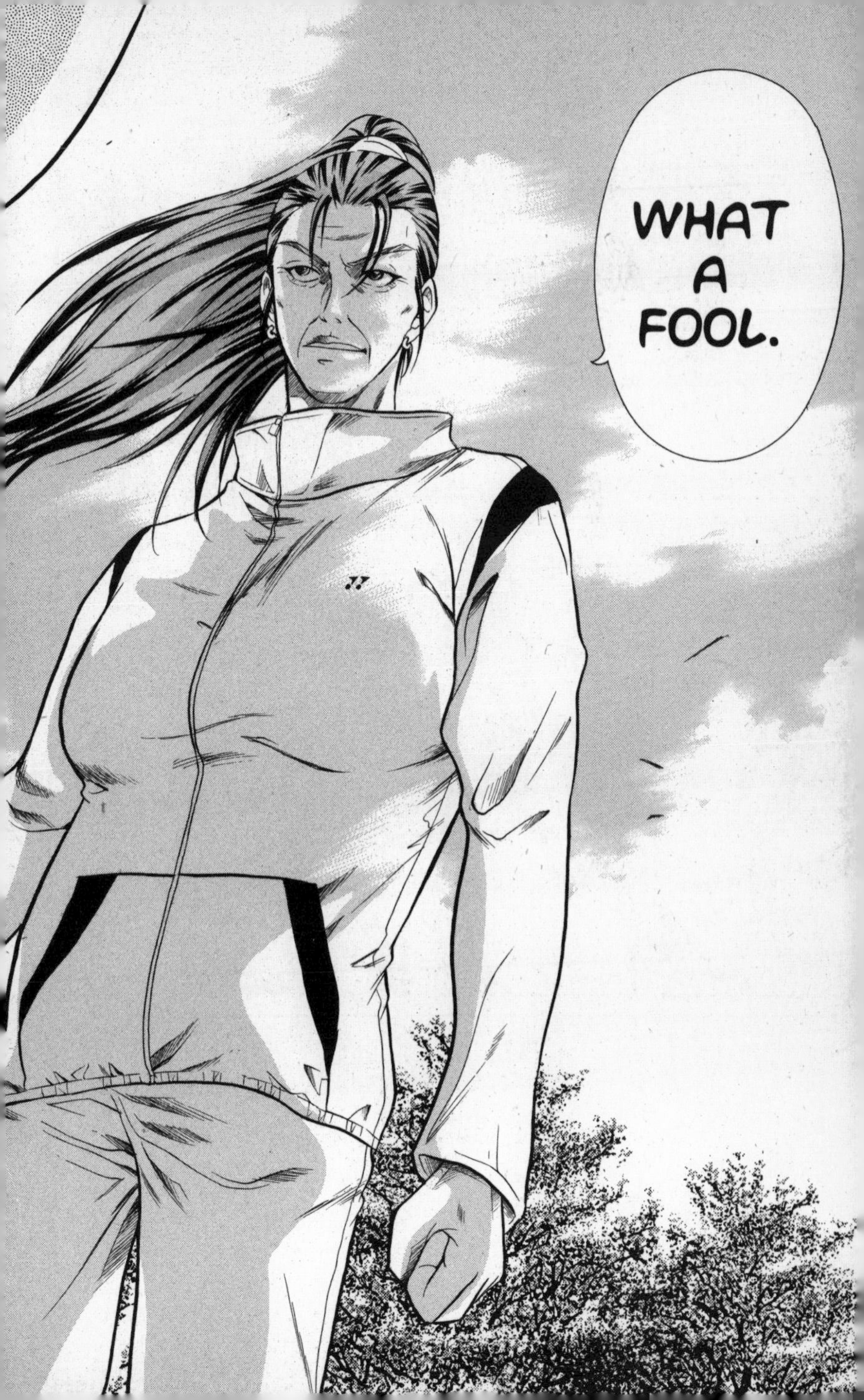
WHAT A FOOL.

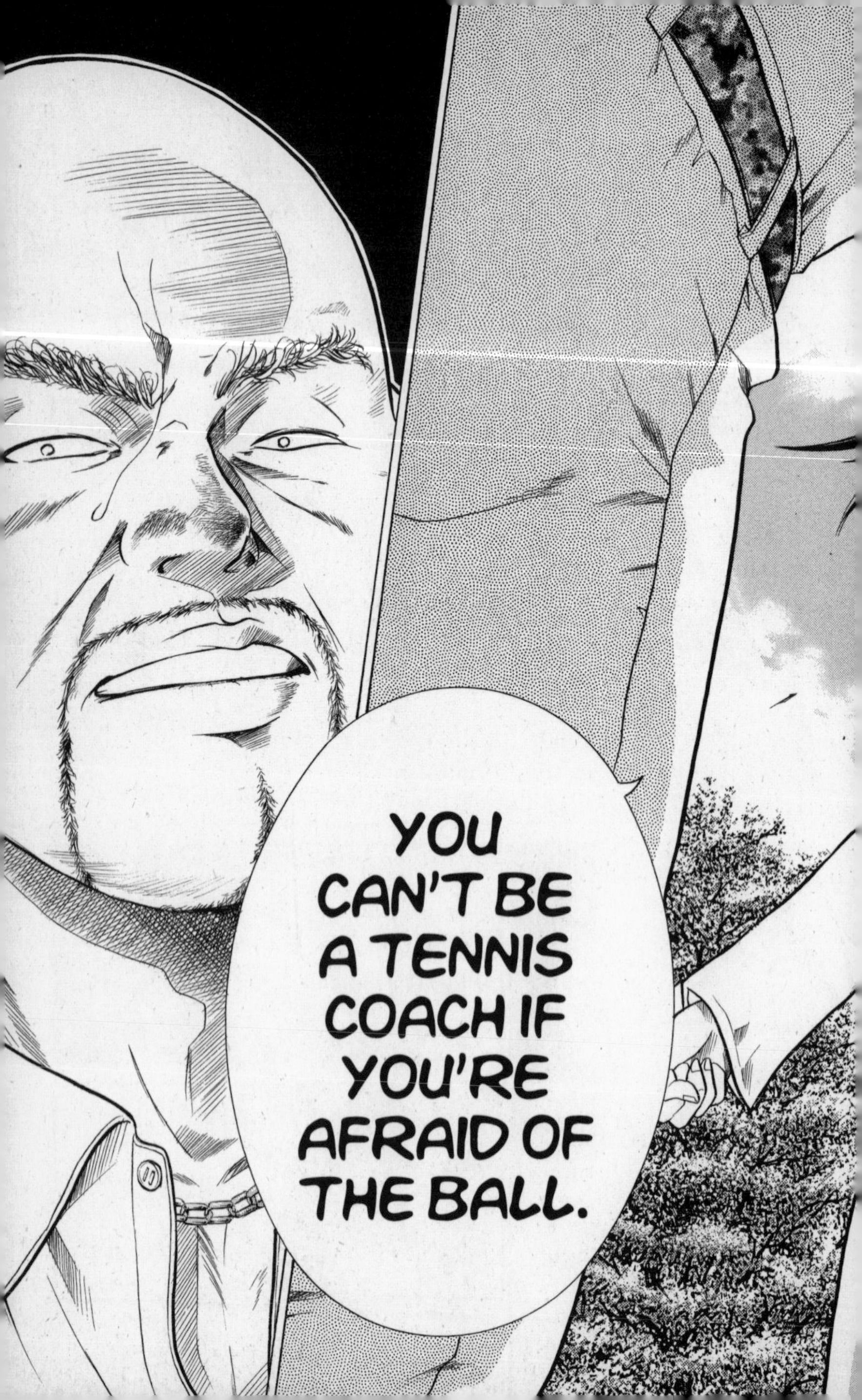
YOU CAN'T BE A TENNIS COACH IF YOU'RE AFRAID OF THE BALL.

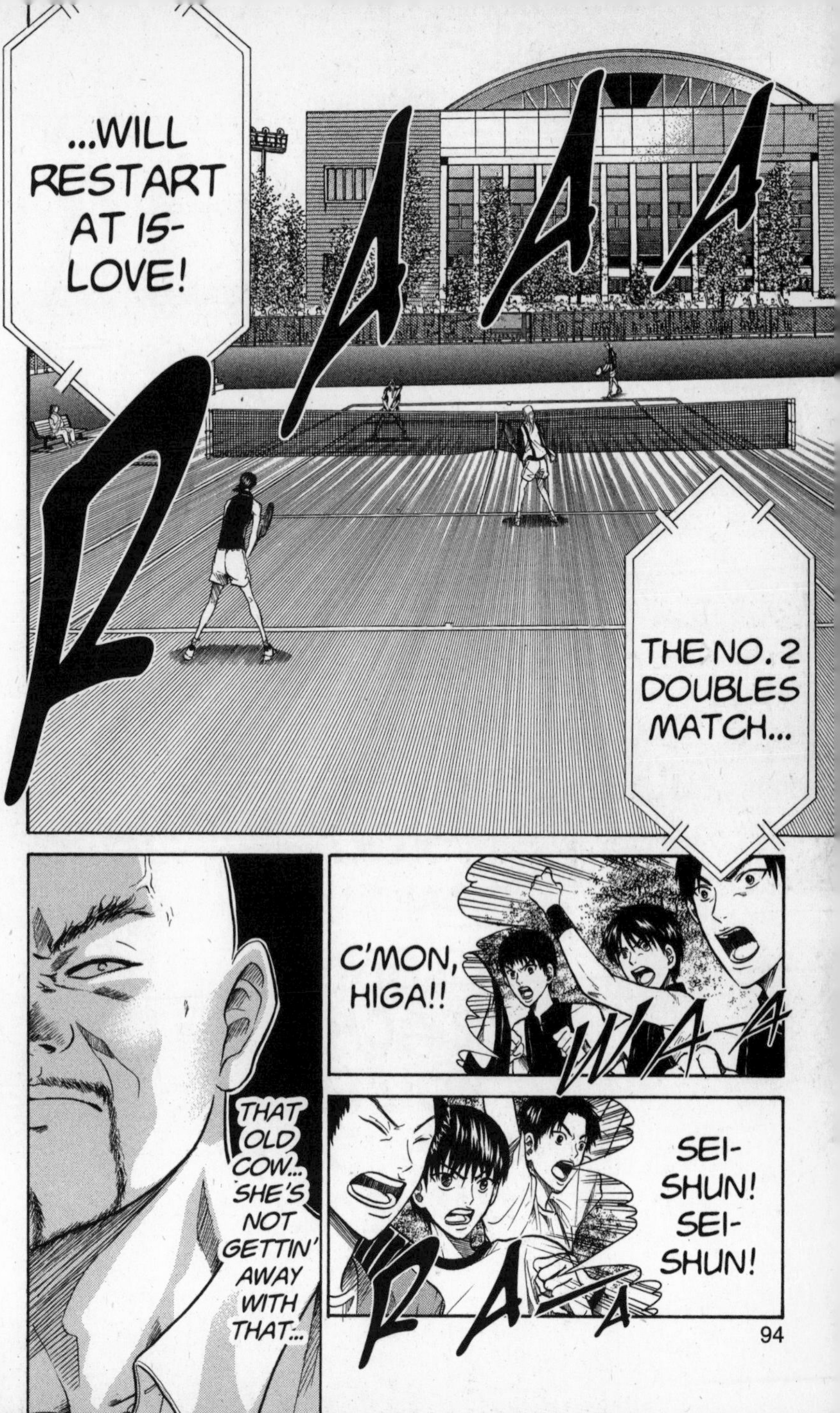
THE NO. 2 DOUBLES MATCH...
...WILL RESTART AT 15-LOVE!
RAAA
C'MON, HIGA!!
WAAA
SEI-SHUN! SEI-SHUN!
RAAA
THAT OLD COW... SHE'S NOT GETTIN' AWAY WITH THAT...

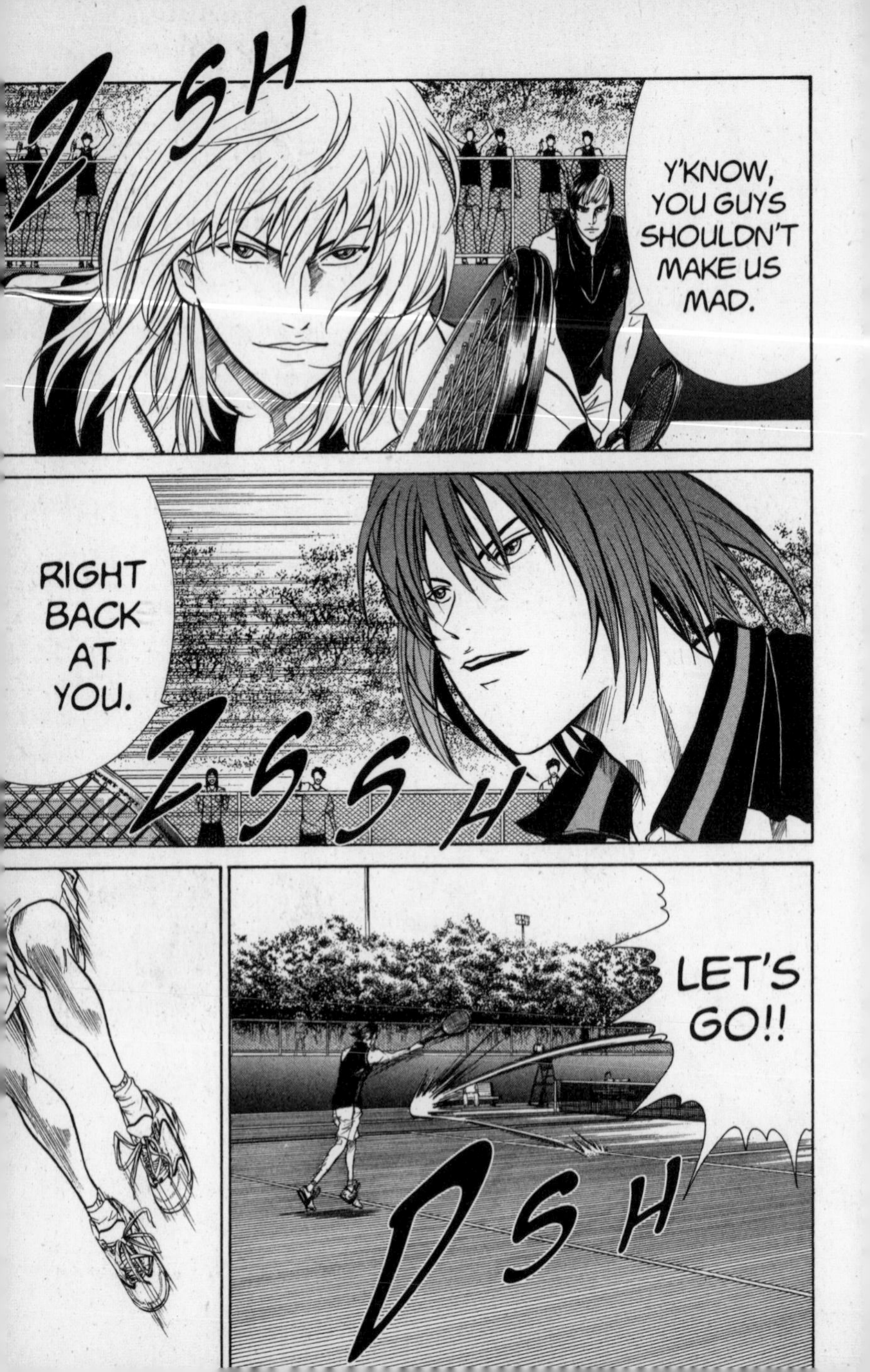
ZSH
Y'KNOW, YOU GUYS SHOULDN'T MAKE US MAD.
RIGHT BACK AT YOU.
ZSSH
LET'S GO!!
DSH

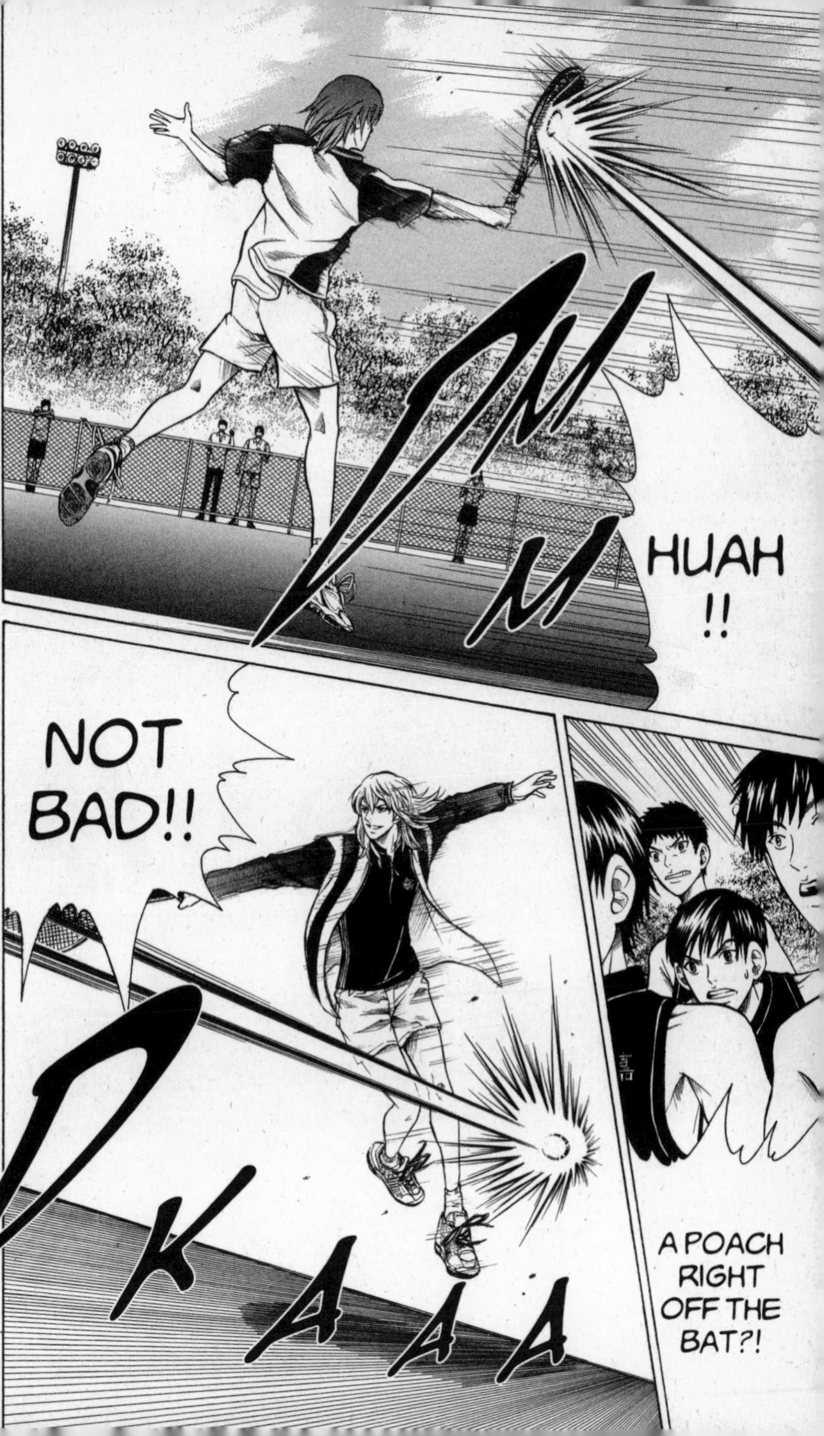
MM
HUAH!!
NOT BAD!!
DKAAA
A POACH RIGHT OFF THE BAT?!

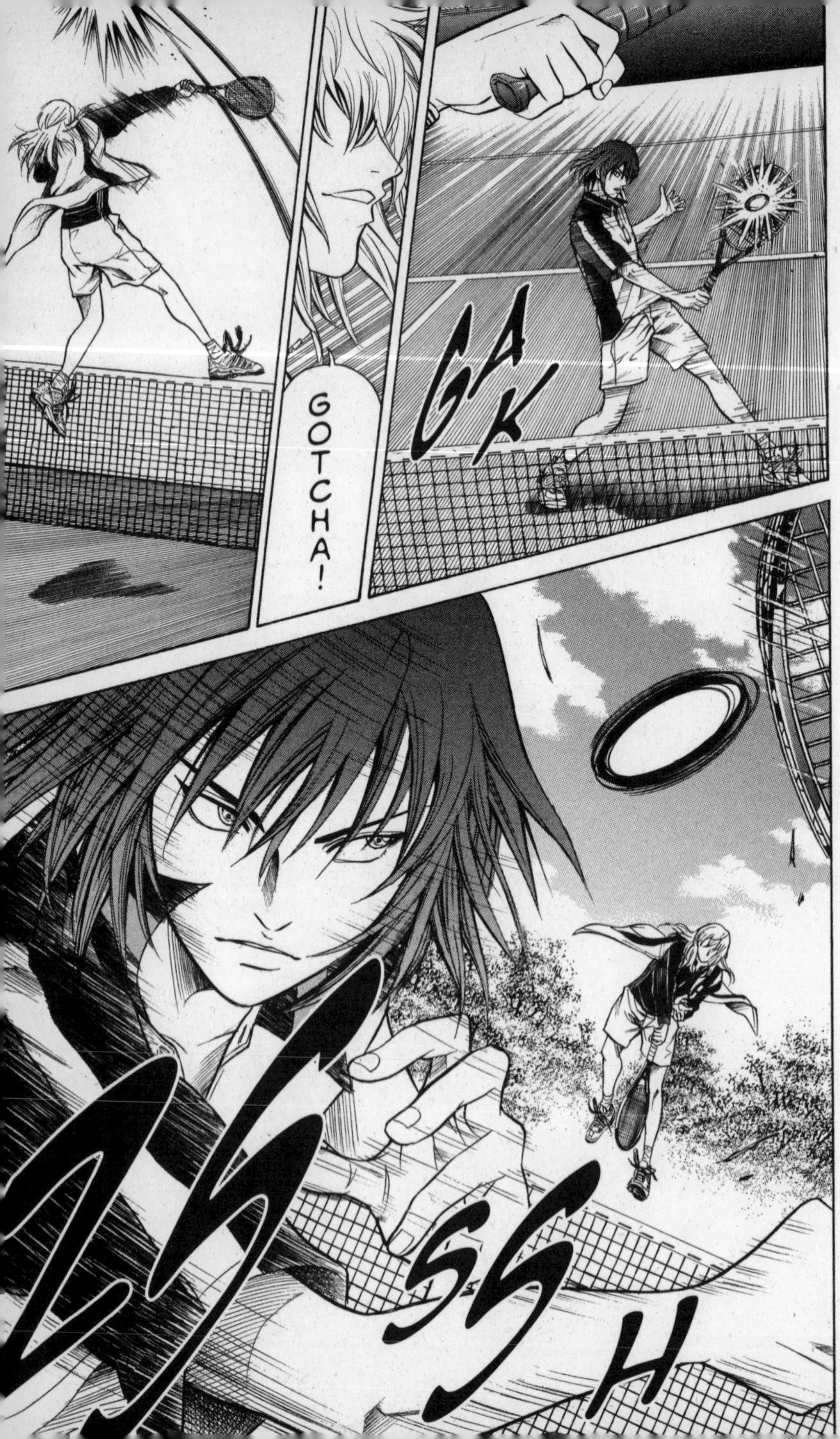
GAK
GOTCHA!
SSH

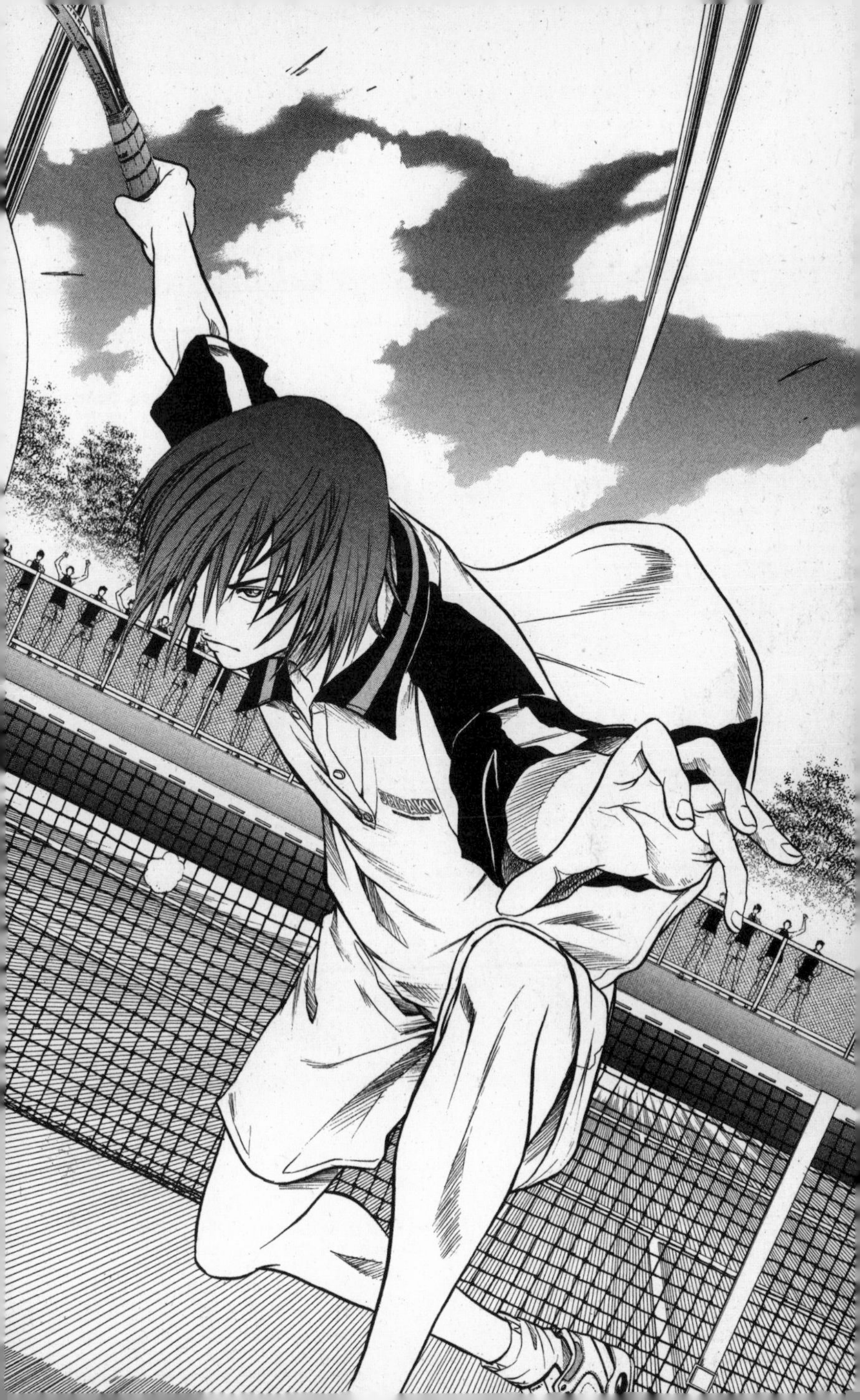
SEIGAKU

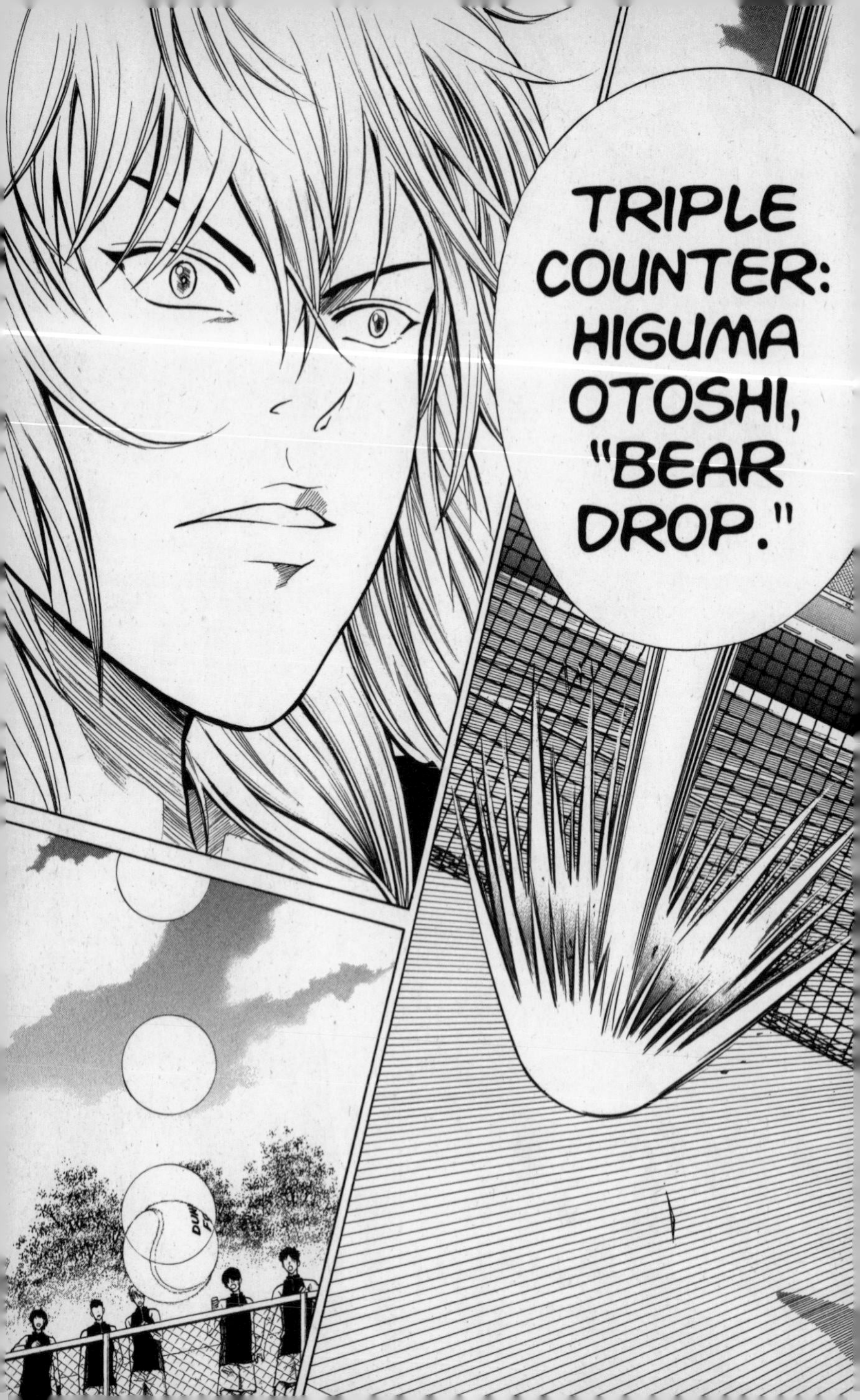
TRIPLE COUNTER: HIGUMA OTOSHI, "BEAR DROP."

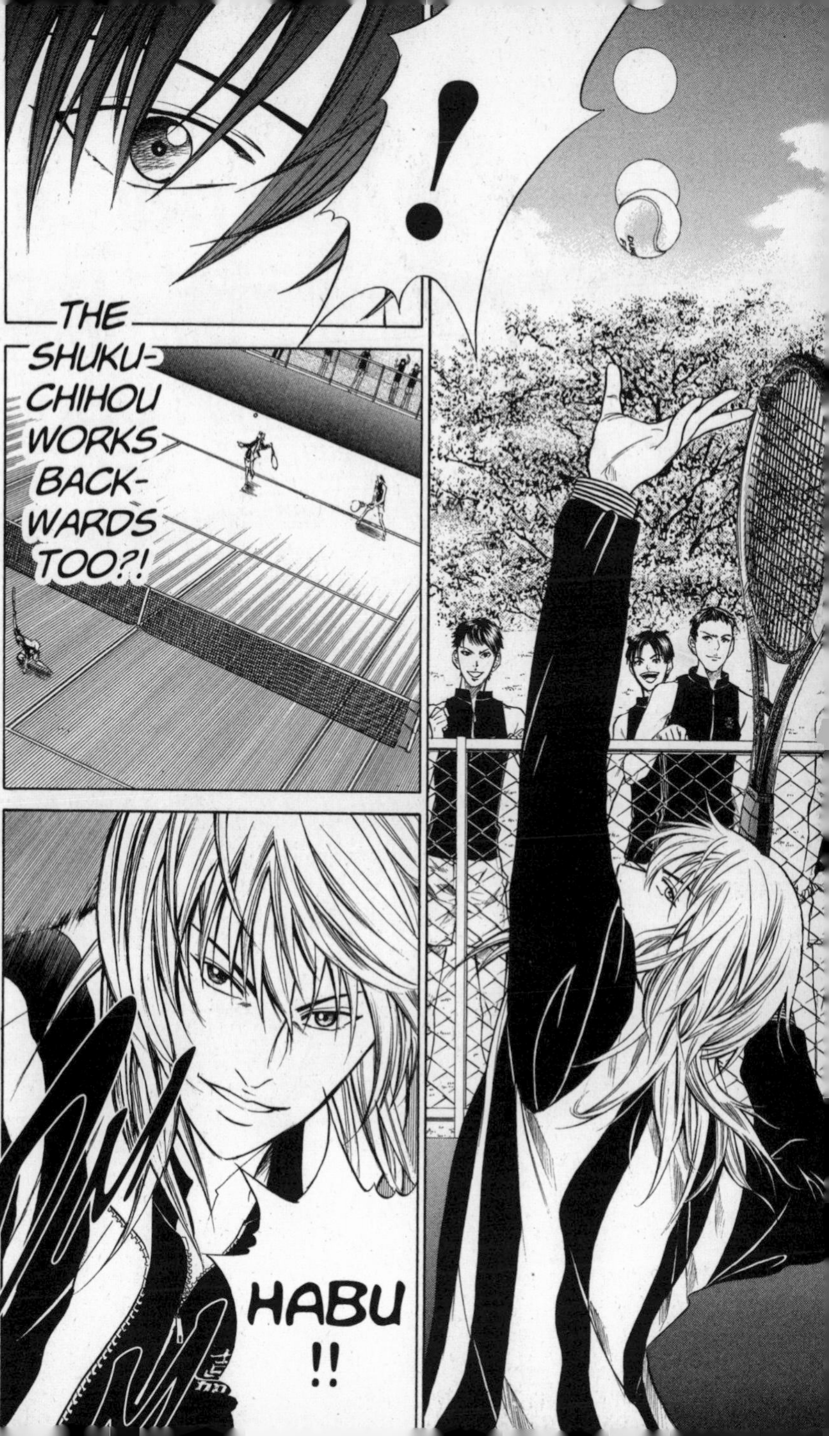
!
THE SHUKU-CHIHOU WORKS BACK-WARDS TOO?!
HABU !!

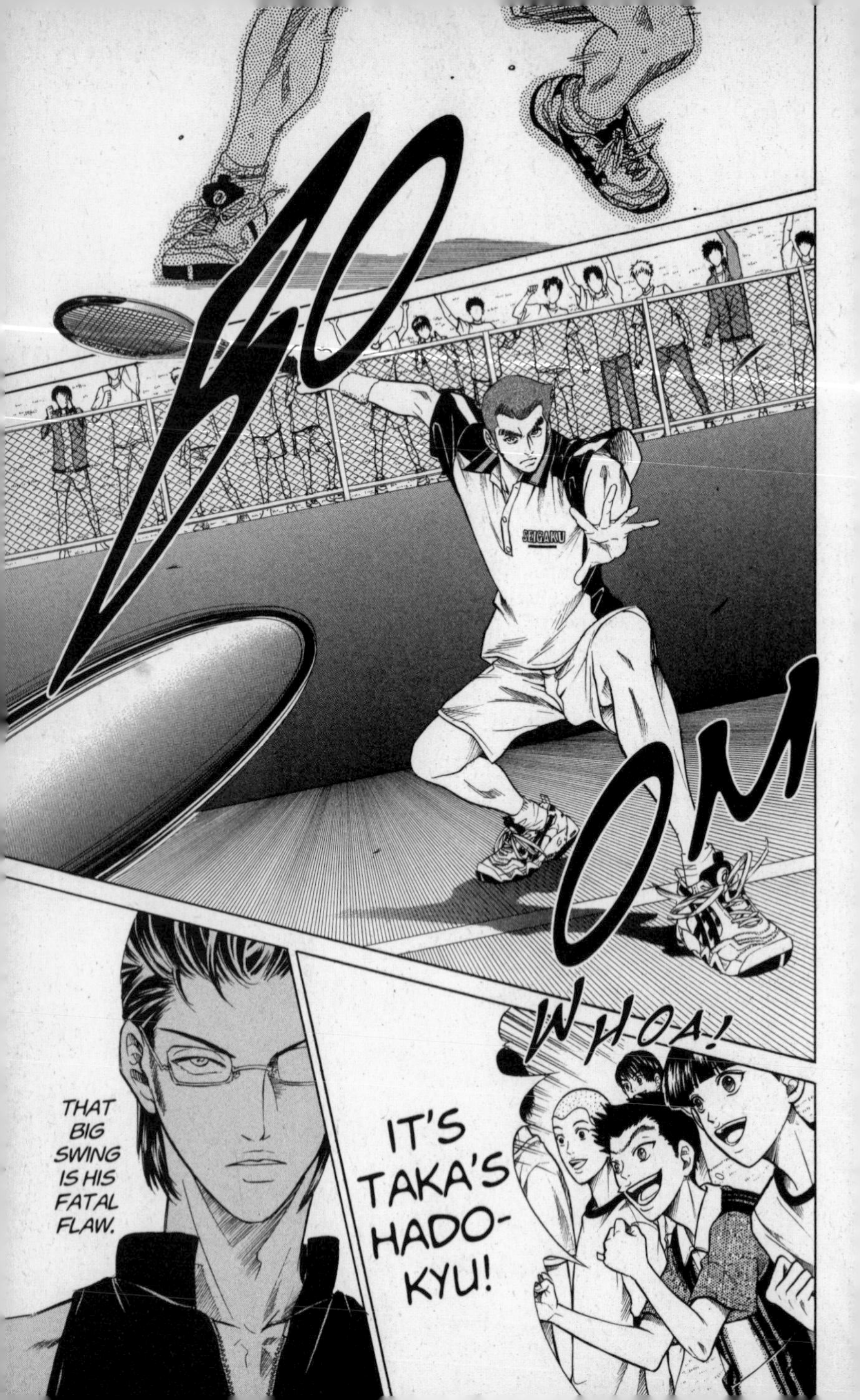
SEIGAKU
ZOOM
WHOA!
IT'S TAKA'S HADO-KYU!
THAT BIG SWING IS HIS FATAL FLAW.

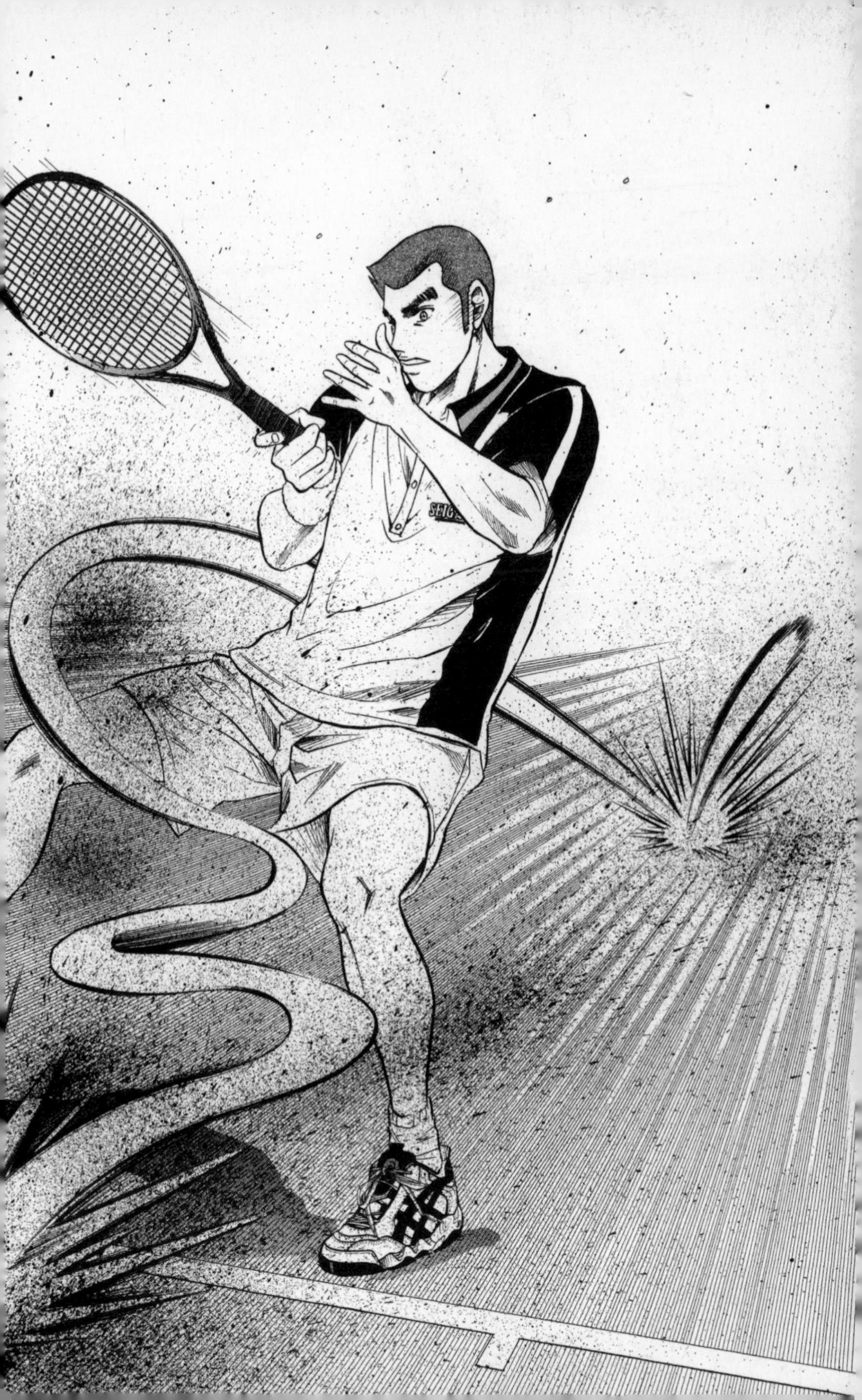

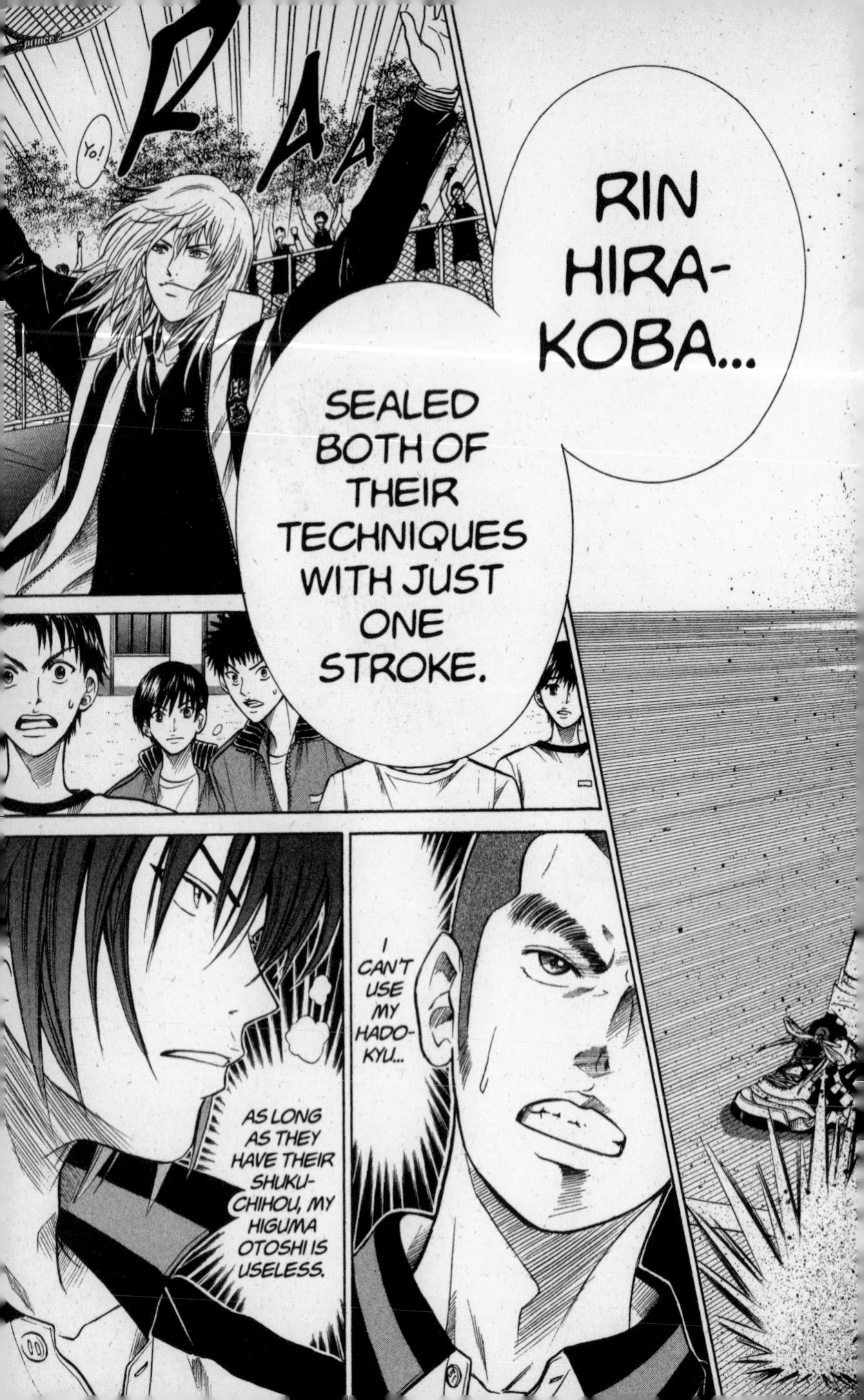
RIN HIRA-KOBA...
SEALED BOTH OF THEIR TECHNIQUES WITH JUST ONE STROKE.
PAAA
Yo!
I CAN'T USE MY HADO-KYU...
AS LONG AS THEY HAVE THEIR SHUKU-CHIHOU, MY HIGUMA OTOSHI IS USELESS.

テニスの王子様

THE PRINCE OF TENNIS

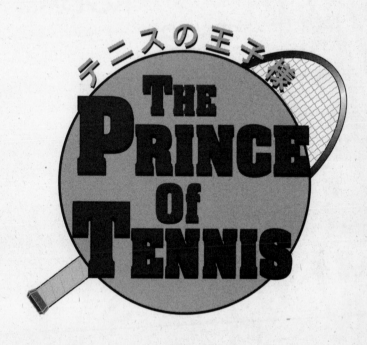

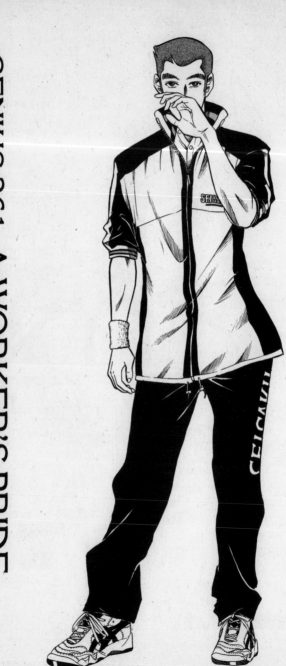

GENIUS 261: A WORKER'S PRIDE

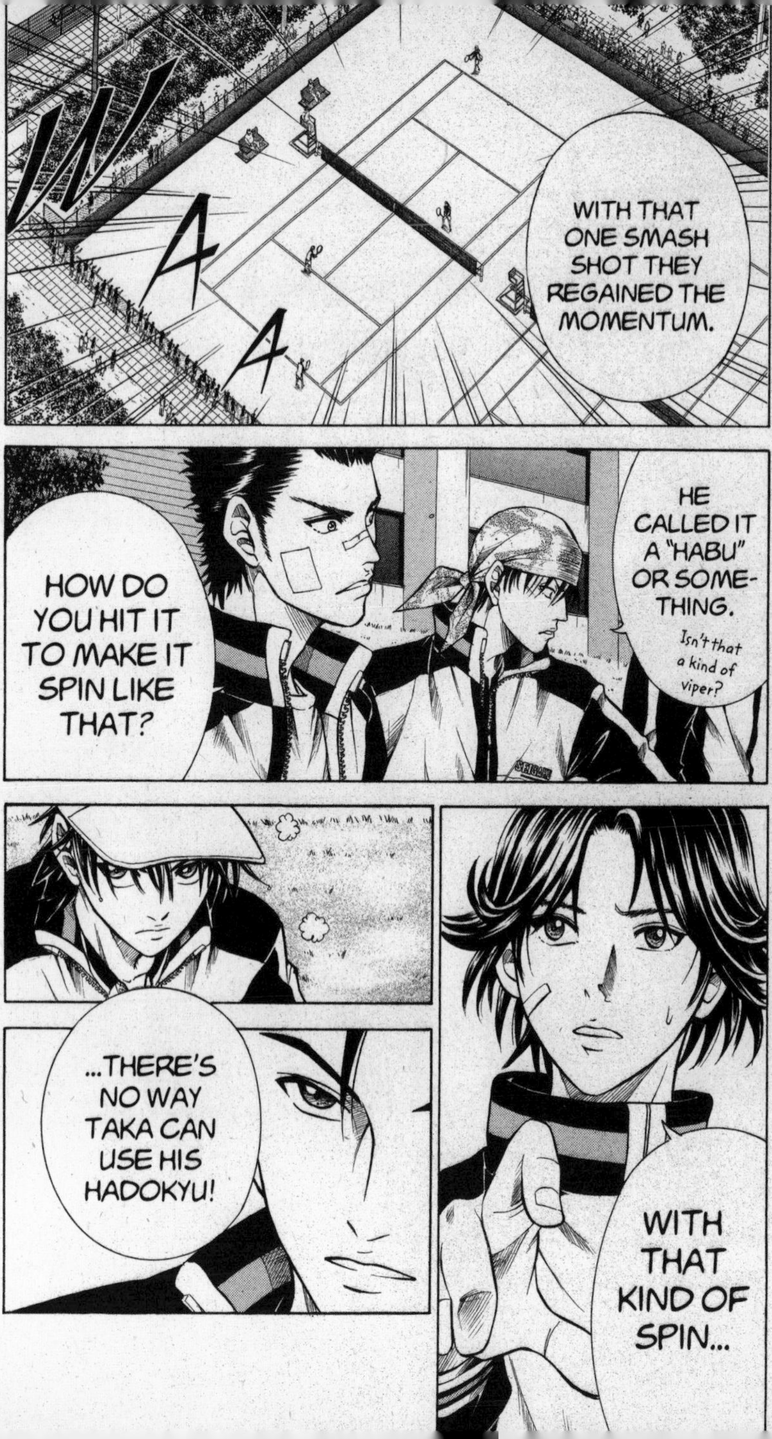
WAA
WITH THAT ONE SMASH SHOT THEY REGAINED THE MOMENTUM.
HE CALLED IT A "HABU" OR SOME-THING.
Isn't that a kind of viper?
HOW DO YOU HIT IT TO MAKE IT SPIN LIKE THAT?
SEIGAKU
WITH THAT KIND OF SPIN...
...THERE'S NO WAY TAKA CAN USE HIS HADOKYU!

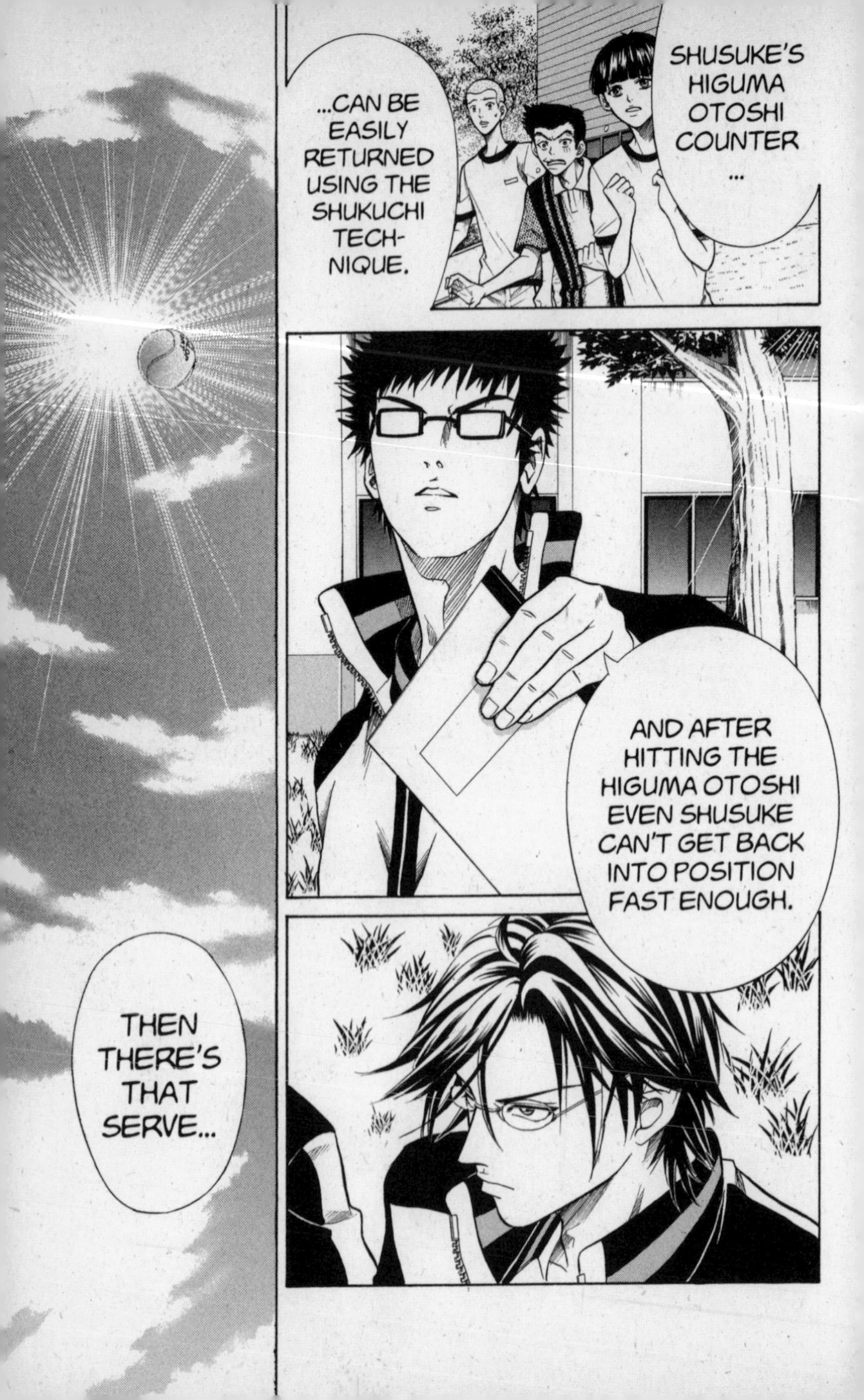
SHUSUKE'S HIGUMA OTOSHI COUNTER ...
...CAN BE EASILY RETURNED USING THE SHUKUCHI TECH-NIQUE.
AND AFTER HITTING THE HIGUMA OTOSHI EVEN SHUSUKE CAN'T GET BACK INTO POSITION FAST ENOUGH.
THEN THERE'S THAT SERVE...

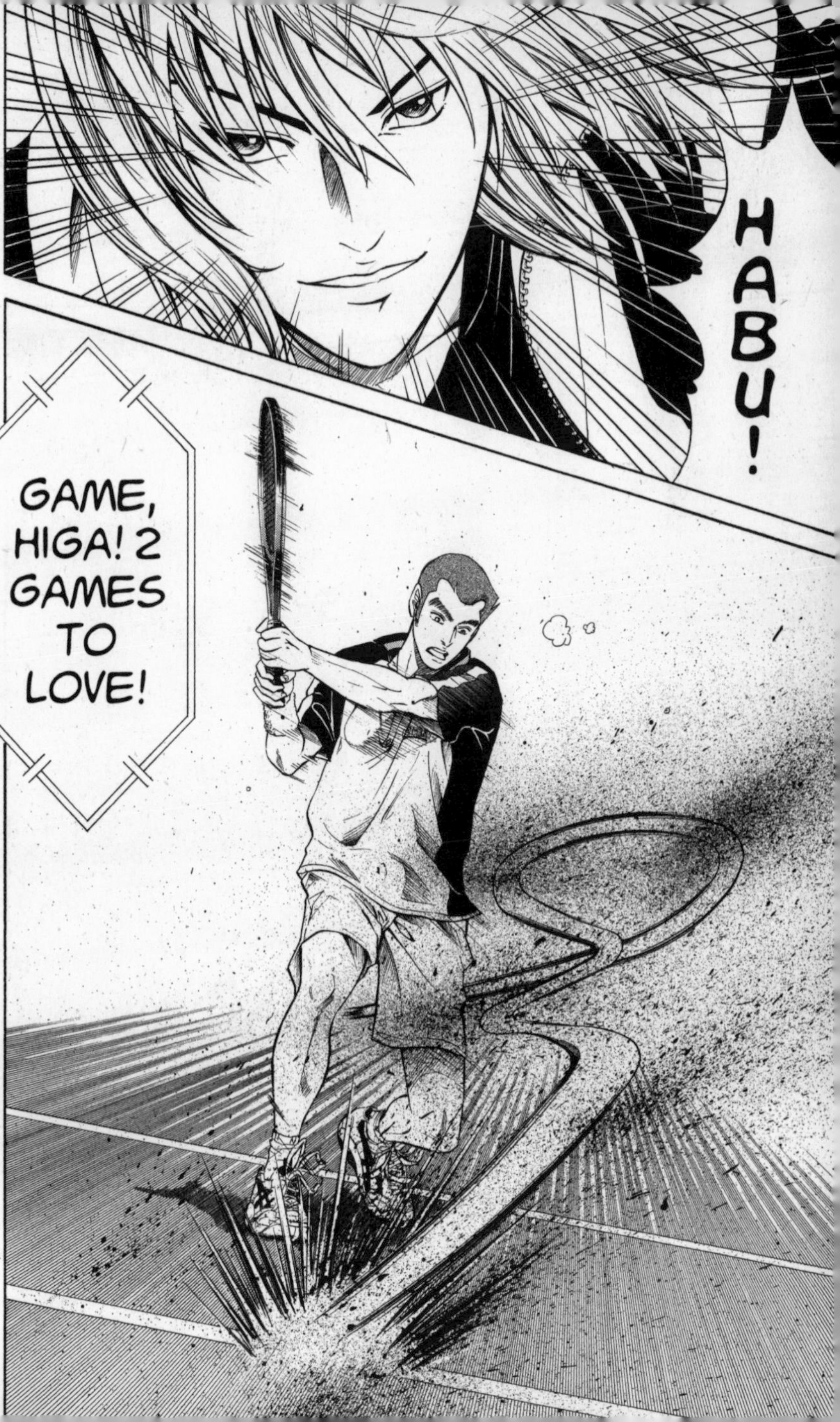
HABU!
GAME, HIGA! 2 GAMES TO LOVE!

READ THIS WAY

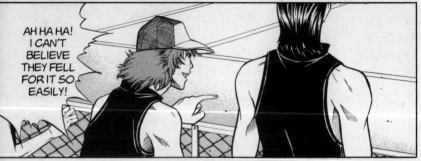

AH HA HA! I CAN'T BELIEVE THEY FELL FOR IT SO EASILY!
ONCE MR. KAWA-MURA'S HADOKYU IS CON-TAINED...
HE IS AS GOOD AS FINISHED.
THE ONE WE NEED TO WATCH OUT FOR IS...
...MR. FUJI, THE ONE THEY CALL A "GENIUS."

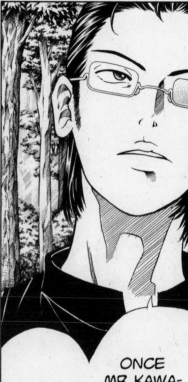

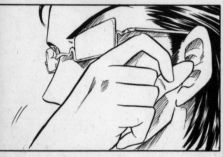

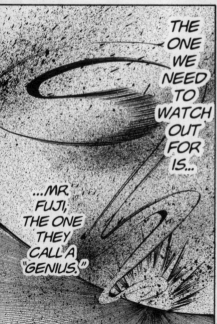

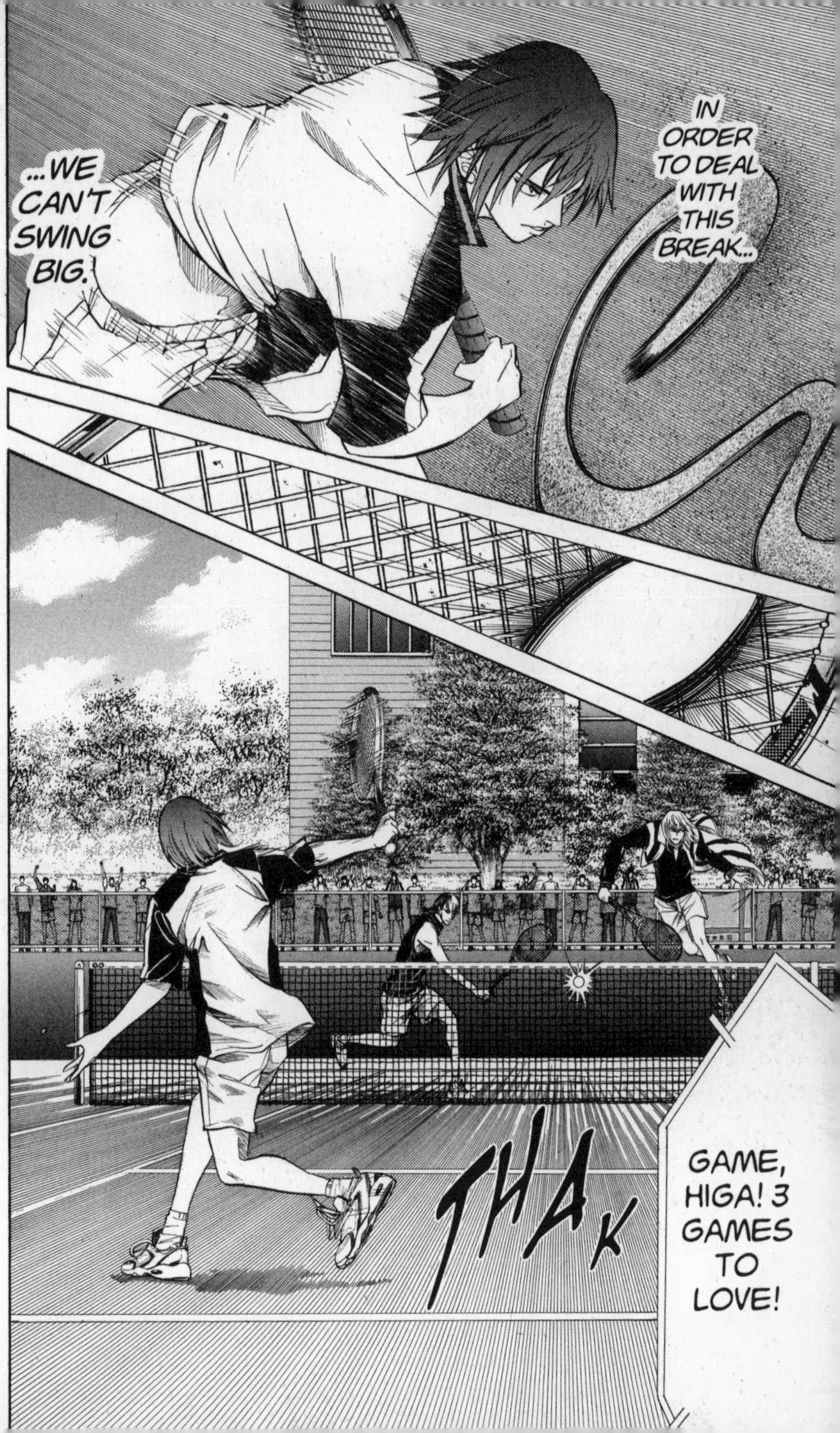
IN ORDER TO DEAL WITH THIS BREAK...
...WE CAN'T SWING BIG.
THAK
GAME, HIGA! 3 GAMES TO LOVE!

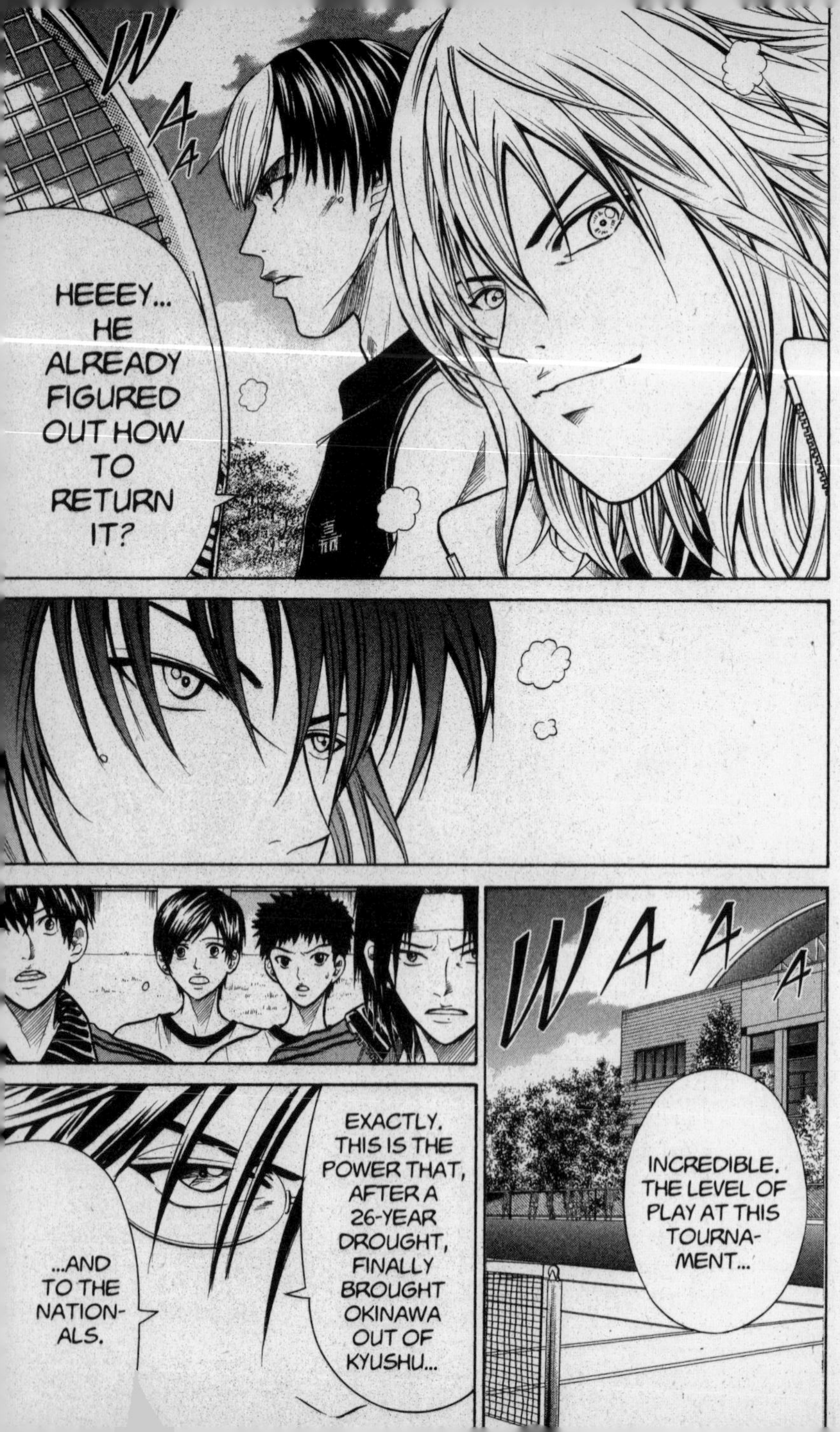
WAA
HEEEY... HE ALREADY FIGURED OUT HOW TO RETURN IT?
WAAA
INCREDIBLE. THE LEVEL OF PLAY AT THIS TOURNA-MENT...
EXACTLY. THIS IS THE POWER THAT, AFTER A 26-YEAR DROUGHT, FINALLY BROUGHT OKINAWA OUT OF KYUSHU...
...AND TO THE NATION-ALS.

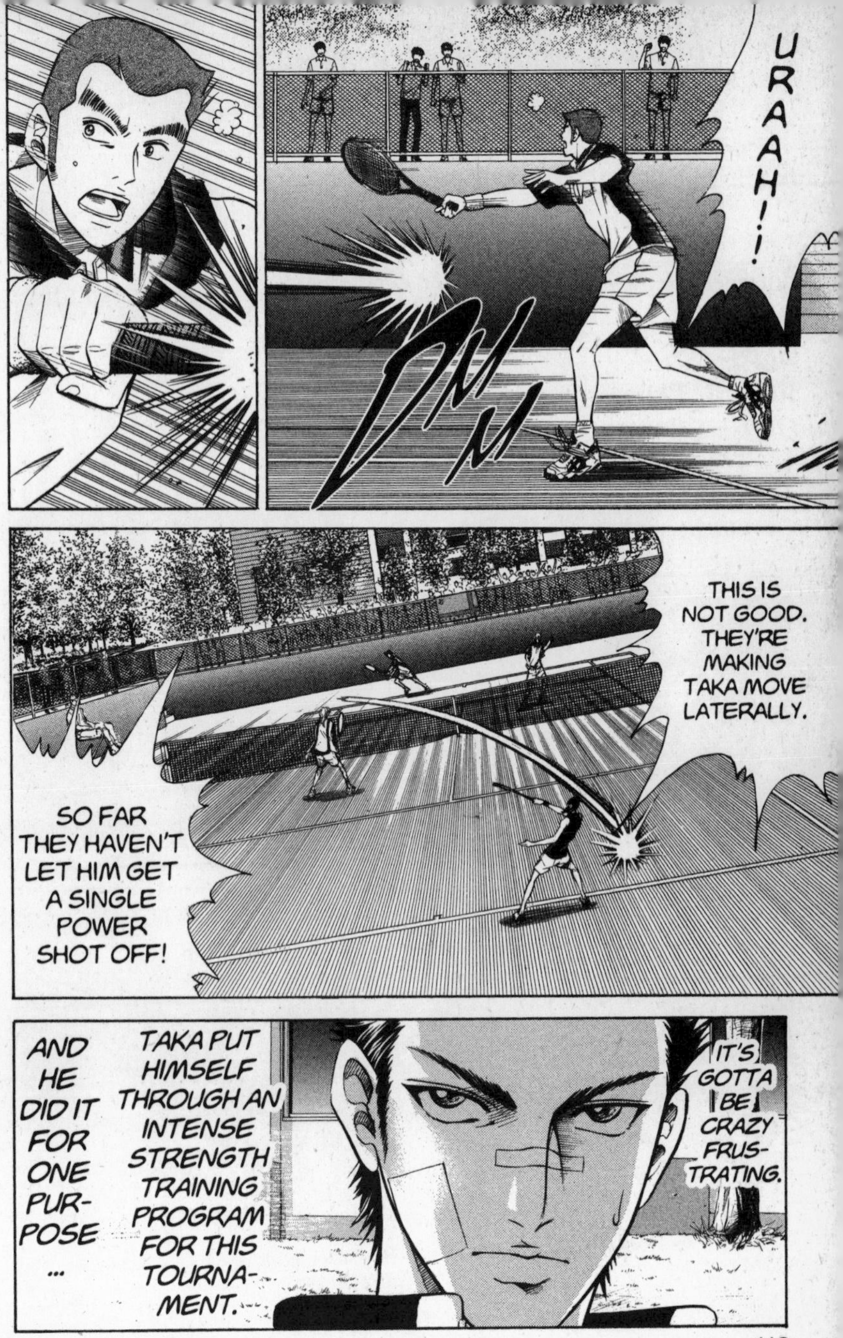
URAAAH!!
DMM
THIS IS NOT GOOD. THEY'RE MAKING TAKA MOVE LATERALLY.
SO FAR THEY HAVEN'T LET HIM GET A SINGLE POWER SHOT OFF!
IT'S GOTTA BE CRAZY FRUS-TRATING.
TAKA PUT HIMSELF THROUGH AN INTENSE STRENGTH TRAINING PROGRAM FOR THIS TOURNA-MENT.
AND HE DID IT FOR ONE PUR-POSE ...

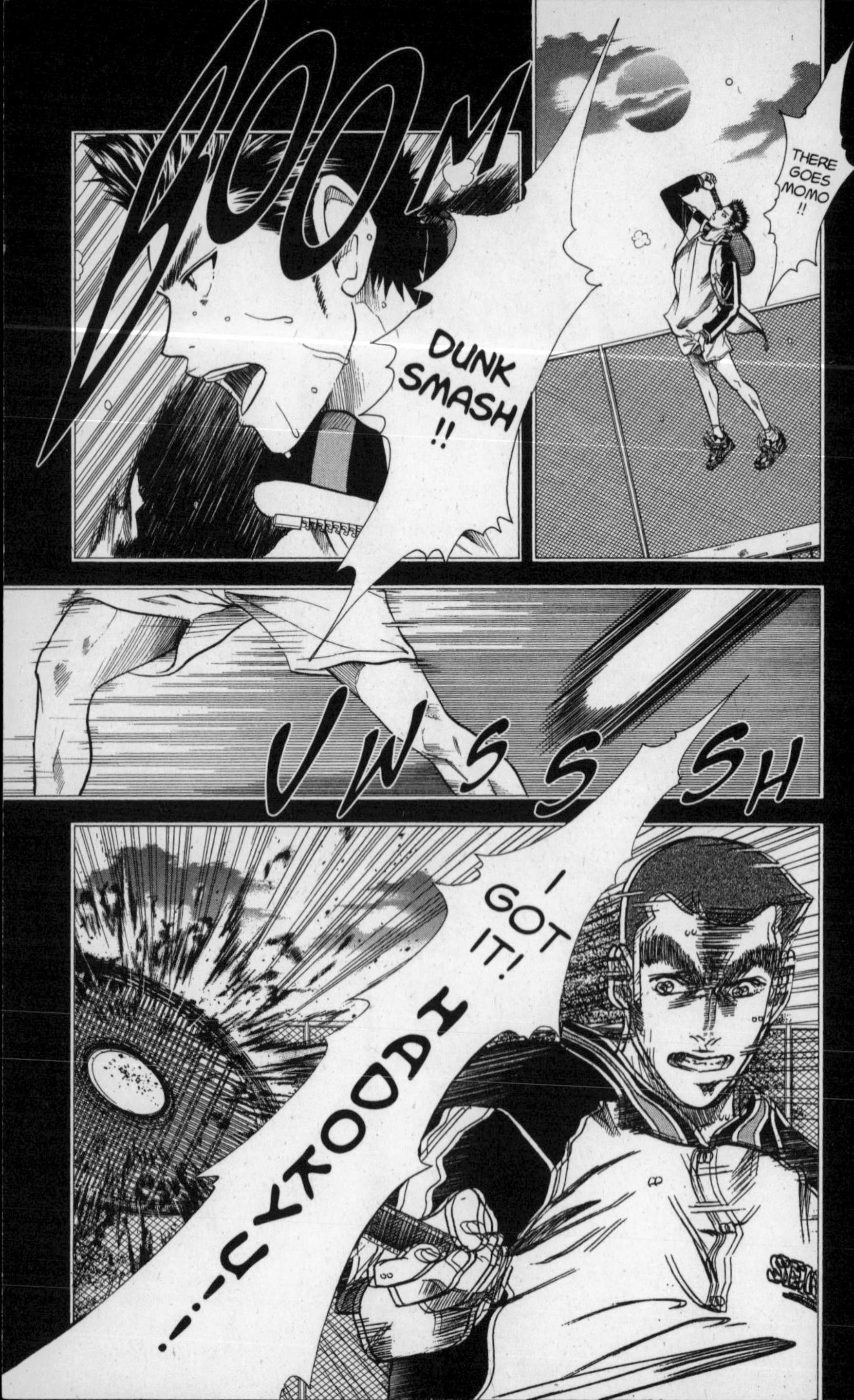
THERE GOES MOMO!!
VOOOM
DUNK SMASH!!
VWSSSH
I GOT IT!
HADOUKYU--!!

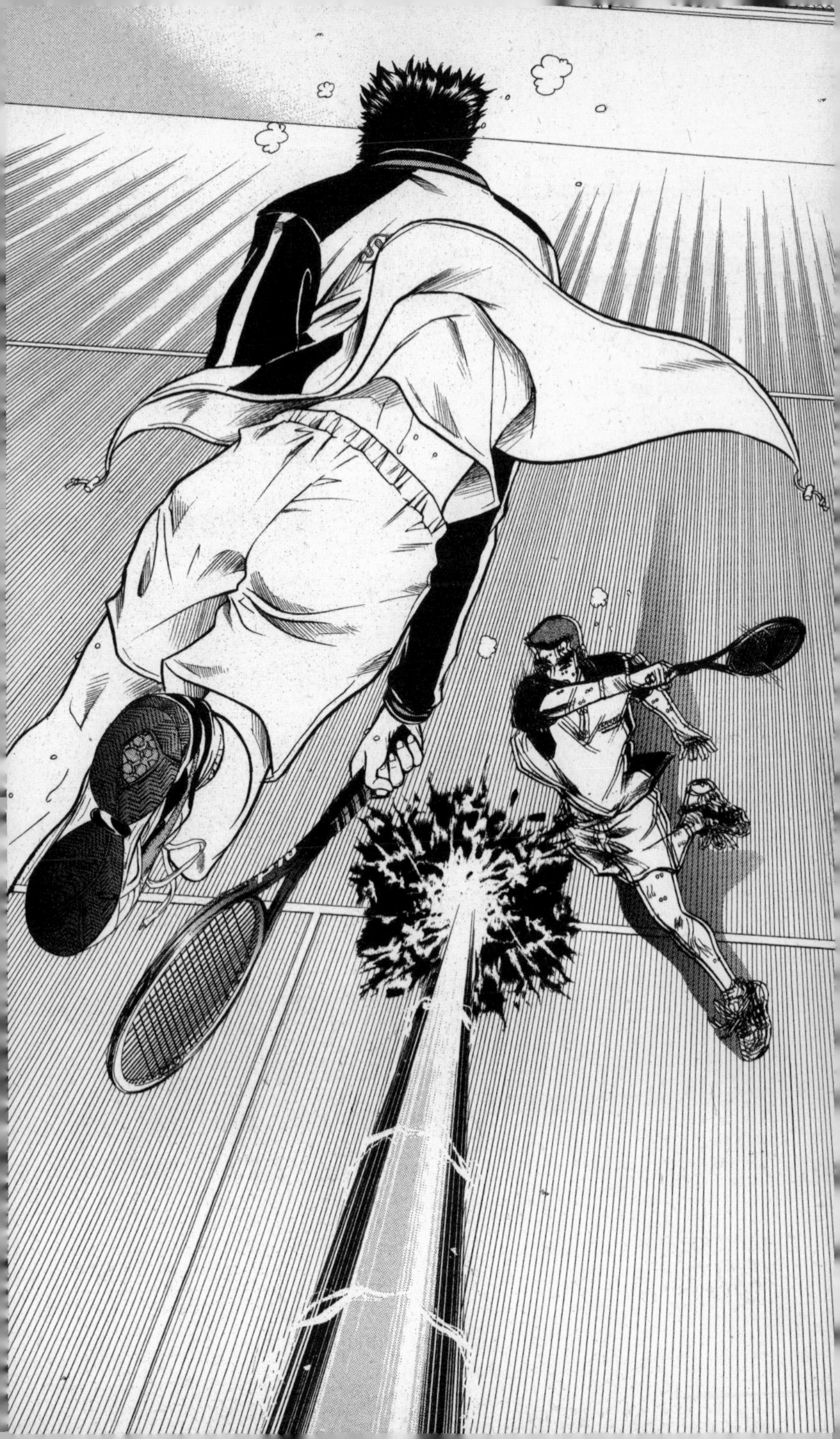

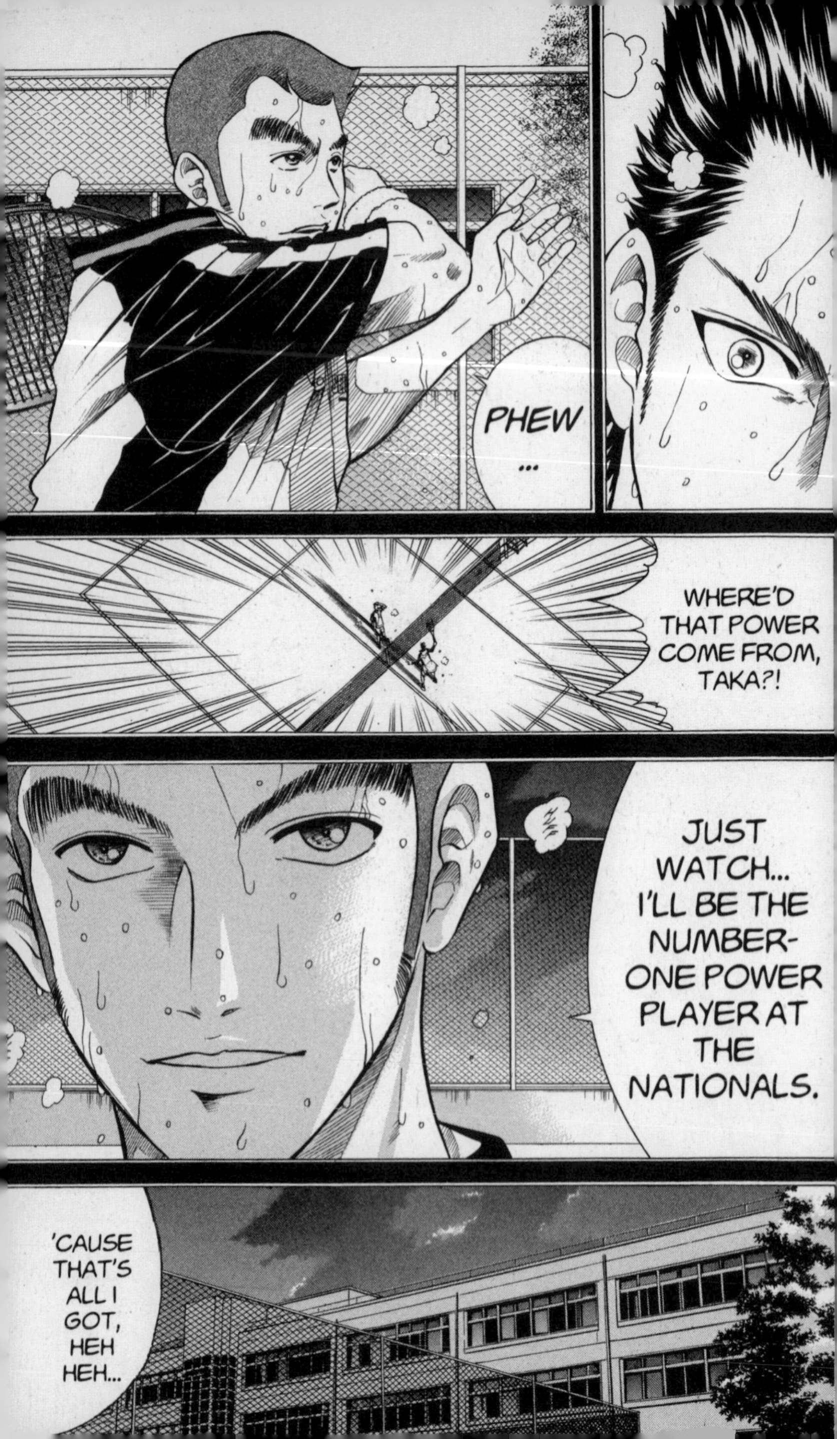
PHEW
...
WHERE'D THAT POWER COME FROM, TAKA?!
JUST WATCH... I'LL BE THE NUMBER-ONE POWER PLAYER AT THE NATIONALS.
'CAUSE THAT'S ALL I GOT, HEH HEH...

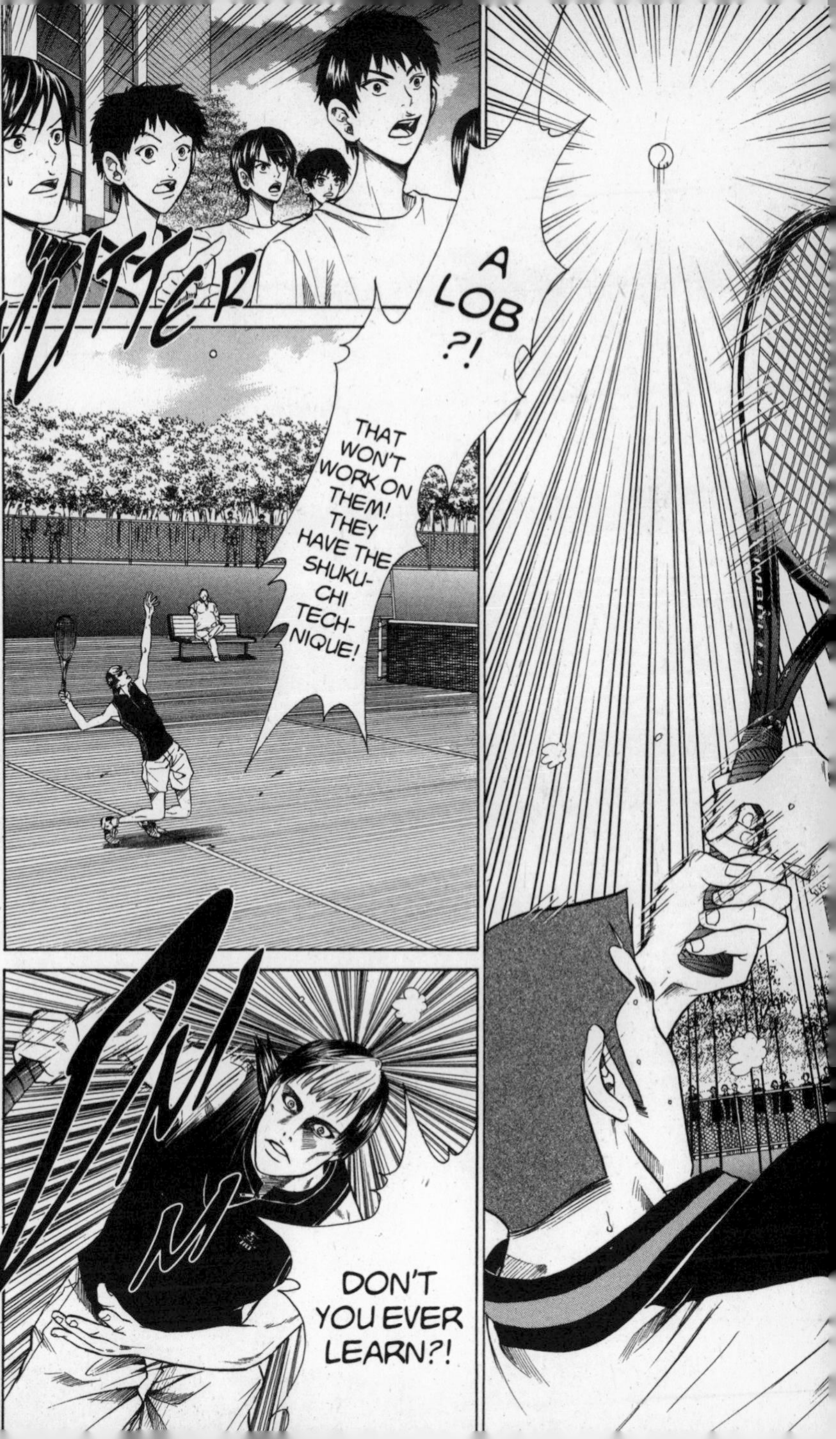
A LOB ?!
MUTTER
THAT WON'T WORK ON THEM! THEY HAVE THE SHUKU-CHI TECH-NIQUE!
DON'T YOU EVER LEARN?!

READ THIS WAY

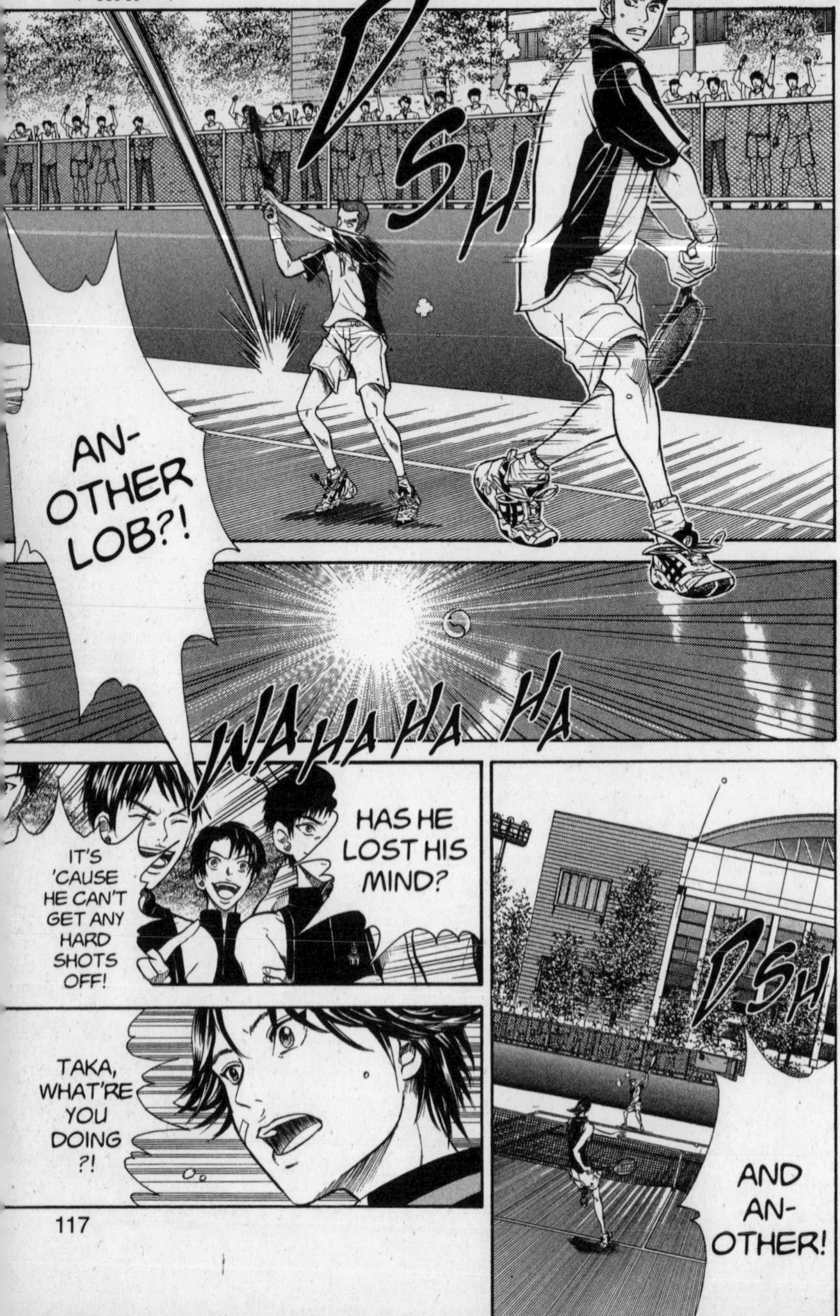
DSH
ANOTHER LOB?!
WAHAHA HA
DSH
AND ANOTHER!
HAS HE LOST HIS MIND?
IT'S 'CAUSE HE CAN'T GET ANY HARD SHOTS OFF!
TAKA, WHAT'RE YOU DOING?!

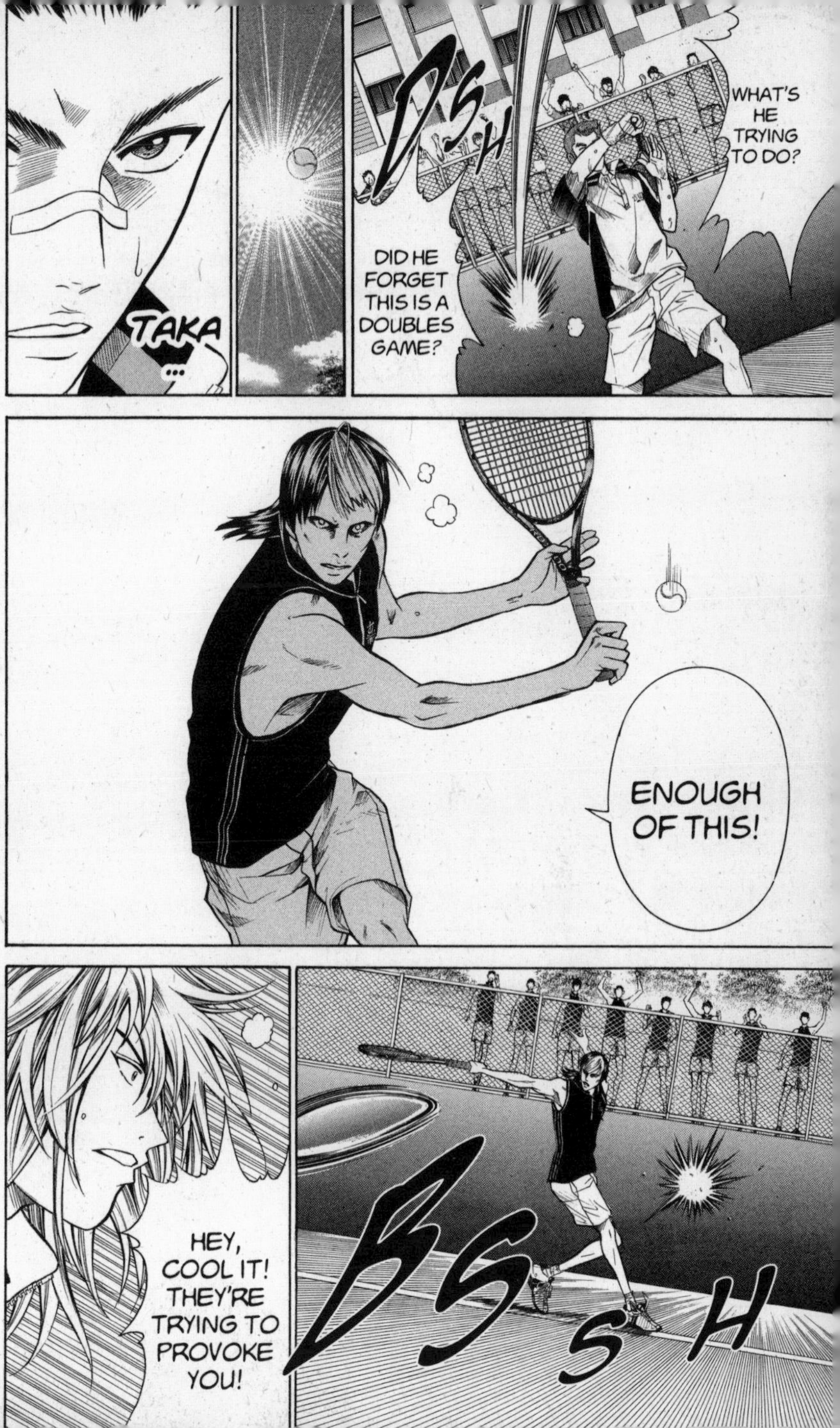
DSH
WHAT'S HE TRYING TO DO?
DID HE FORGET THIS IS A DOUBLES GAME?
TAKA ...
ENOUGH OF THIS!
BSSH
HEY, COOL IT! THEY'RE TRYING TO PROVOKE YOU!

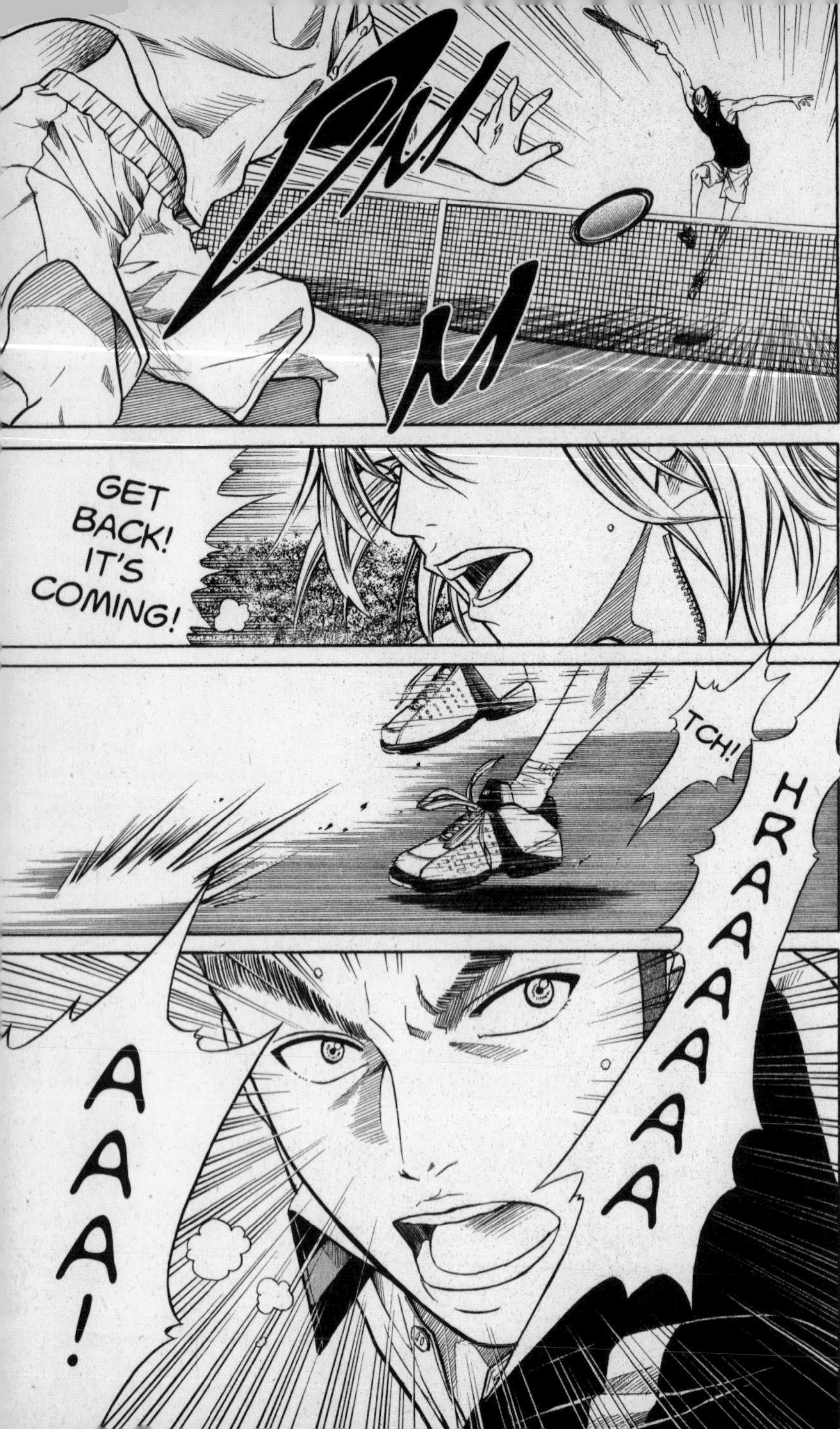
GET BACK! IT'S COMING!
TCH!
HRAAAAAAAAA
AAA!

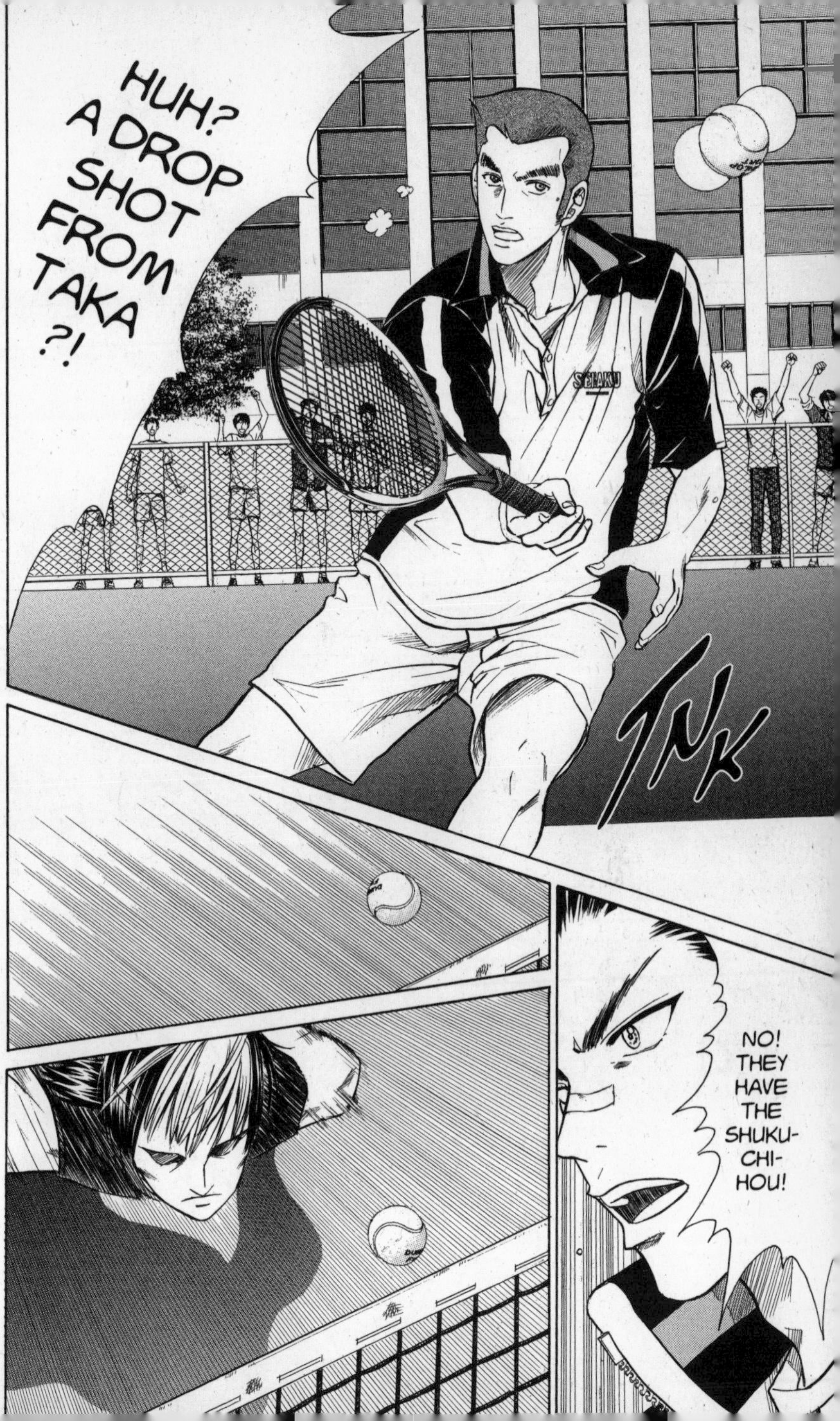
HUH? A DROP SHOT FROM TAKA ?!
SEIGAKU
TNK
NO! THEY HAVE THE SHUKU-CHI-HOU!

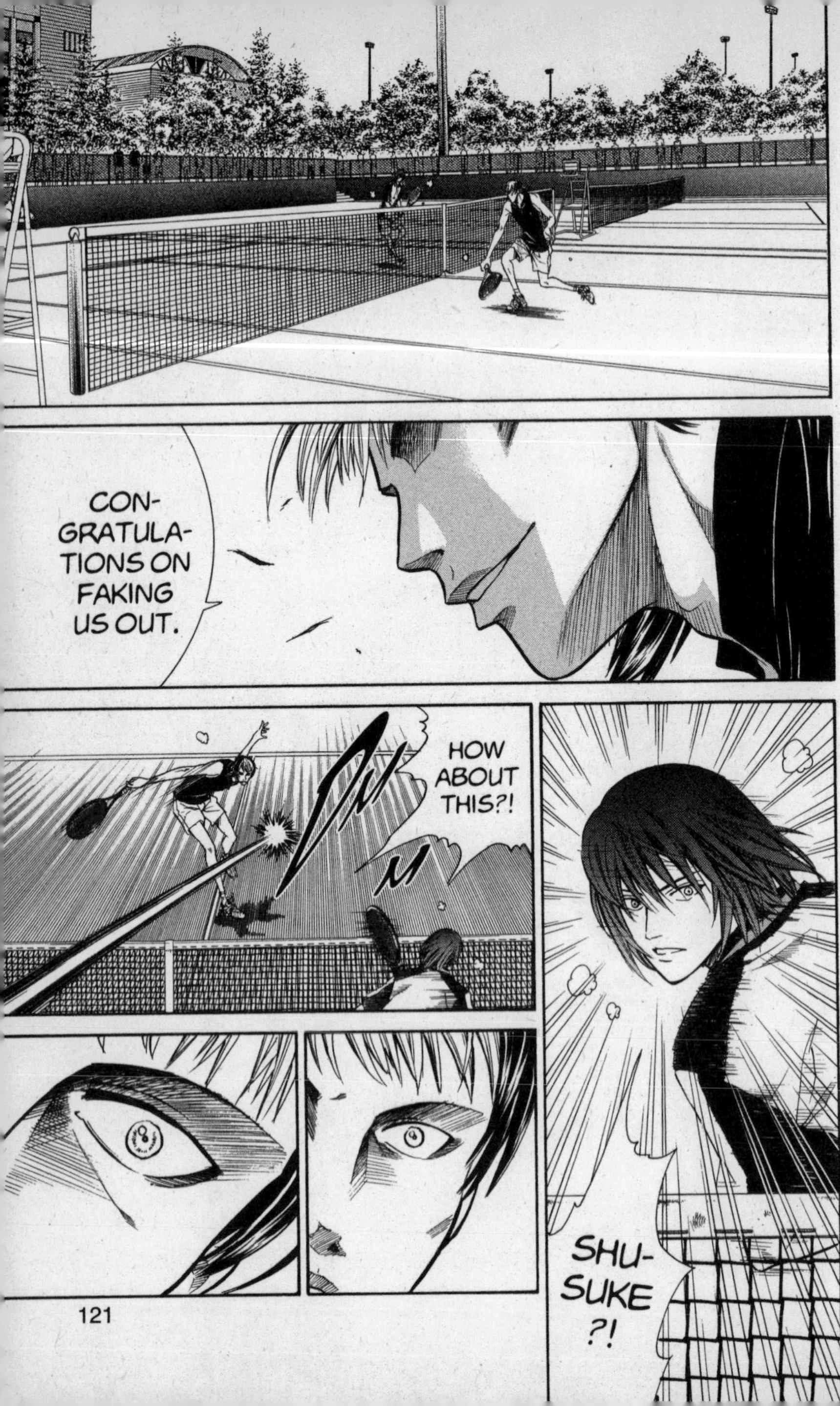
CON-
GRATULA-
TIONS ON
FAKING
US OUT.
HOW ABOUT THIS?!
SHU-
SUKE
?!

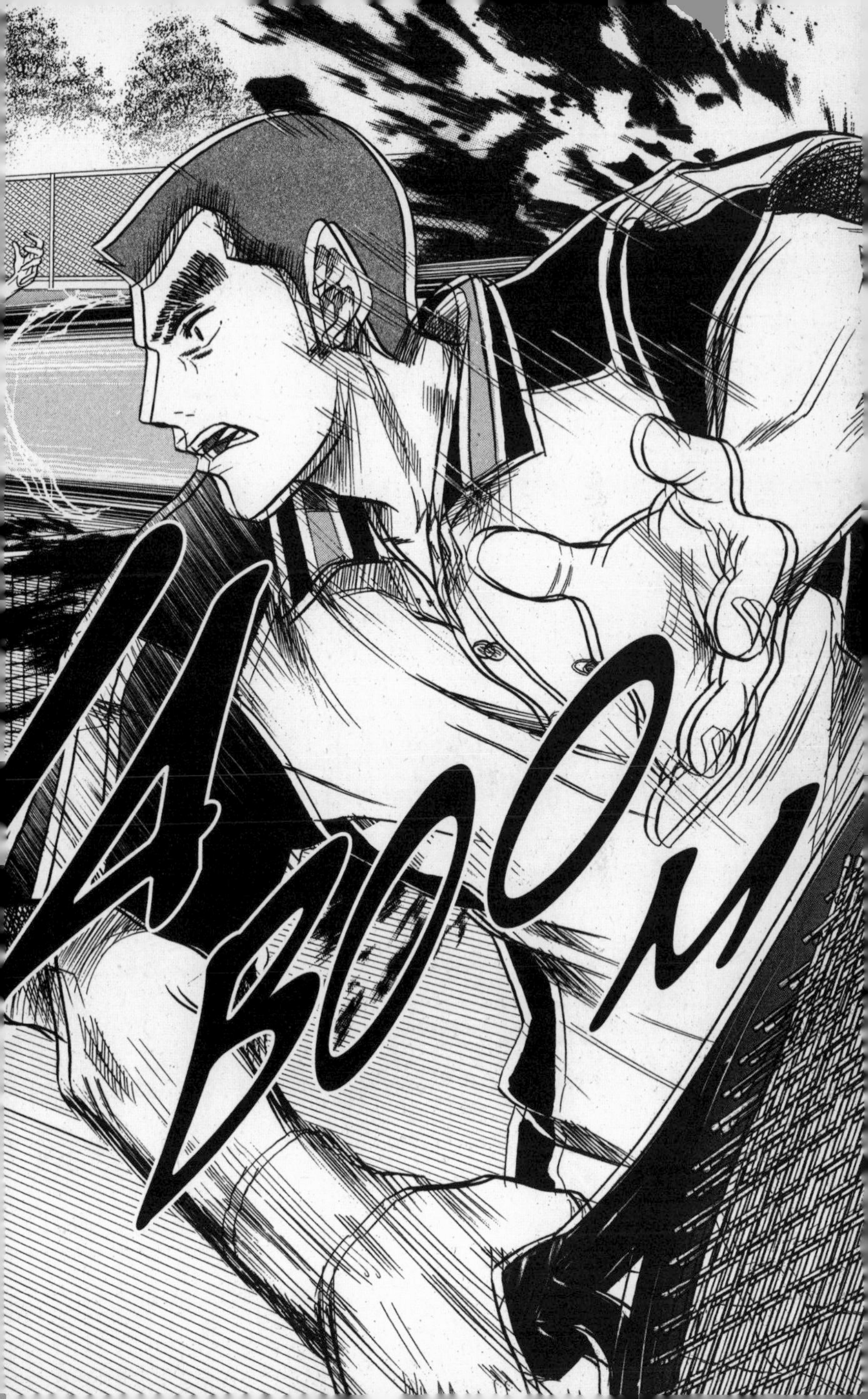
BOOM

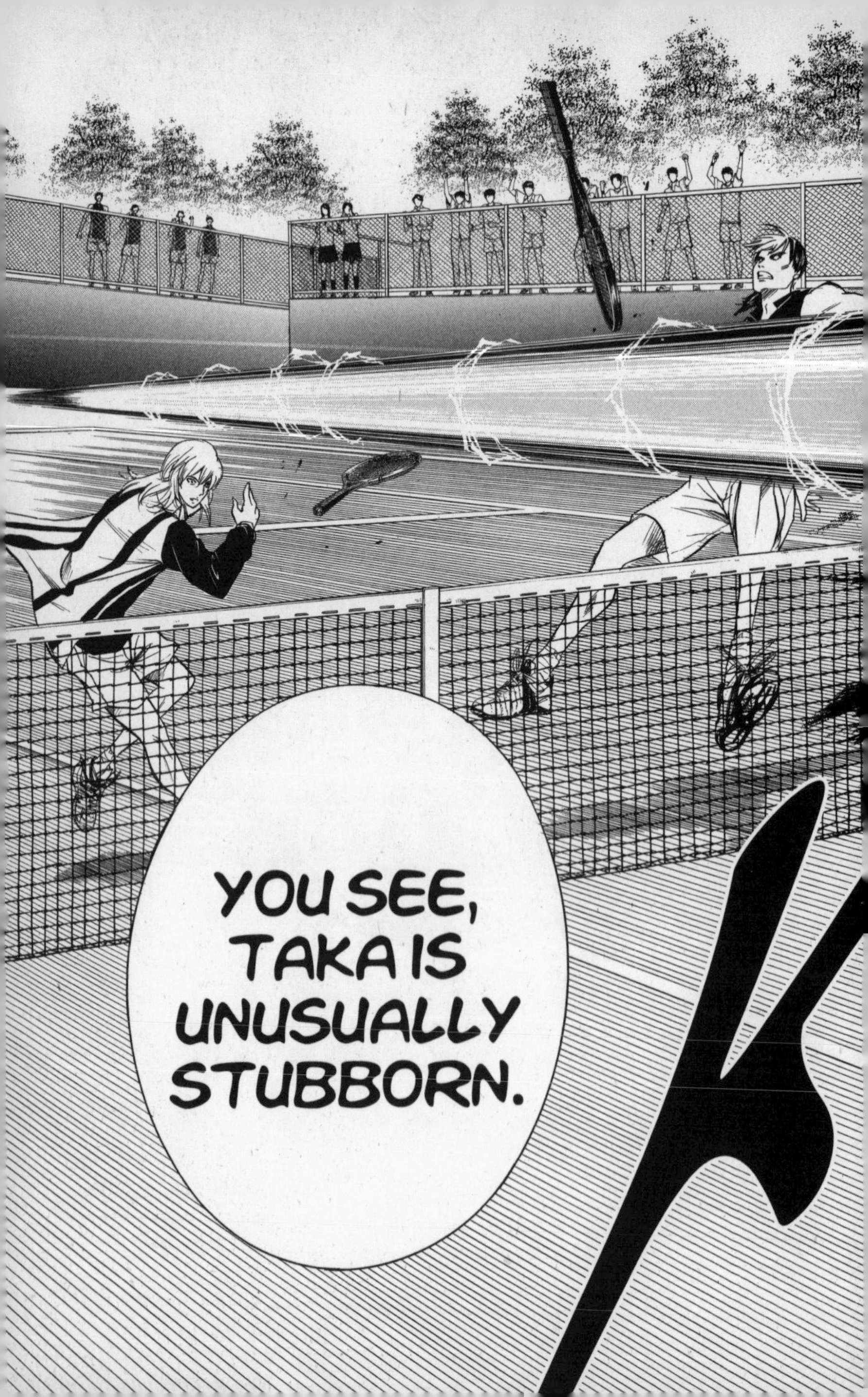
YOU SEE, TAKA IS UNUSUALLY STUBBORN.

テニスの王子様

THE PRINCE OF TENNIS

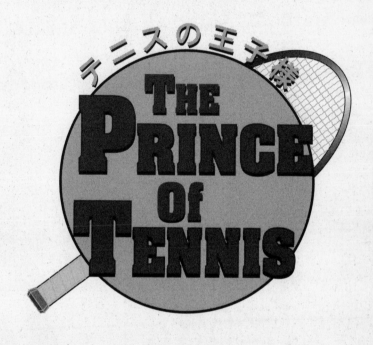

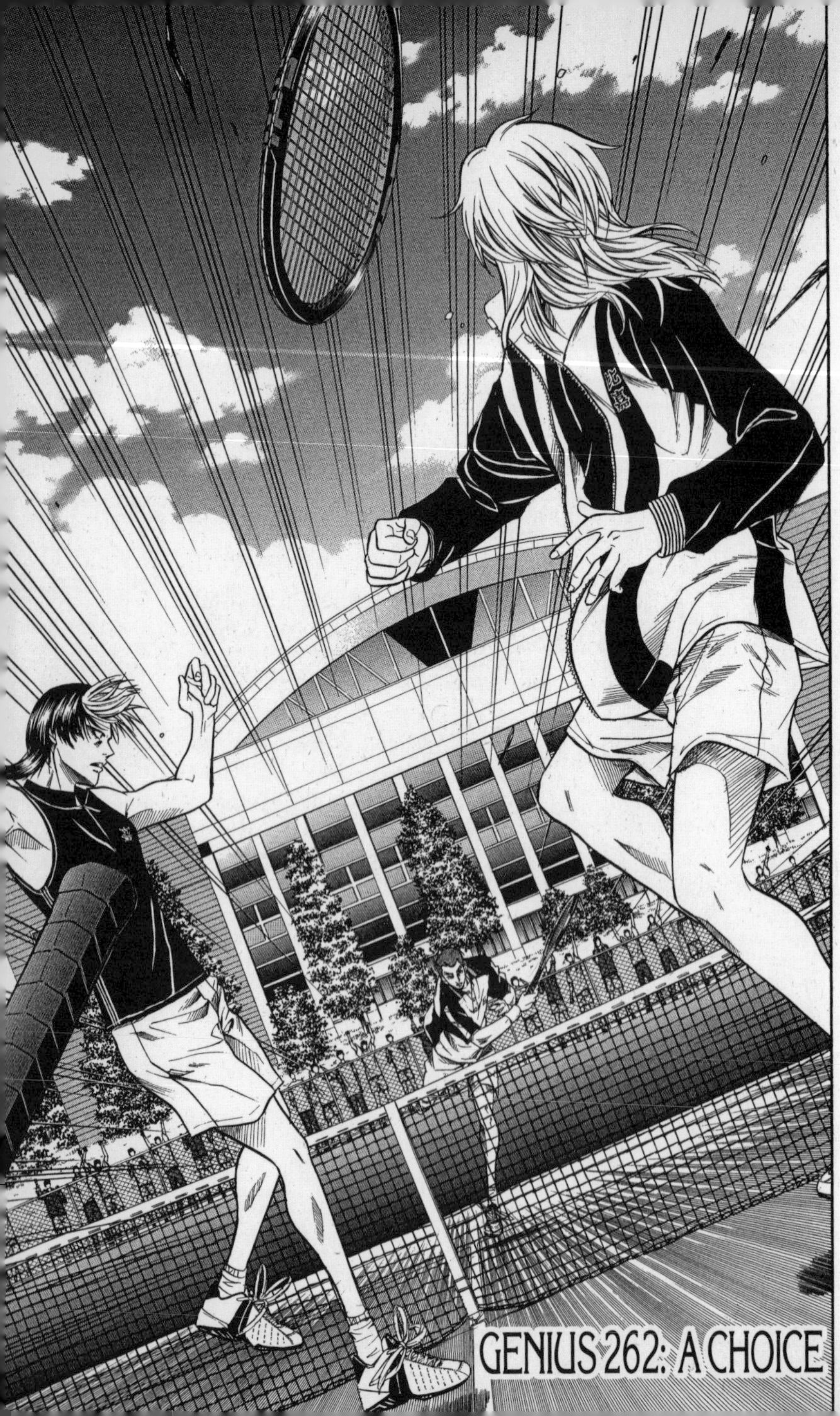
GENIUS 262: A CHOICE

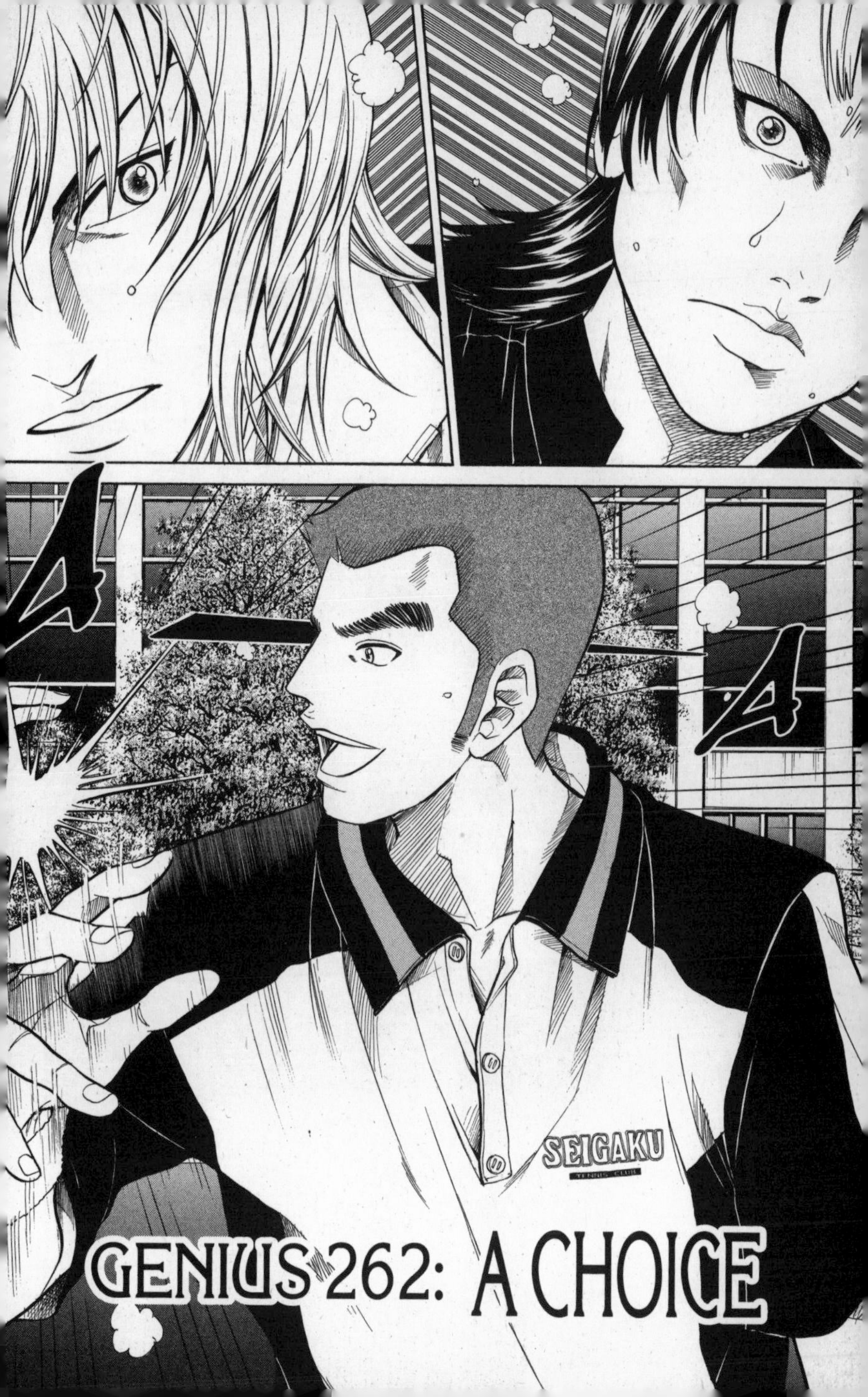
SEIGAKU
TENNIS CLUB
GENIUS 262: A CHOICE

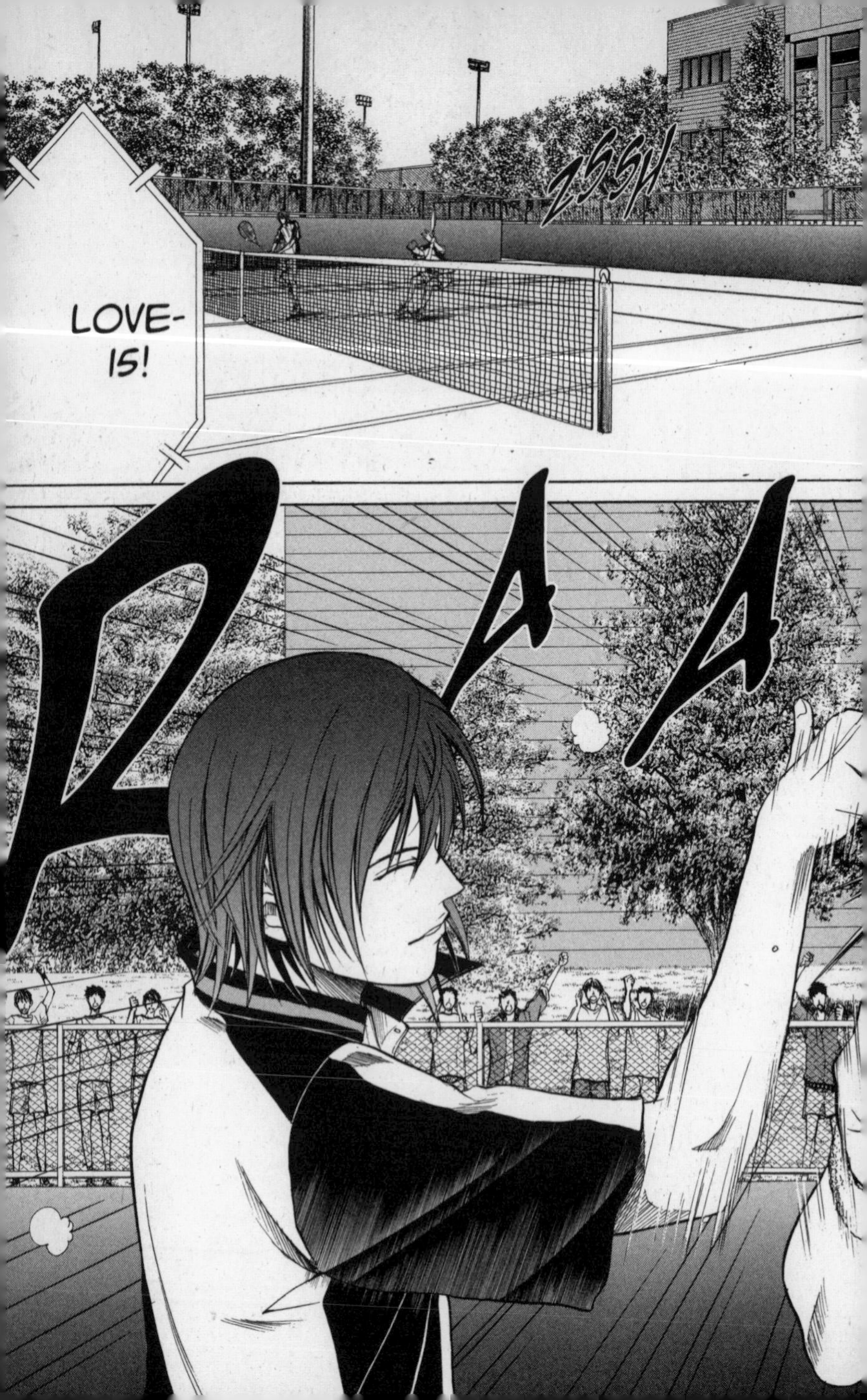
ZSSH
LOVE-15!
DAA

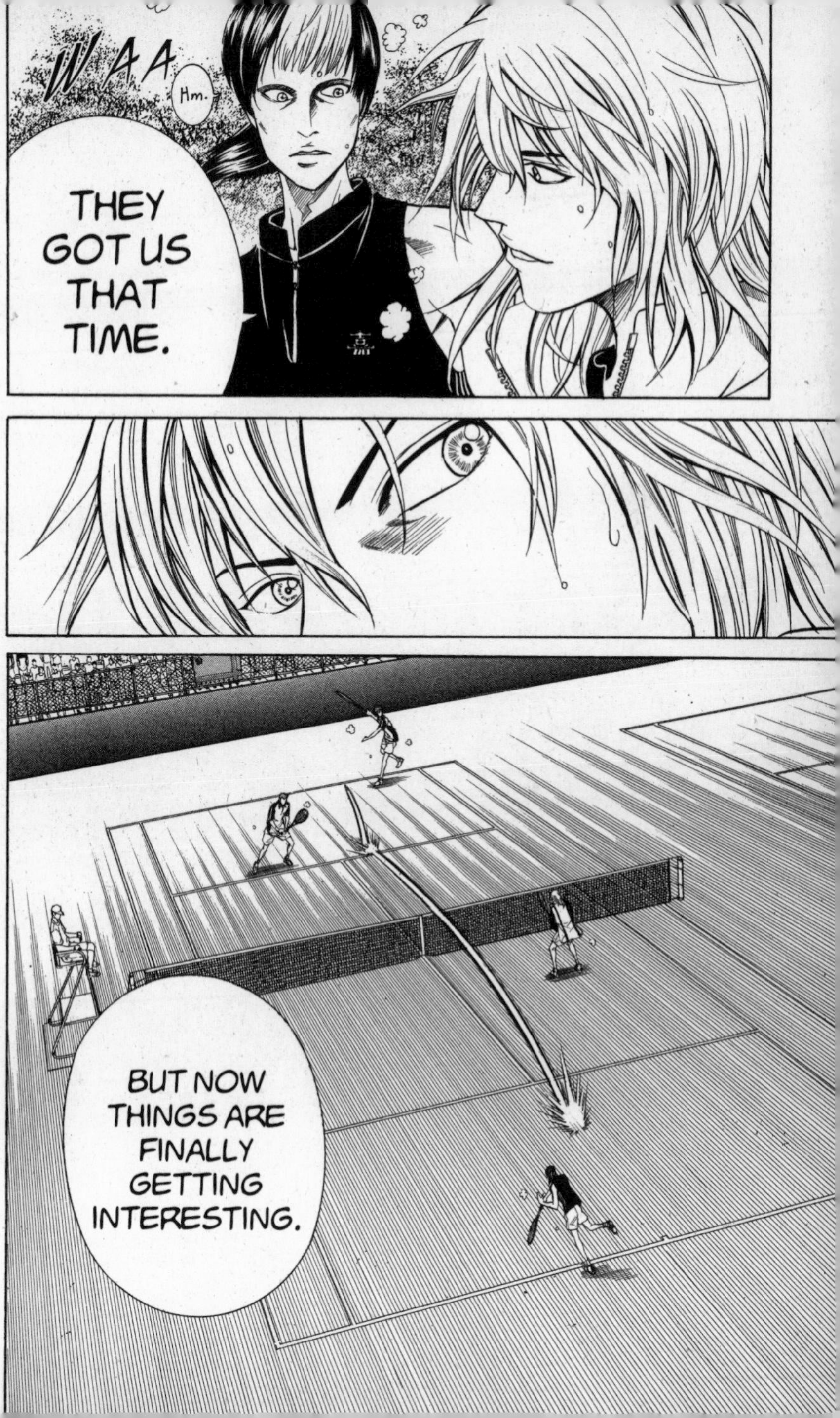
WAA
Hm.
THEY GOT US THAT TIME.
BUT NOW THINGS ARE FINALLY GETTING INTERESTING.

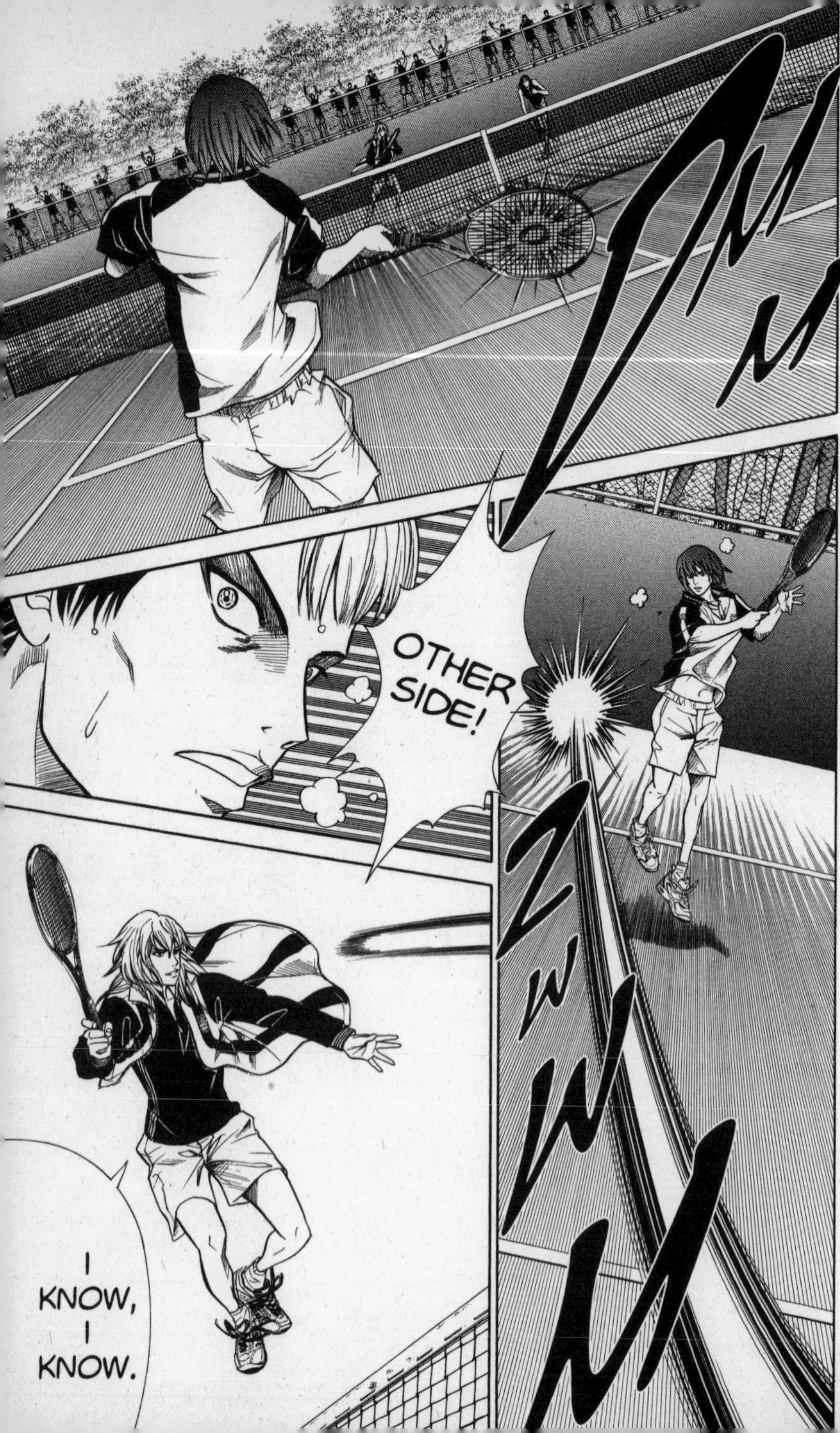
OTHER SIDE!
I KNOW, I KNOW.

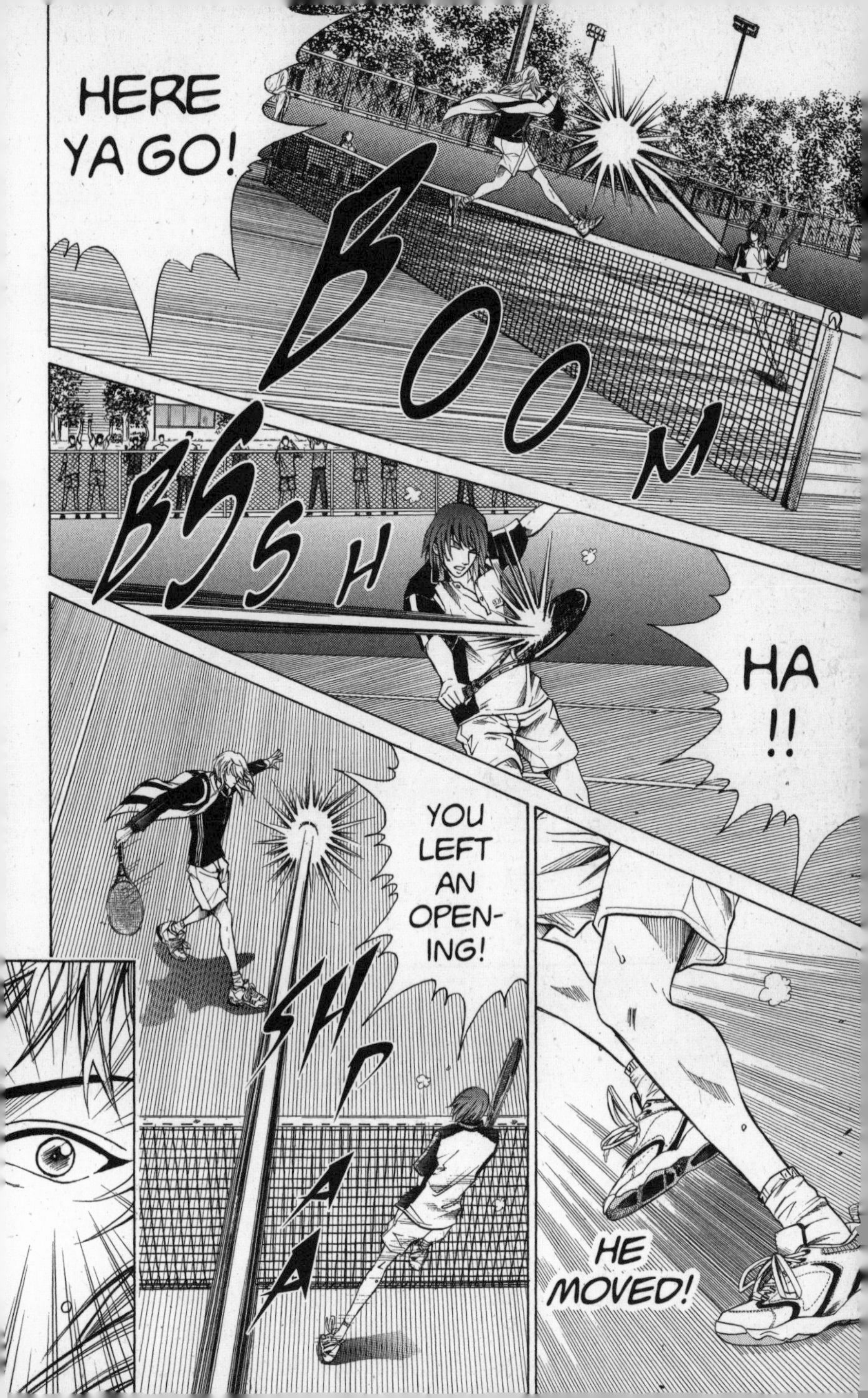
HERE YA GO!
BOOOM
HA!!
BSSH
HE MOVED!
YOU LEFT AN OPEN-ING!
SHPAAA

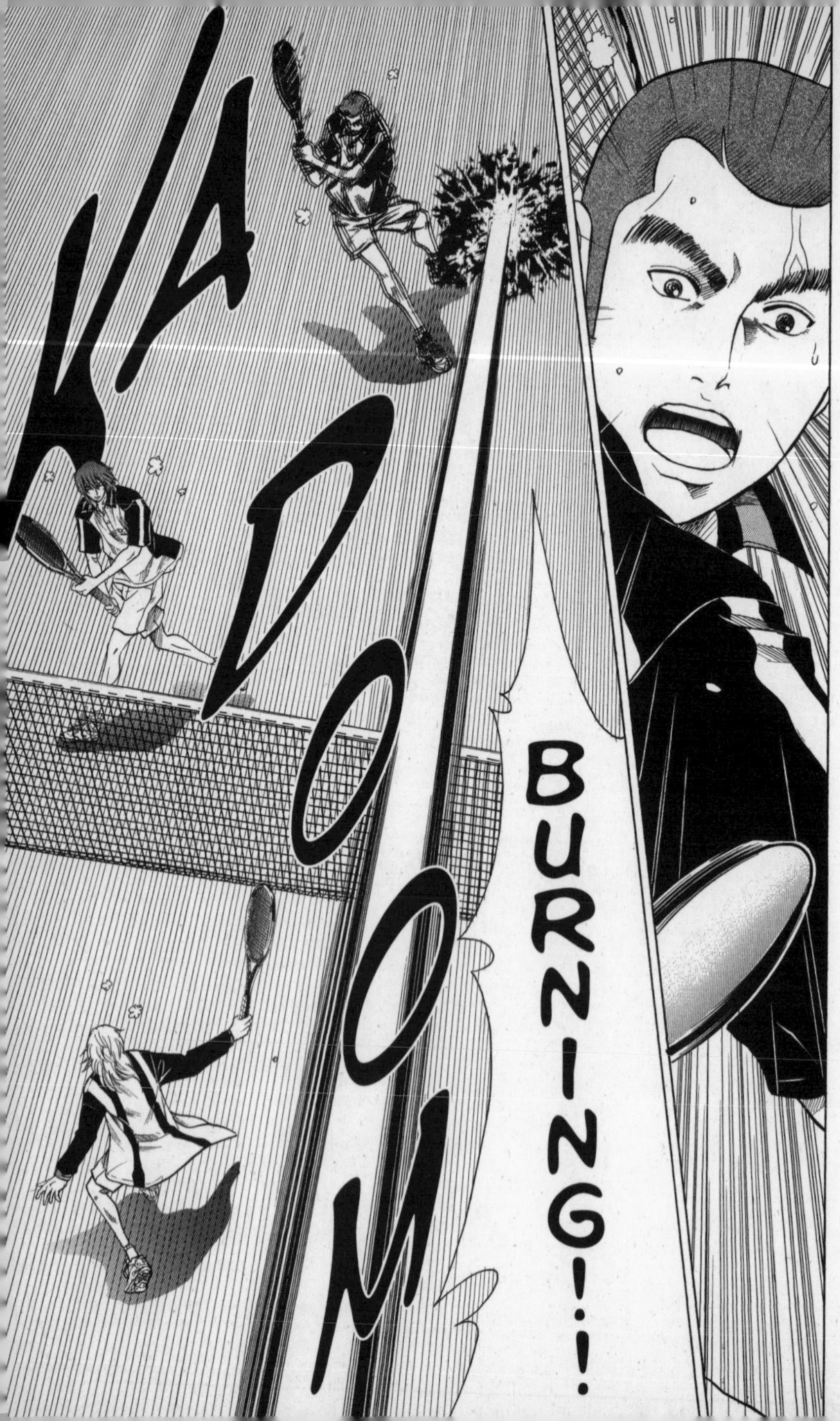
KADOOM
BURNING!!

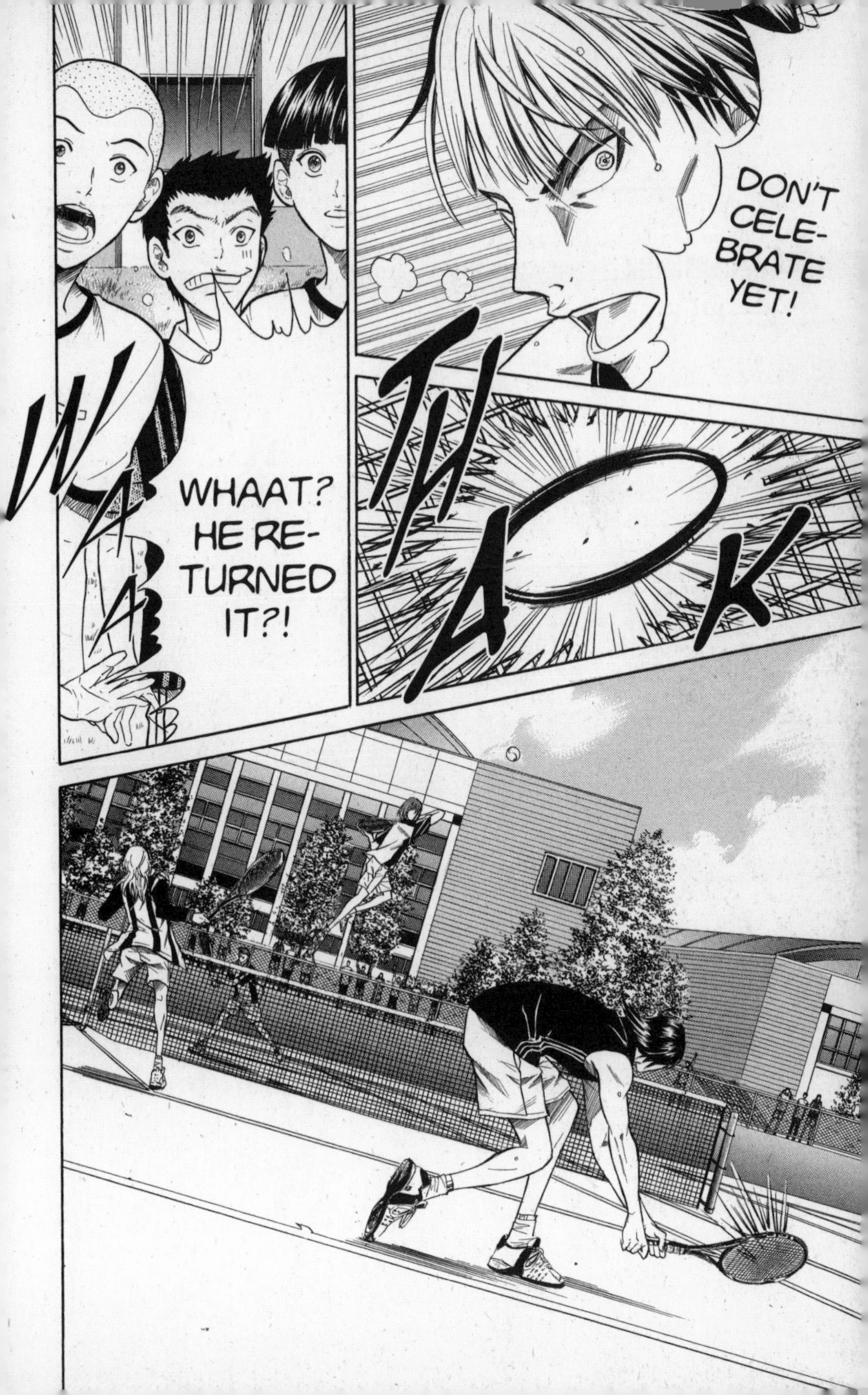
DON'T CELE-BRATE YET!
THWAK
WAAA
WHAAT? HE RE-TURNED IT?!

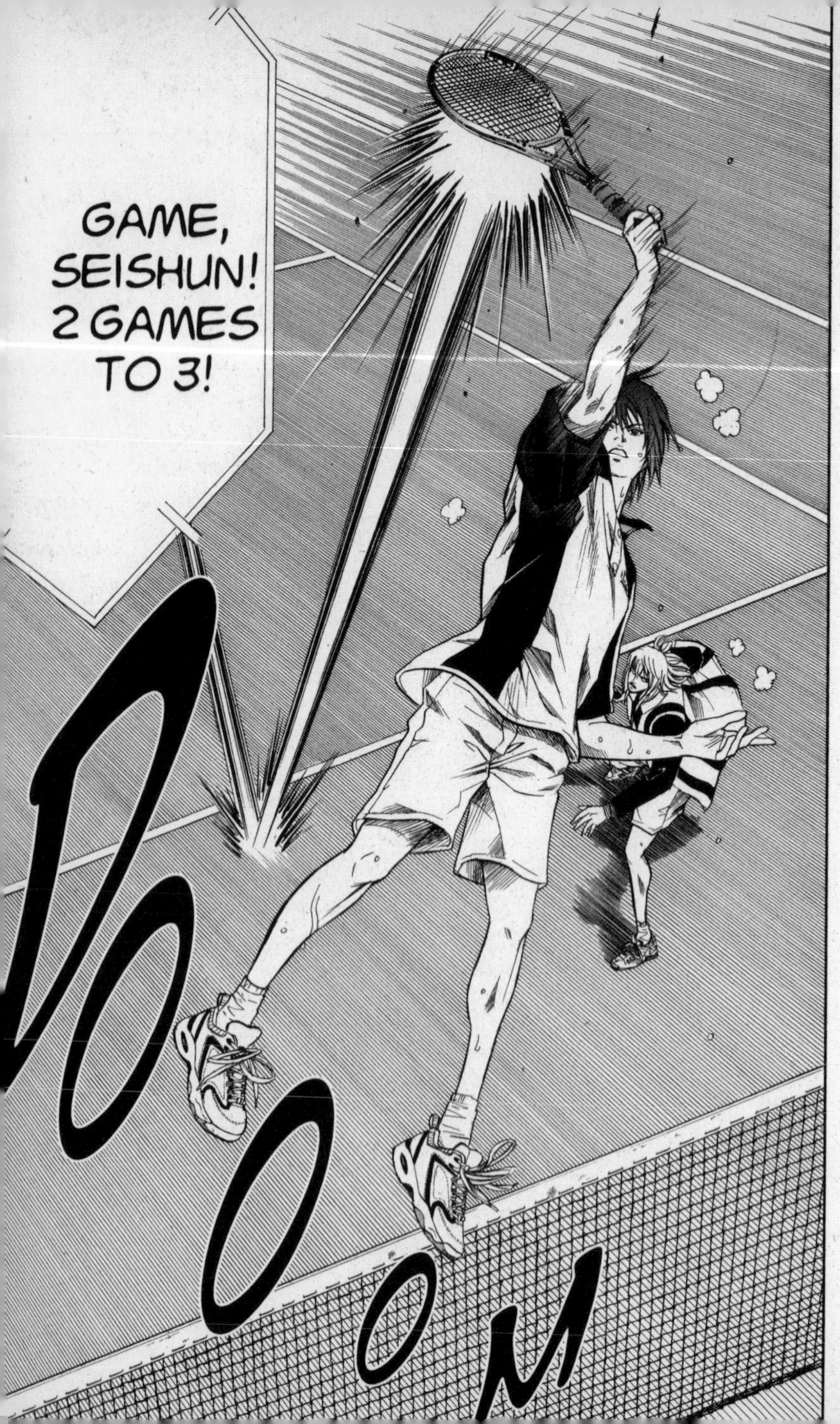
GAME, SEISHUN! 2 GAMES TO 3!
BOOOOM

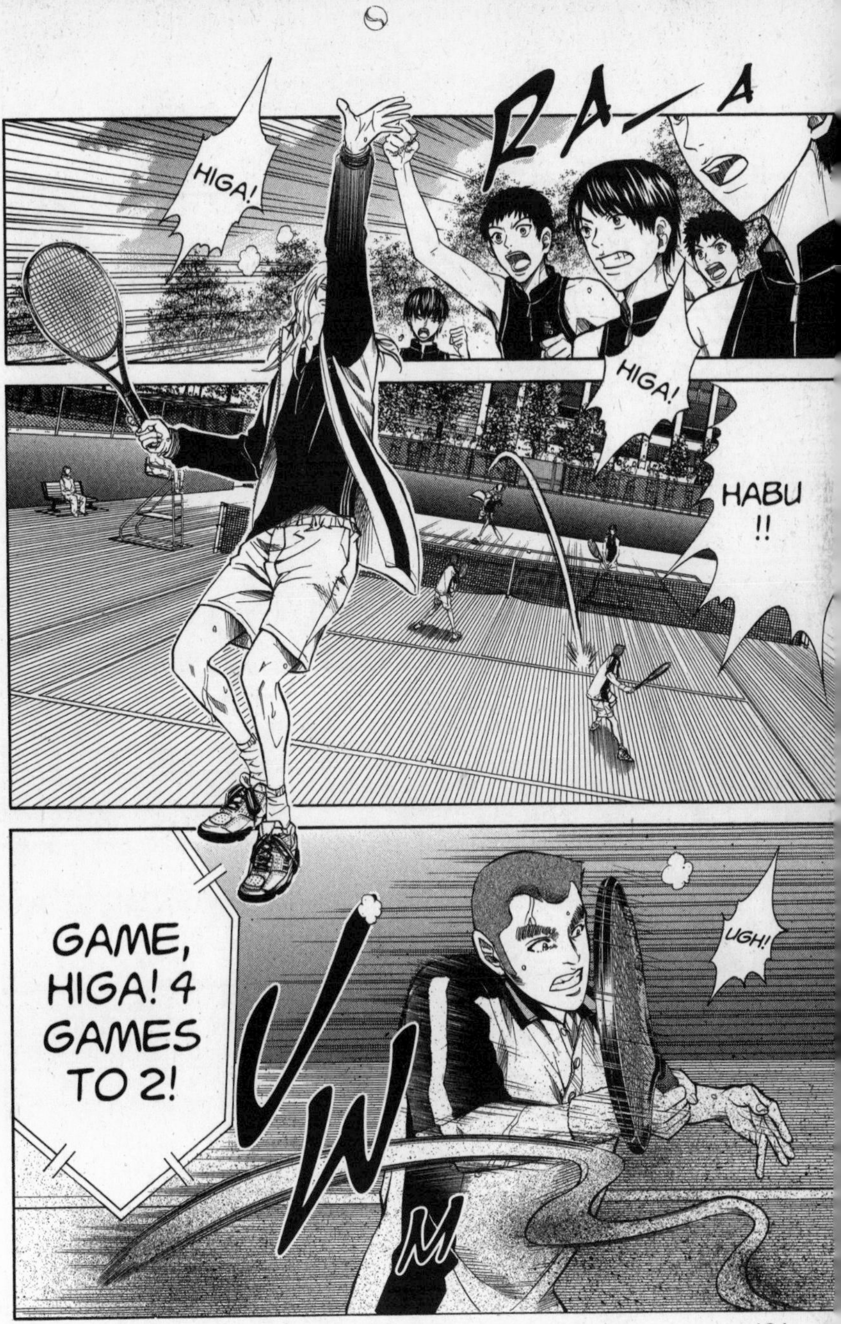
RA—A
HIGA!
HIGA!
HABU !!
GAME, HIGA! 4 GAMES TO 2!
UGH!
VWM

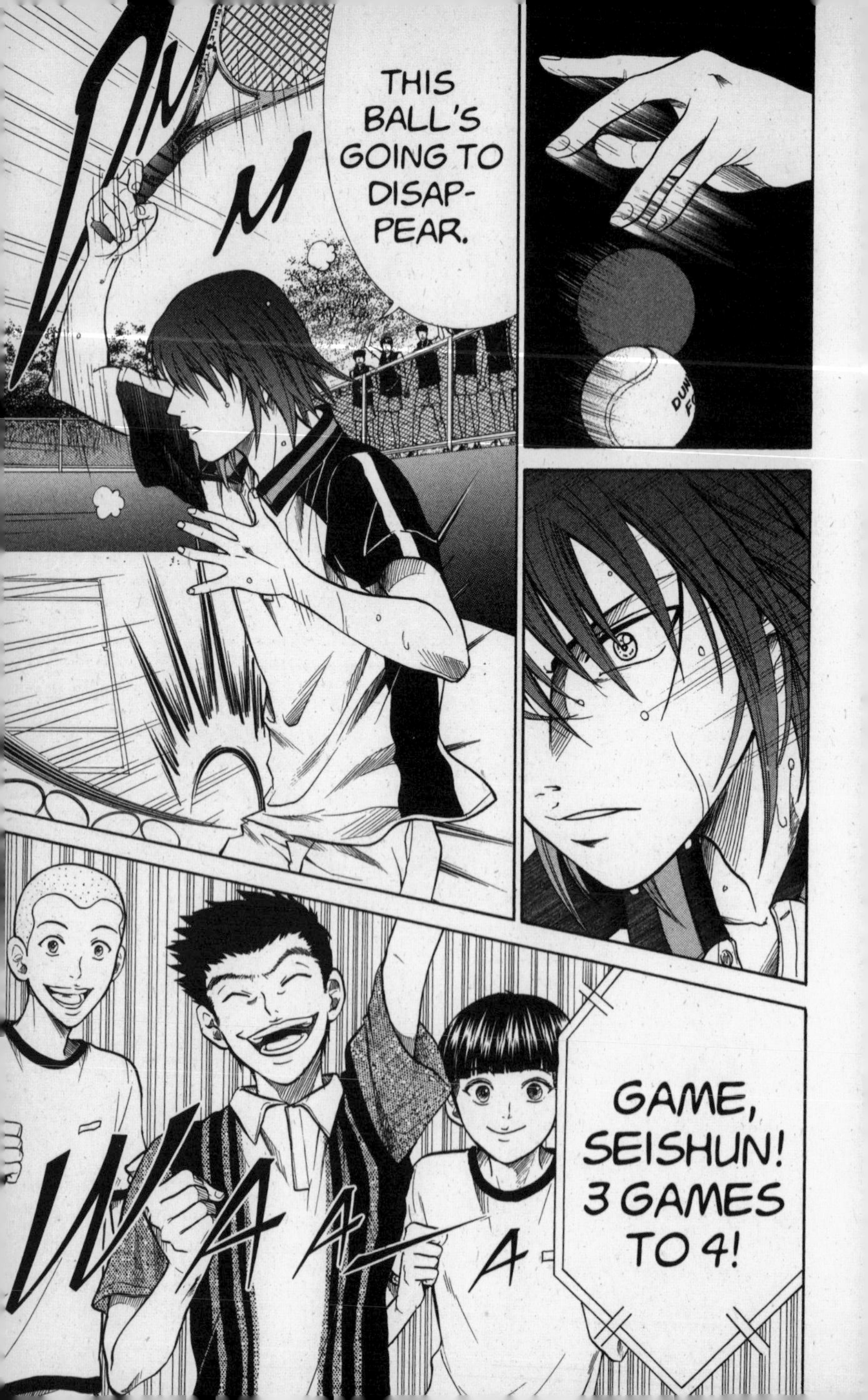
THIS BALL'S GOING TO DISAP- PEAR.
VMM
GAME, SEISHUN! 3 GAMES TO 4!
WAAA

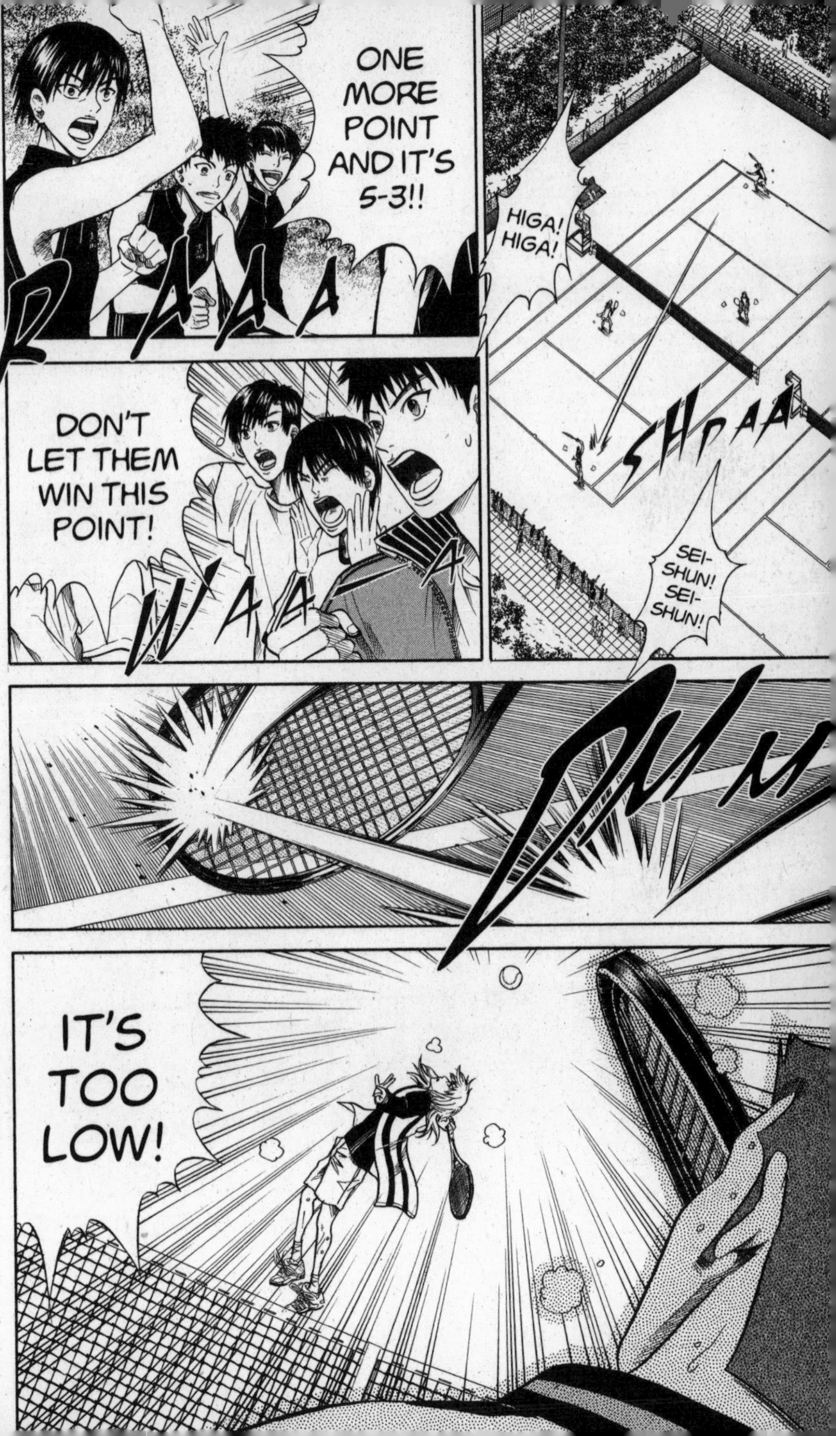
HIGA! HIGA!
SHPAA
SEI-SHUN! SEI-SHUN!
ONE MORE POINT AND IT'S 5-3!!
RAAAA
DON'T LET THEM WIN THIS POINT!
WAAAA
IT'S TOO LOW!

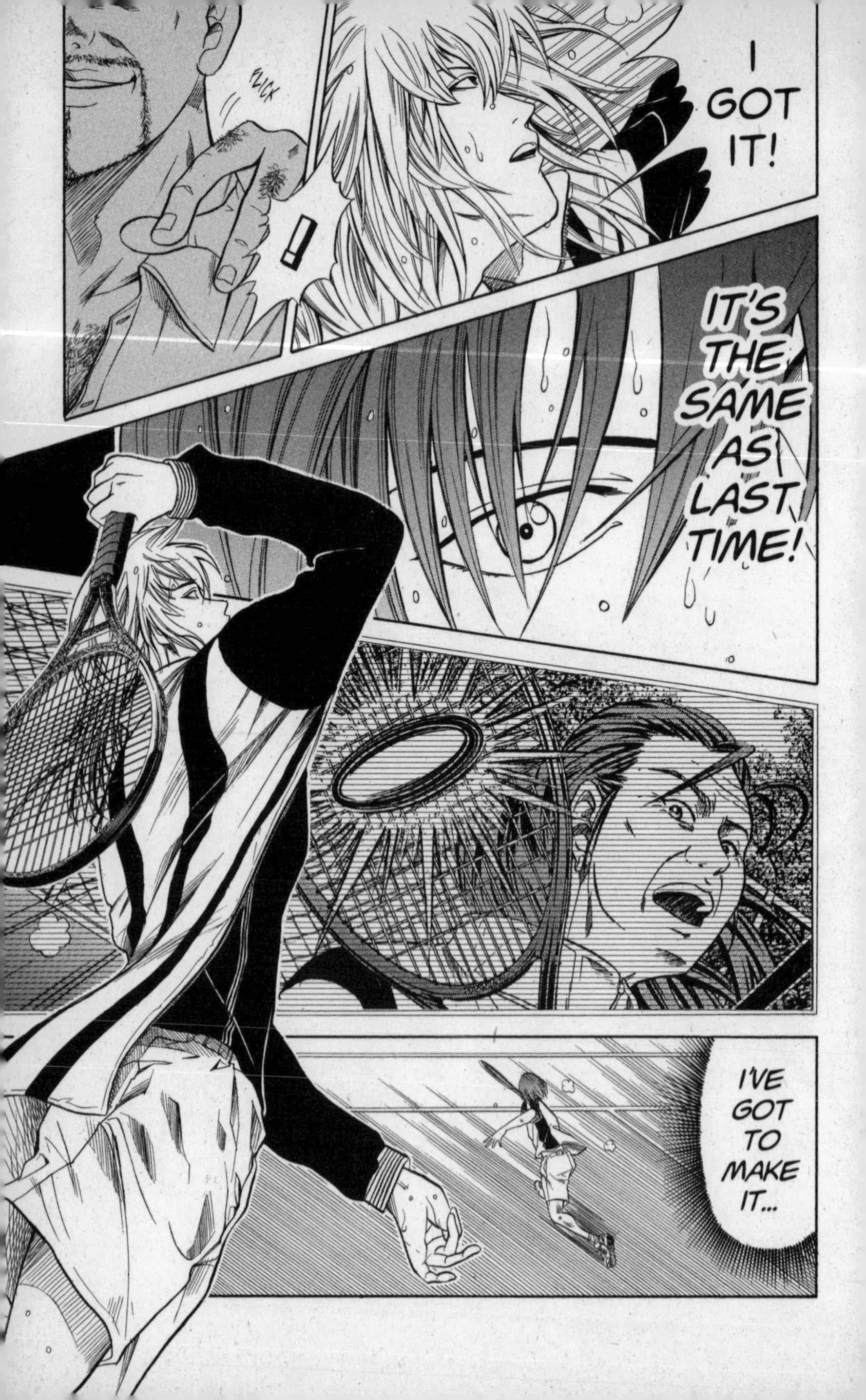
I GOT IT!
FLICK
!
IT'S THE SAME AS LAST TIME!
I'VE GOT TO MAKE IT...

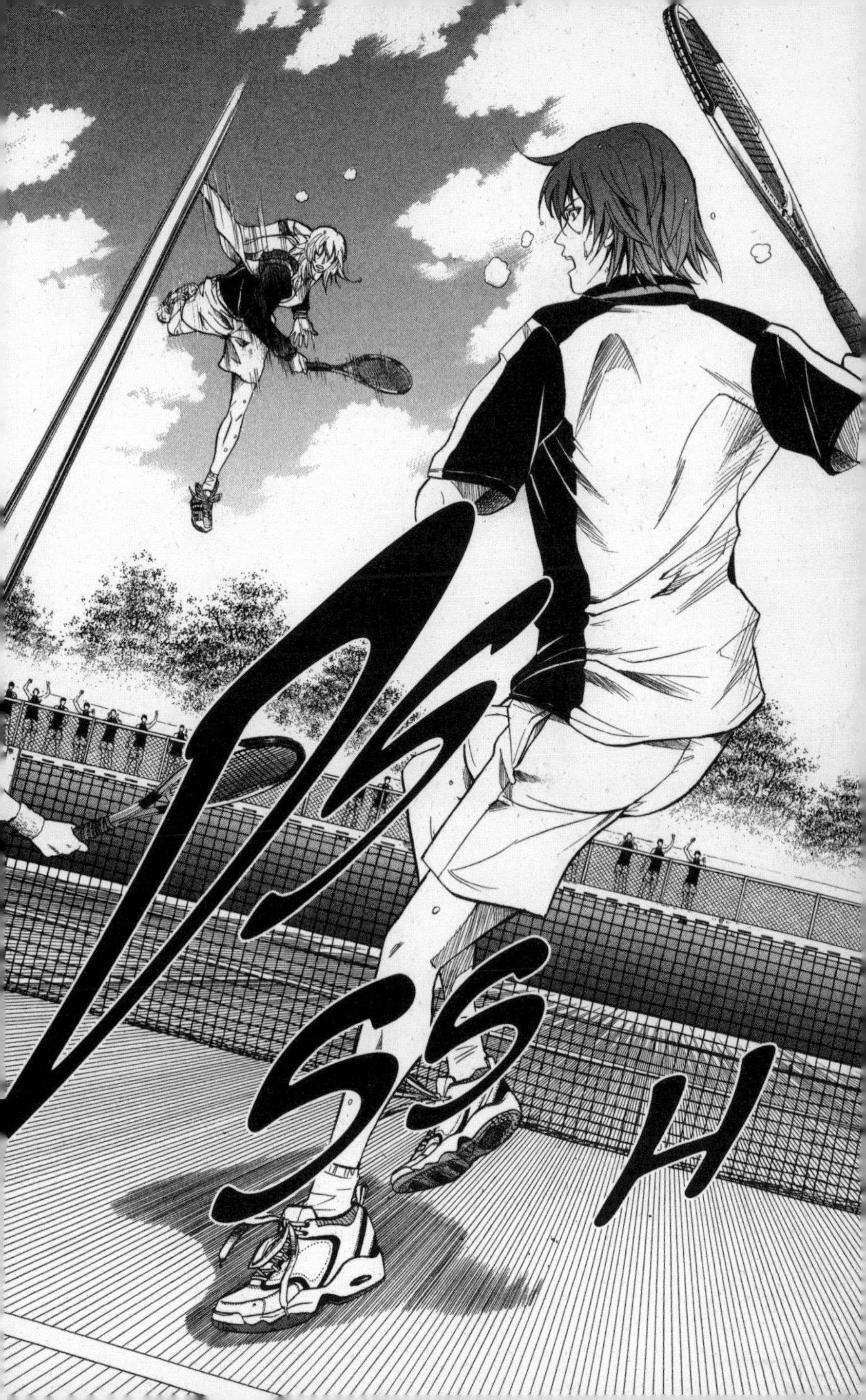
VSSH

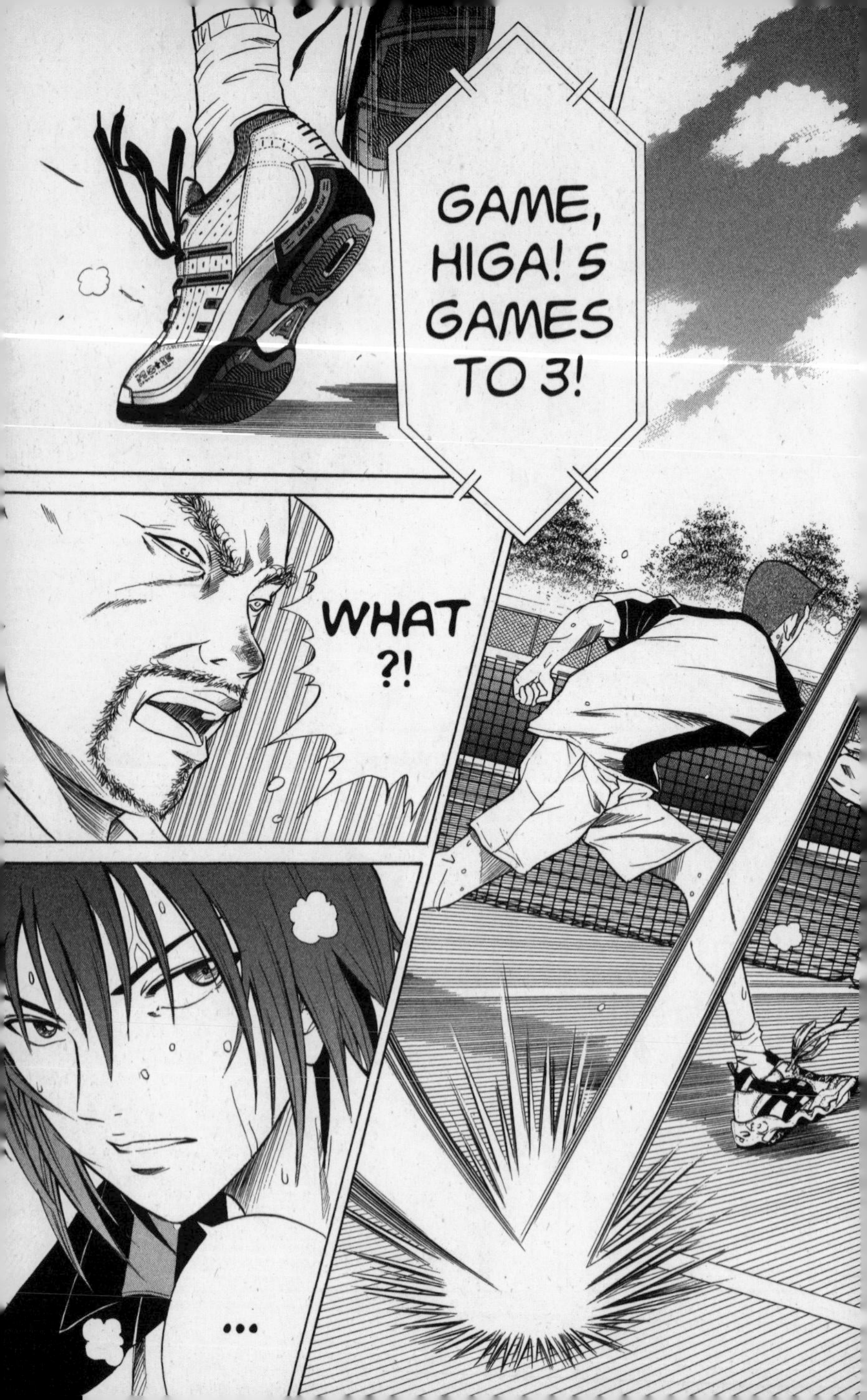
GAME, HIGA! 5 GAMES TO 3!
WHAT ?!
...

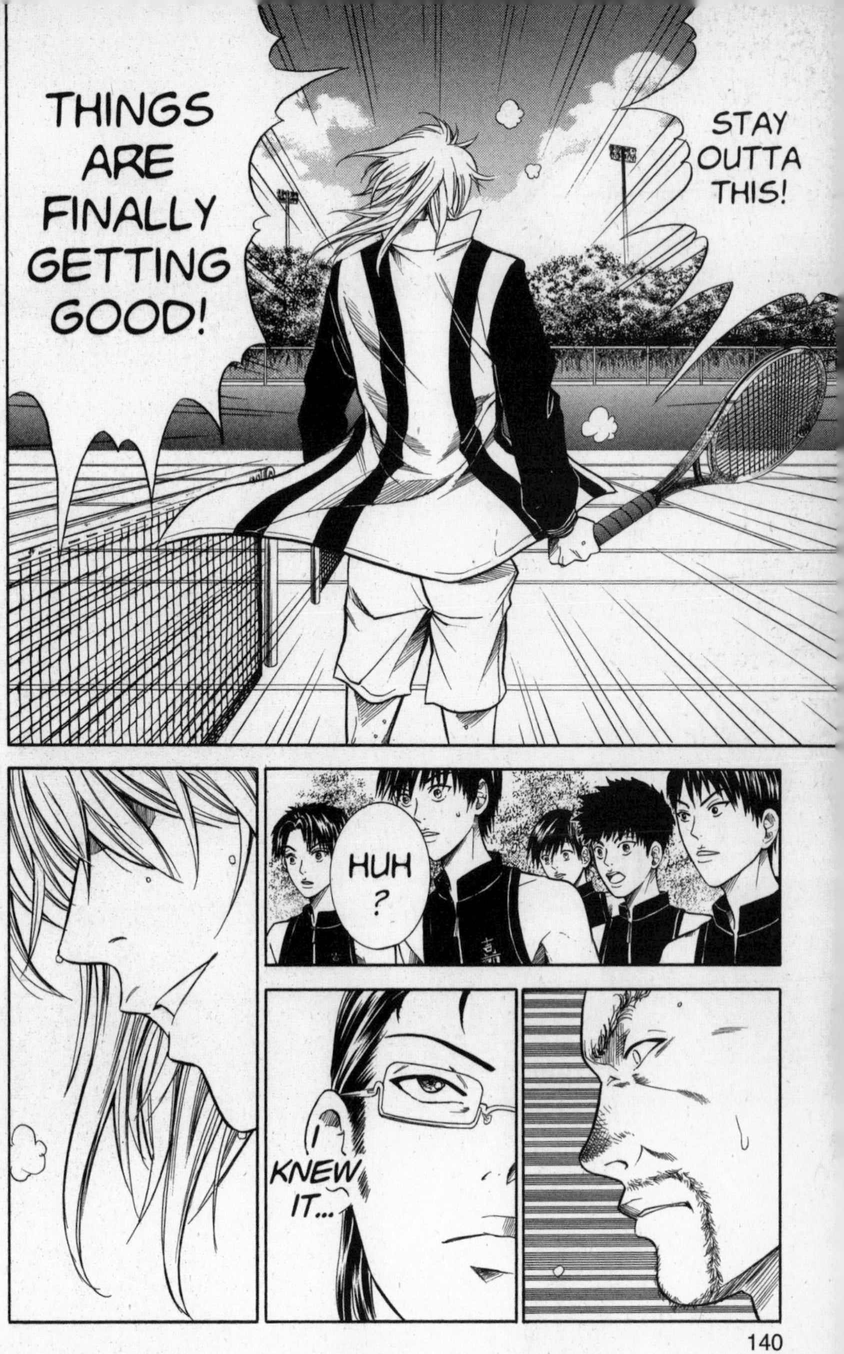
STAY OUTTA THIS!
THINGS ARE FINALLY GETTING GOOD!
HUH?
I KNEW IT...

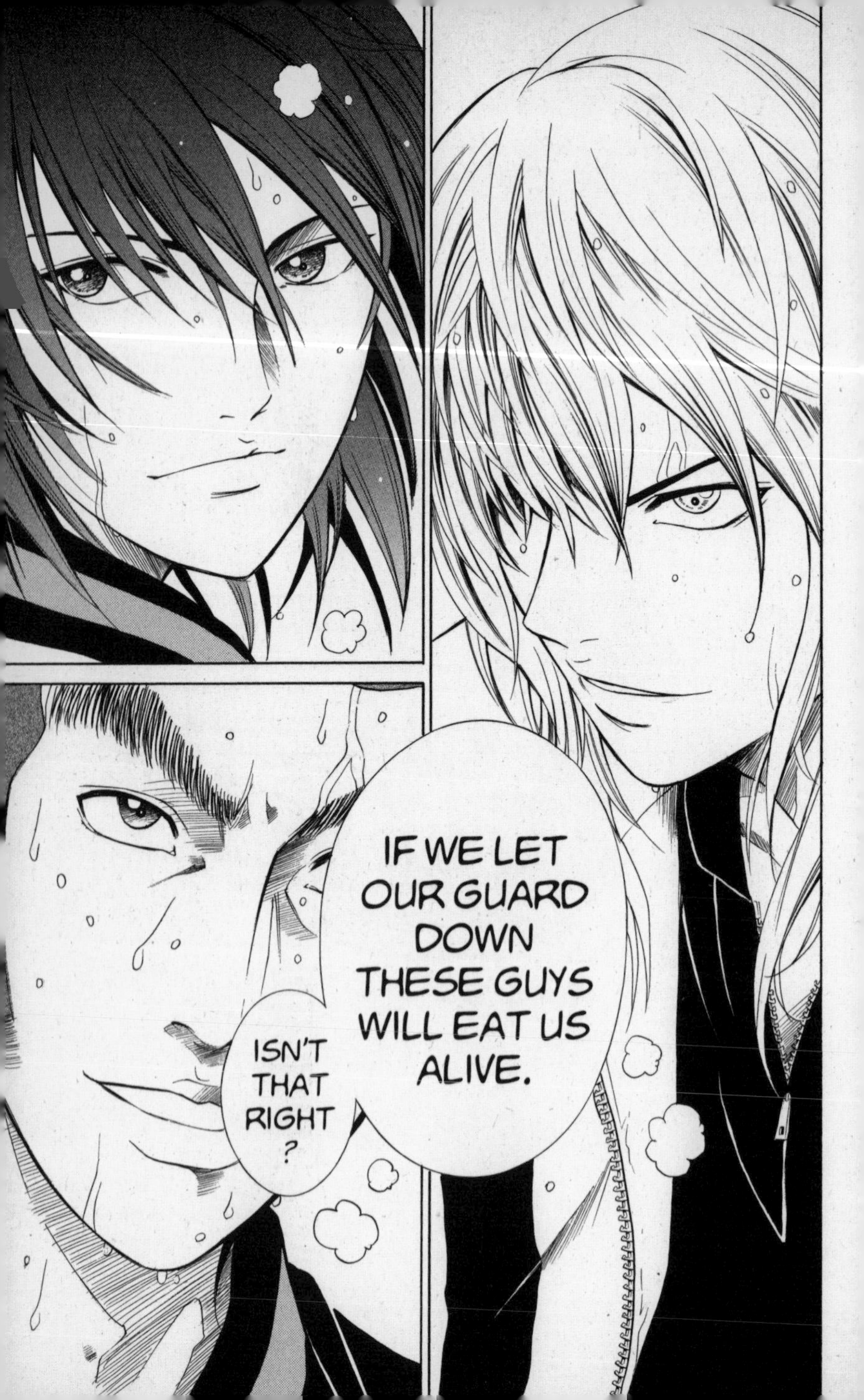
IF WE LET OUR GUARD DOWN THESE GUYS WILL EAT US ALIVE.
ISN'T THAT RIGHT?

テニスの王子様

THE PRINCE OF TENNIS

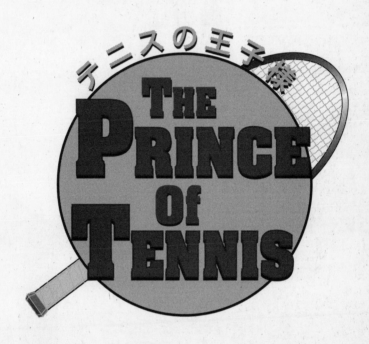

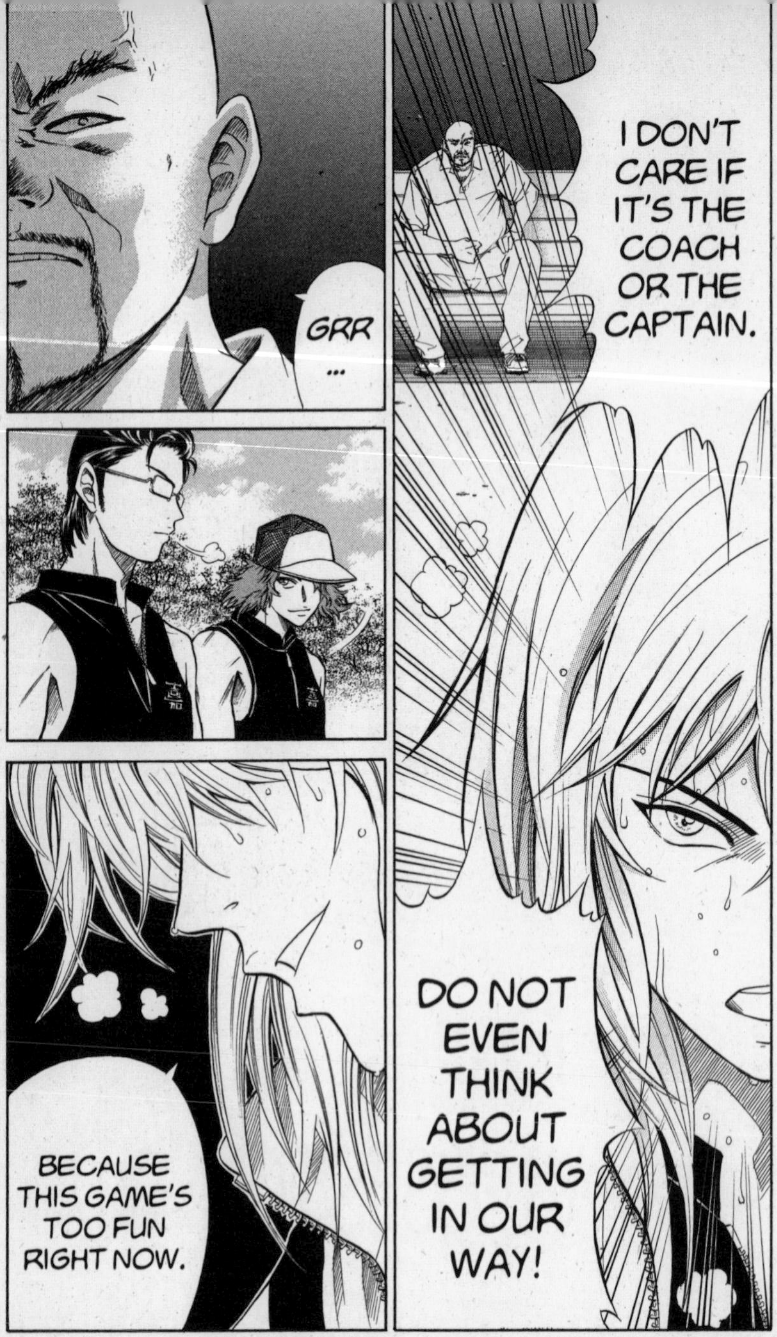
I DON'T CARE IF IT'S THE COACH OR THE CAPTAIN.
DO NOT EVEN THINK ABOUT GETTING IN OUR WAY!
GRR ...
BECAUSE THIS GAME'S TOO FUN RIGHT NOW.

GENIUS 263: AN OBSESSION WITH WINNING

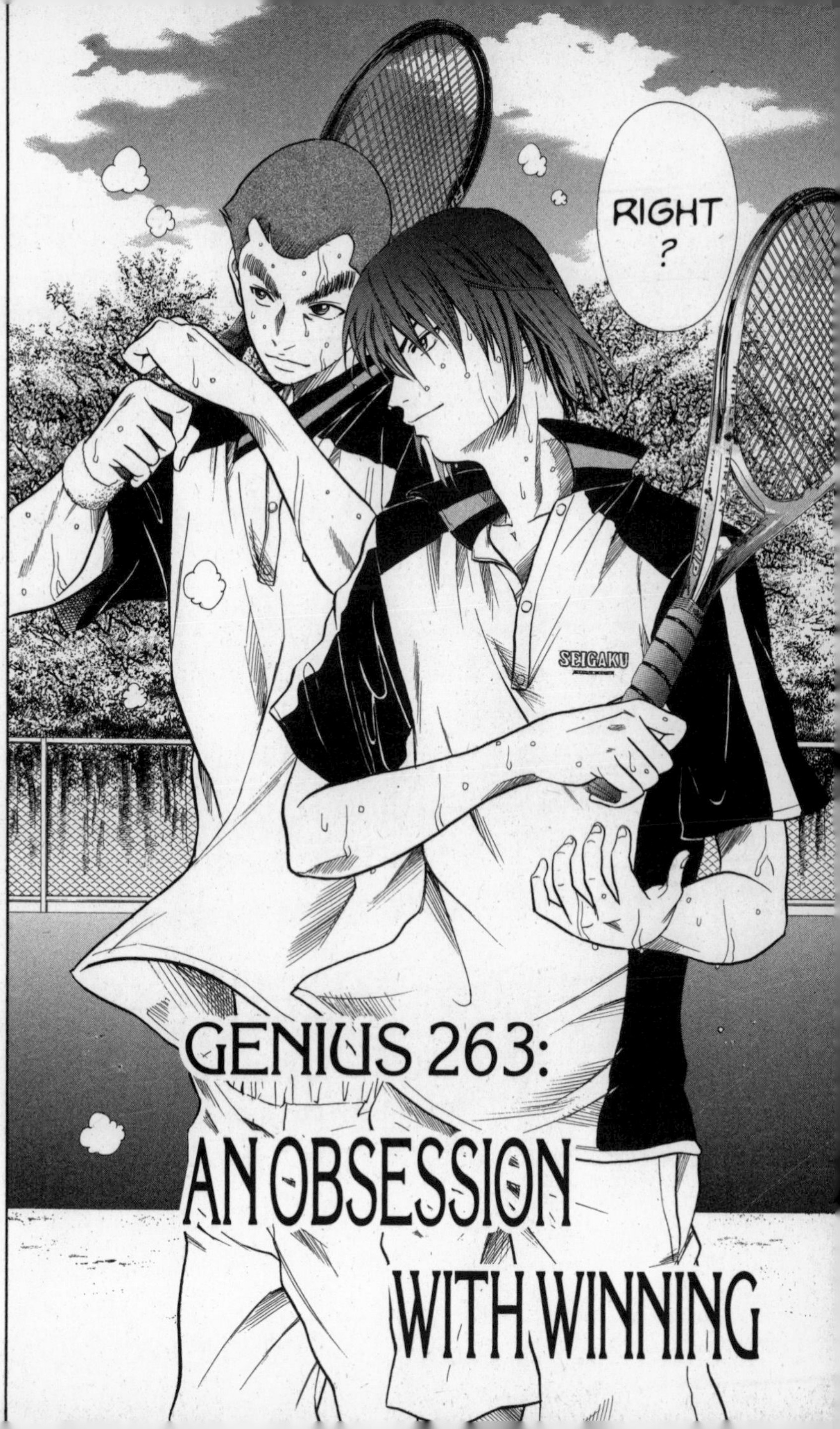
RIGHT?
SEIGAKU
GENIUS 263:
AN OBSESSION WITH WINNING

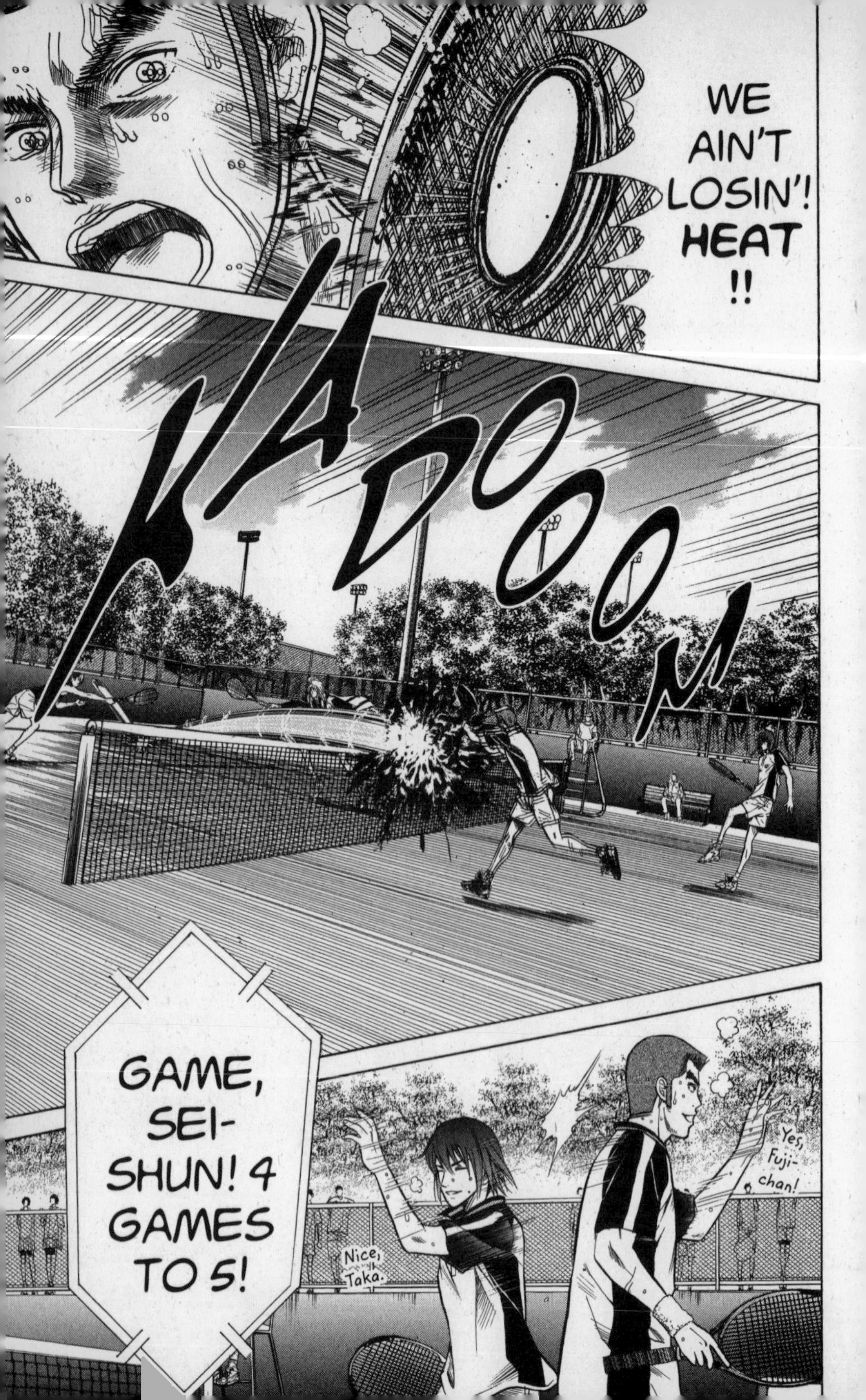
WE AIN'T LOSIN'! HEAT!!
KADOOOM
GAME, SEI-SHUN! 4 GAMES TO 5!
Yes, Fuji-chan!
Nice, Taka.

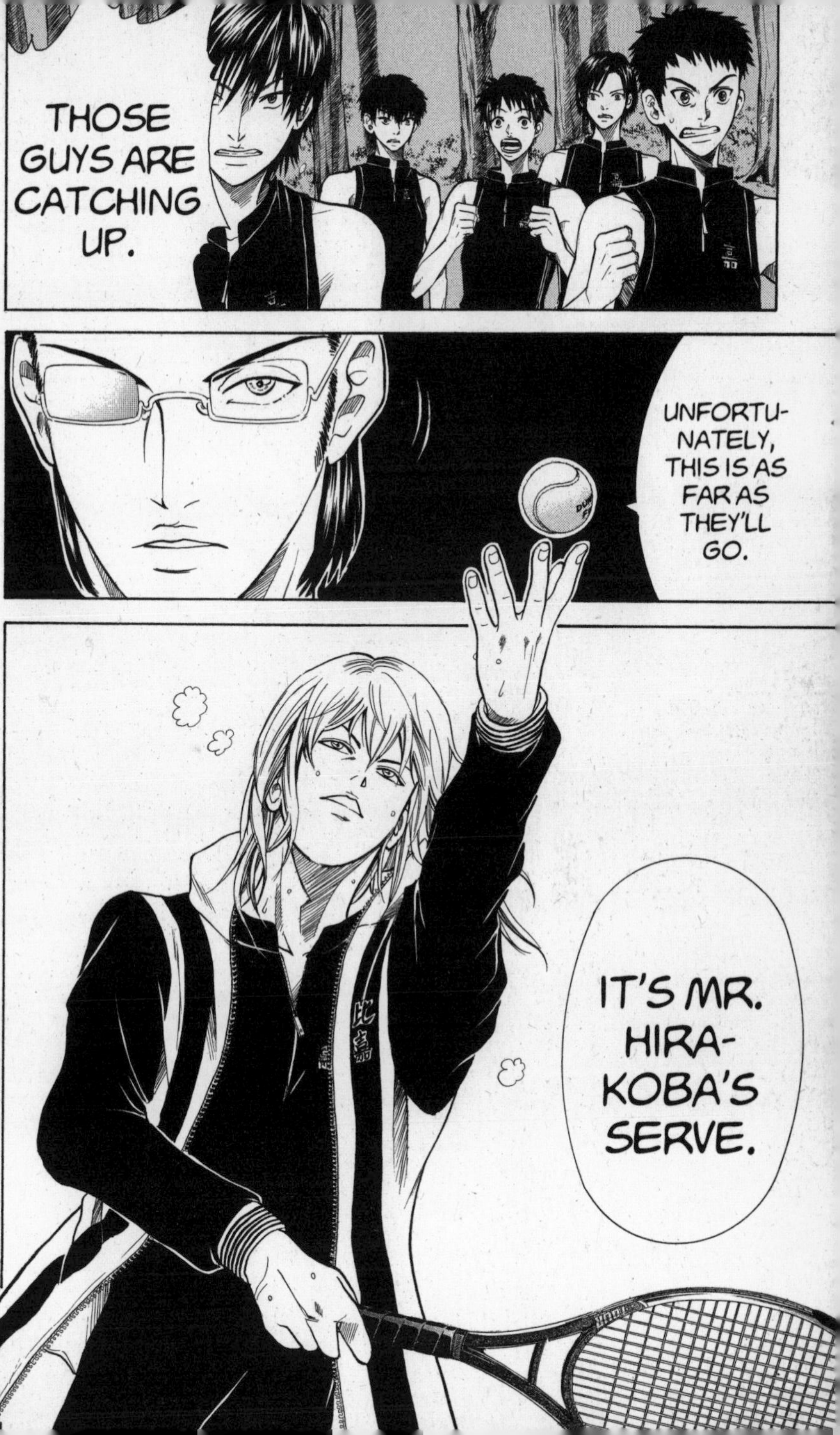
THOSE GUYS ARE CATCHING UP.
UNFORTUNATELY, THIS IS AS FAR AS THEY'LL GO.
IT'S MR. HIRAKOBA'S SERVE.

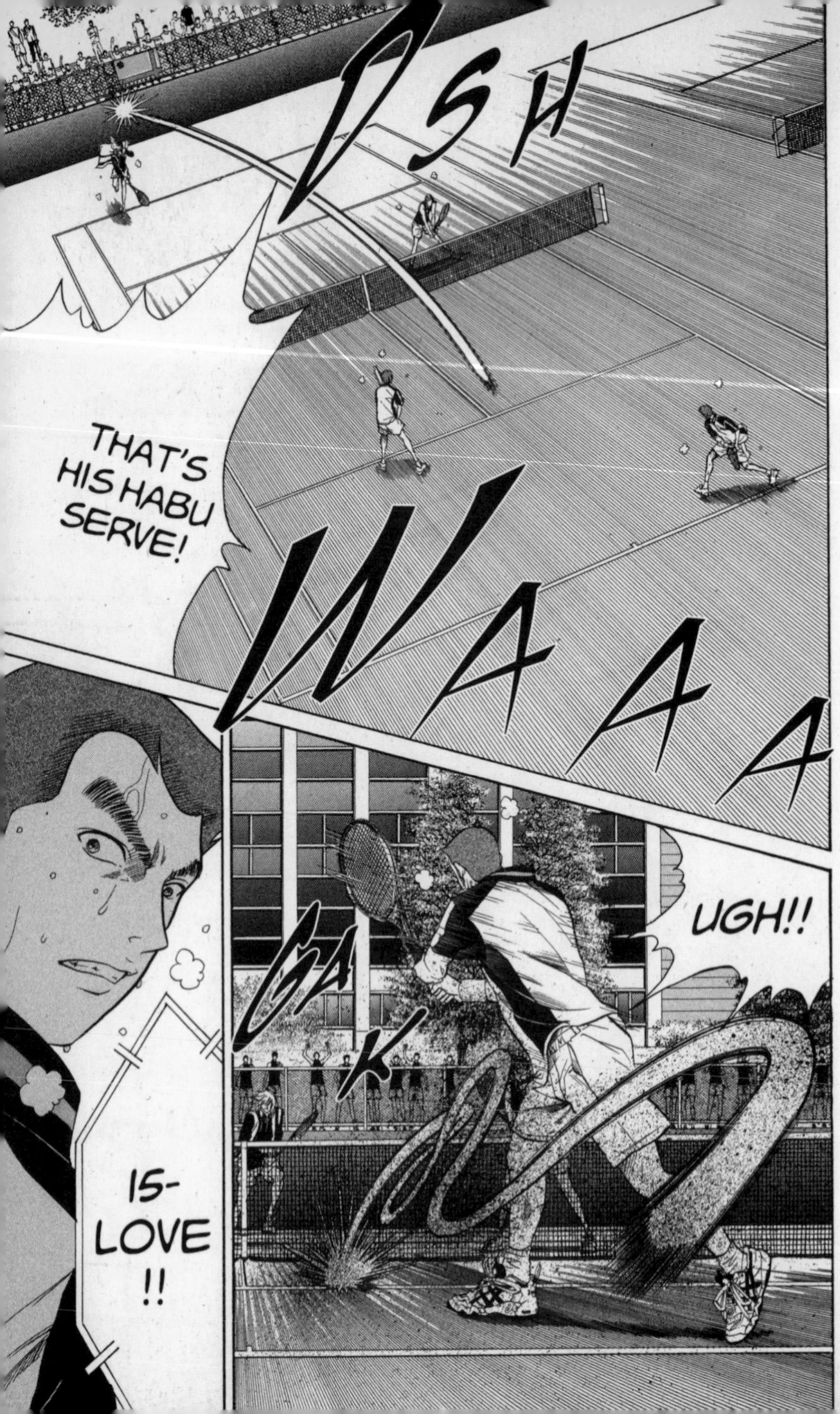
DSH
THAT'S HIS HABU SERVE!
WAAAA
UGH!!
GAK
15-LOVE!!

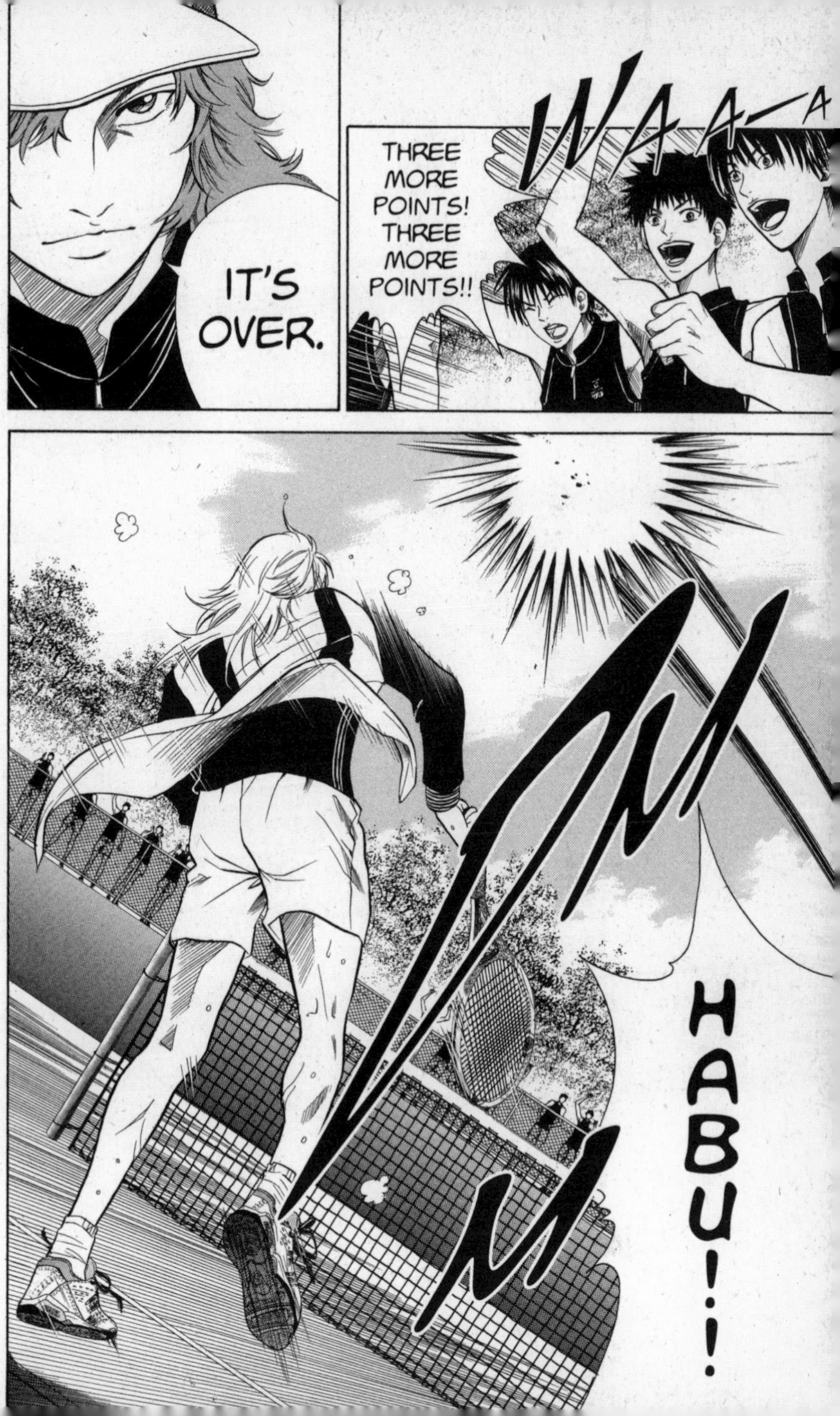
WAA-A
THREE MORE POINTS! THREE MORE POINTS!!
IT'S OVER.
HABU!!!

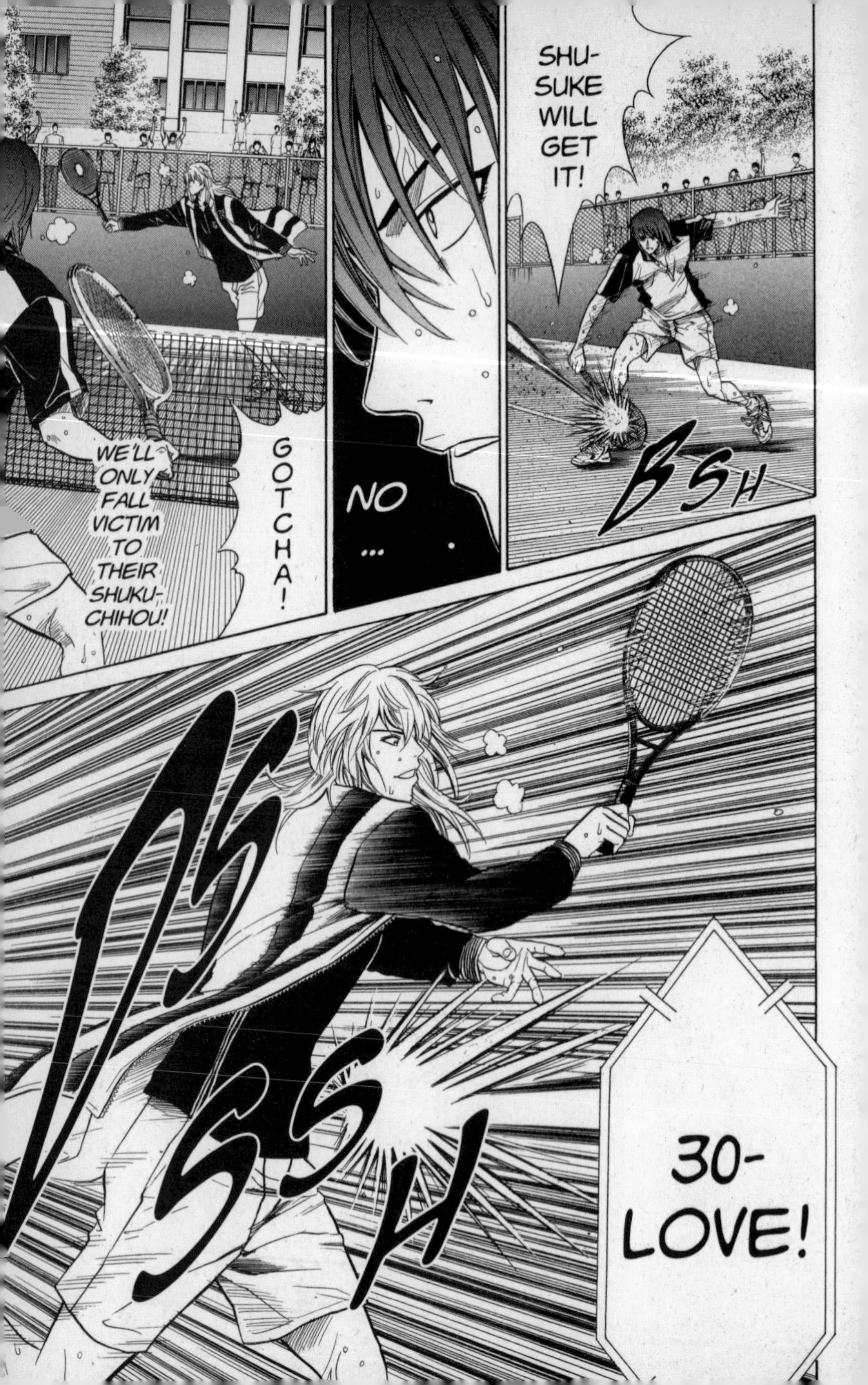
SHU-SUKE WILL GET IT!
BSH
NO ...
GOTCHA!
WE'LL ONLY FALL VICTIM TO THEIR SHUKU-CHIHOU!
30-LOVE!
VSSH

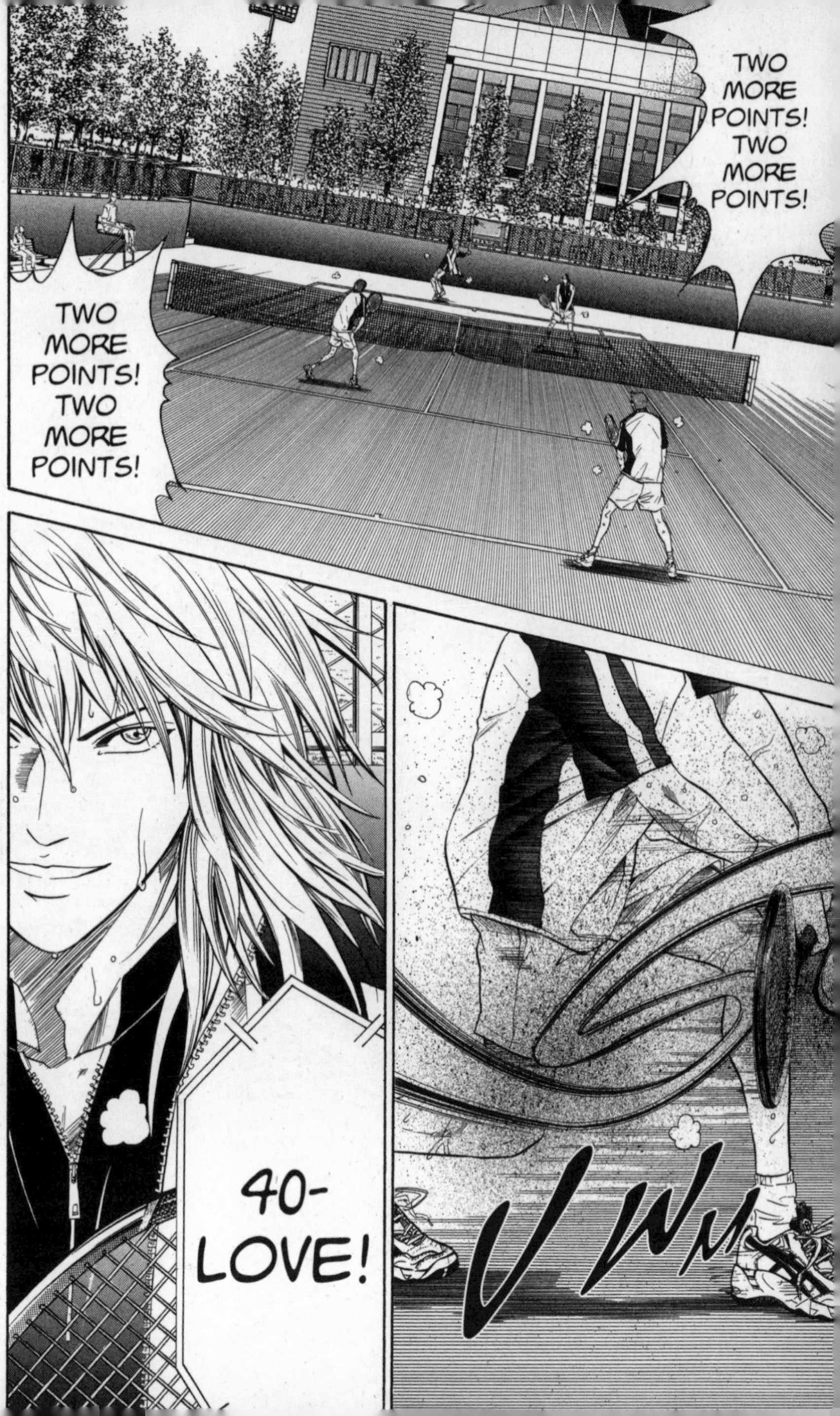
TWO MORE POINTS! TWO MORE POINTS!
TWO MORE POINTS! TWO MORE POINTS!
VWM
40-LOVE!

READ THIS WAY

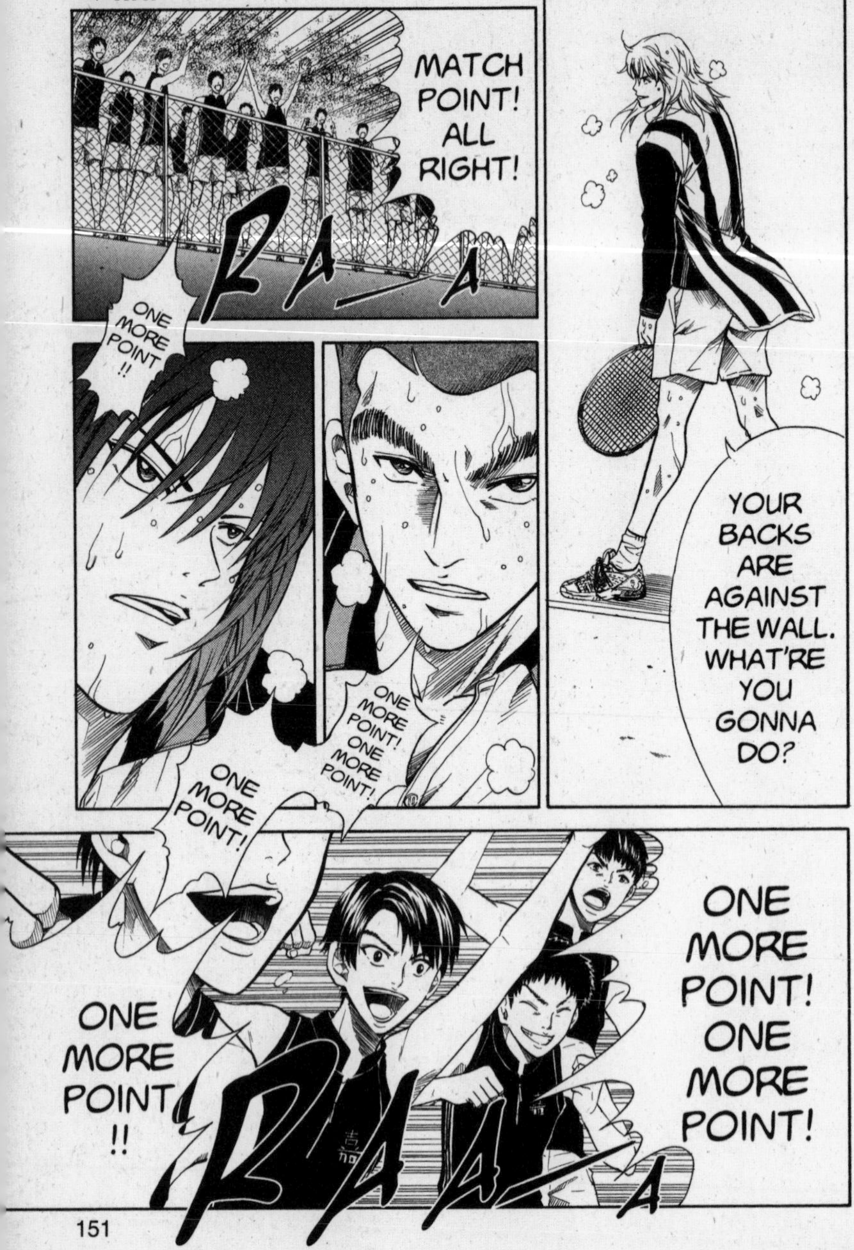
YOUR BACKS ARE AGAINST THE WALL. WHAT'RE YOU GONNA DO?
MATCH POINT! ALL RIGHT!
RAA
ONE MORE POINT!!
ONE MORE POINT! ONE MORE POINT!
ONE MORE POINT!
ONE MORE POINT! ONE MORE POINT!
ONE MORE POINT!!
RAAA

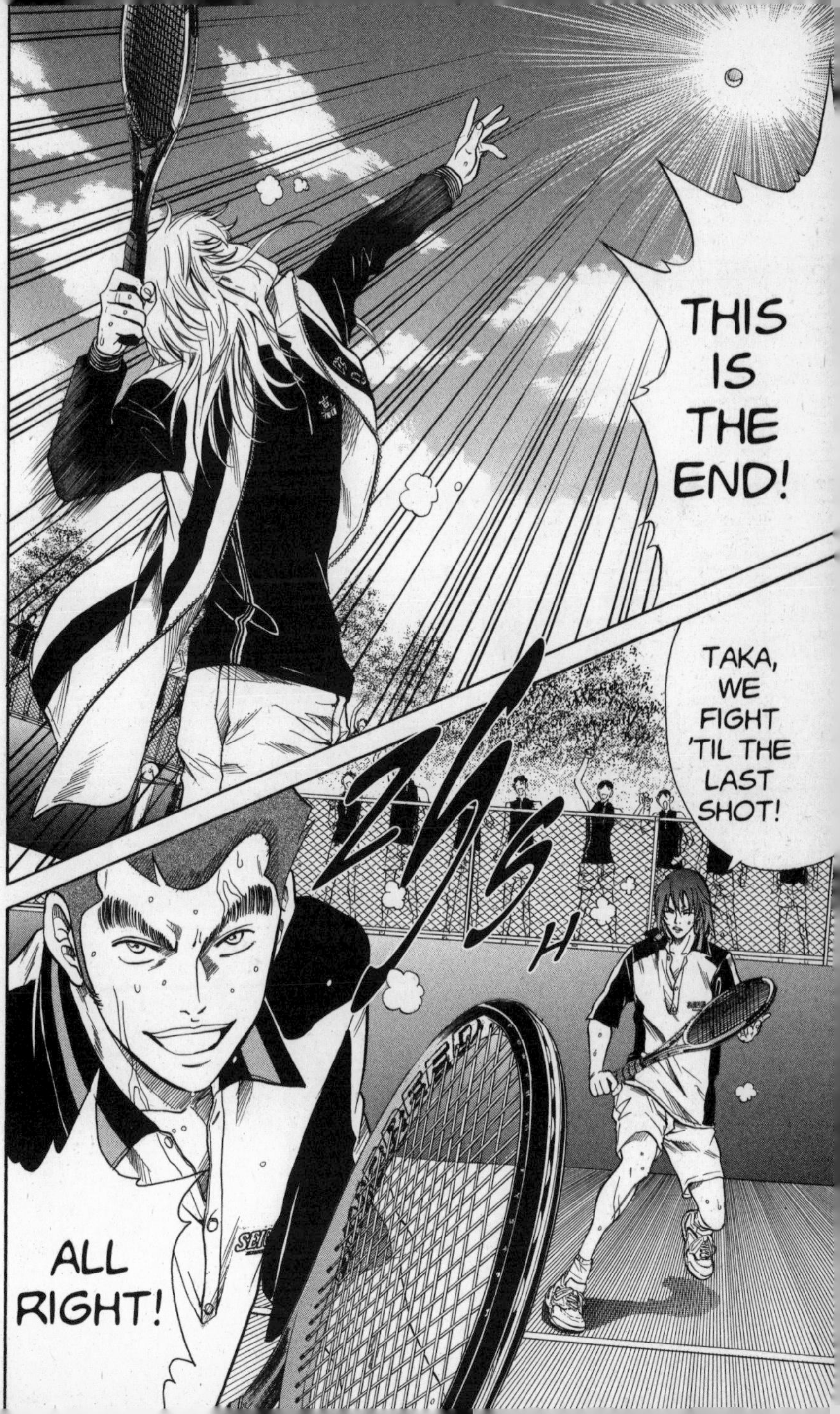
THIS IS THE END!
TAKA, WE FIGHT 'TIL THE LAST SHOT!
SWISH
ALL RIGHT!

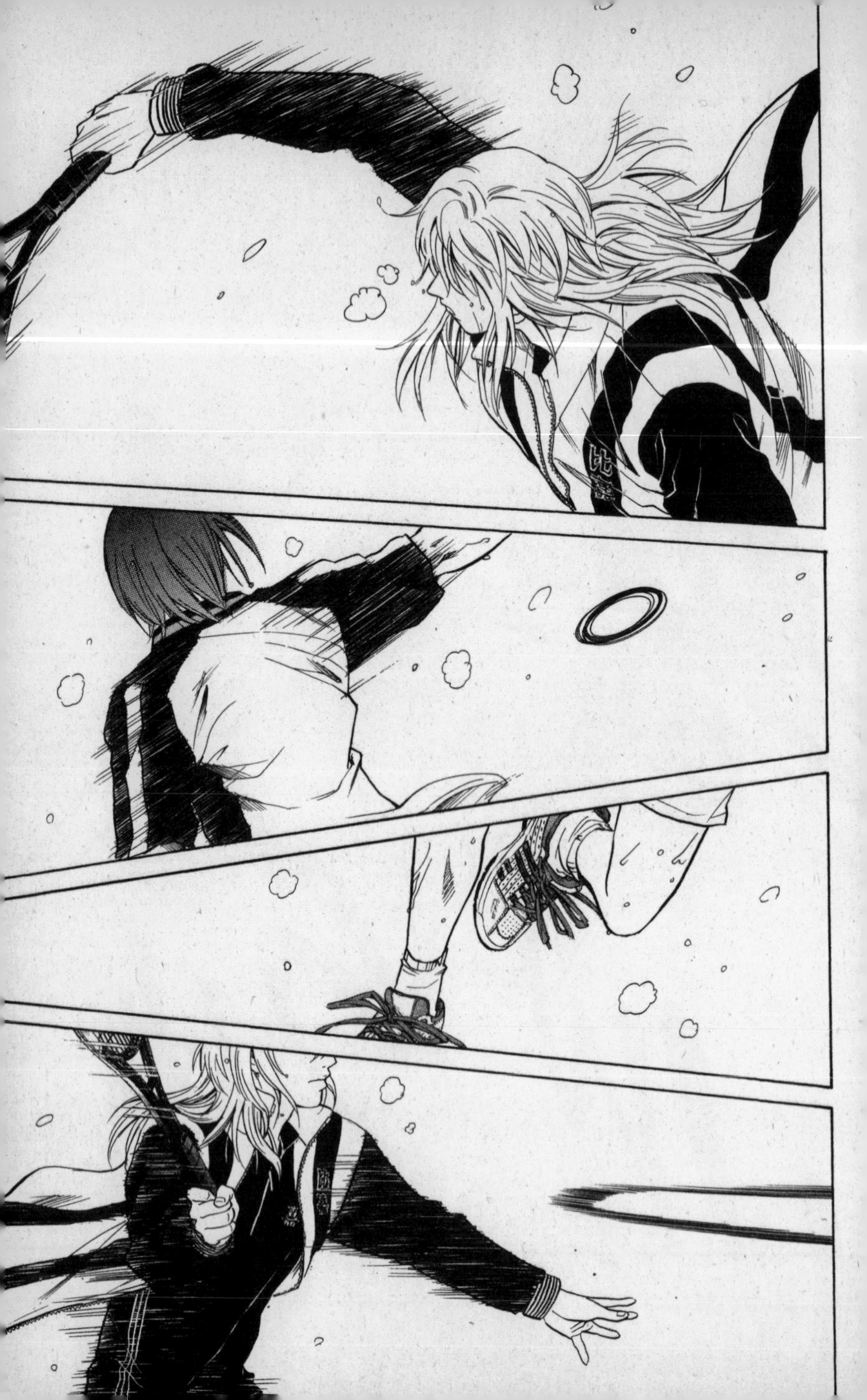

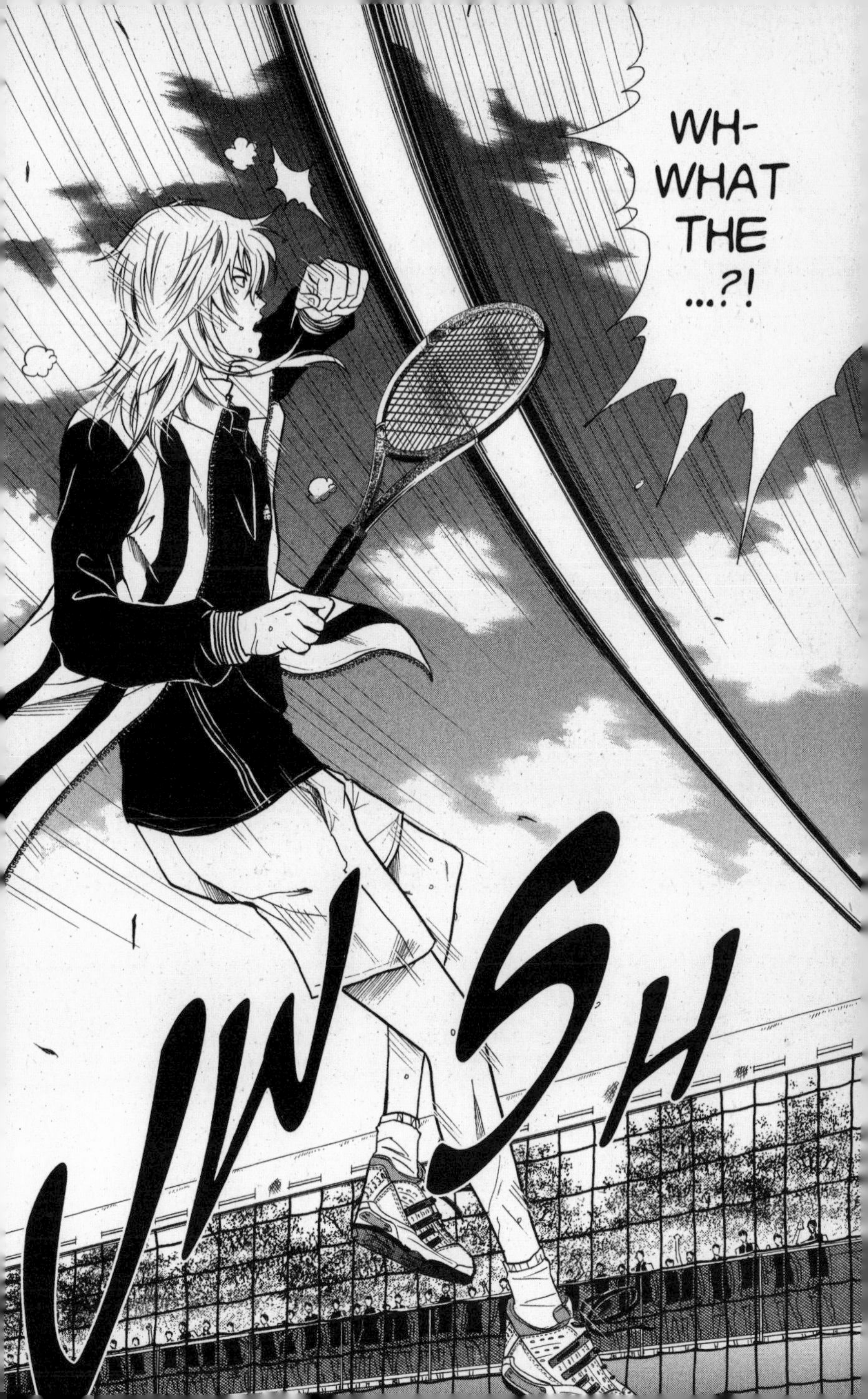
WH-
WHAT
THE
...?!
VWSH

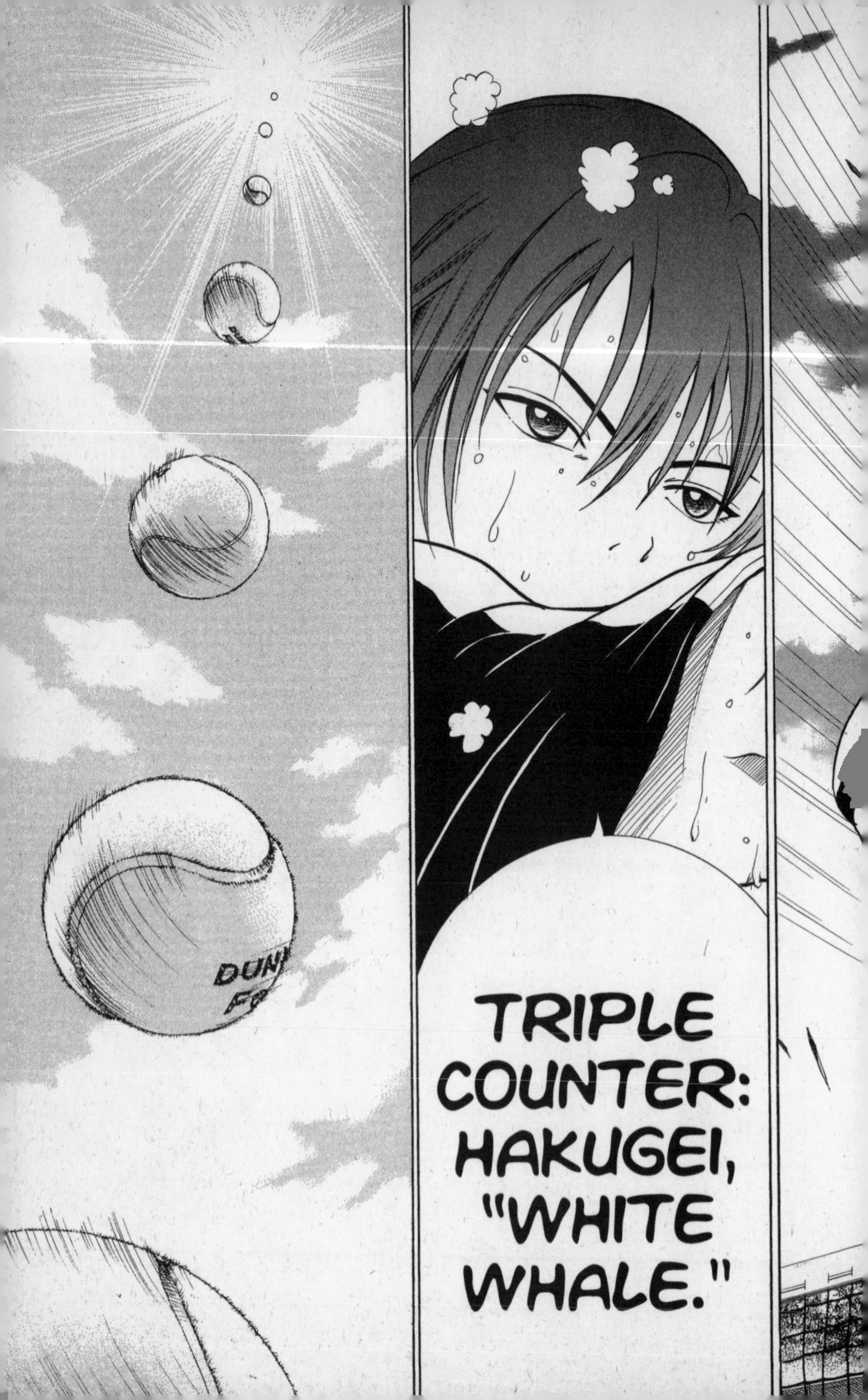
TRIPLE COUNTER: HAKUGEI, "WHITE WHALE."
DUN
F

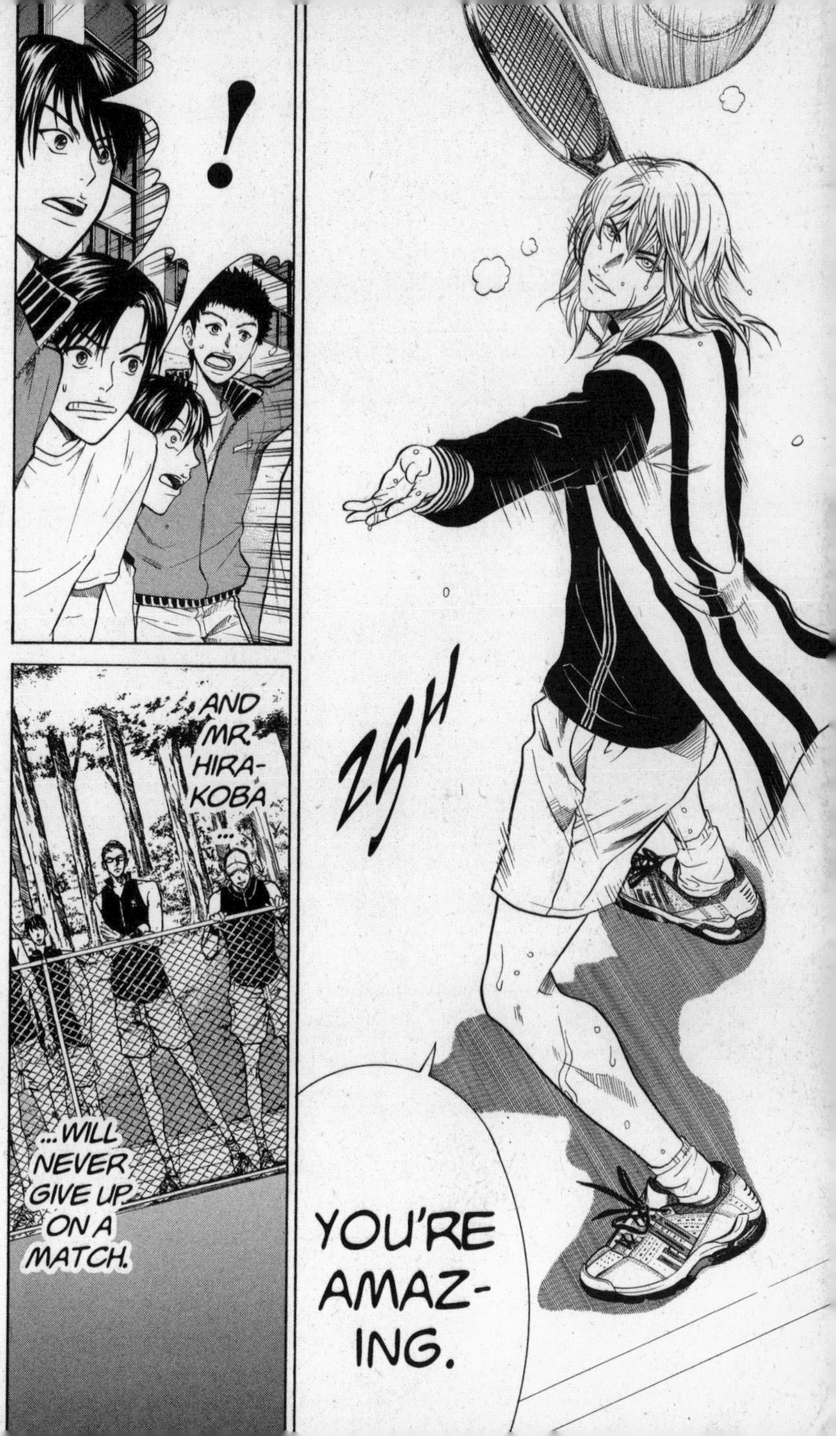
ZSH
YOU'RE AMAZ- ING.
!
AND MR. HIRA- KOBA ...
...WILL NEVER GIVE UP ON A MATCH.

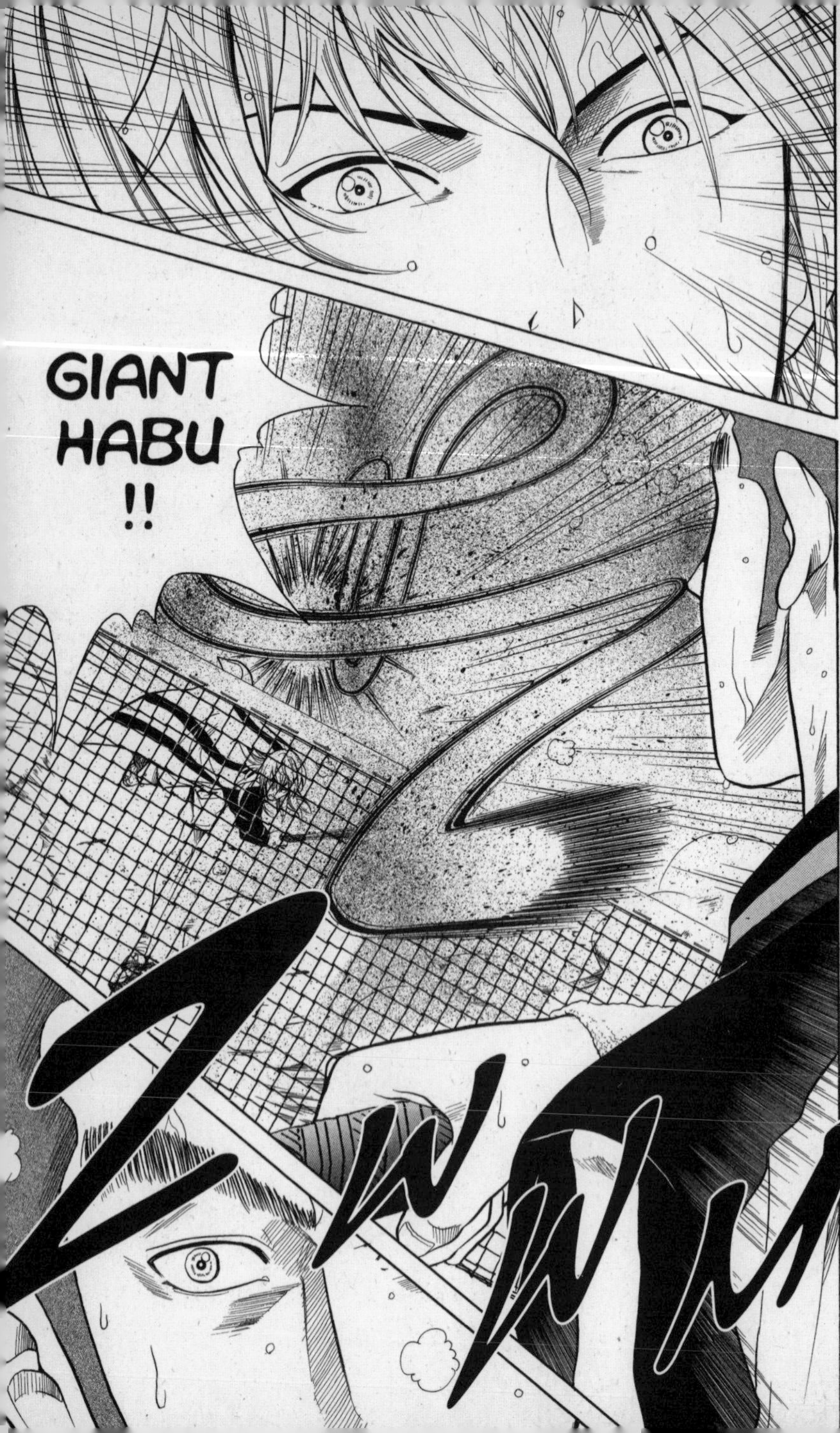
GIANT HABU !!

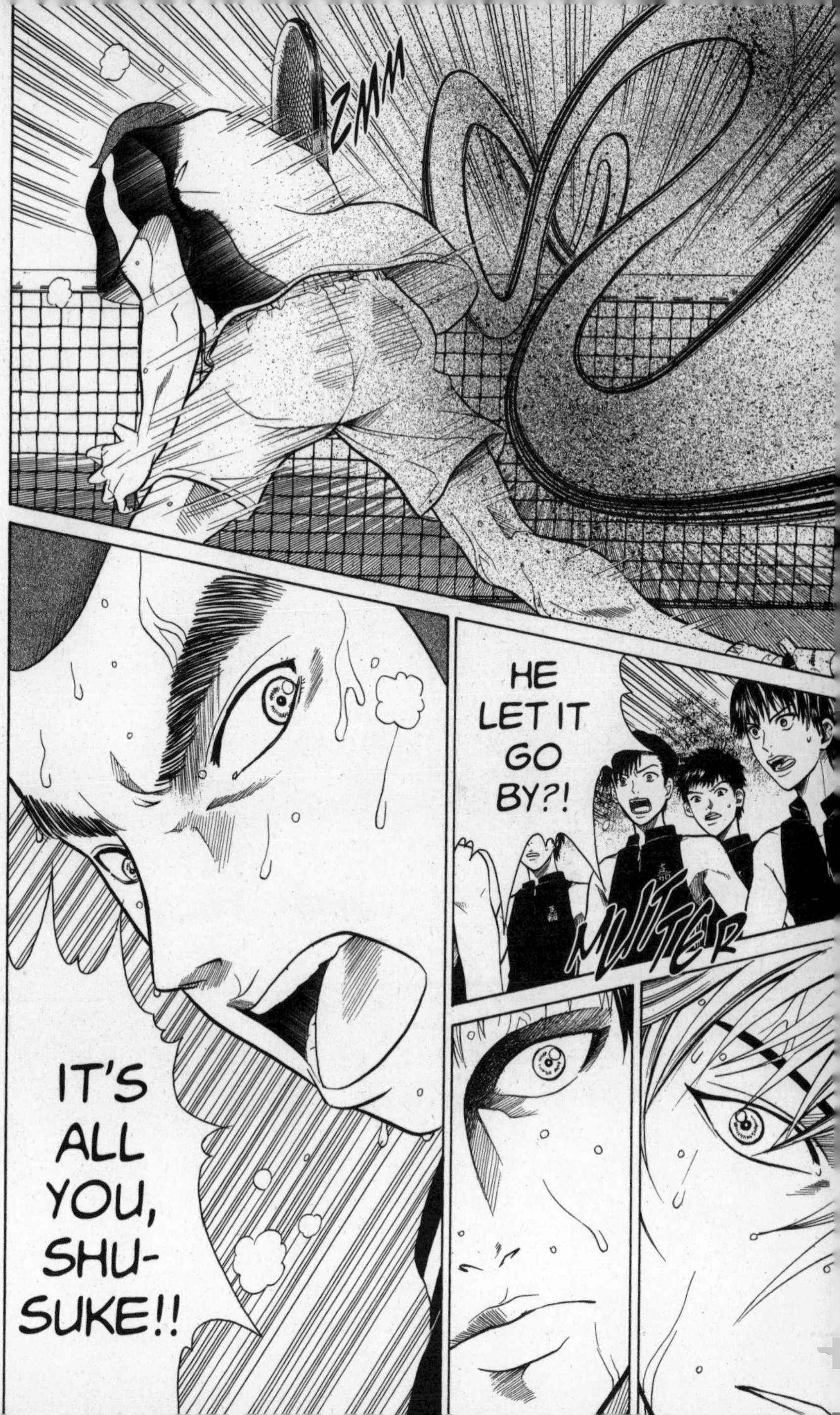
ZMM
HE LET IT GO BY?!
MUTTER
IT'S ALL YOU, SHUSUKE!!

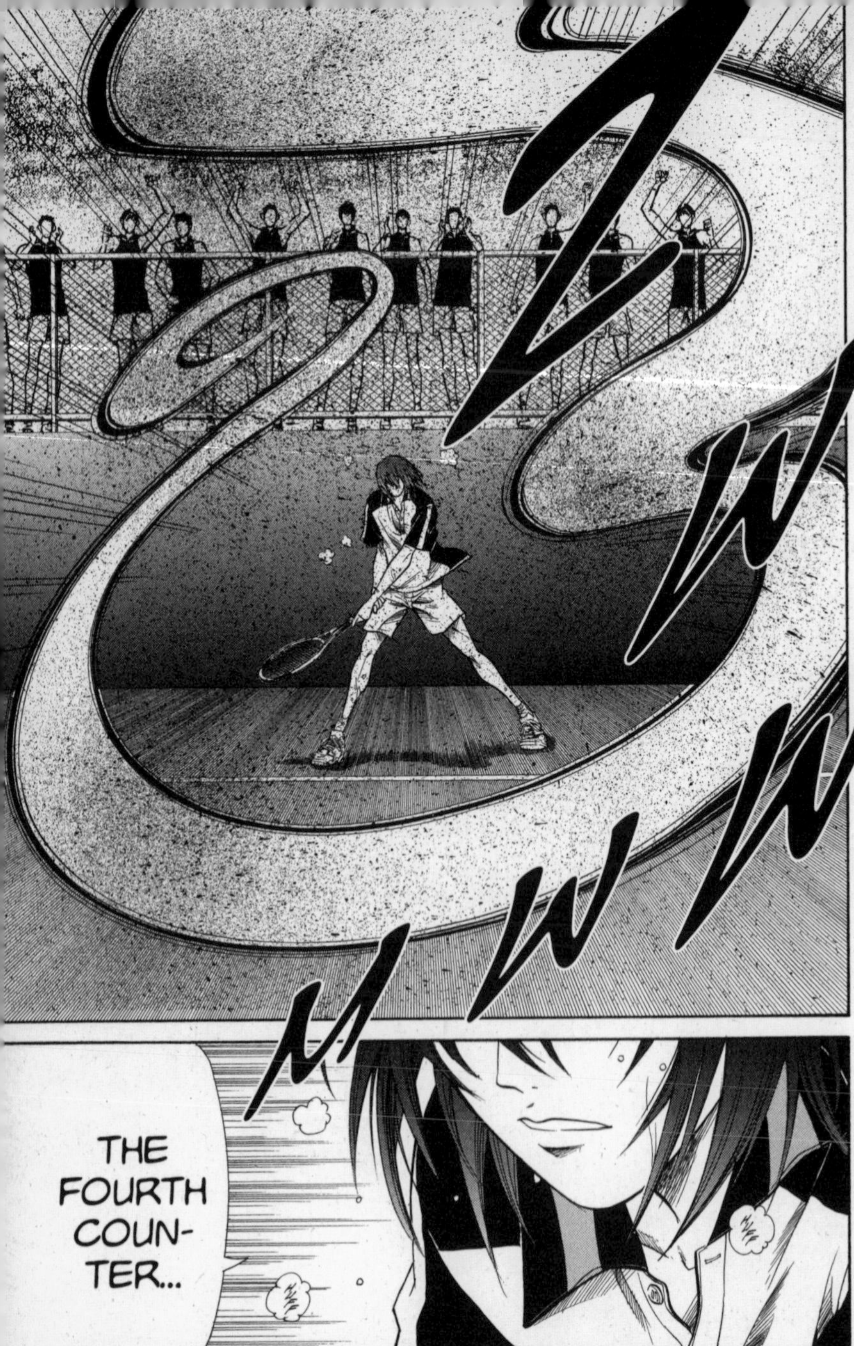
THE FOURTH COUNTER...

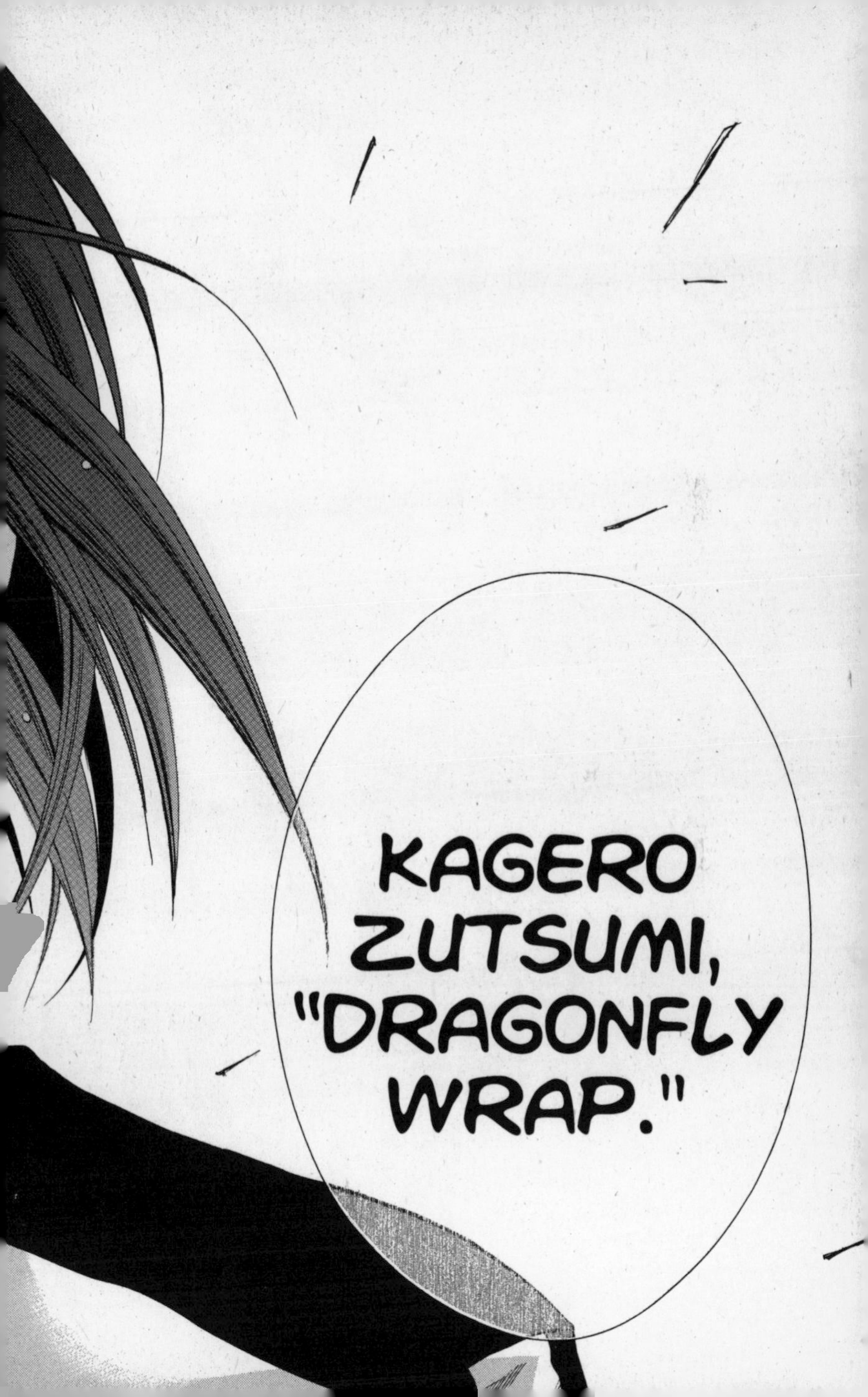
KAGERO ZUTSUMI, "DRAGONFLY WRAP."

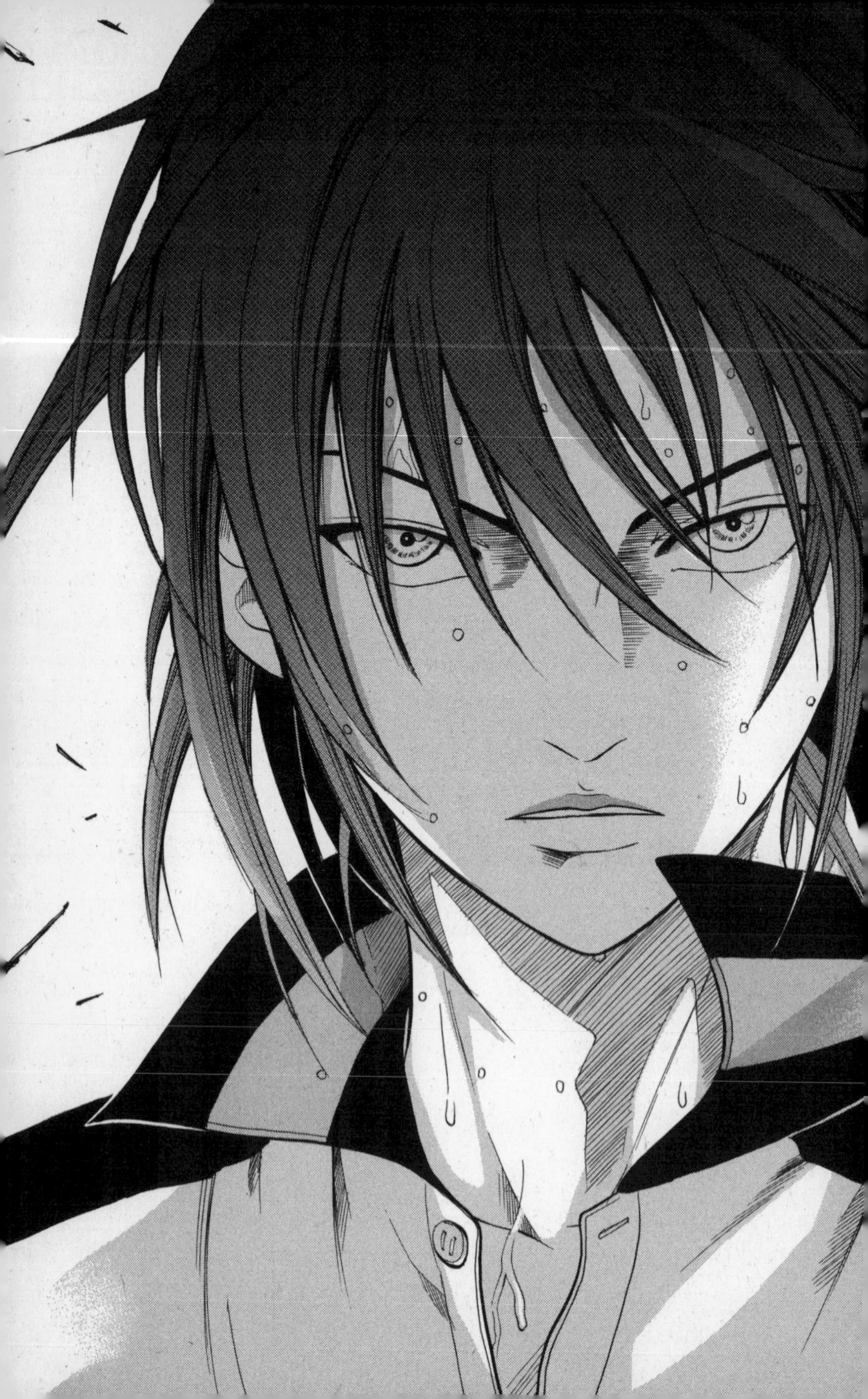

テニスの王子様

THE PRINCE OF TENNIS

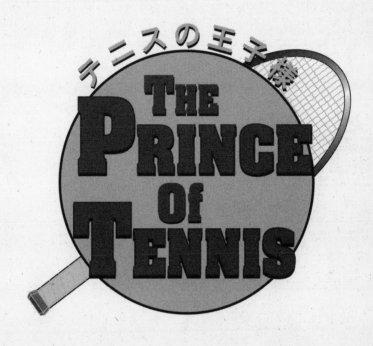

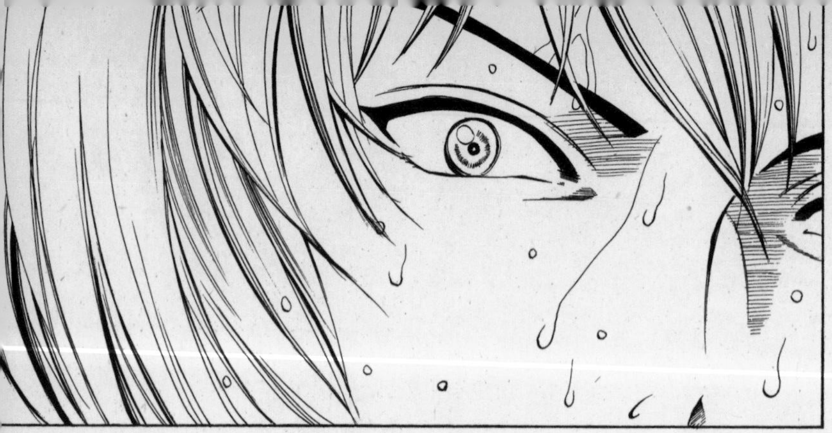

GENIUS 264:

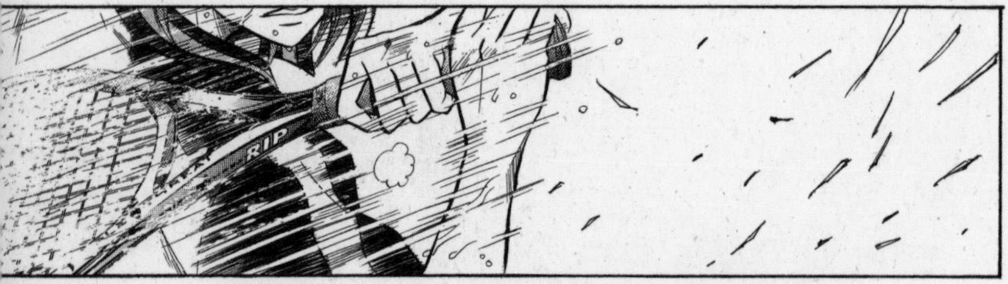

THE FOURTH COUNTER:
KAGERO ZUTSUMI

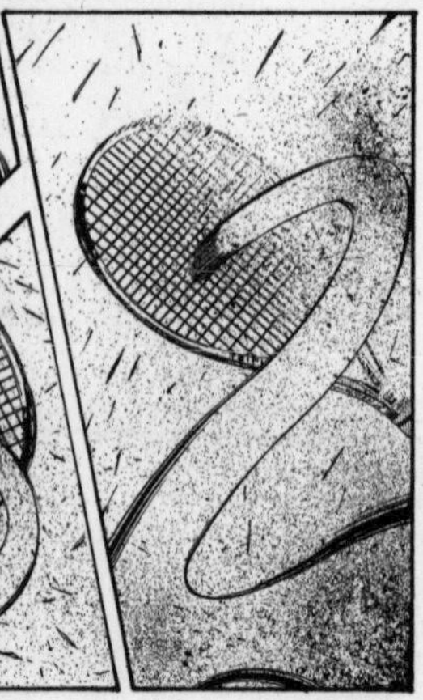
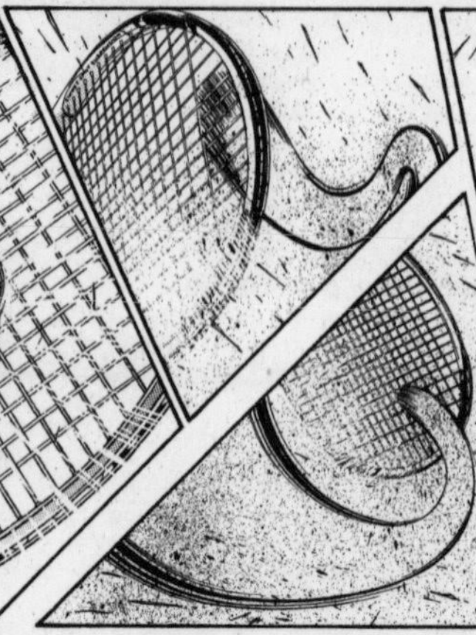
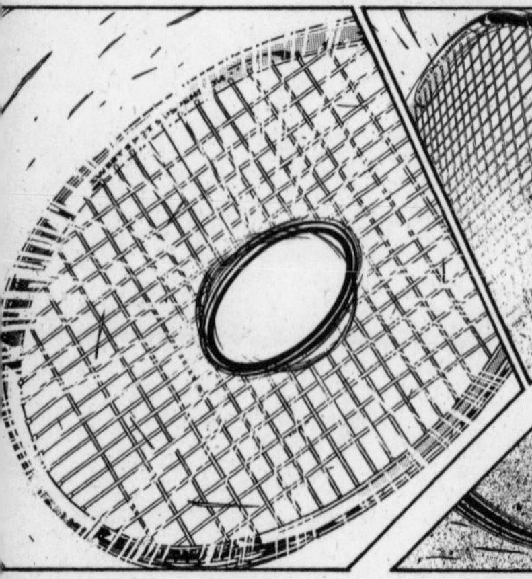

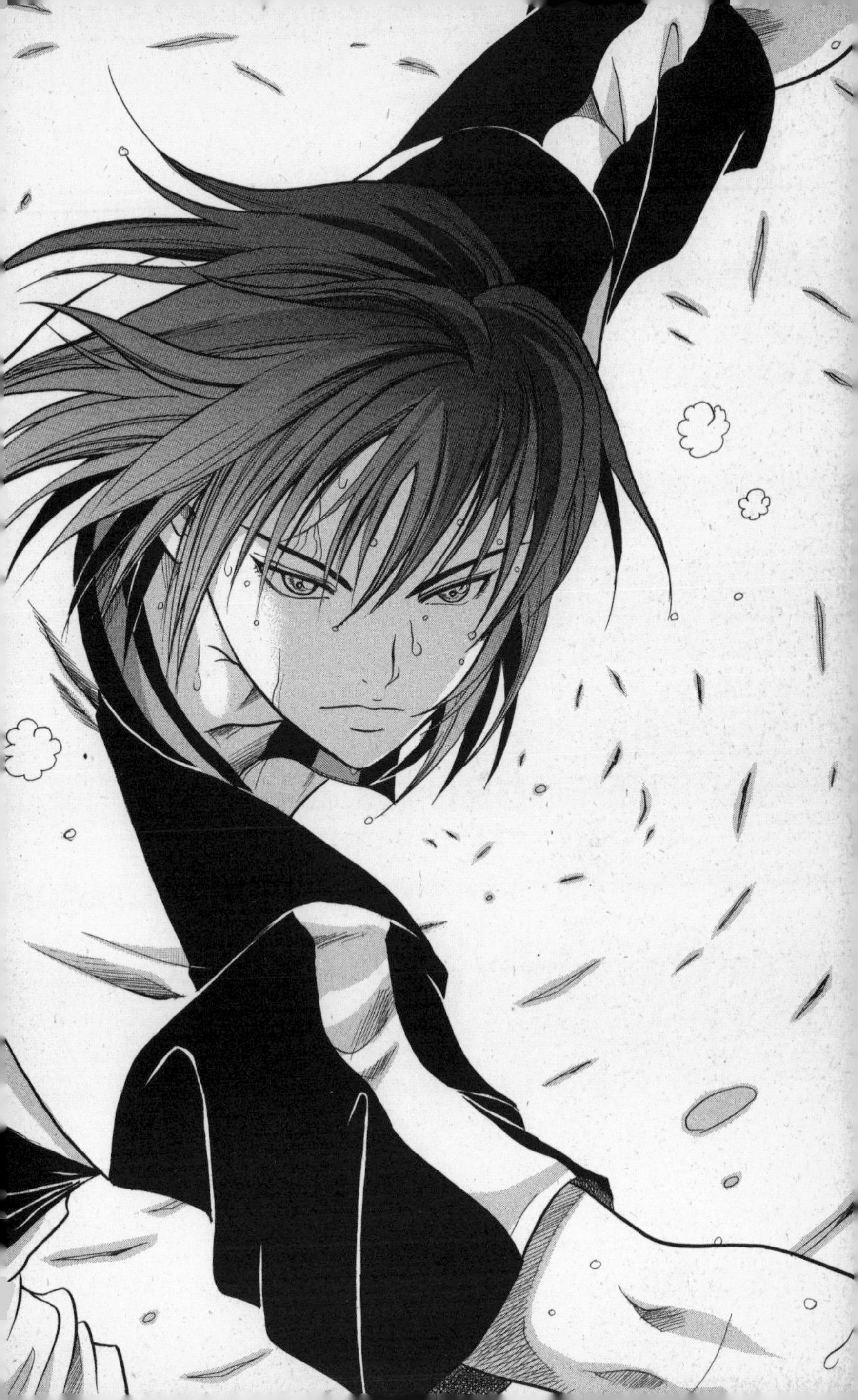

GENIUS 264:
THE FOURTH COUNTER: KAGERO ZUTSUMI

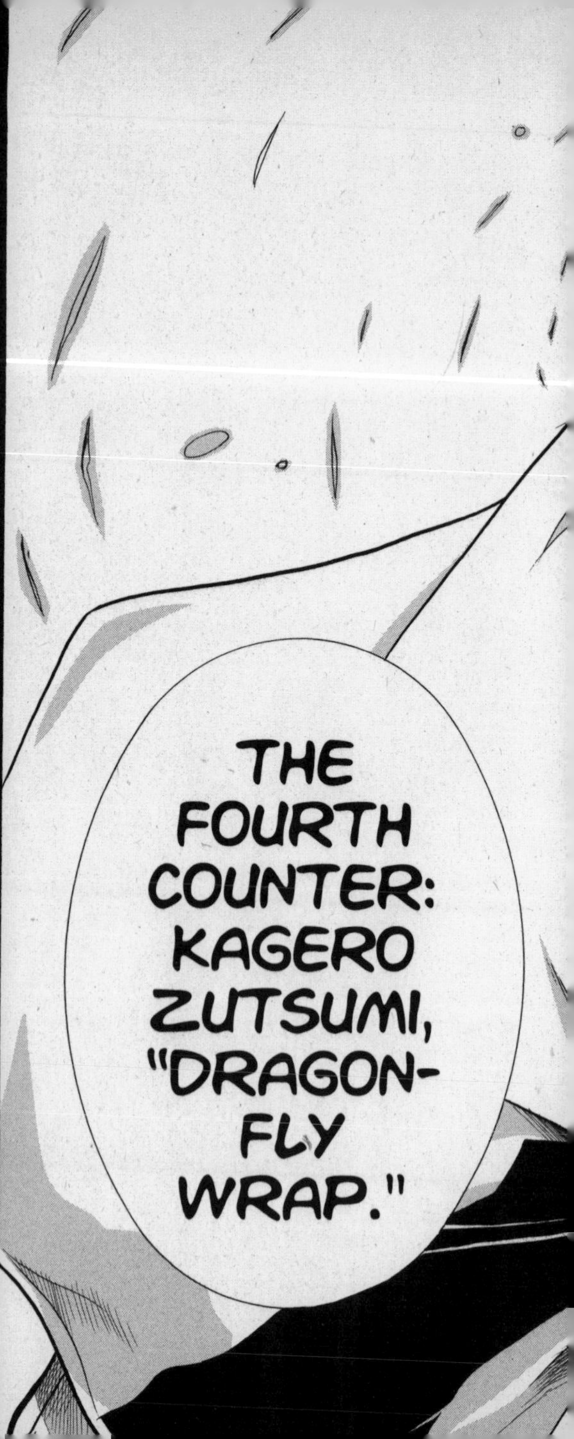

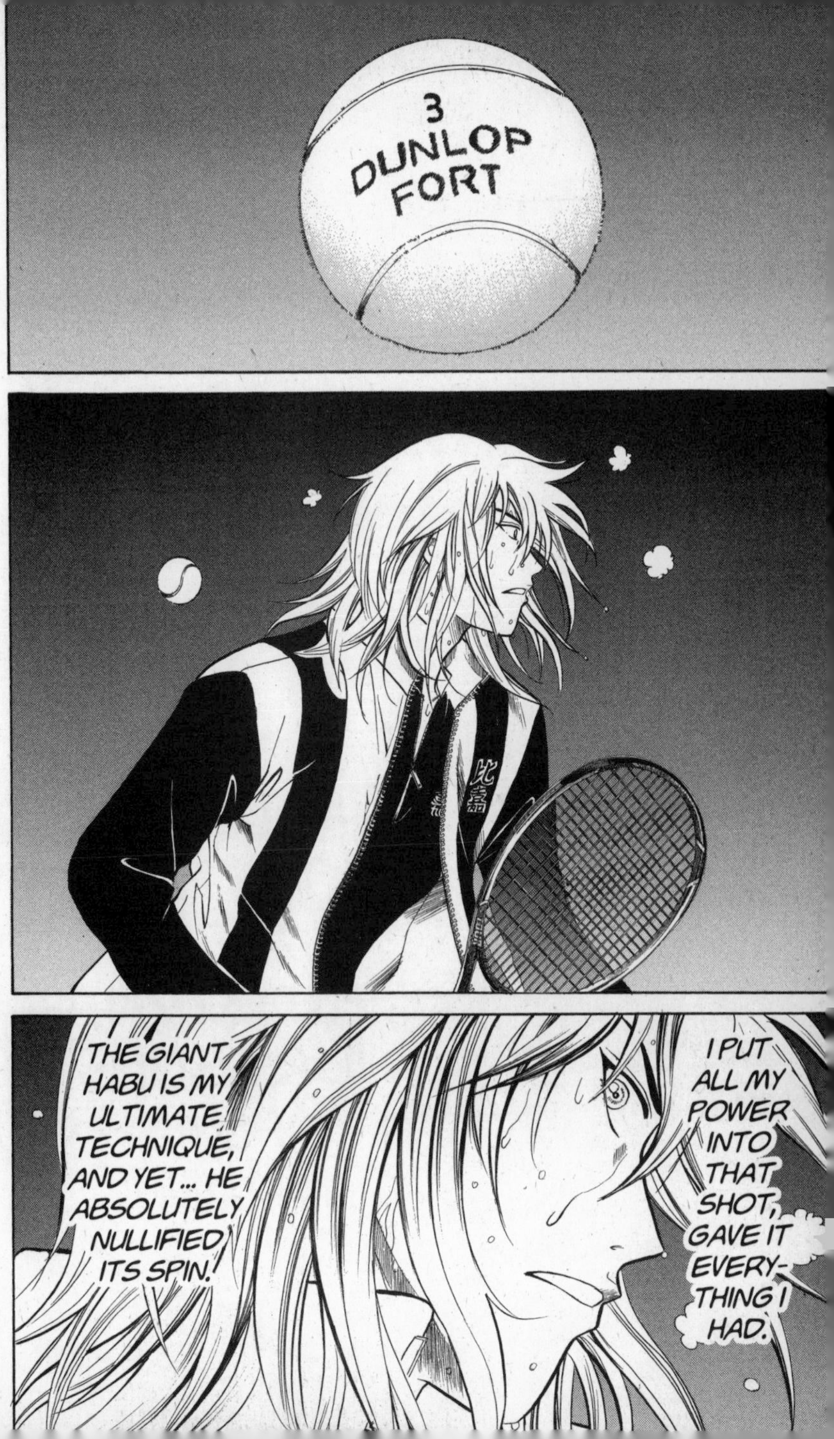
3
DUNLOP
FORT
I PUT ALL MY POWER INTO THAT SHOT, GAVE IT EVERY-THING I HAD.
THE GIANT HABU IS MY ULTIMATE TECHNIQUE, AND YET... HE ABSOLUTELY NULLIFIED ITS SPIN.

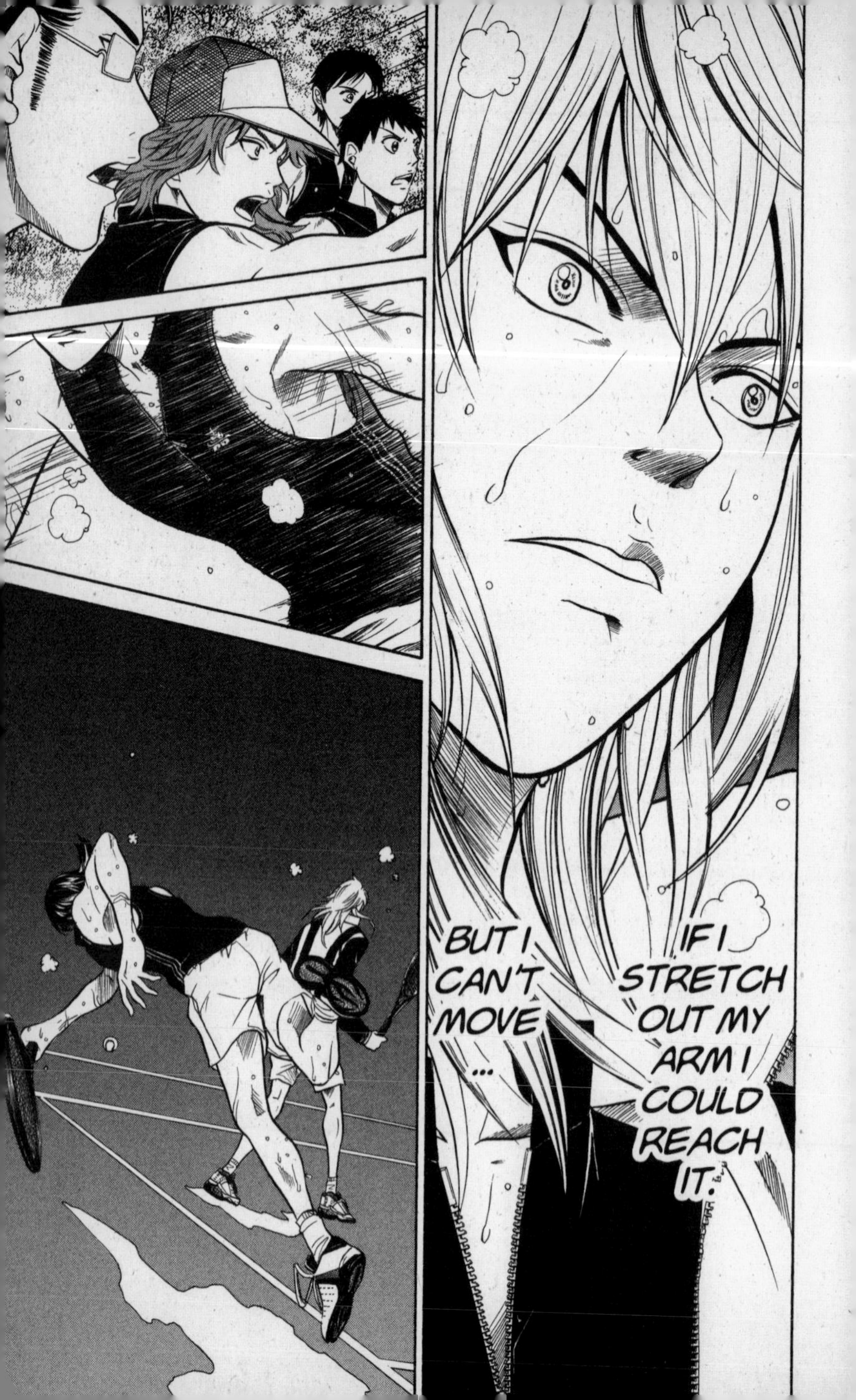
IF I STRETCH OUT MY ARM I COULD REACH IT.
BUT I CAN'T MOVE ...

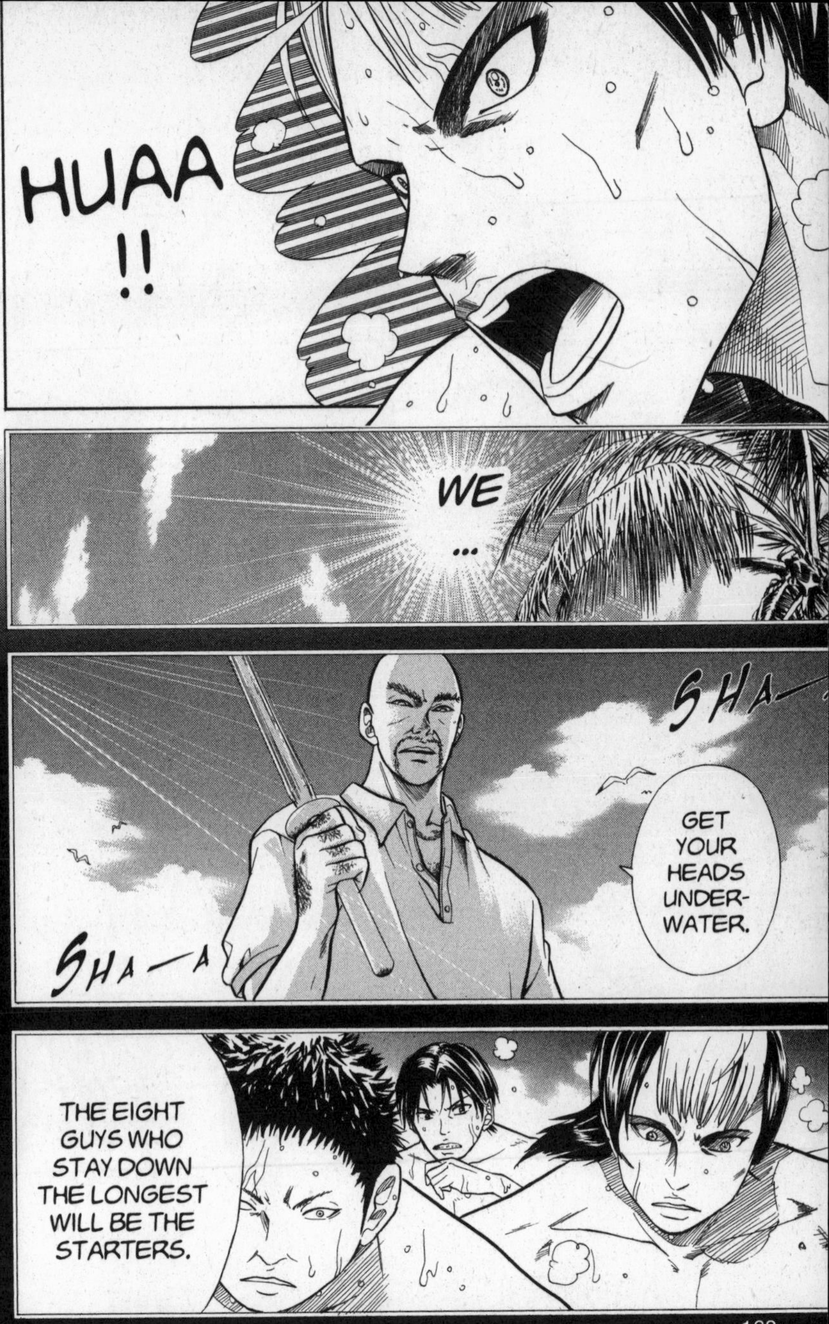
HUAA !!
WE ...
SHA—
GET YOUR HEADS UNDER-WATER.
SHA—A
THE EIGHT GUYS WHO STAY DOWN THE LONGEST WILL BE THE STARTERS.

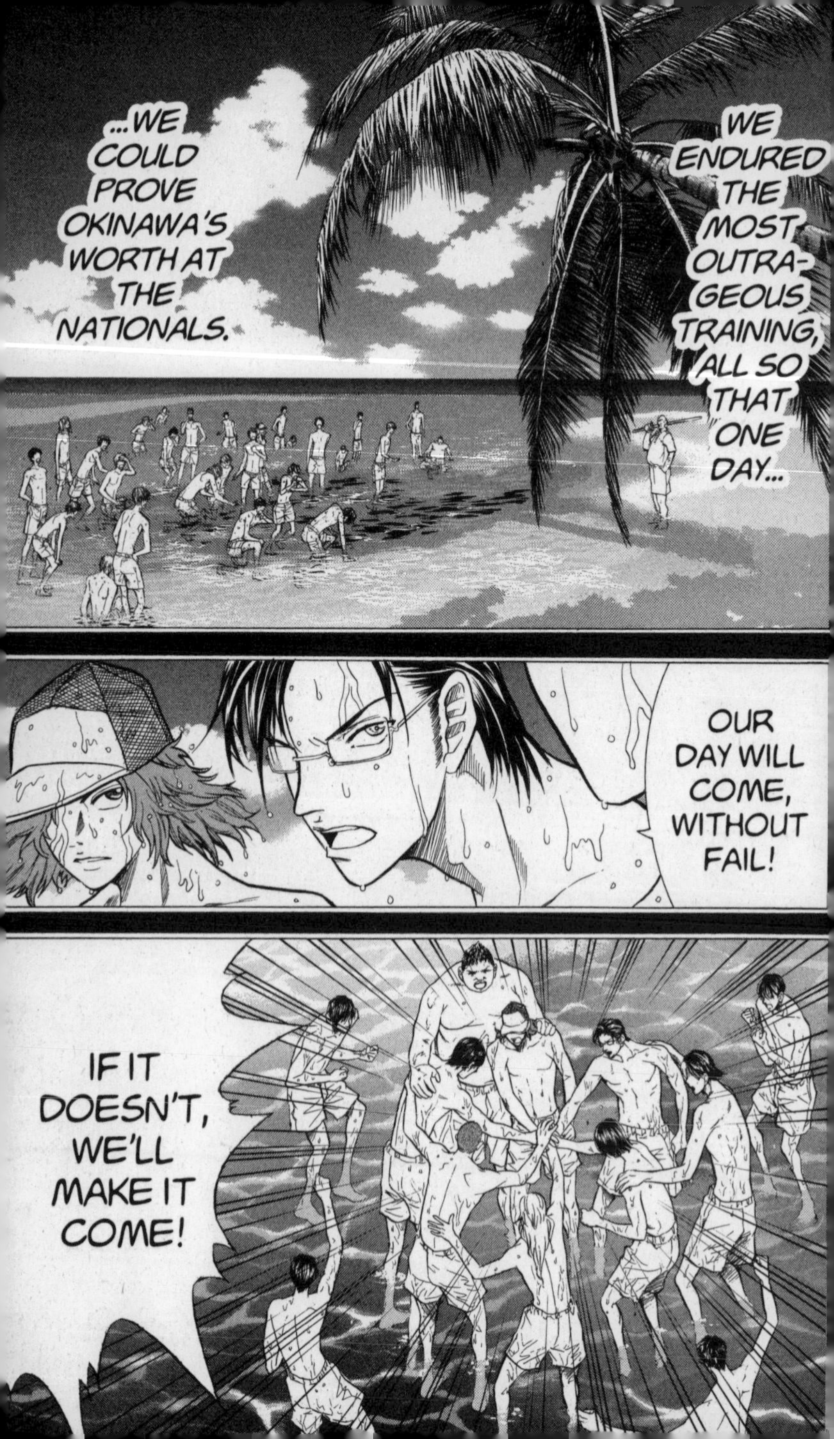
WE ENDURED THE MOST OUTRAGEOUS TRAINING, ALL SO THAT ONE DAY...
...WE COULD PROVE OKINAWA'S WORTH AT THE NATIONALS.
OUR DAY WILL COME, WITHOUT FAIL!
IF IT DOESN'T, WE'LL MAKE IT COME!

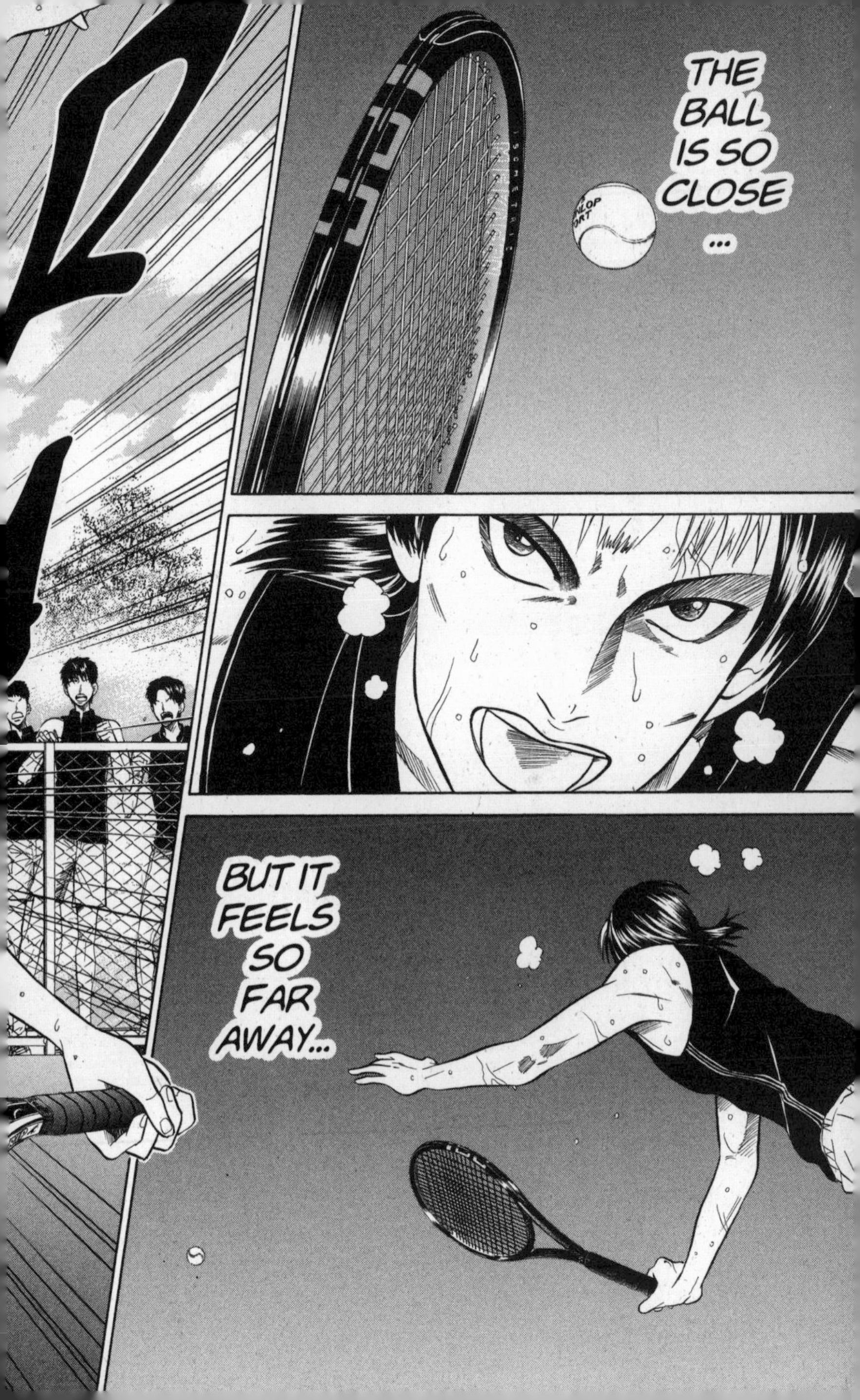
THE BALL IS SO CLOSE ...
BUT IT FEELS SO FAR AWAY...

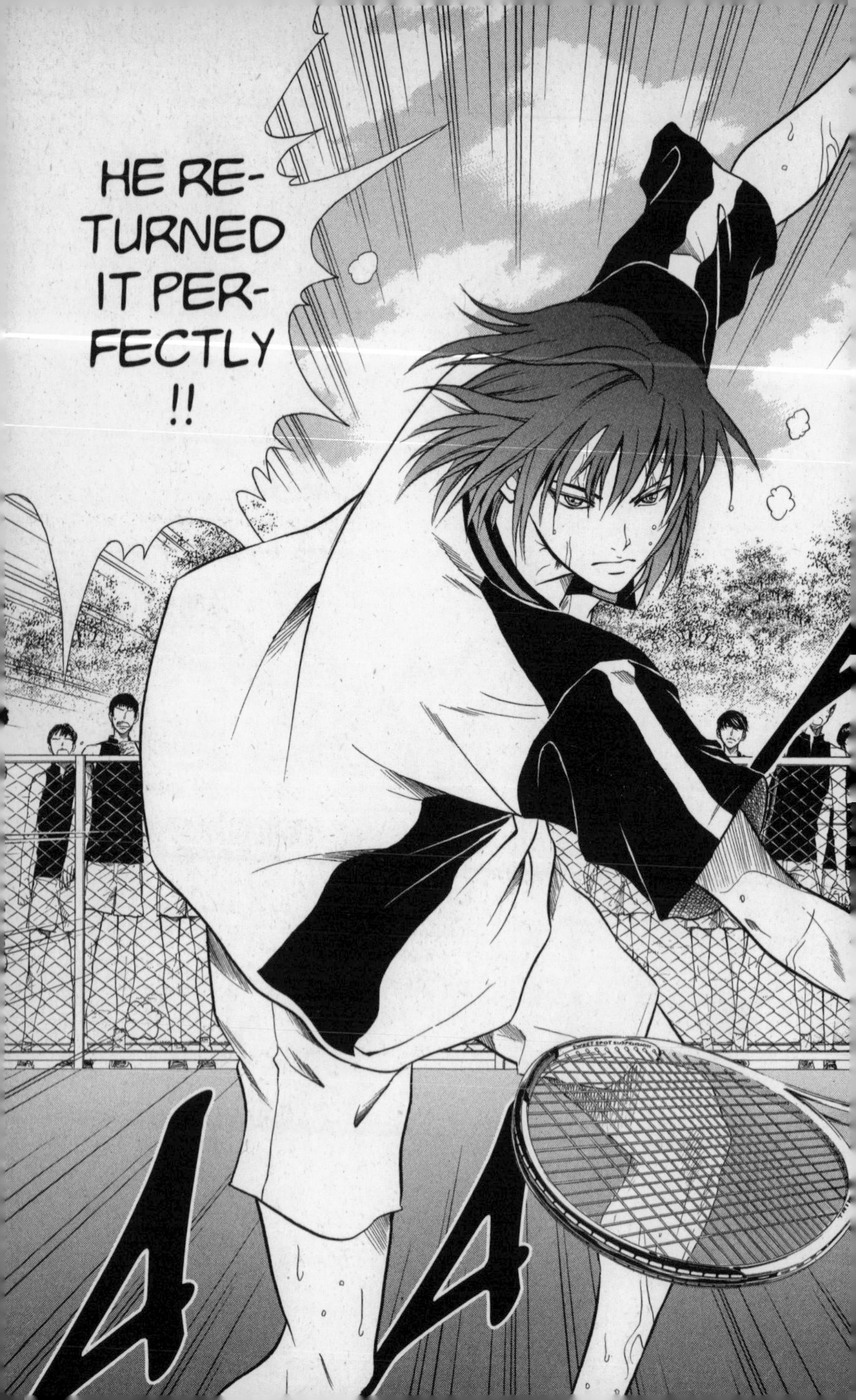
HE RE-
TURNED
IT PER-
FECTLY
!!

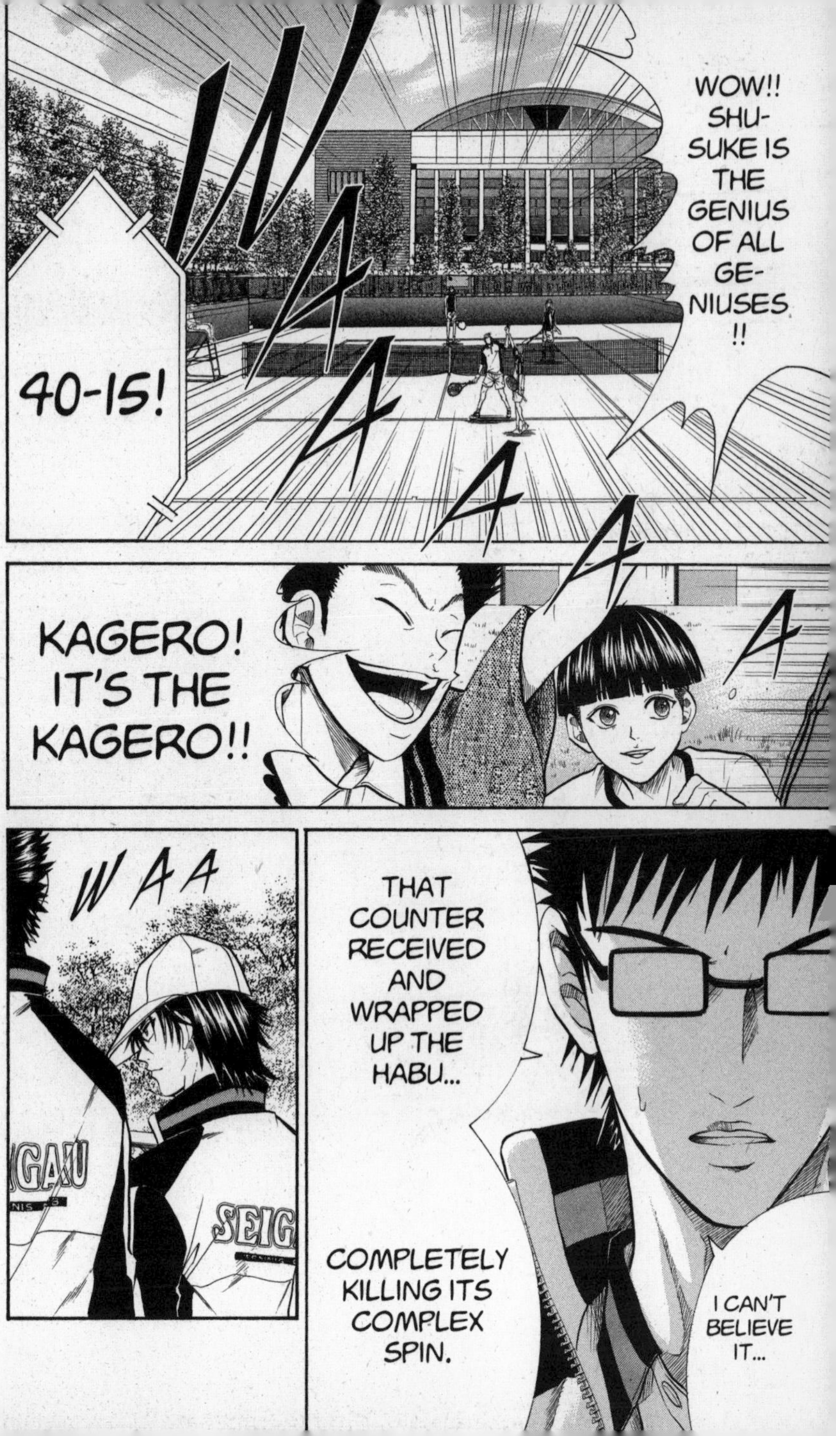
WOW!! SHUSUKE IS THE GENIUS OF ALL GENIUSES!!
WAAAAAA
40-15!
KAGERO! IT'S THE KAGERO!!
THAT COUNTER RECEIVED AND WRAPPED UP THE HABU...
COMPLETELY KILLING ITS COMPLEX SPIN.
I CAN'T BELIEVE IT...
WAA
SEIG

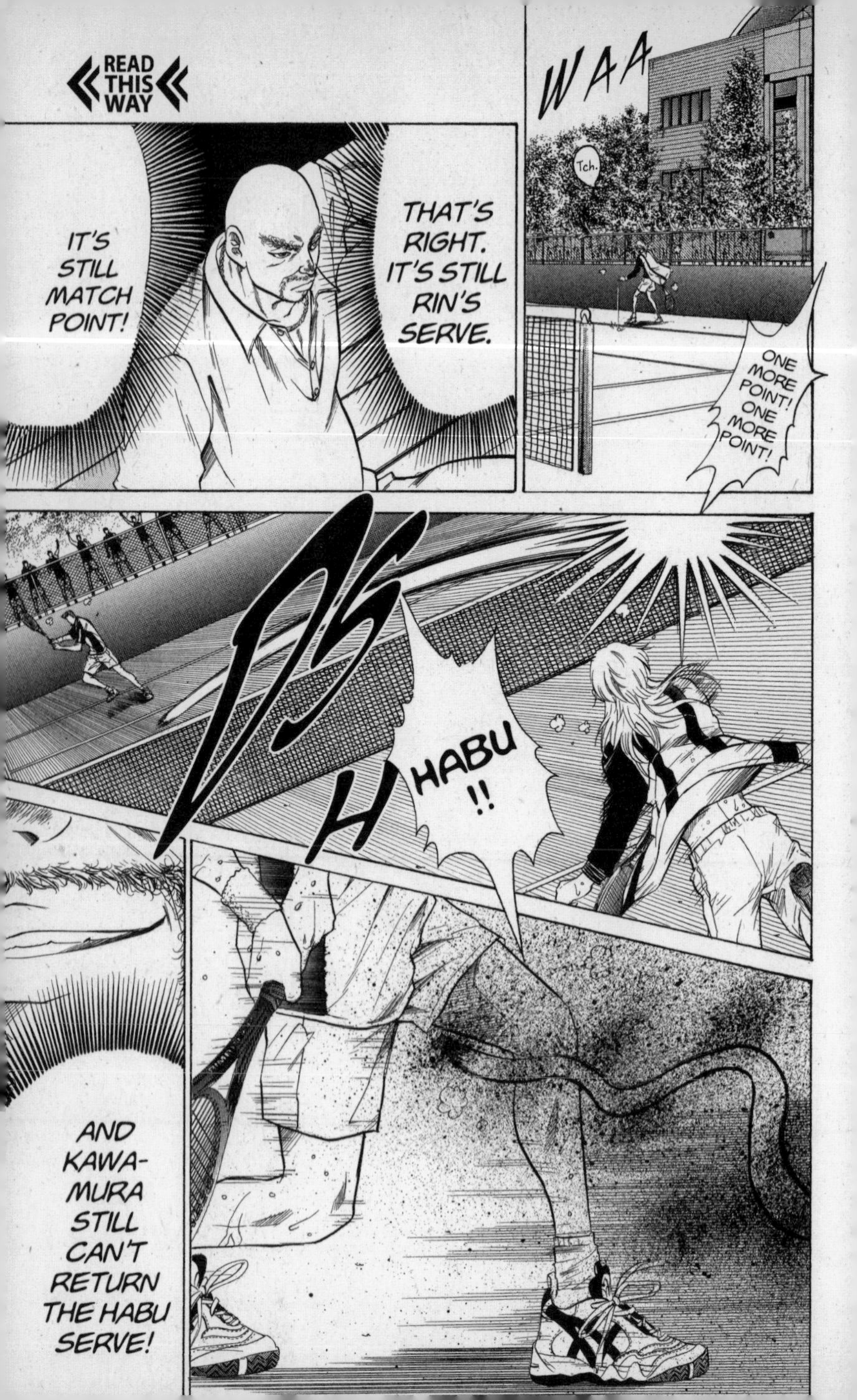
READ THIS WAY
WAA
Tch.
ONE MORE POINT! ONE MORE POINT!
THAT'S RIGHT. IT'S STILL RIN'S SERVE.
IT'S STILL MATCH POINT!
HABU!!
SSH
AND KAWAMURA STILL CAN'T RETURN THE HABU SERVE!

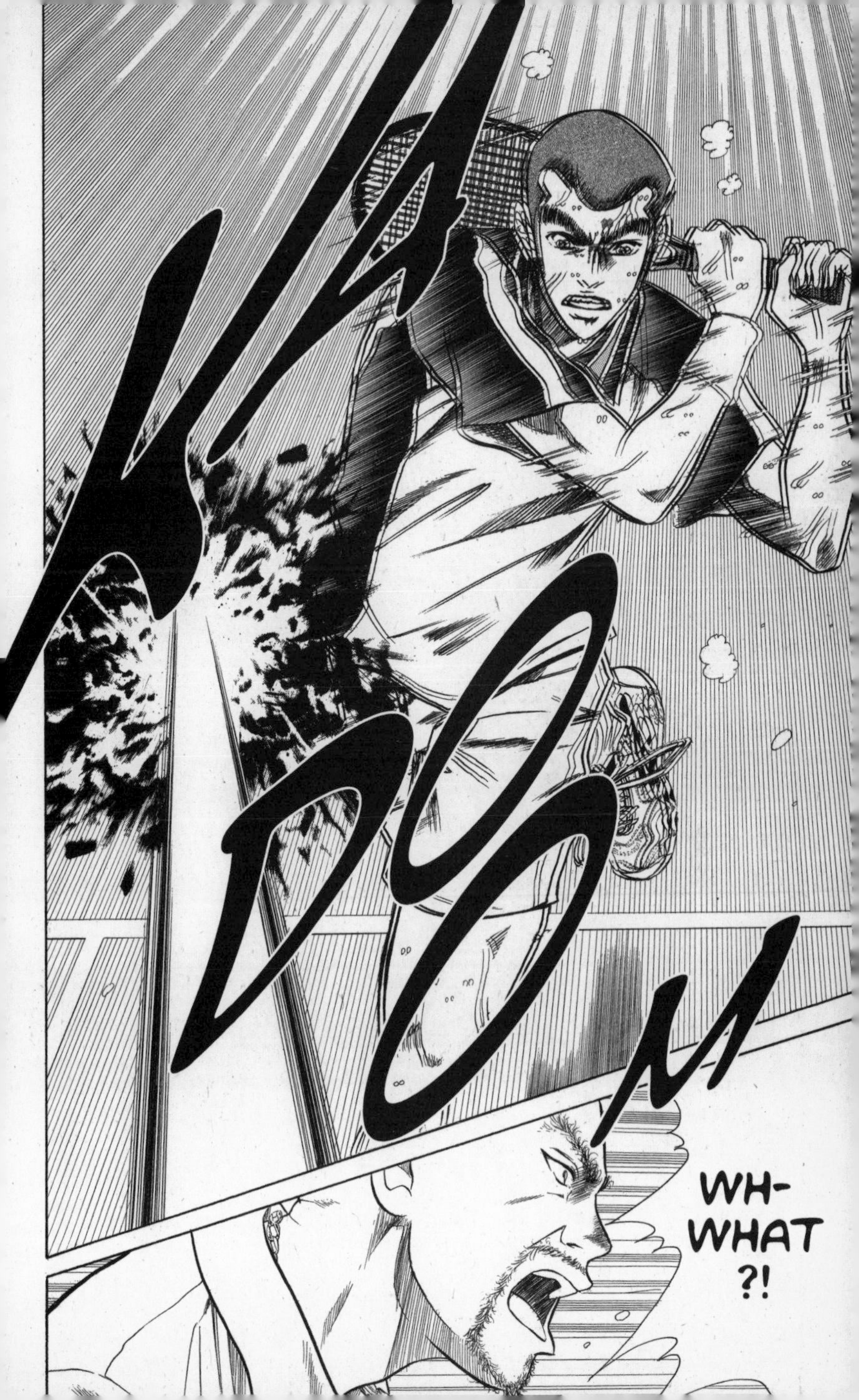
WH-
WHAT
?!

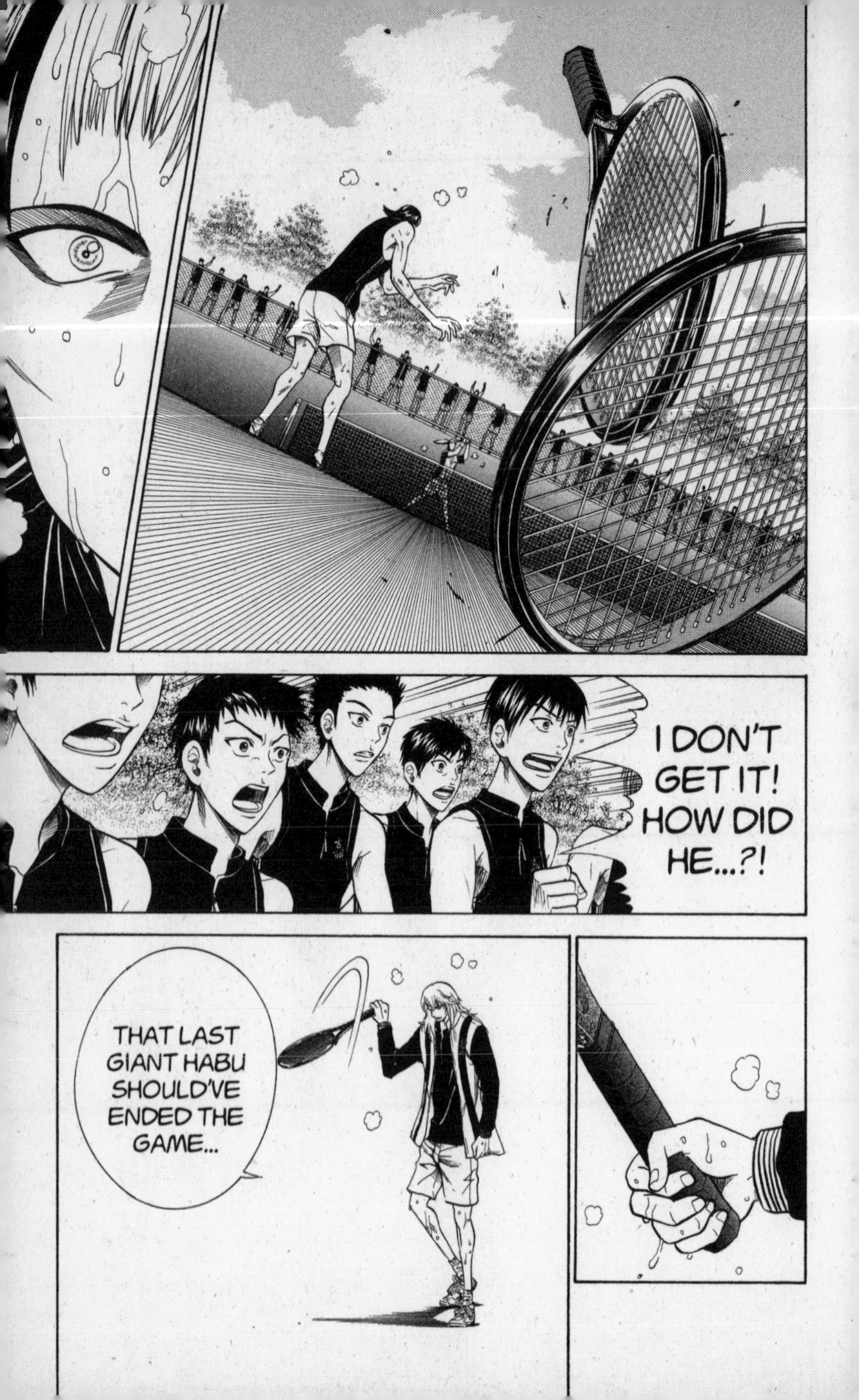
I DON'T GET IT! HOW DID HE...?!
THAT LAST GIANT HABU SHOULD'VE ENDED THE GAME...

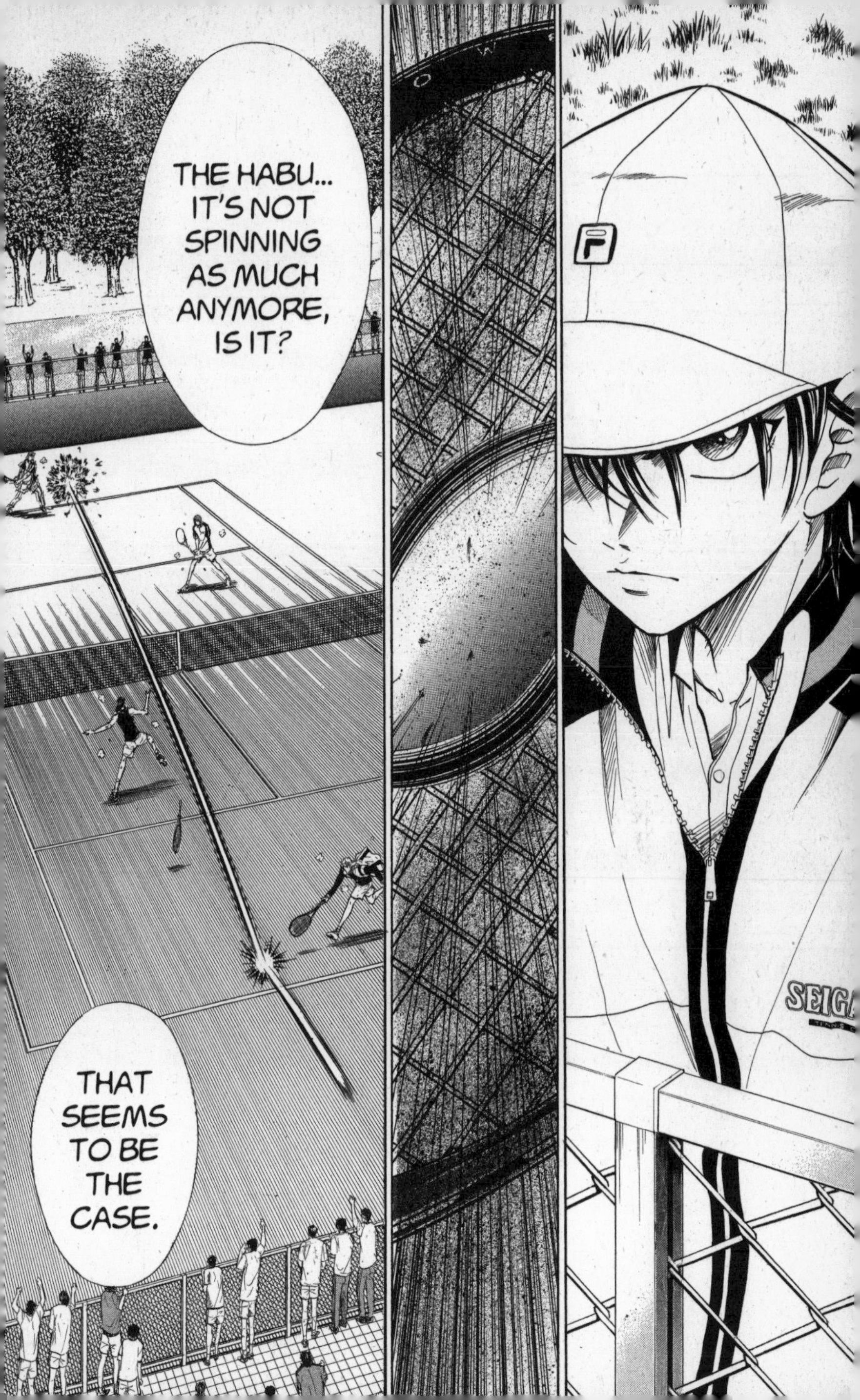
THE HABU... IT'S NOT SPINNING AS MUCH ANYMORE, IS IT?
THAT SEEMS TO BE THE CASE.

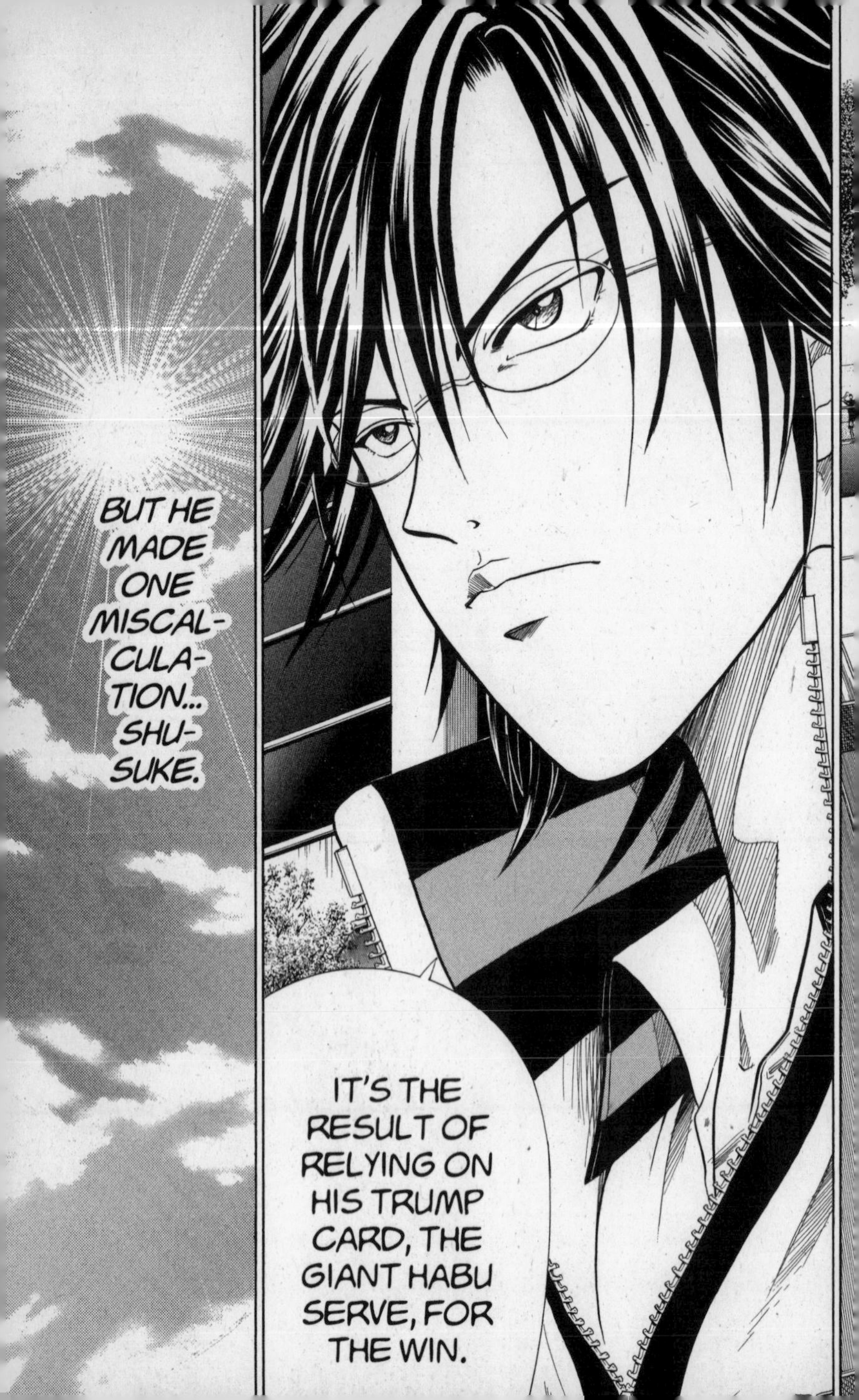
IT'S THE RESULT OF RELYING ON HIS TRUMP CARD, THE GIANT HABU SERVE, FOR THE WIN.
BUT HE MADE ONE MISCAL-CULA-TION... SHU-SUKE.

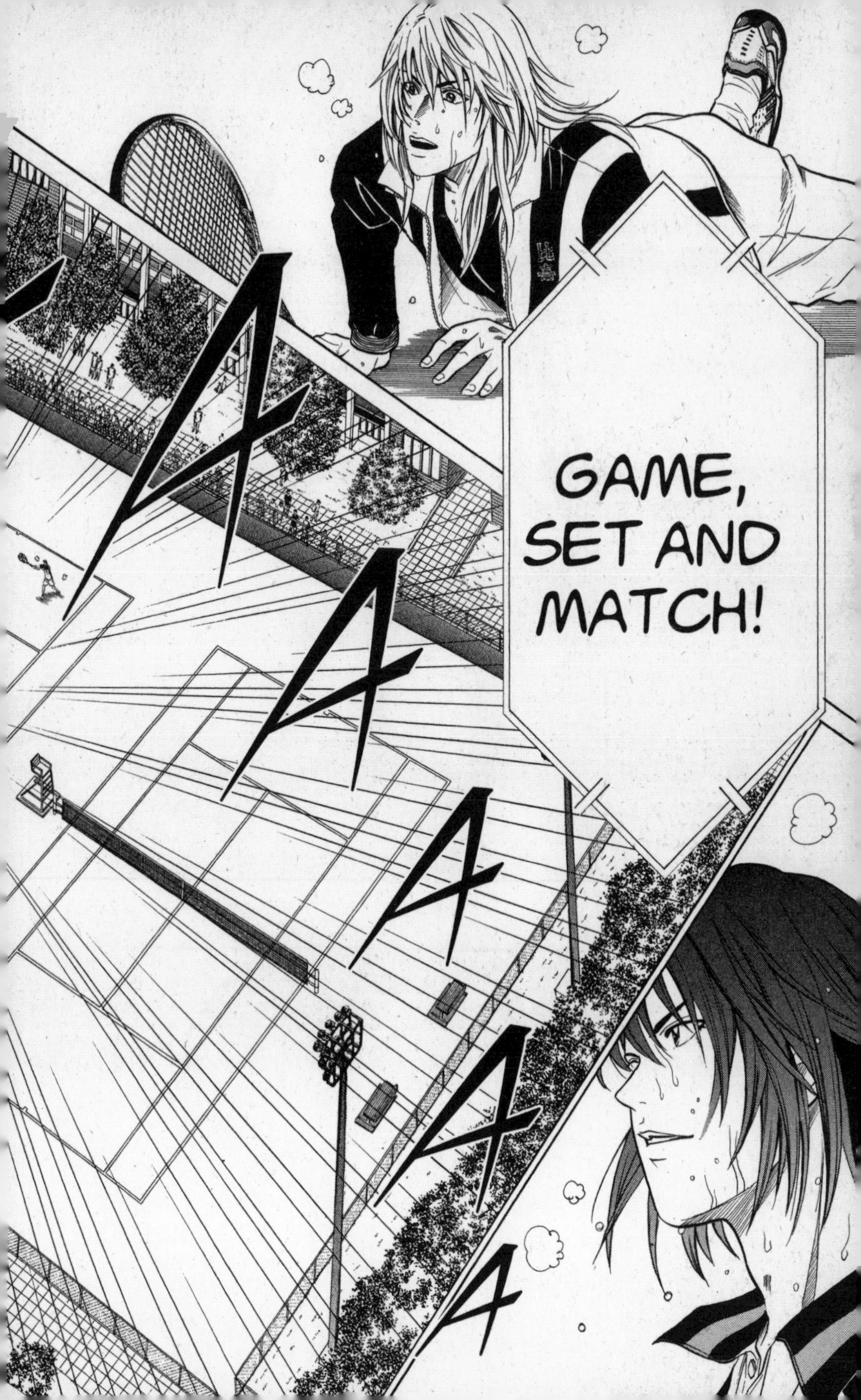
GAME, SET AND MATCH!

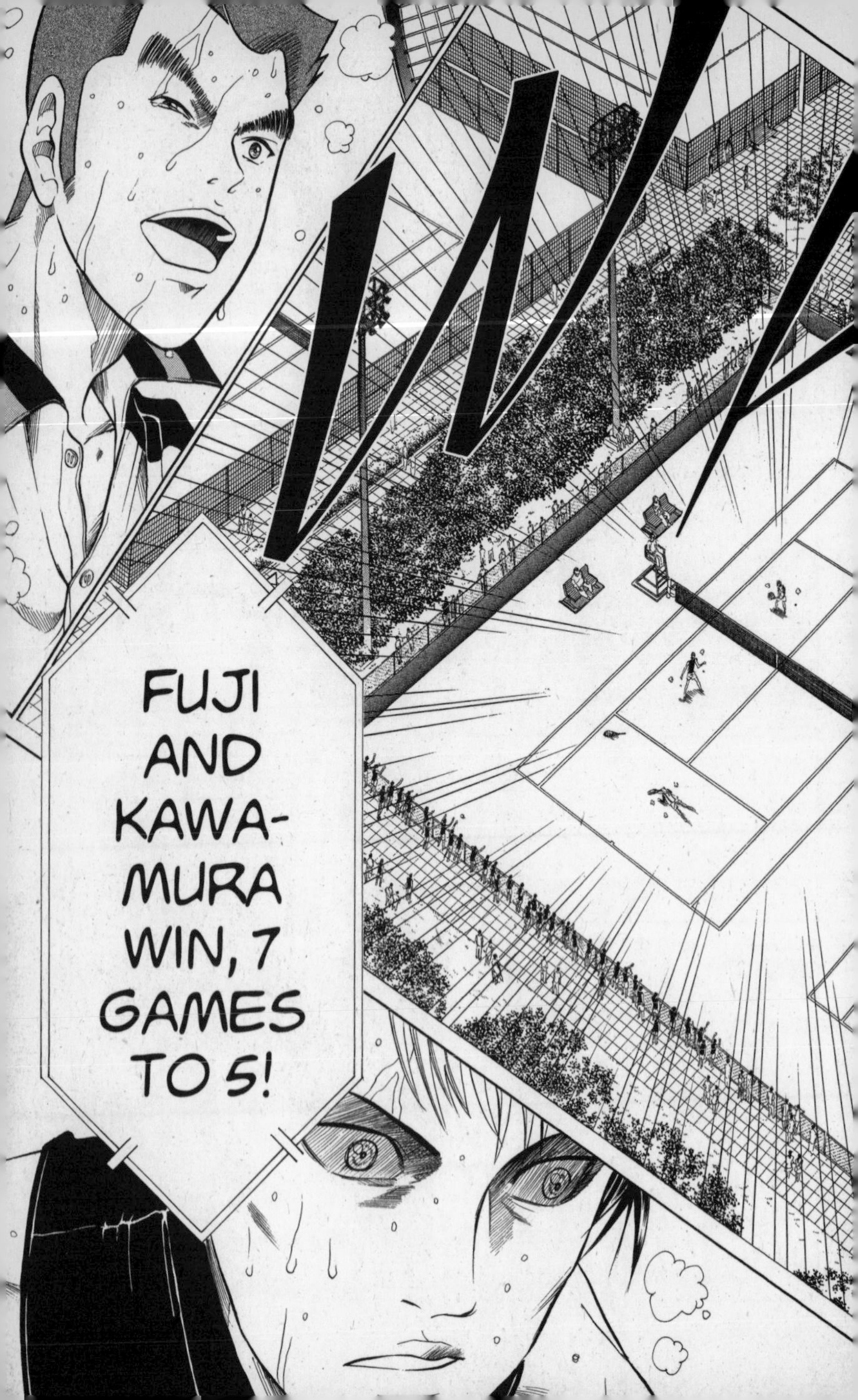
FUJI AND KAWA-MURA WIN, 7 GAMES TO 5!

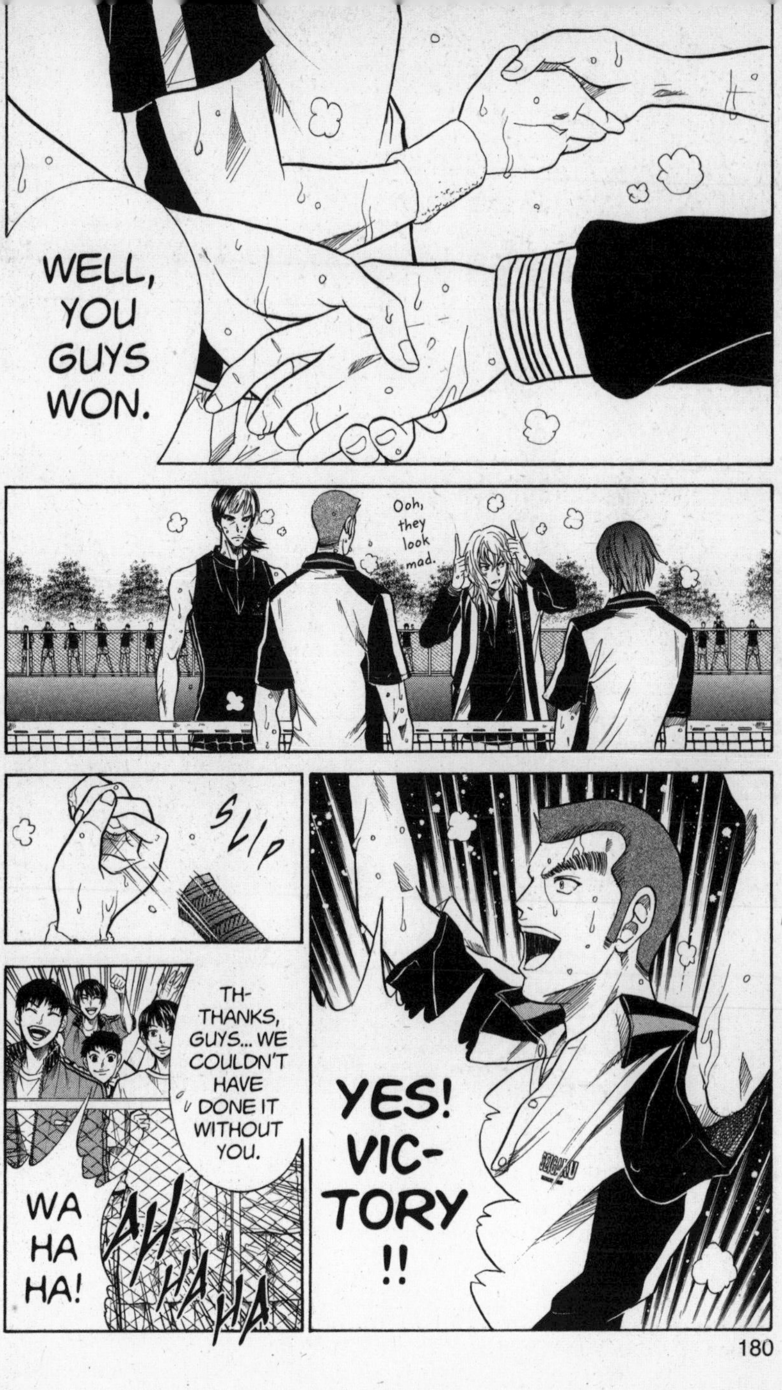
WELL, YOU GUYS WON.
Ooh, they look mad.
YES! VIC-TORY!!
SLIP
TH-THANKS, GUYS... WE COULDN'T HAVE DONE IT WITHOUT YOU.
WA HA HA!
AHAHAHA

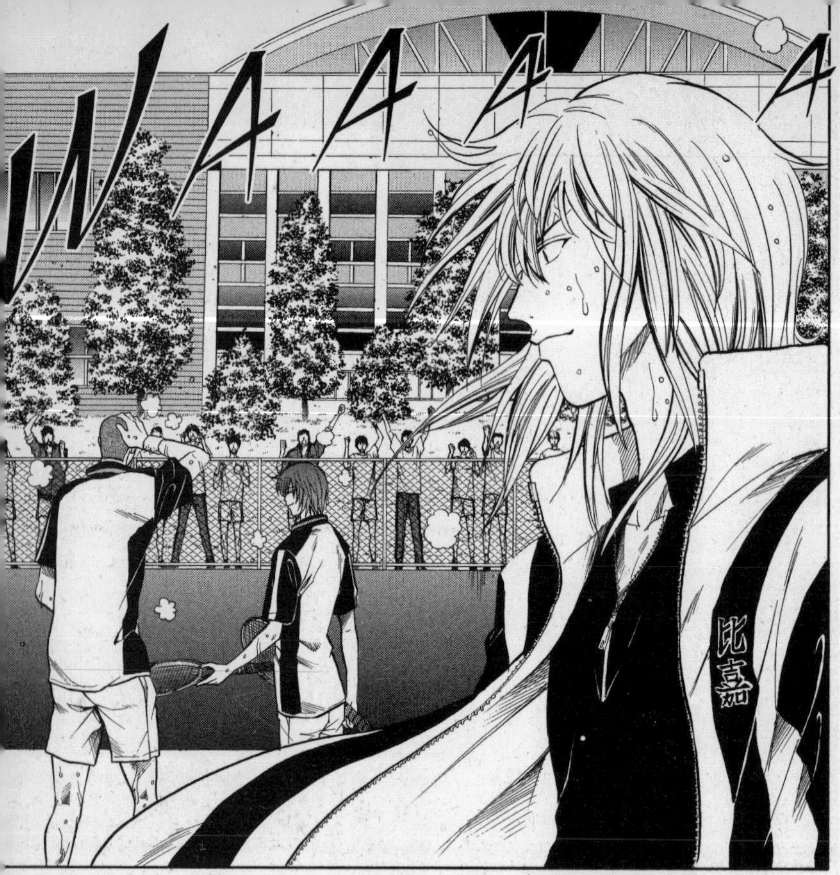
WAAAA
比嘉

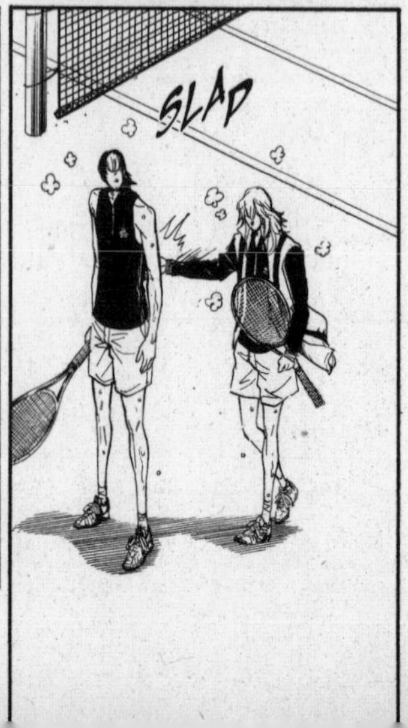
SLAP

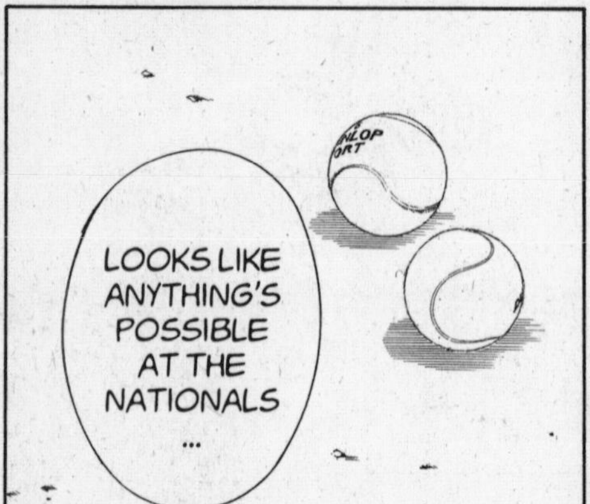
LOOKS LIKE ANYTHING'S POSSIBLE AT THE NATIONALS ...

TO BE CONTINUED IN VOL. 31!

In the Next Volume...

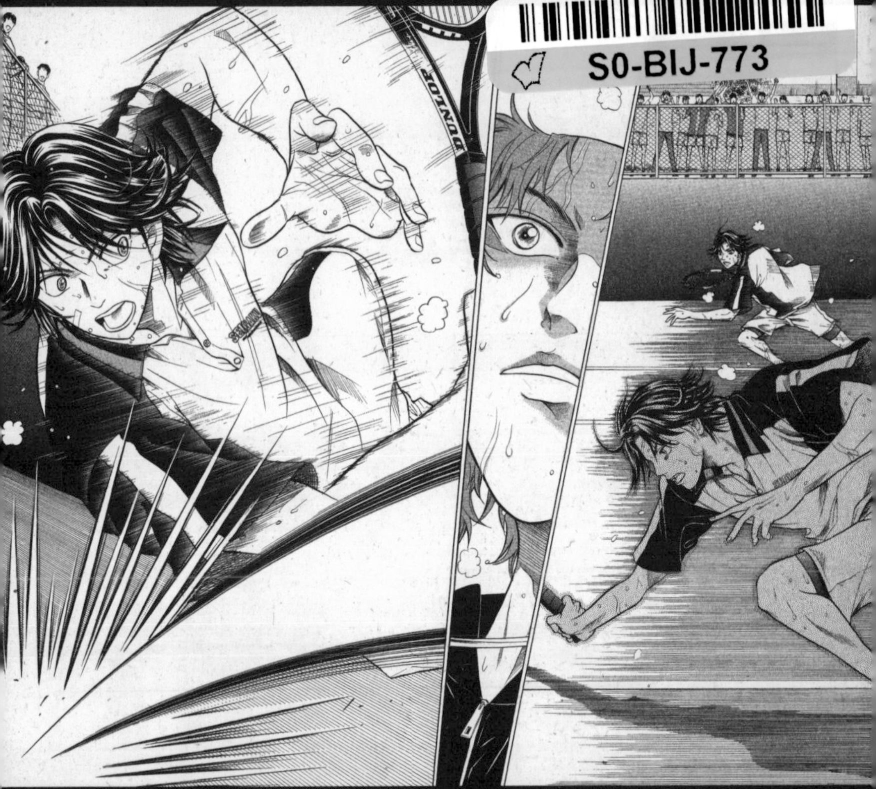

A Surprise Strategy: Eiji Plays Singles

With Shuichiro out of play, the other half of Seishun's Golden Pair faces off against Higa's Yujiro Kai in No. 2 Singles. Can Eiji bring Seishun a victory without his partner's support? The final match of the round, No. 1 Singles, pits captain against captain: Kunimitsu, in his first game back from injury, versus Eishiro "Killer" Kite.

Available May 2009!